Coming into McPhee Country

Coming into McPhee Country

John McPhee and the Art of Literary Nonfiction

Edited by

O. Alan Weltzien

and

Susan N. Maher

The University of Utah Press

Salt Lake City

" 'The Size and Shape of the Canvas': An Interview with John McPhee" by Jared Haynes is excerpted from *Writing on the Edge* 5(2) and 6(1) (Spring and Fall 1994).

"Giving Good Reasons: Environmental Appeals in the Nonfiction of John McPhee" by Brian Turner appeared previously in a slightly different form in *Rhetoric Review* (Fall 1994).

"John McPhee Balances the Act" by Kathy Smith appeared previously in a slightly different form in *Literary Journalism in the Twentieth Century,* edited by Norman Sims (New York: Oxford University Press, 1990).

 The Defiance House Man colophon is a registered trademark of the University of Utah Press. It is based upon a four-foot-tall Ancient Puebloan pictograph (late PIII) near Glen Canyon, Utah.

Printed on acid-free paper

08 07 06 05 04 03
5 4 3 2 1

LIBRARY OF CONGRESS CATALOGING-IN-PUBLICATION DATA

Coming into McPhee country : John McPhee and the art of literary nonfiction / edited by O. Alan Weltzien and Susan N. Maher.
   p.   cm.
Includes bibliographic references and index.
   ISBN 0-87480-746-8 (pbk.: alk. paper)
   1. McPhee, John A.—Literary art. 2. Prose literature—Technique.
3. Wilderness areas in literature. 4. Environmental protection in literature.
I. Weltzien, O. Alan (Oliver Alan) II. Maher, Susan Naramore.
PS3563.C38875 Z64 2003
808'.0092—dc21

                    2002152320

Contents

III. The Writerly Challenges of McPhee

Acknowledgments

This book was born following a session devoted to John McPhee at the Western Literature Association (WLA) meeting in Sacramento, California, in October 1999. Guided in part by the tradition of festschrifts, the editors decided to join forces to bring the project to fruition; and they received encouragement from Theodore Humphrey, a fellow panelist and now contributor. We both believe McPhee merits more recognition, particularly now that he has passed his biblical allotment of three score and ten years. Working together has proven a deep pleasure, mostly conducted via e-mail, in which we have learned steadily from one another. Additionally, our labor has been enhanced by support from several sources.

We wish to thank all our contributors, particularly those who have already published essays on McPhee, for eagerly joining us in preparing this book that honors his career. Maher also acknowledges the help of Isabel Barros, a University of Nebraska research assistant who tracked down McPhee bibliographic material. In addition we thank our editor, Dawn Marano, for her interest and encouragement. Sue Maher thanks her partner, Al Kemmerer, and Alan Weltzien thanks his wife, Lynn Myer Weltzien, for their patience and support of this project. And most of all we salute John McPhee, whose dozens of books have spoken so deeply to ourselves and his wide readership. The present volume represents a small gesture of thanks for a huge, and hugely successful, career.

Introduction

I

L iterary nonfiction has long played a part in the American literary
scene, though it has sometimes remained in the shadows while other
genres assumed center stage. The umbrella term applied to the form has
negative connotations (e.g., other than or less than fiction) that have
tended to obscure its significance. Its heritage, however, can be traced
back at least as far as the *Essays* of Michel de Montaigne, published in
1580. Nonfiction's diverse and wide-ranging history encompasses the
rise of British and colonial American journalism in the seventeenth and
eighteenth centuries, paralleling a growing interest in varying modes of
nonfiction and an implicit recognition, on the part of writers and readers, of their own claims to truth and high literary standards. More recently, the period between 1890 and 1940 produced an "abundance of
literary journalism" (Hartsock, 19). It is no coincidence that the first
heyday of literary journalism prospered in its connection to literary realism and naturalism, grounded as it is in the grain of the real world.
Many prominent American writers of this period (for example, William
Dean Howells, Mark Twain, Stephen Crane, Theodore Dreiser, and
Ernest Hemingway) worked in journalism before or during their careers
in fiction. In recent decades literary journalism has come to be commonly regarded as a subcategory of nonfiction, alongside the emerging
subcategory of creative nonfiction. This latter term is intended to grant
license for the use of fictional and dramatic devices in nonfiction. In the
past two generations, no writer has proven the value of its coinage more
than John McPhee.

Certainly, literary nonfiction assumed a new status in the second half
of the twentieth century, boosted by the work of those literary journalists who rose to prominence in the 1960s. In fact the few historians of
New Journalism, as it is called, such as Chris Anderson, Norman Sims,

Thomas B. Connery, Phyllis Frus, and John C. Hartsock, contend that this development inspired the surge in literary nonfiction's popularity that is still evident. Indeed, Hartsock persuasively argues that narrative literary journalism is "among our most compelling contemporary commentary" (10–11). After books such as Truman Capote's *In Cold Blood* (1965), a widely heralded "nonfiction novel," writers began exploring new connections between fiction and nonfiction, and scholars began to give notice to their mutual influence. Literary nonfiction borrows generously from other kinds of writing, including journalism, autobiography, travel writing, and fiction. While nonfiction has always attracted legions of readers, "the critical attitude up to the new journalism has been ambivalent" (Hartsock, 204). Literary scholar Barbara Lounsberry declared "the art of fact" to be "the great unexplored territory of contemporary criticism" (xi). Only recently has literary nonfiction commanded greater attention from scholars and college curricula. Several emergent voices in New Journalism, including Tom Wolfe, Norman Mailer, and Joan Didion, have developed into major American writers with distinct signatures marking all their work. The same can certainly be said for John McPhee, who is in some respects a more conservative writer than these (insofar as he resists foregrounding the writer's own subjective presence), but one whose career looms, if anything, larger.

The present volume salutes McPhee's enormous, and enormously varying, oeuvre and confirms in however modest a way his stature as a major American writer of the late twentieth century, which shows no signs of diminishing in the new millennium. In subject matter and breadth, McPhee's career is staggering. Between 1965 and 2002 he published twenty-seven books, in addition to the two *Readers* published twenty years apart (1976 and 1996). McPhee has been subject to two anthologies of his own work, which gives some measure of his ongoing productivity. None of his books are out of print, and first editions of early titles such as his first book, *A Sense of Where You Are* (1965), a profile of Princeton basketball star and later New Jersey senator (and presidential candidate) Bill Bradley, now command high prices. McPhee cut his teeth as a writer at *Time* (1957–64), and after a seven-year apprenticeship he quickly emerged at the *New Yorker* as a mature and distinct writer. Since 1963 McPhee has been a trademark name for the *New Yorker,* where he still works, and regular readers can hardly imagine the magazine apart from McPhee. Yet through his publisher, Farrar, Straus & Giroux, McPhee has become a well-known writer among legions who know nothing about the *New Yorker.* During four banner years—1967, 1975, 1976, and 1984—McPhee published two books annually. Within a few years of the first *John McPhee Reader,* edited by McPhee's Princeton University colleague William Howarth, it was already out of date. That book, with its well-known introduction by Howarth, spread McPhee's reputation among many who did not already know his books; in 1977 McPhee published *Coming into the Country,* his longest book and still among his most popular. Given his panoramic range of subjects and interests—what Lounsberry calls his "panoptic perspective" (66)—McPhee defies cataloging, and his work occupies a shelf.

By 1980 McPhee's pace of publication had slowed slightly as he turned to what he has repeatedly called his most daunting series of assignments: that sequence of four books on the geologic history of the United States collectively published as *Annals of the Former World* (1998), which won him a Pulitzer Prize in 1999. McPhee first conceived this project in 1978 and initially intended it to be a small piece; but as with Richard Wagner and his *Ring of the Nibelungs,* one foray turned into a tetralogy. Yet even during the dozen years (1981–93) when McPhee was publishing the four books that constitute *Annals,* he published five other books, including another essay collection, *Table of Contents* (1985), and his portrait of the American Merchant Marine, *Looking for a Ship* (1990).

Annals has its critics. In the *New York Review of Books,* Stephen Jay Gould has objected to what he regards as McPhee's skewed, semihagiographic treatment of geology fieldwork in the tetralogy; and David Quammen bristles impatiently in his *New York Times Book Review* essay, "Rocks of Age," accusing McPhee of "adamantine reserve" and "impeccable caution" (10). Furthermore, some readers wander, lost in sections of explanation and strata of specialized vocabulary. We suspect that such voices and readers are in the small minority, however. Most have eagerly followed McPhee and his geologist guides along Interstate 80; and professional geologists have heaped accolades on McPhee, for they recognize his profound talent for enlarging the common understanding of their discipline. McPhee has been rightly dubbed a "rhapsode of deep time," and it is hard not to deem *Annals* the crowning achievement in his prolific career.

For many, McPhee's career as an environmental writer matches the emergence of environmentalism as a household concern and major political force in the twentieth century's second half. In his recent book *Landscape with Figures* scholar Kent Ryden salutes McPhee's central position as an environmental writer: "Of all American writers working today, John McPhee most fully and assiduously explores the melding and interdependence of the human and the nonhuman in the natural world, a pursuit that he achieves not only through his choice of subject matter but also through his technique" (54–55). More recently, the emergence of ecocriticism and environmental literary studies as major movements in scholarship and college curricula has led to new and more exacting assessments of McPhee's "outdoors" books and his place in the environmental movement. McPhee's own discomfort with the "environmental writer" label and interest in urban landscapes, as well as recent revisionist theories qualifying received notions of "wilderness," suggest the value of reassessing his outdoors books in relation to his overall career as well as the diversified environmental movement at the dawn of the twenty-first century.

Both editors first encountered McPhee during their respective graduate school careers. As Susan N. Maher confesses in the opening of her essay, she picked *Oranges* (1967) off the shelf of a fellow graduate instructor in the same crowded office and has been reading back and forth across the oeuvre ever since. O. Alan Weltzien first heard about McPhee from a friend in graduate school who enthusiastically discussed *The Survival of the Bark Canoe* (1975) and from his father, always a good reading guide. Like most McPhee readers, Maher and Weltzien increasingly sought that tight style and unobtrusive yet firm structure—that marked play of irony—characteristic of this writer, no matter what his subject. After the first *John McPhee Reader,* scattered scholars began paying increasing attention to McPhee in the 1980s and early 1990s. Michael Pearson published a critical biography, *John McPhee,* in the Twayne series in 1997. Several of these scholars, including Howarth, Maher, Pearson, Sims, and Lounsberry, have written new appraisals of McPhee for the present volume: the first book with a range of voices examining the sweep of McPhee's career.

The sheer quantity and consistent quality of the oeuvre justify the volume's subtitle, in the opinion of the editors. For just as J. S. Bach closed his career with *The Art of the Fugue* and Henry James climaxed his with his New York edition and collected (and in some cases revised) prefaces, *The Art of the Novel,* so we believe the McPhee shelf yields some essential wisdom about literary nonfiction—about the factual as literature. We intend this collection to further interest in McPhee and to extend the scholarly and popular conversation concerning him. McPhee's steady example displays a signature style as respected as that of any significant American writer of the past century. Certainly he has carved out some of the territory in literary journalism (at least as that term was understood in the twentieth century's final decades). McPhee broke new ground and helped us all see anew its contribution to the wide field known as literary nonfiction. A number of literary nonfiction writers claim him as a mentor or inspiration. We suspect a large part of McPhee's appeal derives from the novelistic techniques of his art. His books extend the edge of literary realism, as his expository burden—however looming, as was the case with *Assembling California* (1993)—always remains tucked within the web of human interest stories. Information stays in the service of portraiture and even persuasion.

McPhee's place in American literary history feels secure, among other reasons, because of his fascination with the American West (and Alaska) and, occasionally, locations well beyond U.S. borders. As Michael Pearson describes it in *John McPhee,* McPhee enacts a fundamental American, home-away-home pattern in many of his books. Though occasionally he studies his back yard, notably in *The Pine Barrens* (1968), "The Atlantic Generating Station" (in *Giving Good Weight,* 1976), "A Textbook Place for Bears" (in *Table of Contents,* 1985), "In Virgin Forest" (in *Irons in the Fire,* 1997), and *The Founding Fish* (2002), McPhee typically travels far from his East Coast, Princeton, New Jersey, milieu, immersing himself in new and sometimes remote landscapes, only to return home, where his material ferments as he further researches and repeatedly rewrites. This writer's archetypal journeying powerfully attracts readers even as it explains, on some level, the source of much of his writing. McPhee's place seems secure as well because of the kind of human portrait he is drawn to and repeatedly draws. Others have described McPhee as a descendant of Ralph Waldo Emerson, particularly the Emerson who extols native genius and self-sufficiency (e.g., "Self-Reliance"). Over and over, McPhee limns men and women who have mastered their trades or fields and who value and represent traditional lore and craft—often those who have consciously turned away from contemporary cultural assumptions and become self-sufficient. In James Stull's words, "The people who populate McPhee's world . . . are representative of a particular cultural model—the 'authentic' or 'ideal' American—and they are identified by a number of American character traits —among them, self-reliance, individualism, and 'innocence' " (184). McPhee celebrates old-fashioned virtues and self-reliance, and his inscriptions locate him well inside the American grain. He happily courts the risk of being judged old-fashioned.

The habits of discipline and obsessions with form and his example of self-effacement rather than self-aggrandizement recommend him to many; others grow tired of his caution and ostensibly neutral stance, as if McPhee remains reporter and never editorialist. His effect, though, never seems as simple as this facile, either-or dichotomy suggests. McPhee's distancing of himself from noisy environmental advocacy serves as a good example. For many, he writes as eloquently and forthrightly as any robust environmentalist; yet he disdains the label, asserting, in the Jared Haynes interview reprinted in this volume, that he avoids both pulpit and ballot box. There are many green roads, of course, and in our judgment McPhee walks more than one.

The McPhee shelf contains titles and topics that—because of their very range—will not excite every reader equally, but he never disappoints by lapses in quality; his consistently high standard and even performance may prove his most remarkable achievement. His readers learn much about writing from him, and the editors hope this book might enlarge our conception of literary nonfiction based on his sustained example. For instance, what we earlier called his novelistic appeal derives in good part from his ability to evoke worlds more factual than imaginary, dressed out with human characters similar in their effects to the protagonists inhabiting novels. Such an analogous achievement derives from his extreme control, wherein a chaos of travel notes and research (those myriad small notebooks) passes through the crucible of form and emerges into an inevitably perfectly cast structure. McPhee's control manifests itself at many levels, from his preferred length (comparable to the novella) to his well-turned sentences. For example, by his own admission he continued to follow the same outline for *Assembling California* that he had drawn up more than a decade earlier, when he first plotted what became *Annals.*

McPhee insistently leavens his expository burden with wit and humor and sympathy; and as rhetoricians such as Brian Turner (in the present anthology) demonstrate, he usually presents his guides as exempla with whom readers ally themselves. As Kent Ryden remarks, "The signature of McPhee's technique" inheres in the way he "filters the landscape and interprets its meaning through the eyes, hands, mind, and life of a second persona . . . someone who has come over a period of many years to live on terms of comfortable intimacy and cooperation with that landscape, who has crafted a life shaped by the qualities and capacities of the natural world" (56). In most cases, readers like McPhee's human subjects, if not their particular niches. But as Barbara Lounsberry (in the present anthology) and others argue, McPhee challenges himself in his career by occasionally presenting unlikable guides, beginning with Norman Graebner in *Levels of the Game* and Henri Vaillancourt in *The Survival of the Bark Canoe*.

McPhee reads novelistically as well because of his well-known avoidance of didacticism and deference to the reader. In more than one interview, he professes his belief that the reader does almost all the work in making meaning and drawing judgments. His tendency to avoid overt personal judgments and skip the pulpit, instead leading by indirection (e.g., through his guides), suggests a journalist-essayist in common cause with the practitioners of prose fiction. At the least, most elements of McPhee's style such as his particular habits of implication and irony, his compression and nuance, demonstrate his supple exploration of the vast landscape between the factual and the imaginary. He has enlarged the possibilities of literary nonfiction by transforming—inverting his famous Princeton University biannual course title, imitated frequently in many college curricula—"fact" into "literature." That transformation, of course, can assume myriad shapes, as many contemporary writers testify. As one of our primary models, McPhee repeatedly takes his readers into new spaces between the domains of the journalist and the novelist.

More conspicuously, McPhee continually challenges himself with more complicated structures. Critics have remarked his deliberate complications from early portraiture such as Bill Bradley in *A Sense of Where You Are* and Thomas Hoving in "A Roomful of Hovings" (1967) to the double focus of *Levels of the Game* (1969)—a title that can describe his formalist penchant—to the refractions of *Encounters with the Archdruid* (1971) and beyond. We earlier referred to McPhee's own sense of challenge with content in his geology tetralogy, particularly his sense of ignorance with Anita Harris in *In Suspect Terrain* (1983) and his sense of disjunction with the seemingly random pieces of California's geologic history (he struggled to assemble California and thereby splice all geologic and human stories along Interstate 80 into *Annals*). In interviews, McPhee has described his sense of the complex structure of *Looking for a Ship*, which assumed a shape he had not originally conceived. Across his oeuvre we witness the writer continually raising the level of his own game—and given its quantity and length, that proves a remarkable performance.

McPhee's newest book, *The Founding Fish*, might be subtitled—following Wallace Stevens—Thirteen Ways of Looking at American Shad, though McPhee writes sixteen chapters. If Norman Maclean's *A River Runs through It* takes the reader from casting to eventually landing trout, McPhee's tour de force begins with casting and finally, in the appendix, seats us at the table, ready to savor shad in the mouth. His first title since *Annals*, this work has grown out of his long love affair with shad fishing, particularly in the Delaware River; in it the reader travels up and down the east coast of North America, learning the intimate history and variety of shad fishing and physiology of shad. Its longest, title chapter, appearing in the book's center, highlights an obscure chapter of colonial American history. As with so many McPhee titles, this one evolved from a serious hobby, a personal passion, and a few sections from it were first published in the *New Yorker*. Longer than most of his books at 354 pages, it generously reveals all the McPhee trademarks: the daunting range of research and graceful exposition, the surprising anecdote, the well-limned portraits, the rhetorical and ethical appeal of expert guides, the wit and self-mockery, the playful irony and occasional satire, the environmental concerns. Often *The Founding Fish* sees McPhee back in a canoe—his favorite mode of outdoors travel. Contrary to his practice in many earlier books, McPhee has now named and numbered his chapters. Occasionally he quietly gestures to many of his earlier titles, and the personal or family references show him appearing in front of his usual self-imposed curtain. The appendix exhaustively surveys possible ways of cooking shad and roe shad, with and without the legions of bones, and leaves the reader hungry. The ambitious range and structure, and erudition and humor, of *Founding Fish* reveal a master whose work is not yet done.

II

The present volume contains, we hope, all the virtues and few of the faults of a critical anthology. With McPhee's twenty-seven books and assorted miscellany, it would be impossible to cover his oeuvre comprehensively even with twice as many scholars contributing to the enterprise. So our book of necessity treats the McPhee shelf unevenly, skipping many titles worthy of extended comment. We have remarked that, until the past few years, McPhee scholarship has been scattered and surprisingly small in light of his production and influence. Because of that, our volume occasionally runs the risk of incestuous cross-referencing, as many contributors cite one another's earlier McPhee scholarship. In addition, a critical anthology provides a varied menu for readers who bring diverse appetites and tastes to the table. As already mentioned, this book includes most of the leading McPhee scholars as well as several new voices, which together constitute a rich and rigorous ensemble. Of the fourteen essays, eleven are original, and the other three, including a published interview with McPhee, have been slightly revised and edited for this volume.

We have divided the book into three sections: "The Evolving Writer," "McPhee and the Natural World," and "The Writerly Challenges of McPhee." Since McPhee favors triptychs himself, we wanted to imitate his preference, which also reflects narrative's three-part structure (i.e., beginning, middle, end) recommended by Aristotle in the *Poetics*. We believe our careful symmetry is fitting for a writer as conscious of form as McPhee. The first and third sections, containing four essays apiece, frame the larger, central section. Since McPhee outdoors is for many of his readers the essential McPhee, we have grouped six essays, including the two that most focus upon *Annals,* into the book's center. We have conceived our structure according to McPhee's chronology as well, although particular essays range back and forth. The order is not strict, as the first two essays in part three, for example, treat earlier McPhee titles. Part one emphasizes earlier McPhee writing, however, and the second half of the book's final essay, Susan N. Maher's " 'Pentimento in the Hide,' " focuses on *Assembling California* and *Irons in the Fire.*

As William Howarth, a friend of McPhee's for over three decades, introduced McPhee to so many with the first *Reader,* published in 1976, we felt it appropriate for Howarth to introduce this book with his lengthy survey—his first substantial reassessment of McPhee in more than twenty-five years. Howarth briefly reviews the history of their friendship and the genesis of the first *Reader;* "this second introduction" emphasizes what he calls "textual genealogy." As he admits, McPhee "is far better known" now than in 1976; the intervening quarter of a century enables him a richer, longer gaze. Howarth moves easily in and out of biography, stressing, for example, McPhee's varying fortunes under changing editorships and preferences at the *New Yorker.* He studies McPhee's working methods—a theme addressed at times by other contributors—and reviews and rebuts three sources of criticism leveled against McPhee: a tendency toward hagiography, an avoidance of controversy and advocacy, and too much attention to geology. Those criticizing McPhee for one or more of these reasons may not be persuaded by Howarth's arguments, which other contributors echo. In the process, Howarth discusses certain McPhee texts—*The Crofter and the Laird* (1970), *The Deltoid Pumpkin Seed* (1973), *The Curve of Binding Energy* (1974), *The Founding Fish* (2002)—not touched upon by other writers.

Howarth's generous reassessment is followed by Jared Haynes's interview of John McPhee, " 'The Size and Shape of the Canvas,' " originally published in *Writing on the Edge* (1994). For this volume, O. Alan Weltzien has edited the interview to approximately three-quarters of its original length. Unsurprisingly, McPhee's portrait of himself as a writer complements those habits and emphases studied by Howarth and Barbara Lounsberry, whose essay follows the interview. McPhee, a part-time professor, holds clear views about his craft, and his own voice serves as the base on which the other essays in part one make critical elaborations.

Lounsberry and Norman Sims have written about McPhee before, like Howarth, and in their present essays they take complementary positions on his emergence as a mature literary journalist. McPhee is known above all else for his profiles, a *New Yorker* staple he has shaped into his own mold. Lounsberry thoroughly traces the origins of McPhee as "portrait painter," assessing his journeyman pieces for *Time* and then studying his increasingly mature and diverse portraits. She contrasts McPhee with another New Jersey literary journalist, Gay Talese, to sharpen her own portrait. One of the chief values of her contribution is her depiction of McPhee negotiating through certain "postmodern snares" eagerly embraced by other kinds of literary nonfiction writers. She sensitively discusses his negative portraiture in the context of the familiar McPhee verities of balance and even temperament; and her concluding figure, likening the portrait painter to the "multiradial sun," is both felicitous and persuasive. Sims's essay, which rounds out part one, relies primarily on interviews to probe McPhee's biography and highlight those experiences that formed the writer who in 1963 realized his long-standing ambition to become a staff writer for the *New Yorker.* From these essays, taken together, emerges an accurate and detailed understanding of McPhee both before and after that first book in 1965. These writers explain how experiences in childhood and adolescence, and at *Time* and in his early *New Yorker* years, explain so much about the emerging oeuvre.

By McPhee's own admission, no earlier experience proved more essential for him than his repeated summers at Camp Keewaydin in Vermont. In this setting he first learned to appreciate lakes and rivers, canoeing and hiking. Here he fell in love with the outdoors and commenced a lifelong habit of journeying out from home, only to return and distill the experience; the unending desire for "Keewaydin" has taken McPhee beyond American borders at times. For many readers his "Keewaydin Stories" are his best; as much as any, they confirm his excellence in what Howarth calls his place-based prose. Though he shies away from the environmentalist label, McPhee has repeatedly proven himself an eloquent spokesman; and as a result some readers are unaware of his essays and books set in urban or suburban locales. Yet since *Coming into the Country,* if not earlier, McPhee has had to face charges of neutrality, of insufficient partisanship on behalf of the natural world. O. Alan Weltzien takes on the charges and addresses the question of environmental advocacy, tracing in the process McPhee's "green writing" from *The Pine Barrens* on and closely reading *The Control of Nature* (1989). Weltzien concludes that McPhee certainly writes as an environmentalist, though his approach is not the conspicuous, confrontational one applauded by many—in some respects, for good reasons—in the past generation. *Control* marks an unusual case in the oeuvre, appearing three-quarters of the way through *Annals,* in that McPhee's irony spills over into satire and, occasionally, sarcasm. It becomes difficult to reconcile the accusations of neutrality with the bristling energy animating *Control.*

The issue of advocacy poses one way to read "McPhee and the Natural World," the centerpiece section of the anthology, which Weltzien's essay introduces. American literary history becomes another context for reading McPhee's outdoors books. *Coming into the Country* exists at the center of the McPhee shelf and distills all his "Keewaydin Stories." Michael Pearson, who a few years ago wrote the first book on McPhee, now focuses his attention on this pivotal McPhee work. Pearson locates *Coming into the Country* in American literary history, and literary nonfiction in particular; as his eye ranges across its three sections, he probes McPhee's romantic and realist inclinations as well as the "pastoral vision" at its heart. For some, *Country* remains McPhee's best book, though some scholars (notably Susan Kollin in *Nature's State*) have critiqued his simultaneous endorsement and subversion of particular

Alaska stereotypes. Pearson's contribution is contextual, defining the book's place in enduring American literature. "McPhee and the Natural World" can be understood in terms of rhetorical analysis as well as environmental advocacy and American literary history.

Brian Turner's rhetorical study of McPhee originally appeared in *Rhetoric Review* (1994) and has been slightly revised for this volume. Drawing upon Wayne Booth's rhetoric of assent, Turner studies McPhee's "epideictic appeals" as the basis for the "suasive function" in his writing, which Turner believes complements the "expository and epistemic functions." Turner's study broadens our understanding of the guide-portraits described by Lounsberry; it enables us to see the guides not only as alter egos for the writer but as a primary source of McPhee's power. Readers can sense how McPhee's firm commitment to moderation might cause him to lose favor among more polemical environmentalists and environmental writers.

If canoeing represents McPhee's oldest and favorite outdoor activity, it comes as no surprise that experiences on rivers and lakes thread through his writing. Theodore C. Humphrey's essay traces McPhee's love affair across six river essays that collectively span most of his career. Beginning with McPhee's "Lifetime of Descending Rivers," Humphrey writes an appreciation that culminates in a discussion of McPhee's "immersion journalism" and an assessment of his attractive "authorial persona." Moving across water links McPhee's life outdoors.

Norman Maclean reminded us all that any river "runs over rocks from the basement of time" (104), and perhaps McPhee's obsession with rivers and lakes inevitably led to a similar obsession with geology. If *Annals* is McPhee's magnum opus, it is appropriate to feature two essays that focus upon its achievement. In "A Plate Tectonics of Language," Rick Van Noy, following McPhee's well-known fascination, studies post–plate tectonics geology as a "vernacular science." Early in *Basin and Range* (1981) McPhee pronounces geology a "fountain of metaphor" (24), and Van Noy probes the ways in which he creates a vocabulary of metaphors to serve as imaginative bridge and intermediary between professional geological jargon and lay understanding. Van Noy assesses the success of this bridge vocabulary and, along the way, discusses the conceptual challenge of explaining the brave new world in geology after plate tectonics (ca. 1968). In his artful braiding of modern human history with geologic history across the American landscape, McPhee steers between the poles of professional accuracy and a wider comprehensibility. Barbara Stevens's essay scrutinizes McPhee's steerage from other theoretical vantages, aligning his treatment of plate tectonics with postmodern geographical theory, particularly the work of Edward Soja and Derek Gregory. In Stevens's analysis, plate tectonics geology and postmodern geography with its "dialectical and conflictive space" share many conceptual affinities, which *Annals* reflects.

The title of part three, "The Writerly Challenges of McPhee," suggests ways in which McPhee encourages readers to new modes of understanding; the final four essays all highlight particular challenges he creates. Meta G. Carstarphen defines McPhee's brand of literary journalism by locating him within certain traditions in British and American journalism, particularly travel writing, dating from the eighteenth century. Carstarphen then focuses her attention upon two works, *Levels of the Game* and "In Search of Marvin Gardens" (1976), from earlier in McPhee's oeuvre to define and illustrate a mode of social criticism that he hazards. She argues that McPhee blends old and contemporary journalistic habits to anatomize "an inverted rhetoric of privilege." The title of Kathy Smith's essay, "John McPhee Balances the Act," expresses a sentiment shared by the contributors and other McPhee critics. Smith's essay originally appeared in Norman Sims's anthology *Literary Journalism in the Twentieth Century* (1990). Smith closely reads McPhee's first book, *A Sense of Where You Are,* and briefly contrasts him with Tom Wolfe to define "the new contract written by literary journalists" and argue that McPhee "leans into the 'fictional space' of the novel." Her essay probes the interstices between the objective standards of journalism and imaginary standards of the novel; she sees McPhee challenging his readers to recognize the contours of the intergeneric space he inhabits with them.

Dan Philippon's essay begins by glancing at Kathy Smith's contentions and McPhee's subsequent dismissal of some of them as "academic air." Philippon's focus upon *The Control of Nature* complements Weltzien's reading, but his emphasis upon the pedagogical challenges of McPhee adds a new dimension to our volume. Philippon describes the course in which he features *Control,* which becomes a vehicle for discussing "comparative bioregionalism" and the entire issue of teaching environmental issues. Echoing Turner in his portrayal of McPhee's "rhetoric of objectivity," Philippon sustains an analogy between the writer's rhetorical preferences and his own, as a professor who carefully distinguishes between sustainability and environmentalism in his classroom, reassuring his students in the process. Finally, Susan Naramore Maher takes a metaphor from early in the title essay of McPhee's most recent collection, *Irons in the Fire,* to explore another kind of challenge that he provides us. Maher traces the "pentimento in the hide" across four texts spanning the most recent phase of McPhee's career (1989– 97), focusing her lens upon the whole metaphor of code and decoding. Reminding us of the semiotic essence of coding/decoding, she assesses McPhee's varying linguistic experiments with arcane codes (e.g., foren- sic geology) in these texts. In evaluating McPhee's work as "cultural code" bearer and breaker, Maher's treatment overlaps with the analysis of plate tectonics as a vernacular science in *Annals* studied by Van Noy and Stevens and the "social spaces" explored by Carstarphen. She dis- cusses McPhee's success as reader follows after writer, entering unfamil- iar worlds in each of these texts, and generalizes from these to the oeu- vre, arguing that readers confront the task and anticipate the pleasure of "scanning and unraveling diverse aspects of human production and nat- ural history." As with many literary nonfiction masters, the work and the fun have always been one.

Our triptych lacks the tautness of McPhee's own structures; never- theless, the editors believe its inherent logic offers a worthy echo of McPhee. The writer turned seventy in 2001, and with this volume we honor a living writer whose work is not done. We intend it to further McPhee's reputation and inspire further scholarly work. After all, the McPhee shelf, at the beginning of the twentieth-first century, contains many lasting lessons in the art of literary nonfiction.

Works Cited

Anderson, Chris. *Literary Nonfiction: Theory, Criticism, Pedagogy.* Carbondale: Southern Illinois University Press, 1989.

Bach, J. S. *The Art of the Fugue.*

Capote, Truman. *In Cold Blood.* New York: New American Library, 1965.

Connery, Thomas B. *A Sourcebook of American Literary Journalism: Represen- tative Writers in an Emerging Genre.* New York: Greenwood, 1992.

Frus, Phyllis. *The Politics and Poetics of Journalistic Narrative: The Timely and the Timeless.* Cambridge: Cambridge University Press, 1994.

Gould, Stephen Jay. "Deep Time and Ceaseless Motion." *New York Review of Books* (14 May 1981): 25–28.

Hartsock, John C. *A History of American Literary Journalism: The Emergence of a Modern Narrative Form.* Amherst: University of Massachusetts Press, 2000.

James, Henry. *The Art of the Novel.* New York: Charles Scribner's Sons, 1934 (rpt. 1984).

Kollin, Susan. *Nature's State: Imagining Alaska as the Last Frontier.* Chapel Hill: University of North Carolina Press, 2001.

Lounsberry, Barbara. *The Art of Fact: Contemporary Artists of Nonfiction.* New York: Greenwood, 1990.

Maclean, Norman. *A River Runs through It and Other Stories.* Chicago: University of Chicago Press, 1976.

McPhee, John. *Annals of the Former World.* New York: Farrar, Straus & Giroux, 1998.

———. *Assembling California.* New York: Farrar, Straus & Giroux, 1993.

———. *Basin and Range.* New York: Farrar, Straus & Giroux, 1981.

———. *Coming into the Country.* New York: Farrar, Straus & Giroux, 1977.

———. *The Control of Nature.* New York: Farrar, Straus & Giroux, 1989.

———. *The Crofter and the Laird.* New York: Farrar, Straus & Giroux, 1970.

———. *The Curve of Binding Energy.* New York: Farrar, Straus & Giroux, 1974.

———. *The Deltoid Pumpkin Seed.* New York: Farrar, Straus & Giroux, 1973.

———. *Encounters with the Archdruid.* New York: Farrar, Straus & Giroux, 1971.

———. *The Founding Fish.* New York: Farrar, Straus & Giroux, 2002.

———. *Giving Good Weight.* New York: Farrar, Straus & Giroux, 1976.

———. *In Suspect Terrain.* New York: Farrar, Straus & Giroux, 1983.

———. *Irons in the Fire.* New York: Farrar, Straus & Giroux, 1997.

———. *The John McPhee Reader.* Ed. William Howarth. New York: Farrar, Straus & Giroux, 1976.

———. *Levels of the Game.* New York: Farrar, Straus & Giroux, 1969.

———. *Looking for a Ship.* New York: Farrar, Straus & Giroux, 1990.

———. *Oranges.* New York: Farrar, Straus & Giroux, 1967.

———. *The Pine Barrens.* New York: Farrar, Straus & Giroux, 1968.

———. *The Second John McPhee Reader.* Ed. Patricia Strachan with an introduction by David Remnick. New York: Farrar, Straus & Giroux, 1996.

———. *A Sense of Where You Are: A Profile of William Warren Bradley.* New York: Farrar, Straus & Giroux, 1965.

———. *The Survival of the Bark Canoe.* New York: Farrar, Straus & Giroux, 1975.

———. *Table of Contents.* New York: Farrar, Straus & Giroux, 1985.

Pearson, Michael. *John McPhee.* Boston: Twayne Publishers, 1997.

Quammen, David. "Rocks of Age." *New York Times Book Review* (5 July 1998): 9–10.

Ryden, Kent. *Landscape* with *Figures: Nature and Culture in New England.* Iowa City: University of Iowa Press, 2001.

Sims, Norman. *Literary Journalism in the Twentieth Century.* New York: Oxford University Press, 1990.

Stull, James, "Self and the Performance of Others: The Pastoral Vision of John McPhee." *North Dakota Quarterly* 59(3) (1991): 182–200.

I

The Evolving Writer

The four essays in part one study McPhee's biography and plot his emergence as a writer who works beyond the boundaries of most conventional journalism. William Howarth introduced John McPhee to a wide audience with his *John McPhee Reader* (1976). He introduces our book and a more widely known writer with his long survey that shifts gracefully between biography and literary criticism. This "second introduction" also reviews and refutes three sources of criticism sometimes leveled against McPhee. The next three essays elaborate themes enumerated by Howarth. Jared Haynes's (edited) interview, " 'The Size and Shape of the Canvas,' " provides us with McPhee's own voice and reinforces judgments rendered by Howarth. Barbara Lounsberry's essay traces in depth McPhee's predilection for the literary portrait, contrasting his emerging form with that developed by other nonfiction writers. Norman Sims, like Howarth a personal friend of McPhee's, uses interview material to echo biographical issues touched upon by Howarth. Together, these essays document McPhee's early ambition to become a writer as well as his long apprenticeship at *Time*. By 1963, when he realized his ambition of joining the *New Yorker* staff, McPhee (in his early thirties) had become the writer we know today. The subsequent career and shelf of twenty-seven books elaborate but do not substantially change that signature.

William Howarth

Introducing John McPhee

When Will He Write a Novel?

I first encountered John McPhee in 1967, when a friend lent me a book with a cover design of bright orange orbs, gathered around the title *Oranges*. "It's about oranges," he said, helpfully. "I can't believe I read a whole book about oranges, but there it is." A year later I was teaching at Princeton and a colleague asked me to review a book, any book, for the alumni magazine. Recalling those oranges, I proposed to write about John McPhee, '53.

McPhee had then published five volumes of nonfiction, ranging from profiles of Bill Bradley and Deerfield's headmaster to a study of the New Jersey Pine Barrens. He was an alumnus of the Princeton English department, where he read Joseph Conrad and William Faulkner and caused a stir by asking to write a novel for his senior thesis: a 65,000-word, never-published epic called "Skimmer Burns." This early achievement fixed his reputation with the professors. With each new nonfiction book, they would fretfully ask: "But when will he write a novel?"

My essay declared that he was writing literary nonfiction, the hot genre of the 1960s. In the hands of other contemporaries, like Norman Mailer, Tom Wolfe, Joan Didion, and Hunter Thompson, literary nonfiction was a feverish blur of reportage, opinion, imagination, and attitude. McPhee's version was steadfast, cooler, more obviously sustained by method and craft. His reporting was accurate, yet his sentences had an austere clarity that hinted at layers of meaning, even when focused on basketball or malt whisky.

In response to that essay I received a note from McPhee himself, who closed: "I read your review with . . . a sense of unexpected sharing, as if we were looking over the same fence into the same field." I liked that image, and perhaps he liked hearing at last some praise from his old department. A few days later we met.

McPhee was a small, trim man with dark hair and no beard—one later appeared and took up permanent residence. He dressed in tweed jackets and thick sweaters, and he spoke rapidly, between intervals of wary silence, in a low, emphatic baritone. He wore large, horn-rimmed glasses that magnified watchful eyes. He called his friends, prep-school fashion, by their last names: McGlynn, Bingham, Crow. We became exercise pals, playing squash or going for a run before lunch. I visited the McPhee home, a rambling colonial set on wooded acres north of Princeton, and met his wife, Yolanda Whitman, an attractive, witty partner who took his work seriously—his 1950s habits of thrift and chivalry, less so.

Their marriage created a blended family—six girls, two boys—and McPhee supported this brood by working remarkably long hours, reaching the office early and rarely leaving before 8 P.M. He preferred to work "down-town," first in rented space in the Princeton business district and later on the university campus. His day began slowly, with reading mail and making phone calls, then taking breaks for lunch and a run. Late in the afternoon came a zone of time that few could interrupt, about five hours when he typed steadily away on the latest project. This habit of playing the day as a long crescendo, he said, came from years spent at *Time* magazine, where writers famously procrastinated up to deadline hour.

Journalism has always nurtured McPhee's career, yet today he has earned a level of fame granted chiefly to novelists. In four decades he has produced twenty-seven books, entered the American Academy of Arts and Letters, received the 1999 Pulitzer Prize for Nonfiction, and accepted eight honorary degrees. He also has won honors for distinguished teaching at Princeton, where since 1975 he has trained a host of successful magazinists, including the present editors of *Time* and the *New Yorker*.

McPhee resists acting as a public voice, yet he has exerted a pervasive influence on the undervalued genre of literary nonfiction. The tradition reaches back to early British periodicals, with Daniel Defoe and James Boswell considered primal ancestors; and in America many writers have used nonfiction as a bread-and-butter venue, from Ben Franklin to Willa Cather, while newspaper and magazine work has trained novelists from Mark Twain to John Updike. Contemporary reporters view McPhee as a hero, for he is taught widely in schools, featured at literary festivals, and often cited as having the best job in journalism. The age of the Internet has only extended McPhee's fame, with several websites attracting breathless fans, including one devoted keeper of a "John McPhee Shrine." All his books remain in print, with steady sales. A book that I edited in 1976, *The John McPhee Reader,* has seen four editions and over thirty printings. (Profits go to the publisher: as an eager young academic, I worked for a flat fee of $600.)

The John McPhee Reader was a collaborative effort. The first edition was for Vintage Books at Random House, where Gail Collins supervised production. Two editors at Farrar, Straus & Giroux, Tom Stewart and Pat Strachan, helped me select the excerpts, which we passed to McPhee for approval. His only stipulation was that we not butcher his books. I wrote headnotes for each selection, also vetted by McPhee, and then an introduction. That essay went through several drafts, as I learned from his close editing how hard it is to compose an accurate piece of nonfiction. I called the book a *Reader,* in deference to school and anthology traditions, but also for those who might one day read McPhee as carefully as he read me.

In this essay I seek to introduce McPhee once more, though now he is far better known and we both have longer perspectives. I am in a curious position, trying to be an honest critic and also a good friend. I respect his privacy and would not betray confidences; at the same time, I was trained to be frank, especially when assessing what E. B. White called "the-man-on-paper" (402). In truth, that is the McPhee whom I know best. My sole distinction among his many friends is a deep interest in literary nonfiction, especially when it depicts natural history and science. In what follows, I have tried to use my personal knowledge of McPhee carefully, while paying his books the compliment of close attention. My studies have often featured textual genealogy, explaining how words reach print and speak to readers, and that process remains my focus here.

Another element now guiding me is the passage of time. The *McPhee Reader* first appeared in the Bicentennial year of 1976, between *The Survival of the Bark Canoe* (1975) and *Coming into the Country* (1977). That interval currently marks a mid-point in McPhee's career: in 1976 he had published thirteen books, and now fourteen more are in print. (Some fifty translations and limited or illustrated editions of his writings have also appeared.) This moment of symmetry will pass, but it allows me to reflect on how the last quarter-century affected him and to consider how some cultural trends may shape future views of his writings.

The Literature of Fact

Readers in the twenty-first century will regard McPhee as a man of letters, thanks to greatly expanded views of canon. Most literary anthologies now include a wide range of nonfiction writers and genres, from diary to manifesto. Yet some old habits prevail: libraries still categorize nonfiction books by content, scattering McPhee from Recreation to Environmental Studies, when he clearly deserves a shelf of his own. He also does not fit academic taxonomy; at Princeton, a Writing Program teaches expository prose while a Creative Writing Program covers poetry, drama, and fiction. McPhee dwells in his own venue, offering a Humanities course called "The Literature of Fact," on the art of writing essays, profiles, and stories of travel and place. This segregation is peculiar to Princeton, for elsewhere nonfiction is a healthy field of study, sustained by advanced-degree programs, scholarly journals, and frequent conferences.

An earlier Princetonian, F. Scott Fitzgerald, '17, once observed that "an author ought to write for the youth of his own generation, the critics of the next, and the schoolmasters of ever afterward" (25). Over a long career McPhee has mastered that hat trick, all the more rare because his books are nonfiction. The gold standard of his craft is reporting and fact-checking. He gives his students strict writing tips: cut the fluff; verify all quotations; do not interview dead people.

The label "nonfiction" also remains inadequate (though widespread), for it defines through negation, implying that nonfictional prose is also not creative, imaginative, or inventive. In this bias, we hear the echo of McPhee's professors: "But when will he write a novel?" The word "fiction" is from Latin *fictio* or *fingere,* which mean to feign or make up, as opposed to "fact," from *facere* or to do, meaning a deed or event. The contrast is between pretense and action or illusion and reality. As Tobias Smollett wrote, facts are "stubborn things" (188), distinct from belief or opinion. Facts express the past and present; the future is the realm of fiction. When reporters seek facts, they mean undeniable deeds, indisputable events.

These distinctions become slippery when applied to writers of literary nonfiction, since they use facts imaginatively, collecting and arranging them to tell stories and hint at larger implications. Emily Dickinson writes: "Tell all the truth—but tell it slant, / Success in circuit lies" (506), and that formula—gather, redirect, imply—often characterizes

McPhee's prose. If he knows all, he rarely tells all in numbing detail. Instead he selects, adjusts, and shapes. His use of literary devices, the purity of his style, and his devotion to form all help him to make feature writing—the "human interest" stories of daily journalism—into art, so that a miscellany of facts about quarter-horses or a Swiss army regiment becomes compelling narration.

Another literary aspect of McPhee's writing is that it endures, with little of it becoming dated or topical. Over a quarter-century, his books have outlived most of yesterday's newspapers and magazines, whose generic accounts of calamity or celebrity quickly sink, only to surface with new names and faces. Most ambulance-chasing "news" evaporates, because it spotlights attention-grabbing events and then moves on to the next sensation. "Read not the Times," Henry Thoreau once suggested, "Read the Eternities" ("Life without Principle," 175). McPhee is not writing scripture, but he rarely attends to subjects with timely news angles. Instead, he focuses on little-noted aspects of life—not the tennis matches played at Wimbledon, but the man who grows its grass. This attention to facts that other writers miss is a large part of McPhee's appeal, at least to readers drawn to subtlety and shadow, to the borders of a picture rather than its center.

McPhee has also descended from a tradition known as "documentary," in which the investigative methods of journalism merge with the narrative styles of literature and mass media. Documentary is a didactic art that has a hard surface but a warm heart; it affects a reader by gathering pieces of authentic evidence, then giving them affective force through arrangement and juxtaposition. In America, documentary tends to flourish in periods of grave social crisis: wars, depression, prolonged scandal. From the Civil War to Vietnam, tumultuous events have made the public clamor for documentation, for sober and honest readings of indisputable facts. When the World Trade Center towers fell into the ashes of history on 11 September 2001, just such an era may have begun again.

If McPhee has stretched the dimensions of reportage, he has always maintained a reporter's transparent persona. He has shied from any tendency to project a public identity or act as a public voice. Flickers of self-revelation and private allusion abound in his pages, yet those are what Thoreau called the secrets in a writer's trade, "inseparable from its very nature" (*Walden*, 15). Unlike Twain or Hemingway, writers with boisterous stage presence, McPhee avoids publicity. He has no agent, gives few interviews, and poses for even fewer photos. His portrait has never appeared on a book jacket—and never will, if he has his way.

Modesty and privacy, like implication and indirection, often dominate McPhee's books, which depict isolated figures who pursue high standards of craft. His attention goes to people who spend years learning to play tennis, build a canoe, or read a rock face, since they echo the writer's solitary discipline. McPhee is able to move easily through crowds, looking harmless, absorbing names, details, snatches of talk, and undercurrents. The subjects of his writing recall him fondly, if not well, for most of the time he has not given them much back. Each piece and each book resembles a roadcut, a layered exposure of the way we live now.

McPhee rose to fame through steady production, averaging since 1965 a new book every sixteen months. His publisher, Farrar, Straus & Giroux, keeps all the titles in print in both hardcover and paperback editions. This mutual enterprise creates a steady supply of McPheeviana, and consumer word-of-mouth sustains the demand. Readers make gifts to friends; new fans may buy McPhee's entire canon. Few living authors enjoy that kind of security, which verifies that a steady, long-term strategy in publishing may benefit a writer more than trying to create quick best-sellers, if the writer is by nature a marathon runner.

Even nonfiction celebrity brings considerable traffic, but McPhee guards his time by turning down most offers and queries that reach him. Few readers understand how long it takes to write the pages they can skim so swiftly. Over the years he has declined requests to write screenplays, deliver lectures, endorse products, and write blurbs. Although corporations and individuals often suggest stories that are thinly disguised advertising, McPhee has evaded checkbook journalism, though once he was sorely tempted by the offer of an expense-paid trip to cover a litter cleanup on Mount Everest.

The Writing Life

A good part of McPhee's emotional and professional security rests on having deep roots in one place. He was born in Princeton in 1931 and, except for brief interludes, has lived there all his life. During his youth, Princeton was more a small town than a suburb. He grew up in the modest "tree streets" (Maple, Linden, Pine, Chestnut, Walnut) near the campus, where his neighbors included a policeman, a doctor, a janitor, a newspaper editor, two football coaches, a butcher's cashier, and the dean of the School of Engineering. A decade later, the McPhee house became home to Earl Browder, former presidential candidate of the American Communist Party. Today this diversity has declined, thanks to warp-speed growth in central New Jersey. Sprawl has eaten local fields and woods, giving way to McMansions with quadruple garages. The tree streets have gentrified, and Nassau Street now sports a honking, gaseous, daylong crush of traffic. McPhee eyes these changes grimly, opting to spend his free time at a fishing retreat on the Delaware River.

Harry McPhee and Mary Ziegler McPhee instilled in their children (Roemer, Laura Anne, and John) a stubborn, anxious determination to strive. Dr. McPhee, a pioneer in sports medicine, tended Princeton athletes and several U.S. Olympic teams. McPhee was a sports-minded boy: he attended Princeton football games (often heading for the end zone to catch extra-point kicks) and local public schools, earning distinction in basketball and English. His most influential teacher, Mrs. Olive McKee, assigned three essays a week, each to include a detailed outline of its beginning, middle, and end. Summers he passed at a canoe camp in Vermont, eventually becoming a counselor.

After high school McPhee spent an extra year at Deerfield Academy, where he took first-rate courses in literature and geology, before entering Princeton in the fall of 1949. He played basketball his first year and also became a media celebrity. During his four collegiate years he appeared on *Twenty Questions,* a weekly television and radio program originating from New York. The producers wanted one young person on the show's panel. Fond of games, McPhee rapidly mastered the art of identifying mystery items—animal, vegetable, or mineral—with questions that required yes or no answers. This may have been useful literary training, as he learned to interview quickly, arrange evidence, and infer new lines of thought.

At Princeton, McPhee worked on the staffs of intermittently witty student publications like the *Nassau Literary Magazine* and the *Princeton Tiger.* He avoided the grind of day-to-day, "scoop" journalism, writing only two brief reviews, of a book and a movie, for the *Daily Princetonian.* As a senior he wrote "On the Campus," a page about student life, for the *Princeton Alumni Weekly.* The *PAW* circulates to a large readership, and this exposure encouraged him to turn professional. His fondest dream was to write for the *New Yorker,* but its editors persistently rejected his early submissions.

After college, McPhee took a year to read literature at Cambridge University, where he joined the school basketball team and played throughout Britain. Returning to Princeton, he tutored at a prep school, wrote television scripts (mainly for *Robert Montgomery Presents*), and tried to sell to the *New Yorker*, with no success. In 1957 he joined the staff of *Time*, where he worked in the back of the book: as writer of the "Show Business" section, he produced cover story profiles that ranged from Jackie Gleason to Richard Burton.

Work at *Time* was lucrative, exhausting, and formulaic. Given an opportunity to join the "National Affairs" section, a sure route to the top, McPhee declined and continued to solicit attention from the *New Yorker*. By 1960 that magazine's founding generation—Harold Ross, James Thurber, Dorothy Parker, Robert Benchley, Alexander Woollcott—was gone, but figures like Ogden Nash, S. J. Perelman, Edmund Wilson, and E. B. White still wrote for editor William Shawn, who had built a celebrated nonfiction staff with the talents of Alva Johnston, A. J. Liebling, and Joseph Mitchell, whom McPhee regarded as models. Shawn's taste for doom expanded the magazine's postwar range to include long-form works on social and political issues, including John Hersey's *Hiroshima* (1946), Rachel Carson's *Silent Spring* (1962), and Truman Capote's *In Cold Blood* (1965).

In 1963 the *New Yorker* finally accepted a McPhee story (a memoir of his basketball days at Cambridge) but then declined a subsequent proposal on Bill Bradley, saying the magazine had just run another basketball profile, on Bob Cousy of the Boston Celtics. McPhee looked it up: the Cousy story was dated 1959. He then wrote and sent to the *New Yorker* a 5,000-word letter describing Bradley. Shawn promised to read a full submission, but nothing more. McPhee delivered a 17,000-word piece in December 1964; it was accepted and printed the following month. Shortly thereafter he extracted an offer from Shawn to join the magazine as a staff writer.

Although the *New Yorker* advanced McPhee's career, he maintained his freelance status by working chiefly in Princeton and choosing topics that suited his range of experience. He wrote on basketball, tennis, canoes, Deerfield, Princeton, Cambridge, Scotland—and on all manner of animals, vegetables, and minerals. His passion for fresh orange juice inspired the piece that became *Oranges*, while *The Curve of Binding Energy* sprang from an after-tennis conversation with a law professor. The dividend on these diverse projects was *Coming into the Country* (1977), his first best-seller, a triptych portrait of Alaska that explores its people, towns, and deep wilderness. Then came an ambitious epic: four volumes on geological change along the route of Interstate 80. Conceived in 1978, this project took nearly two decades to complete, eventually winning the Pulitzer Prize as *Annals of the Former World* (1998). During that long interval McPhee wrote seven books on other topics, from haute cuisine to tramp steamers. Yet his professional landscape was erupting, for in 1985 Condé Nast bought the *New Yorker.*

The *New Yorker* hit its peak ad revenue in 1968 and then began a long decline. Its last profitable year was 1984, just before the Condé Nast sale; since then—through editors William Shawn, Robert Gottlieb, Tina Brown, and David Remnick—the losses have topped 200 million dollars. The major cause is a changing public. According to the *New York Times,* average Americans now spend less than 43 minutes a day reading. They are outdoors for 47 minutes, groom for 49 minutes, and watch television for 154 minutes (Hamlin, C1, 6). A Darwinian algorithm is at work here, suggesting that a general magazine for sophisticated readers has only faint prospects for survival.

Shawn was forced out in 1987, a move protested by 150 of the magazine's writers. McPhee's career then entered a difficult phase. Editor Gottlieb (1987–92) published the entire geology quartet, while editor Brown (1992–98) commissioned essays on Russian art, exotic autos, and scrap tires. McPhee never capitulated to tabloid sleaze or of-the-moment vulgarity, but the Brown-era pieces seem notably joyless. In McPhee's best work, the fabric and texture of a story reflect his own stubborn character, a dangerous quality in a *New Yorker* under unsympathetic management. For McPhee, style is the man: wherever his prose is compact, brisk, and edgy, the words mirror his own basal metabolism.

A Working Method

On the subject of his methods, McPhee has been far less private. He gives interviews, talks to writing classes, and, as a Ferris Professor of Journalism at Princeton, teaches sixteen seminar students in two of every three years. McPhee requires them to interview visitors, to research set pieces, and to "green" published texts, removing lines until they fit in less space. They also submit six or seven compositions, which he discusses in private conferences.

As a *New Yorker* staff writer under William Shawn, McPhee enjoyed both company benefits and free-agent independence. At the old head-quarters on 43rd Street, he had a small private office, rarely used. Staff writers did not cover assigned beats or write for special issues, but instead submitted story ideas to Shawn for "reservation." A reserved story was an optioned property, its topic and approach entered in a binder and held in perpetuity for the author. Writers could also submit sketches for "The Talk of the Town," the breezy opening section, and over thirty-eight years McPhee has contributed eleven unsigned Talk pieces. Mostly he works in Princeton on longer projects, developed with the counsel of Shawn and other editors, chiefly the late Robert Bingham. The *New Yorker* holds a first option on all of McPhee's work. He is free to choose a subject; the editors may criticize, accept, or reject his proposal. If rejected, he may still write the piece and sell it elsewhere. The magazine pays him monthly advances, plus all travel expenses.

A large portion of McPhee's early work on a project is field research. He prefers to drive, ideally with a canoe strapped on top, while listening to recorded books, the novels and classics he might not read at home. Hearing cadences of Dickens or Le Carré is probably a calisthenic exercise, since he often reads aloud when composing. At his home McPhee once kept a world map on which he drew rectangles, marking the range of his travels; today only Asia and the South Pacific remain virgin terrain.

McPhee conducts interviews equipped with basic knowledge but free of preconceptions. This open point of view helps him to learn more quickly, alert for surprises in the unfolding evidence. Because most stories have unsuspected complexities, he neither fakes ignorance nor puts phrases into an informant's mouth. His objective is to hear something that is fresh, a knotty and unconventional response.

Once McPhee interviewed me for part of a book; during our conversation his speech slowed, his brow knit, and he asked the same questions over and over. When repeating questions, he was apparently seeking a more printable reply. I began to work harder, eventually speaking in loose, free terms to the reporter. McPhee insists that his air of density is no ruse, but it also has useful results. Subjects may be timid or hostile until they feel comfortable with a writer. By repeating and even fumbling their answers, McPhee encourages informants to embroider a topic until he has it entire. In an ideal interview he listens silently, taking notes without framing repartee or inserting conversation.

Nearly all of McPhee's topics, from aircraft to canoes, are subjects that interested him in boyhood. For any topic beyond his youth, he turns to the Princeton faculty. He is listed in the university catalog as a visiting professor—a misnomer, since he is neither visiting nor a professor. (The Ferris appointment does not entail tenure.) Being raised among experts has advantages for an attentive journalist: McPhee lives surrounded by world-class authorities (in astrophysics, in geology, in classical and modern literature), and he works them as a prospector, mining the scholars for nuggets of suggestive or significant fact.

McPhee's stories often develop from interviews with a principal informant, a strong personality who provides skeletal framing for the work. Finding this character may be an act of serendipity: while working on *The Pine Barrens,* he accidentally met the indispensable Fred Brown, who knew all the people and nameless sandy roads of his region. Profiles built around a single character, like headmaster Frank Boyden or museum director Thomas Hoving, were more planned from the outset; but in the cases of physicist Ted Taylor and canoe-builder Henri Vaillancourt, McPhee was led to his central figure on the advice of informants, who play minor roles in the stories. At first he did not use tape recorders, fearing they would inhibit people, but later he found that mini-cassettes help to preserve accuracy. Whether on tape or a notebook page, his writing begins with words—a scrap of talk, bits of description, odd facts and inferences.

During some interviews McPhee seems to play mental chess, anticipating answers or plotting questions, but usually he builds on what he has previously seen and heard. Although he writes in a clear, left-handed script, the notes are unintelligible to an outsider. They are not indiscriminate jottings, since some may reach the final text with little change. The notes reflect his passion for physical details, bits of actuality that no one could make up. Mark Twain once wrote: "Truth is stranger than fiction . . . because Fiction is obliged to stick to possibilities; Truth isn't" (108). In nonfiction, the impossible often rules. Traveling in Alaska, McPhee heard several stories about a military aviator whose plane crashed in deep bush in December 1942. No one could remember his name, only that he survived the arctic winter and walked out after eighty days. The story intrigued McPhee, so he launched a line of inquiry that took several months, winding from Alaska to Alabama and then to Philadelphia, where he found the survivor, named Leon Crane. Thirty-five years after the crash, Leon filled in the gaps of his story: he survived by finding an unlocked cabin, full of supplies, abandoned by its owner four years earlier.

Given close attention, facts may flower into tropes that express character and theme. Instead of sermonizing on thrift or extravagance, McPhee notes that islander Donald Gibbie's teapot is plugged with thirteen wood screws or that the light in Lt. Arthur Ashe's closet at West Point is always burning. In rhetoric this figure is *synecdoche,* the part that represents all. Hence McPhee may infer a history of civilization from the botany of oranges. In writing about basketball, he builds a sense of the game around Bill Bradley by learning and projecting the player's knowledge. He credits Bradley with the book's articulation, yet reporting talk well is not transcription but an act of ventriloquism. In *The Deltoid Pumpkin Seed,* McPhee more obviously arranges the story, for his climax reports the inner thoughts of a test pilot—as told to him later by the pilot—while attending to the facts of air speed, stability, angle of attack, and rate of climb.

When he begins to hear the same stories a third time, McPhee stops interviewing, returns to Princeton, and launches the arduous process of composition. His working methods vary with projects, and in 1984 he began to write with computers, but the tasks remain constant. He first transcribes the notebooks by typing entries in order, occasionally adding other details or current thoughts as he goes. He likens this process to a magnet's attraction of iron filings; as the notes take shape, they suggest new ideas about placement, phrasing, or possible analogies. When finished, he may have a printed sheaf of notes, enough to fill a spring binder. He makes a copy and shelves it for later use. He then reads and rereads the binder, looking for areas he needs to flesh out with research and reading. Reading produces more notes, added to his binder pages. Finally, he makes notes on possible structures, describing patterns the story might assume.

While its structure is forming, or when he senses how a story may end, McPhee often writes a first draft of "the lead" or story opening. In newspaper writing the lead is often a one-sentence paragraph, imparting the story's who-what-where particulars. McPhee's leads are longer, more dramatic, and more oblique. He establishes a mood, a setting, perhaps some characters or events, but does not nutshell the story or even hint at its full dimensions. In "Travels in Georgia" the lead conveys tone, style, characters, and theme in a few dramatic actions. Three people are riding in a Chevrolet across back Georgia roads. They share a snack, exchange good-humored insults, and then halt to inspect a turtle lying dead on the road. The action begins *in medias res* and continues without flashbacks or helpful exposition for several pages. When readers finally hit a backward loop, they have a subliminal sense of who-what-where, and fulfilling that expectancy becomes McPhee's task in planning the rest of his story.

Having read the lead aloud to his wife, friends, and editors, McPhee goes back to the binder and begins to code it with structural notes, using titles like "Voyageurs" and "Loons" or acronyms: "GLAT," "LASLE." These topics are formal story segments, which he writes on index cards. After assembling a stack, he fans them out and plays writer solitaire, studying the possibilities of order. Decisions come slowly, for a story has many possible sequences, and each arrangement yields a chain of desired or undesired effects. When he has the cards in a satisfactory arrangement, he thumbtacks them to a large bulletin board. The shade of Mrs. Olive McKee smiles upon this array: beginning, middle, end. McPhee calls the outline logical, but its logic is of no ordinary, abecedarian variety, running from A to Z or 1 to 10.

With cards on the board, committed to their structure, he next codes the duplicate set of notes and then sorts them into file folders, one folder for each topical index card on the bulletin board. These folders are the narrative segments that he will refine when writing a first draft. With the folders squared away in a vertical file, he is ready to write. Once he kept a large steel dart to mark his progress, stabbing it into one card after another on the bulletin board. The dart has long since disappeared, though it remains in spirit. For each card he opens a folder, further sorting its notes until this segment also has a structure. Then he begins to type his first draft, picking up where the lead ends. When he finishes a folder he moves to the next card, gets its folder, sorts it out, and continues to type.

Outlined in this fashion, McPhee's writing method may seem mechanical, almost programmed to sort and retrieve data bits. The purpose of his routine is both practical and aesthetic: it runs a line of order through the chaos of his notes, leaving him free to write on a given parcel of work at a given time. Other sections do not come crowding in to clutter his desk and mind; structure spares him that confusion, creates a design that will not come tumbling down. The process also provides no easy exit from the work at hand, which is to confront that silent and humorless partner, the blank computer screen.

As readers begin a piece, they can be sure that McPhee knows how it will end, where the center lies, how that middle spans its members, and where the point of balance lies. At the center of *The Pine Barrens* stands a chapter on Chatsworth, "The Capital of the Pines," and Chatsworth itself stands but six miles from the region's geographical center. The dead-even spot of *Levels of the Game* is not at dead center, however, but twenty pages from the end. At that moment Ashe and Graebner have each won ninety-three points, and they rush on to a swift denouement—"the next four points they play will decide it all" (128). The closing chapters are often antiphonal, setting echoes from the past against future rumbles. New Jersey's legendary pines steadily shrink before the press of urban development. The fresh citrus market of old Florida wanes; a booming industry in concentrate rises. Atlantic City crumbles, but Monopoly goes on forever. Near the end of *Encounters with the Archdruid,* dam-hater David Brower and dam-builder Floyd Dominy ride through the Colorado River's Lava Falls, their ceaseless quarrel silenced momentarily by the roar of pounding water.

Coming into the Country is a tour de force in structural planning, for McPhee shrinks vast Alaska into three places—wild, urban, bush—where life is less political than bioregional, governed by terrain and water. Book I, "The Encircled River," begins and ends in the same place, signaled by allusions to a bandanna, "rolled on the diagonal" around McPhee's head (5). That square rolled into a circle wraps the story, which begins at a moment just before the ending, when the bandanna has begun to dry. Written in present tense to preserve the illusion of time streaming forward, the story moves with the river current; yet against that line of action appear constant references to circles, from the oval shapes of fish and their spawning craters to the cycles of plants and animals, making endless rings of life through encircling seasons and years.

The story actually involves two rivers, Salmon and Kobuk; but McPhee makes those spaces fluid so that past, present, and future will touch and flood each other. Near the story center, he comes to the journey's end and shifts into past tense: "Children were fishing when we were here before" (*Coming,* 40). That earlier time he now recalls, when he flew up-river to the headwaters region and headed downstream. Descending the Salmon, he looked for bears, heard hunting stories, learned the paradox of raw, repellent Nature: "It was no less strongly attractive—with a beauty of nowhere else, composed in turning circles" (93). Then he drifts toward closure, which becomes a moment just before the story opens. A grizzly bear is at play in the river, whirling salmon into the air, "end over end" (94), before he heads upstream toward the boats. A stick snaps, the bear comes alert, and the boats drift into his focus: "If we were looking at something we had rarely seen before, God help him so was he" (95). This moment of contact closes the story circle, connecting human narrative to natural history. The bear is central because he is at risk, like the river that no longer runs clear, like the country that may not live forever wild. Form here offers not a solution but an incarnation of problems, giving them shape through linked events and leading as an introduction to books II and III of the volume.

The hallmark of McPhee's craft is that his work always has inherent form. A potter and carpenter seek form; Aristotle asked writers to reach a similar goal. But writers have infinite options for order, and McPhee seems to delight in making any that do not violate story logic. A book on tennis may imitate the game's back-and-forth, contrapuntal action; but it might also resemble a mountain climb, with an ascent, climax, and descent arranged in pyramidal form. The choice is clear: find an idea for order *in* the material, but do not impose one *upon* it, favoring what Samuel Taylor Coleridge called the "organic" over "mechanic" principles of structure. McPhee is careful to make a distinction between situation and structure. In *Encounters with the Archdruid,* he plans the situation, a series of confrontations between David Brower and three arch-foes, but within each story a structure emerges that was not planned *a priori*. A novelist might elect to create a highly elaborated plot, but good nonfiction presents rather than invents order. Too much shuffling of those index cards would lead to fussy, baroque patterns, suggesting self-indulgence. Yet McPhee does not allow subject matter to dictate his narrative forms. The story of a horse race need not run in an oval; nor must a canoe trip curve at its ends—those limited formal objectives are dull and pious, like the shaped verse of seventeenth-century poets.

McPhee seems also to want to stay loose, free to exploit surprises. At times he manipulates order: recounting Thomas Hoving's discovery of an ivory cross, McPhee cuts and reshapes time like a sculptor. In *The Deltoid Pumpkin Seed,* he often digresses from the story's forward motion to suggest an experiment in progress, lurching ahead ten yards and then sideways for twenty. The pattern makes readers oscillate between straight and ironic estimates of the probable fate of the airship Aereon 26. Yet McPhee will not trim evidence to fit a narrative pattern. When trouble begins on a canoe trip, "it comes from the inside, from fast-growing hatreds among the friends who started" (*Survival*, 68). That change is beyond the writer's control; he appears to accept it as an athlete respects the impartial rules of a game.

Writing a first draft is painful work, whether it moves quickly or slowly. McPhee retreats to his office, not writing constantly, but distilling research into prose. Some authors overwrite and later boil down; he culls before typing. He likens this method to the sport of curling, sweeping the ice clean to advance a gliding stone. Writing requires endless decisions, mostly on what *not* to say. The process is nerve-racking and lonely. Sometimes he talks to others about problems but then generally follows his own counsel. Facing the screen for long stretches, he generates excess energy. Over the years he has shifted from racket sports to cycling, which he attacks with a dogged fury. Writing is a similar self-challenge: he has spent years learning to move *against* a habitual thought or phrase, avoiding old ruts in the road.

The resulting prose style is fresh, strong, unaffected, and idiosyncratic. McPhee's phrases and sentences come in many guises. A basic mode is simple declaration, arranged in strings of laconic grace: "Every motion developed in its simplest form. Every motion repeated itself precisely when he used it again" (*A Sense*, 5). He can also invoke eloquence, as when Tom Hoving recalls his adolescence: "At noon we ate sandwiches and field tomatoes, and drank iced tea; then we slept off lunch in the cool earth of the corn furrows. The corn had a kind of mystery. You were out there and it was very high, all around you" (*A Roomful*, 18). On student papers, McPhee sometimes writes in the margins: "Busy." The goal is to waste not a word, as in this description of Havasu Canyon, a chain of stairstep pools set in a baking desert: "The pools were as much as fifteen feet deep, and the water in them was white where it plunged and foamed, then blue in a wide circle around the plunge point, and pale green in the outer peripheries" (*Encounters*, 236).

Part of his craft rests on knowing the language of a subject. He masters its vocabulary and syntax, even the jargon of atomic destruction—ploot, shake, jerk, kilojerk, megajerk. "A cross-section for neutron capture was expressed in terms of the extremely small area a neutron had to hit in order to enter a nucleus—say, one septillionth of a square centimeter—and this was known as a 'barn'" (*The Curve*, 115–16). Mostly the prose succeeds because it is as unsparing as an engineer's report, until a bomb ignites. Here is a description of Clark Graebner's neighborhood: "The houses of Wimbledon Road appear to be . . . almost too big for the parcels of land allotted to them. They are faced with stratified rock, lightened with big windows, surrounded with shrubbery, and lined up in propinquous ranks like yachts at a pier" (*Levels,* 59).

Persistent good humor—the tennis-mad Graebners live on "Wimbledon Road"—is another strong aspect of McPhee's style. He can skewer a blowhard, like the Carranza Day speaker in *The Pine Barrens,* who "had recently spent 'an unprecedented hour with the President of Mexico'" (105). At times he reports in *New Yorker* style, using trademarks— L. L. Bean, Adidas, The Glenlivet—to specify a scene, sharpen an observation. This affection for labels produces in *The Crofter and the Laird* two pages of Gaelic place names, each with English translation: "Sguid nam Ban Truagh (the Shelter of the Miserable Women)" (54).

McPhee's jokes are often brief asides that puncture hyperbole. One awestruck fan of David Brower, meeting him in the desert, draws this thrust: "I wondered if the hiker was going to bend over and draw a picture of a fish in the sand" (*Encounters,* 207). Later on, the rafting party fearfully approaches the Upset rapids: "People say it as if they were being wheeled toward it on a hospital cart" (220). "Travels in Georgia" creates an ironic motif by repeating an acronym. Carol Ruckdeschel, an environmental biologist, collects animals accidentally killed by traffic and found Dead on the Road or "D.O.R." Barely explained in the story's lead, "D.O.R." begins to appear in other contexts, like a traffic jam around Newark Airport: "thousands and thousands of murmuring cars, moving nowhere, nowhere to move, shaking, vibrating, stinking, rotting, *Homo sapiens* D.O.R." (*Pieces,* 26). Ultimately the phrase becomes an emblem of cultural decay: "D.O.R. gas station. It was abandoned, its old pumps rusting; beside the pumps, a twenty-year-old Dodge with four flat tires" (46). Elsewhere McPhee uses extreme analogies to provoke shock and laughter. One scene in *The Deltoid Pumpkin Seed* depicts John Kukon's frantic efforts to win a model airplane race. With time running out, he decides to try a high-energy fuel: "Blend 4 had never been used. Kukon had never actually expected to use it. He had conceived of it as a fuel for a situation of extreme and unusual emergency. Its characteristics were that it would almost certainly destroy the engine that burned it, but meanwhile the engine would develop enough thrust to drive a sparrow to the moon" (27).

Moving beyond a first draft, McPhee picks up speed. He prunes and polishes but makes few changes in his original structure. Now his laborious planning and composing pay off, for the hardest stretch is over. He prints clean copies and off they go to the *New Yorker*. No official deadlines are set, but usually he meets self-imposed goals. Editors read the final draft, and the copy gets its closest readings from three offices. The grammarian provides a meticulous parsing of every sentence and point of English usage. The lawyer looks for potential libel. The "checkers" independently verify every assertion of fact. They retrace McPhee's steps, contact his informants, and look up the books he read, as well as many he did not read.

Exactly when his work appears in the *New Yorker* depends on several factors, including the magazine's current backlog and seasonal aspects of the piece. "Firewood" cannot run well in July, for example, but is fine in early March. Like many writers, he proofreads with no visceral pleasure. Shawn often ran McPhee's long pieces in a series of issues, under titles like "Profile" or "A Reporter at Large." Tina Brown kept those rubrics but preferred much shorter lengths. The *New Yorker* copyrights its texts but transfers ownership to McPhee when he has arranged for book publication. He does not revise the book texts, except for minor details or updates. He proofreads these works, too, even when caught up in the field research for his next project.

Looking at Things

Although reviewers have treated McPhee well, three negative lines of comment do recur: he tends to over-praise his heroes, he will not take stands on controversial issues, and he writes too often about rocks. These charges oversimplify his aims and also ignore the course of his career. McPhee has in fact described many kinds of heroes, fools, and blackguards, and they have grown more complex with each new book. Moreover, he always positions heroic figures against strong opponents who offer them tough confrontations. His central figures thus represent many strata of behavior, not a single ideal of excellence.

Bill Bradley seems heroic, for he is talented, disciplined, articulate, and rich. Yet he is also paradoxical, a man both proud and self-effacing; able to analyze five parts of his hook shot, but helplessly addicted to the narcosis of basketball: "It's getting dark. I have to go back for dinner. I'll shoot a couple more. Feels good. A couple more" (*A Sense*, 74). McPhee contrasts Bradley's complete skills to the "aimless prestidigitation" (7) of certain other players, who can make brilliant shots but have no defensive or ball-handling skills. He also catches Bradley in down cycles, hampered by injury or academic fatigue, and thus can show how the Princeton team of 1965 rallied to match its hero. In their final home game, Bradley is replaced by Kenny Shank, whom the crowd has made into a mock hero because Shank is Bradley's substitute, never used in games but the best defender against him in practice. That night Shank reaches a career high of fourteen glorious points, and Princeton's coach pays him the ultimate compliment: "He sent Bill Bradley into the game as Shank's substitute" (110). The crowd cheers Shank's exit, "and the applause was now as genuine as it had ever been for Bradley himself" (110). Shank's triumph tempers Bradley's heroic attributes, established earlier in the profile. The star and his sub reverse their images in the mirror of basketball, which McPhee calls a "multiradial way of looking at things" (49).

In *Levels of the Game,* Ashe and Graebner seem matched as hero and villain, but the choice is not that simple. Ashe is an admirable figure because he also has multiradial vision. Unlike Bradley, Ashe wins because he is inconsistent, disorderly, and unpredictable. His background is less privileged than Bradley's, his mind more layered. Graebner is an exact counterpart, one of McPhee's least likable figures: brutal, bigoted, and predictable, doomed to lose because he cannot adapt to change. By the story's end, he is more to be pitied than feared. Attempting to emulate Ashe, Graebner fails to become another Shank: "An unbelievable shot for me to try—difficult in the first place, and under this pressure ridiculous. Stupid" (150).

McPhee's heroes remain in character, mostly. In *The Headmaster,* Frank Boyden runs his school adroitly but with little apparent strategy. Yet his shallows still sparkle, and Helen Boyden more than compensates with her learning and moral acuity: "When they are together, she makes light of him and he reacts in kind. She is the quicker of the two. He is funnier" (52). In *La Place de la Concorde Suisse,* Luc Massy, member of the Tenth Mountain Division of the Swiss Army, is a winemaker by trade—and everywhere on maneuvers he carries wine, drinking glass, and corkscrew, ever ready, like an armed grenade.

Other heroes in McPhee's canon represent entire social classes. Long characterized as vicious and inbred, the "pineys" of south Jersey prove shrewd and principled. In their world, the barbarians are urban intruders: city thugs build stills or dump bodies, arsonists start fires, poachers slaughter deer, "developers" erase a region's vitality. The crofters on Colonsay are just as tough and face a parallel crisis: history has made them into thrifty recyclers who waste nothing, least of all the laird's sympathy for their anachronistic plight. In Georgia, McPhee discerns two broad classes of people, those who meander and those who straighten. Carol, Sam, and even the governor are heroes with large credentials, winners who endure because of their innate tolerance: "She had no exclusive specialty. She wanted to do everything. Any plant or creature, dead or alive, attracted her eye" (*Pieces*, 24).

The notion that McPhee avoids controversy stems from his habit of walking around a topic many times, to see it from all angles. He does not pursue the old journalistic claim of "objectivity," which evaded the fact of writer-bias; nor will he adopt the newer fashion of advocacy reporting. In McPhee's writings, the standard is not passion or identity but expertise. Many of his books focus on experts who rise above local allegiances, responding instead to the demands of craft. The citrus scientists who sustain Florida's economy are outsiders who ignore profits, focusing on diseased stock and careful fruit inspections. Ted Taylor is a maverick expert, wanting to merge theoretical and applied physics and also to make science politically responsible. An especially cross-grained expert is Henri Vaillancourt, builder of birch-bark canoes. He is all that a master artisan should be: patient, skillful, instinctive in his handling of tools and designs. He also seems a master woodsman who makes his own beef jerky. Yet on a canoe voyage the beef spoils and he proves "as green as his jerky" (*Survival*, 85), a maladroit canoeist, camper, and human companion.

Given this approach to character, McPhee will not take sides in a controversy. His purpose is to put all sides fairly before readers, who then have a responsibility to think. David Brower may be an ardent conservationist, but he is also a prickly, stubborn, vain, cranky SOB. His opponent, Floyd Dominy, is a dam-builder and much more—funny, brave, stoic, and generous, even to Brower. Instead of drawing simple cartoons of his characters, McPhee renders them fully for our judgment by maintaining an artist's distance and catholicity. He liked Bill Bradley for the totality of his play: "He did all kinds of things he didn't have to do simply because those were the dimensions of the game" (*A Sense*, 7–8). The same devotion to skill animates his account of Ed and Stanley Gelvin, a father and son who decide to mine a remote Alaskan stream for gold. The task requires ingenuity and enterprise, from studying the landscape to breaking down a 5,700-pound backhoe and flying it to the site, "like birds carrying straws" (*Coming*, 232). Soon they need a large bulldozer, a 110,000-pound D9 Cat, which they purchase and drive home through blizzards and mountain passes. The Gelvins divert a stream, kill its fish, trash its meadows—all for a jar of gold. Watching them and thinking of a larger context, McPhee delivers what for him amounts to an editorial:

> Am I disgusted? Manifestly not. Not from here, from now, from this perspective. I am too warmly, too subjectively caught up in what the Gelvins are doing. In the ecomilitia, bust me to private. This mine is a cork on the sea. Meanwhile (and possibly, more seriously), the relationship between this father and son is as attractive as anything I have seen in Alaska—both of them self-reliant beyond the usual reach of the term, the characteristic formed by this country. Whatever they are doing, whether it is mining or something else, they do for themselves what no one else is here to do for them. Their kind is more endangered every year. Balance that against the nick they are making in this land. Only an easygoing extremist would preserve every bit of the country. And extremists alone would exploit it all. Everyone else has to think the matter through—choose a point of tolerance, however much the point might tend to one side. For myself, I am closer to the preserving side—that is, the side that would preserve the Gelvins. To be sure, I would preserve plenty of land as well. (430)

McPhee can make this judgment because his portrait of the Gelvins is full and balanced; they are masters of technology yet love their country; they meet it always on its terms, adapting their needs to its seasons, climate, and terrain. The Gelvin passage has stirred some controversy among politically minded readers, no doubt provoked by that swipe at "the ecomilitia," but the literary critic Thomas Bailey takes a longer view, arguing that McPhee's stance is that of a "meta-naturalist" (195, 212), weaned from the old notion of Nature as pastoral to the darker sense that it is a system far more powerful than human politics and economics.

The notion that McPhee erred in writing about geology reflects a narrow view of his career. His early pieces were classic *New Yorker* fare, filling space in a magazine sold to affluent urban readers. Because of his training at *Time,* he specialized in *New Yorker* profiles, the biographical sketches of Bradley, Boyden, Hoving, and travel guru Temple Fielding that appeared in 1965–69. Rooted in McPhee's life experiences, the stories offer self-portraiture in a minor key. "Every motion developed in its simplest form" (*A Sense,* 5), he writes, watching Bradley practice.

"Every motion repeated itself precisely when he used it again." By the time he wrote "A Roomful of Hovings" (first published in 1967), McPhee had advanced into formal experiment, dropping the usual time-line of history to follow Hoving's many pasts, moods, and masks. The profile became a stroll through a gallery, its scenes arranged to suggest both portraiture and provenance, the scattered bits of evidence that form an artwork's genealogy.

The other *New Yorker* genre McPhee mastered is what some publications call the commodity or process story, which takes an object and creates a full account of its origins or production. Such a story, "A Dash of Tabasco," appeared in the *New Yorker* on 13 June 1953, a week after McPhee graduated from Princeton. The piece has a simple opening: seated in a Manhattan restaurant, the author dashes his clams with Tabasco sauce and reads the bottle label. Its reference to a McIlhenny family of New Iberia, Louisiana, sets him pondering, and soon he is traveling south. McPhee's early work in this mode produced *Oranges* (1967) and *The Deltoid Pumpkin Seed* (1973), where his primary focus is on an object, framed by the people who grow or build it. The citrus book recalls *Fortune* and *Life* documentaries: library and field research plotted and pieced like an intricate mosaic. The Aereon 26 story is one of McPhee's few comedies: its characters are odd-lot and their invention hybrid, halfway between airplane and airship. Even the inventors' secrecy is amusing, since the Aereon 26 shape only provokes attention.

McPhee made a large advance in this mode when he wrote *The Curve of Binding Energy* (1974), a book that weds process and profile in a unique literary structure, resembling the letter Y. The book has two story lines: one describes special nuclear materials and how easy they might be to procure; the other depicts Ted Taylor's growth as a physicist and bomb designer. Those lines begin far apart and steadily grow closer, finally converging when McPhee and Taylor retreat to a Maryland cabin and there pursue, "in its many possible forms, the unclassified atomic bomb" (131). This book was McPhee's first extended venture into reporting science, which became compelling narrative because Taylor explained obscure matters with vivid analogies. The subject matter was also timely, for nuclear energy produces materials that can be reprocessed into uranium and plutonium, both essential for bomb-building terrorists. The book was cited at congressional hearings, and it later inspired other authors to write books and films on nuclear terrorism.

McPhee's writings from 1969 to 1979 increasingly combine the profile and process models, laying equal weight on a set of personalities and a contest or journey that brings them together. Some of the conflict is socially ordained, as in *Levels of the Game* (1969), which depicts the 1968 U.S. Open semifinal match between Arthur Ashe and Clark Graebner, who were Davis Cup teammates but now opponents and also opposites in race, culture, training, and style. To write the piece, McPhee obtained a film of the match, studied it closely, and then asked each player to watch as well. As they talked, re-creating their thoughts and emotions with wondrous precision, he took notes. That material allowed him to catch the immediacy of serve and volley rallies, but with room for deep lobs into the past.

A more complex contest governs *Encounters with the Archdruid* (1971), where McPhee pits David Brower against advocates for mines, resorts, and dams. The plan is formulaic, rather like Boswell prodding Johnson to pontificate, but it succeeds because of McPhee's impartiality. For every point Brower scores on the beauties of wildness, his opponents respond with sensible defenses of progress. The four personalities only rumple these issues, since Brower is no mere Druid, a worshipper of trees; nor are his adversaries simply out to exploit the land. *The Survival of the Bark Canoe* (1975) has a simpler two-part pattern, in which the profile is both process and journey, starting with Henri Vaillancourt building canoes in his workshop and then watching him test that product on the waters of Maine. Vaillancourt often alludes to Henry D. Thoreau's writings, so it transpires that a party of six will follow Thoreau's 1857 canoe journey from the west to the east branches of the Penobscot River. The narrative alternates between precise descriptions of craft and the wayward, fluctuating pace of the trip. Although Thoreau's presence in the narrative is incidental, the description of his writing methods suggests a McPhee self-portrait: "With the advantage of retrospect, he reconstructed the story to reveal a new kind of significance that the notes do not reveal. Something new in journalism" (36).

McPhee's later books often rely on profile and process stories, from collections of short pieces like *Giving Good Weight* (1975–79) and *Table of Contents* (1980–85) to the longer narratives of *Heirs of General Practice* (1986), *Looking for a Ship* (1990), and *The Ransom of Russian Art* (1994). All provide densely reported stories about food, medicine, shipping, and art collection, written during intervals between McPhee's ongoing four-part series on geology. Two of the books caused media flaps when McPhee used informants who proved to be less than expert. The chef called "Otto" has a great natural talent for cookery, but he errs in disparaging some fish served at Lutèce, a top New York City restaurant. Norton Dodge is an economist who buys unsanctioned Soviet-era paintings, a few of dubious quality. Defending their professional turf, a food critic and a historian strongly attacked McPhee's veracity. No one mentioned form or style, only content, with the clear assumption that no journalist may attain expertise. Their pique aside, we are more likely to remember the lead for "Brigade de Cuisine," in which McPhee enumerates with sensuous pleasure the fifth-, fourth-, third-, second-, and first-best meals he ever ate, all of them served at an anonymous inn "in the region of New York City" (*Giving*, 181).

In my view, McPhee's most original and lasting books focus intently upon places. He came to this task by drawing on several elements in his background: deep affection for a hometown, years of outdoor sport and travel, training in natural science, and a strong grasp of visual patterns, especially those in maps, land, water, and rocks. It also helped to be shy and withdrawn, since affection for nature often begins with distrust of human racket and clutter. As an eleven-year-old in 1942, he joined the Air Warning Service, which trained him to identify the shapes of passing aircraft. On weekday afternoons he rode in a car from Princeton to Rocky Hill and sat for hours with an adult volunteer in a air-spotter booth. McPhee scanned the skies with binoculars, listed each sighted plane on a chart, and phoned his list to New York. Some seventh-graders might find that a boring assignment; but he felt swept away by excitement, for he was out in the open, reporting back its news.

The *New Yorker* has not often published "outdoor" topics. Manhattan is the most prodigiously developed real estate on earth, and Anne Matthews spoke for many residents when she defined their view of nature as "that big green blur between the lobby and the cab" (7). E. B. White pioneered in a contrarian vein by writing accounts of wildlife in the city, and his later dispatches from Maine on snowstorms and pig funerals appealed to *New Yorker* readers, who by the 1960s increasingly lived in suburbs. McPhee's earliest place-centered book is *Oranges*, set in the landscape of central Florida. A Talk piece, "On the Way to Gladstone" (9 July 1966), describes the once-dwindling bear population of New Jersey. His first major work on place is *The Pine Barrens* (1968), a personal breakthrough in his nonfiction writing.

The Pine Barrens makes a story out of rich and forgotten materials, imparting a sense of place that is rare in works of reportage. It describes a legendary piece of terrain, the "pines" of southeast New Jersey, a great tract of sandy, sparsely populated forest that lies between the state's coastal resorts and its industrial corridor of Interstate 95. Within a day's drive of several million people stands this wilderness, the improbable heart of Eastern megalopolis, set equidistant from Richmond and Boston. In preparing his book, McPhee struggled to find a narrative structure. He recalls lying on a picnic table in his back yard, mulling over different plans, and finally realizing that Fred Brown knew three-quarters of the book's informants. The story thus begins with a visit to Brown's home, a place exactly inventoried to establish character and setting. Each chapter after that takes up a new place, and within that succession McPhee arranges his notes on nature, people, and history. The result is a piece of true place-writing, in which physical environment becomes the active foreground, not a scenic backdrop.

McPhee also envisions the pines as a *locus classicus,* the place in America where cultural traditions of North and South meet, where prerevolutionary history is recorded and postmodern battles will be fought by developers and ecologists. The region is both an archetype and another country, a place so at variance with modern norms that it breeds replicas of America's original stock, "pineys" like Jim Leek: "There ain't nobody bothers you here. You can be alone. I'm just a woods boy. I wouldn't want to live in a town" (*Pine Barrens,* 56). That phrase is both angelus and alarm, since developers are eager to construct jetports and amusement centers for the pines—which sits atop the largest freshwater aquifer in the eastern United States. McPhee weaves these facts with gentle, relentless insinuation, combining narrative, dialogue, and exposition to suggest how a place like the pines sustains its fabled Air Tune, a melody "there, everywhere, just beyond hearing" (73).

Next McPhee produced *The Crofter and the Laird* (1970), based on a season spent with his family on Colonsay—a rocky island in the Inner Hebrides, off Scotland's western coast. At Colonsay the last chief of clan Mhic a' Phi was killed, and by the late eighteenth century many of the other Highland clans were also broken, victims of civil strife or English misrule from the south. Traditional Scots culture further waned during the nineteenth century, as immigrants left for America and other lands. McPhee's return to the home of his ancestors is both sentimental and ritual, an effort to reclaim the Celtic part of his Scots-Swiss heritage. This book celebrates community life, its constant flow and ebb of boast and gossip, daydreams and legends. Colonsay is a microcosmic place, "less like a small town than like a large lifeboat" (48), manned by a crew whose stations bear the archaic titles of crofter (tenant), laird (owner), and factor (overseer). Bound in tangled lines of loyalty and distrust, the islanders sail toward an unpromising future, one that may be as gloomy as his old chieftain's fate. In this place-story, McPhee becomes less a neutral observer and more involved as a character. His anecdotes are funnier, more frequent, less oblique; his learning and tastes (for food or language) more evident. The reciprocal affection of Colonsay also comes through, as the islanders open to his discovery of the place they inhabit but never quite own.

Pieces of the Frame (1975) contains a dozen years of stories written about places, ranging from Scotland to New England and the South. Two in particular stand out. "The Search for Marvin Gardens" (1972) is a portrait of urban blight in Atlantic City, once the resort kingdom of the New Jersey shore. The piece has a boldly experimental air, setting the story of the city's fall within a game of Monopoly, the parlor game built on local place names: Boardwalk, Park Place, Marvin Gardens. Monopoly is "chess at Wall Street level" (83), and its players echo the same heartless rules that built and destroyed Atlantic City. The story works by layering places, on the board and in the city, cutting back and forth, detonating ironic wins and losses. One of the few surviving neighborhoods is Marvin Gardens, a middle-class haven south on the Boardwalk, in Margate, New Jersey.

"Travels in Georgia" (1975) profiles Carol Ruckdeschel, a field zoologist who travels back roads, searching for landscapes and species to preserve. McPhee's journey with her makes a great loop through Georgia, touching its mountains, piedmont, and coastal plain. Yet the trip also "tended to mock the idea of a state—as an unnatural subdivision of the globe" (*Pieces,* 26), for the bogs and creeks of Georgia resist political boundaries and legal claims. People constantly threaten Georgia's wild places, but McPhee does not paint them as stock villains. Chap Causey, the dragline operator who reams a river to provide flood control, is a "world class" performer (13); the dozen folks who live in Georgia's remotest, most beautiful place have an ornery aesthetic of their own: "Lyrical in its effrontery to fact, the name of the valley was Tate City" (29). On his own travels, McPhee hews to the same line of balance, lyrical one moment and then (in the estimate of his companions) an ironic "little Yankee bastard" (3).

These early books about places prepared him to write *Coming into the Country* (1977), his three-part saga of Alaska, in which narrative builds through orchestration of locale. Book III, the title story, depicts three villages—Eagle, Circle, and Central—in the eastern bush, where residents develop a clannish sense of place. Living in a remote area, their climate varying over 168 degrees F, all have odd stories of survival and rebellion; but often McPhee walks off to spend time alone with the country. These moments release beautiful instances of writing: "Great floes coming on from upriver roll, heave, compile; sound and surface like whales" (200). "The difference is also in the winter silence, a silence that can be as wide as the country, and the dreamy, sifting slowness of the descent of the dry snow" (271). "The landscape is softened, in illusion less rough and severe—the frozen rivers flat and quiet where the waves of rapids had been" (409). Against all the chatter from Alaskans, who talk ceaselessly about themselves, each other, and the despised federal government, McPhee sets the implacable country, immense physical surroundings that dwarf the people, barely one human being per square mile of earth. Dick Cook, an irascible trapper with little respect for his neighbors, still reveres Alaska as a place, especially its governing force: "You are close to the land here, to nature, to what the Indians called Mother and I call Momma. Momma decides everything" (267).

By the time Condé Nast bought the *New Yorker*, McPhee was often writing about wild or remote places. His growing knowledge of geology attracted him to mountain landscapes, featured in *La Place de la Concorde Suisse* (1984) and the California "debris slide" chapter of *The Control of Nature* (1989). In a later collection, *Irons in the Fire* (1997), he focused on the art of forensic geology, describing how bits of mineral grain helped to solve murder cases. The book also contains two works of environmental history: "Travels of the Rock," about the Pilgrims' boulder at Plymouth, Massachusetts; and a brief "Talk of the Town" piece, "In Virgin Forest," about a 65-acre patch of woods, a last surviving remnant of the wild East, located north of Princeton. At the other end of an eco-spectrum, he visits the largest tire dump in America, where "a black vista" (151) of 44 million discarded tires offers a potential recovery of 178 million barrels of oil.

These stories about places surround the project that occupied McPhee for most of the 1980s and 1990s, four volumes on North American geology: *Basin and Range* (1981), *In Suspect Terrain* (1983), *Rising from the Plains* (1986), and *Assembling California* (1993). All appeared, revised and augmented with a fifth chapter on the plains ("Crossing the Craton"), as *Annals of the Former World* (1998). *Annals* is an undeniably great work of literary natural history. It readily compares with Alexander von Humboldt's *Cosmos* or Charles Darwin's *Voyage of the Beagle,* admirable not just for ideas and argument but for prose that makes hard science accessible to lay minds. McPhee's achievement also rivals two pioneers of American place-writing, Clarence King and John Wesley Powell, not in matching their explorations but rather their feats of translation and popularization. The main purpose of *Annals* is to describe plate tectonic theory, set within several frames: the work of contemporary geologists, the regions they know best, and the transcontinental course of Interstate 80, where roadcuts reveal geological events. Although sited in North America, the book's overall scope of reference is global, the narrative nonlinear, guided more by deep time than surface space.

Geology is the best natural science for McPhee to explore because it is foundational, devoted to explaining the events that create earth forms. In time, rocks generate all land, soil, plants, and animals as well as atmosphere, climate, clouds, and water forms. We cannot know "the environment" without grasping that its origin is rock, whether in molten, cooling, or solid form. At the same time, the science of geology is *human* expression, developed by physicians and others who gave it a descriptive language borrowed from anatomy (neck, arm, lip, mouth, head) and architecture (pillar, column, dike, shelf). Writing about rocks cannot be impersonal or "inhuman," as some readers have claimed. Modern geology developed as eighteenth- and nineteenth-century observers examined natural conditions and learned their patterns. The progress resembled that of medicine, moving from surface symptoms to hidden causes, and gradually a sense of natural cycles and phases built up, allowing humans to peer deep into time. Just as advances in descriptive geology sustained the work of early naturalists, so after 1960 the tectonic revolution offered a model that unified all phenomena. The key concept is that the earth has a crust and upper mantle, a lithosphere on which surface plates may drift or dive; those actions set off quakes and eruptions. The processes work uniformly all over the globe, in widely separated places and times. Hence the earth is integral, connected, *tectonic:* a word meaning built or constructed, creating the architecture where nature makes a home.

McPhee has a difficult story to tell, for few general readers can envision geology or grasp its human basis. The *Annals* volume adds many helpful supplements, from time charts to maps, illustrations, a foreword, and a detailed index. The foreword, "A Narrative Table of Contents," summarizes his work on the project and explains its method, answering those who ask why a magazine writer should take up rocks. The connection is language: since geology describes hidden structures and inferred events, it must work through verbal analogies. McPhee's interest began with words: "I used to sit in class and listen to the terms come floating down the room like paper airplanes. Geology was called a descriptive science, and with its pitted outwash plains and drowned rivers, its hanging tributaries and starved coastlines, it was nothing if not descriptive. It was a fountain of metaphor—of isostatic adjustments and degraded channels, of angular unconformities and shifting divides, of rootless mountains and bitter lakes" (31).

McPhee's principal informant for the *Annals* series is Kenneth Deffeyes, a Princeton professor and master teacher who emphasizes the linguistic basis of geology. Words describe rocks and rocks tell stories, often ambiguous ones. Learning to read them requires a sharp eye, a command of expert vocabulary and syntax, and a sound interpretive line. The first forensic geologist was a literary detective, Sherlock Holmes. Detection is close reading, which acquires logic and voice through rhetoric; and for McPhee geology is the ultimate *Twenty Questions,* since he has to make complex, unwitnessed events take shape in prose. Some of his most effective moments are paradoxes that take a while to sink in: a clear stream runs toward the Great Salt Lake, "talking so profusely on its way to its fate" (53). Cyanide, a poison born of air and lightning, will bond with water to make amino acid, the source of protein and life. "If by some fiat I had to restrict all this writing to one sentence, this is the one I would choose: The summit of Mt. Everest is marine limestone" (124).

Another reason to write about geology is that it contains heavily disputed knowledge. The Gallup organization runs a poll each year to assess religion-science issues, and repeatedly it finds that about 54 percent of Americans believe the earth was created 10,000 years ago. Apparently no sign of evolutionary change, such as bugs that resist insecticide, will shake literal readings of Scripture. In contrast, geology is reasoned interpretation, gathering and reading evidence to make plausible meanings. McPhee often cites disputes among geologists, especially those concerning tectonics, which only recently earned wide acceptance.

Deffeyes acknowledges that his science evolves through speculation and argument, with much resistance to new ideas: "There are still some people dragging their feet. They don't want to come into the story" (*Annals*, 132).

McPhee notes "the literary timbre" (133) of this remark, for it matches his own formal purposes. As he explains in *Annals*, his plan was to build "the entire composition . . . written in the form of journeys, set pieces, flashbacks, biographical sketches, and histories of the human and lithic kind—intended as an unfolding piece of writing and not as a catalogue of geological topics" (7). Rather than create a linear textbook, he mixes expository, descriptive, and narrative segments that cover five regions and several timelines to create pictures of vanished eras. While his four volumes are integral, their grand structure was less evident when it was unfolding. Now he makes a post-facto survey: *Basin and Range* is a primer set in Nevada, where Ken Deffeyes exposes the geologic scale of time and tectonic process. *In Suspect Terrain* is a counter-story; in one segment, Anita Harris disputes place tectonics as applied by others to the Appalachians; another segment is a "freestanding experiment" (10) linking human and geologic history at the Delaware Water Gap. *Rising from the Plains* sustains the debate by introducing David Love, whose view of the Rockies commutes between exploration and preservation. He is nearly as complex as his schoolteacher mother, who recorded her Wyoming frontier days in a remarkably literate diary. Part four, *Assembling California*, occurs where tectonics make daily headlines, as Eldridge Moores studies parts of the Sierra borne upward from spreading sea floors. "Crossing the Craton" fills the gaps and confirms tectonic shifts by describing the mid-continent from a point in Colorado, where "you see the basement of Nebraska bent up in the air" (13).

McPhee follows this summation with a table of contents for *Annals*—and for the first time he appears to be printing out the index cards, usually tacked up in his office. The structure that he reveals is not linear, like a piece of rhetoric, but jumps around and is multicolored, like the many geological maps he consulted while writing. I am reminded of the table of contents of James Agee's *Let Us Now Praise Famous Men* (1941), which seems a miscellany but also resembles the contents page of a magazine, a kind of skewed inventory of modern life, drawn by exigency into formal lines. Agee said he was seeking to create "a portion of unimagined existence" (xlvi). Whether he (or McPhee) succeeds depends on the patience that readers bring to the texts.

In *Annals of the Former World,* McPhee makes a startling effort to extend the limits of his own craft. Always wary of hyperbole, he has tackled a subject of astonishing depth and scope. Of all his peers (Norman Mailer, Joan Didion, Thomas Wolfe, Philip Roth, John Updike) McPhee may turn out to be the only one who really did write a great American book—but in nonfiction, and about rocks. In writing on geology, he achieves every journalist's dream: creating a story with permanence, even immortality. In its compression and vividness, literary nonfiction is often akin to poetry—in this case, to John Keats's poetry of earth. McPhee hints at this kinship when describing his laborious editing of *Annals of the Former World:* "Reminders and repetitions can be as useful in [geology] as they are in ballads. Rock carries its own epithets, its own refrains" (14).

McPhee's latest book, *The Founding Fish* (2002), is a guide to his favorite pastime of recent years, sport fishing for shad in American waters. Shad is an anadromous species, returning from the sea to its river of birth, there to spawn and die. That mysterious natural cycle has inspired writers from Aristotle to Norman Maclean, the Chicago professor of English and native Montanan whose tales depict fly-fishing as a religion, especially among Scottish Presbyterians. McPhee has that legacy in mind, but his sixteen chapters combine the personal and the historical to explore seaboard rivers from the Bay of Fundy to Mobile Bay, each estuary a place rich in local shad lore that also has national implications: Cotton Mather fished here, Henry Thoreau there; Grover Cleveland and Thomas Eakins followed. The story reels from native and colonial days through the Revolution and Civil War up to the present. In a manner recalling the cetology chapters of *Moby-Dick,* McPhee also cuts deep into the guts and brains of shad, to learn from expert anatomists that the elusive, schooling fish have acute hearing and feeling: when caught, they experience intense pain. This insight leads to a glum meditation on the ethics of fishing, which will please neither anglers nor animal-rights activists, for McPhee concludes that fishing is cruel yet also just, as long as one eats one's catch.

The authorial voice of *The Founding Fish* is personal, animated and funny, less a reporter than a master storyteller, writing with verve about an underrated species, "the planet's largest herring" (13), whose life and times constitute a natural-cultural history of the eastern shores of North America. McPhee has much to say about his own slow learning of this topic, based on decades of fishing, traveling, and staring for days at dark, unreadable waters. That is a humbling but liberating situation for a writer, for his book on shad was less an "assignment," taken to pay rent or tuition bills, than an avocation pursued for its own rewards, as seeking fish, or writing prose, must be. At that personal level, *The Founding Fish* presents McPhee's reflections on his long career as an artist, and also on the lifelong importance to him of the Delaware Valley that spawned and nurtured him.

While the book is rarely nostalgic, it often recalls themes and landscapes from McPhee's earlier works. Finding them is a bit like catching those signature glimpses of Alfred Hitchcock in his films. Even when shad-hunting in the remotest Maritimes, McPhee notes that "this beautiful river in its incised valley is not only reminiscent of—it is much like—the upper Delaware in the general region of Equinunk and Callicoon" (126). Shad fishermen on the Delaware stand "shoulder to shoulder like bears in a river in Alaska" (191). A chapter on dam-busting as a way to turn back piscatorial time rhymes nicely with the river-running debates in *Encounters with the Archdruid,* while the Kennebec setting recalls the inland Maine waters paddled in *The Survival of the Bark Canoe.* Like *The Deltoid Pumpkin Seed* or *The Curve of Binding Energy,* the story of shad is a heroic process narrative, from spawning to fry pan. Like *Oranges,* the fish story anatomizes a commodity McPhee himself adores, fresh or—as in *The Crofter and the Laird*—soundly kippered. When he fishes on the St. Johns River in Florida with Sam Candler of "Travels in Georgia," the McPhee canon begins to loop and link like a literary Möbius strip: "More oranges were floating by, roughly at the rate of one orange per shad. You might have thought you were fishing in the Indian River" (*Founding Fish,* 142). The final word he addresses to chef Alan Lieb, the anonymous "Otto" of "Brigade de Cuisine," who years ago guessed wrongly that the posh New York restaurant Lutèce served frozen fish. McPhee stops by Lieb's Pennsylvania home for lunch, and the menu includes pickled shad. The chef says that he can make shad bones taste delicious, drenched with enough butter, anchovies, and capers. Responds McPhee, at seventy-one, "I will save that one for my old age" (353).

As I end this second introduction to John McPhee, I am inclined to agree that critics, like chefs, may too often insist on boiling authorial bones. McPhee hardly needs augmentation, for his prose has grown richer in time, and also more personally revealing. On occasion, he has referred to a book he may never write, once sketched out as "Six Princetons," an account of one of America's most fraught, beautiful, and complicated locales, in space, across time, through memory. To write the annals of the world that formed him may prove the best way—at long last—of introducing John McPhee.

Acknowledgments

My grateful thanks to David Howarth, Susan Maher, Anne Matthews, John McPhee, and Alan Weltzien for their suggestions. I also thank Farrar, Straus & Giroux for granting me permission to adapt material that first appeared in *The John McPhee Reader.*

Works Cited

Agee, James, and Walker Evans. *Let Us Now Praise Famous Men: Three Tenant Families.* Boston: Houghton Mifflin, 1988.

Bachrach, Judy. *Tina and Harry Come to America: Tina Brown, Harry Evans and the Uses of Power.* New York: Free Press/Simon & Schuster, 2001.

Bailey, Thomas C. "John McPhee: The Making of a Meta-Naturalist." In *Earthly Words: Essays on Contemporary American Nature and Environmental Writers,* ed. John Cooley, 195–213. Ann Arbor: University of Michigan Press, 1994.

Bonney, William. "John McPhee's *Coming into the Country:* The Frontier as Commodity." *Isle: Interdisciplinary Studies in Literature and Environment* 1(1) (1993): 81–95.

Dickinson, Emily. *The Complete Poems of Emily Dickinson.* Ed. Thomas H. Johnson. Boston: Little, Brown, 1960.

Espey, David. "The Wilds of New Jersey: John McPhee as Travel Writer." In *Temperamental Journeys: Essays on the Modern Literature of Travel,* ed. Michael Kowalewski, 164–75. Athens: University of Georgia Press, 1992.

Fitzgerald, F. Scott. In *Writers on Writing,* ed. Jon Winokur. Philadelphia: Running Press, 1986.

Hamlin, Suzanne. "Time Flies, But Where Does it Go?" *New York Times,* 6 September 1995, C1, 6.

Howarth, William. "Levels of John McPhee," *Good Reading* 21 (February 1970): 2–3. Published as an insert in the *Princeton Alumni Weekly* and *University: A Quarterly Magazine.* (This may be the first general essay on McPhee's writings.)

Matthews, Anne. *Wild Nights: Nature Returns to the City.* New York: North Point Press, 2001.

McCarter, John. "A Dash of Tabasco." *New Yorker* (13 June 1953): 31–53.

McPhee, John. *Annals of the Former World.* New York: Farrar, Straus & Giroux, 1998.

————. *Assembling California*. New York: Farrar, Straus & Giroux, 1993.

————. *Basin and Range*. New York: Farrar, Straus & Giroux, 1981.

————. "Basketball and Beefeaters." *New Yorker* (16 March 1963): 186–94.

————. *Coming into the Country*. New York: Farrar, Straus & Giroux, 1977.

————. *The Control of Nature*. New York: Farrar, Straus & Giroux, 1989.

————. *The Crofter and the Laird*. New York: Farrar, Straus & Giroux, 1970.

————. *The Curve of Binding Energy*. New York: Farrar, Straus & Giroux, 1974.

————. *The Deltoid Pumpkin Seed*. New York: Farrar, Straus & Giroux, 1973.

————. *Encounters with the Archdruid*. New York: Farrar, Straus & Giroux, 1971.

————. *The Founding Fish*. New York: Farrar, Straus & Giroux, 2002.

————. *Giving Good Weight*. New York: Farrar, Straus & Giroux, 1979.

————. *The Headmaster: Frank L. Boyden, of Deerfield*. New York: Farrar, Straus & Giroux, 1966.

————. *Heirs of General Practice*. New York: Farrar, Straus & Giroux, 1986.

————. *In Suspect Terrain*. New York: Farrar, Straus & Giroux, 1983.

————. *Irons in the Fire*. New York: Farrar, Straus & Giroux, 1997.

————. *The John McPhee Reader*. Ed. William Howarth. New York: Farrar, Straus & Giroux, 1976.

————. *La Place de la Concorde Suisse*. New York: Farrar, Straus & Giroux, 1984.

————. Letter to William Howarth. 17 April 1970.

————. *Levels of the Game*. New York: Farrar, Straus & Giroux, 1969.

————. *Looking for a Ship*. New York: Farrar, Straus & Giroux, 1990.

————. *Oranges*. New York: Farrar, Straus & Giroux, 1967.

————. *Pieces of the Frame*. New York: Farrar, Straus & Giroux, 1975.

————. *The Pine Barrens*. New York: Farrar, Straus & Giroux, 1968.

————. *The Ransom of Russian Art*. New York: Farrar, Straus & Giroux, 1994.

————. *Rising from the Plains*. New York: Farrar, Straus & Giroux, 1986.

————. *A Roomful of Hovings and Other Profiles*. New York: Farrar, Straus & Giroux, 1968.

————. *A Sense of Where You Are: A Profile of William Warren Bradley*. New York: Farrar, Straus & Giroux, 1965.

————. "Six Princetons and Counting." *Princeton Alumni Weekly* (19 March 1997): 16–21.

————. *The Survival of the Bark Canoe*. New York: Farrar, Straus & Giroux, 1975.

————. *Table of Contents*. New York: Farrar, Straus & Giroux, 1985.

Moore, Leslie S. "The Architectonics of the Personal Essay." *English Journal* 81(6) (1992): 18–25.

Nocera, Joseph, and Peter Elkind. "The Buzz Factory." *Fortune* (20 July 1998): 73–83 (my source for profit and loss at the *New Yorker* since 1984).

Roundy, Jack. "Crafting Fact: Formal Devices in the Prose of John McPhee." In *Literary Nonfiction: Theory, Criticism, Pedagogy*, ed. Chris Anderson, 70–92. Carbondale: Southern Illinois University Press, 1989.

Sims, Norman. "Joseph Mitchell and *The New Yorker* Nonfiction Writers." In *Literary Journalism in the Twentieth Century,* ed. Norman Sims, 82–109. New York: Oxford University Press, 1990.

Smollett, Tobias. In *Webster's New World Dictionary of Quotable Definitions,* ed. Eugene Brussell. New York: Prentice-Hall, 1988.

Stull, James. "Self and the Performance of Others: The Pastoral Vision of John McPhee." *North Dakota Quarterly* 59(3) (1991): 182–200.

Terrie, Philip G. "River of Paradox: John McPhee's 'The Encircled River.'" *Western American Literature* 23(1) (1988): 3–15.

Thoreau, Henry D. "Life without Principle." In *Reform Essays,* ed. Wendell Glick, 155–79. Princeton: Princeton University Press, 1973.

———. *Walden and Other Writings.* Ed. William Howarth. New York: Mc-Graw-Hill, 1980.

Turner, Brian. "Giving Good Reasons: Environmental Appeals in the Nonfiction of John McPhee." *Rhetoric Review* 13(1) (1994): 164–82.

Twain, Mark. *Following the Equator: A Journey around the World.* New York: Gabriel Wells, 1923.

White, E. B. *Letters of E. B. White.* Ed. Dorothy Guth. New York: Harper & Row, 1976.

Yagoda, Ben. *About Town: The New Yorker and the World It Made.* New York: Scribner, 2000 (a meticulous and absorbing account of the magazine's history).

Jared Haynes

"The Size and Shape of the Canvas"

An Interview with John McPhee

I interviewed John McPhee in July 1993, shortly after *Assembling California,* the last of his four books on the geology of the United States, had been published. We met at his office at Princeton University and talked there for a couple of hours then broke for lunch and continued the interview in the afternoon. A large portion of that interview follows; it can be read in its entirety in the journal *Writing on the Edge* 5(2) and 6(1) (Spring and Fall 1994).

Haynes: When did it first occur to you that writing could be your profession?

McPhee: I'm wondering if it is ever going to occur to me. When I was young, I had a driving compulsion to write; I didn't want to do anything else, or I couldn't see myself doing anything else. But I used to wonder what would happen to me if I couldn't make it. I remember how gloomy and in the dark I felt.

And there still hasn't been any point where I could suddenly say, "Hey, I can make a living as a writer." I still worry too much that I might not be able to. I'm only half joking when I say now, at the age of sixty-two, I wonder if I'll ever feel I can make a living as a writer. Your last piece of writing will not write your next one. There's a fear that it will evaporate, or that you'll lose your energy for it as you go along.

Somebody once asked E. B. White why he continued long into his career to write the witty remarks that go along with what the *New Yorker* calls "newsbreaks," those little things at the bottom of columns. When he had long since moved to Maine, they still sent those things to him. He'd write the tag lines and send them back. He said that he never thought—including up to that point—that he could make a living as a writer. He'd always worried. I understand that totally. I mean, you don't have this muscular feeling that you can make a living as a writer. Not if your name is John McPhee, you don't.

Haynes: You submitted quite a number of pieces to the *New Yorker* before you got one accepted.

McPhee: I started submitting them when I was a teenager. I sent them both fiction and nonfiction—I mean anything. Any genre that's in the *New Yorker,* I tried. It was all turned down until I was thirty-two years old. Harold Hayes at *Esquire* had asked me to write a piece. I said I'd been thinking about doing a piece about my own experiences playing basketball in England. He said, "Fine." Then he rejected it. I was filled with gloom, but the *New Yorker* bought it. That was my first piece ["Basketball and Beefeaters"], in 1963.

Haynes: Why do you think they liked that article and not the pieces you gave them before?

McPhee: I think it was very much in the vein of the so-called *New Yorker* casuals—autobiographical pieces, which were bought by the fiction department. This sounded like a "casual" to them. I also don't think they were making any big mistake in turning me down with those other pieces. I mean, I was developing as a writer. By the time I wrote the profile of Bill Bradley ["A Sense of Where You Are"] and started my full-time work on pieces that were aimed at the *New Yorker,* I'd been through a lot of stages and was not a beginning writer. In a way that's lucky, because when I started writing my books, I was not a neophyte.

Haynes: You worked at *Time* for several years before you got the break with the *New Yorker.* Did you get a lot of feedback on your writing there?

McPhee: Yes. It's sort of a force-fed situation. You do four or five stories per week, each with a beginning, a middle, and an end, based on a set of facts; it was a very good training ground in that way. You were exhausted at the end of one week, and a little more at the end of the next week, but after three or four years there I think I'd learned quite a bit.

Haynes: What about earlier influences, in high school and college?

McPhee: High school English teachers in my time had the responsibility of teaching writing and also teaching literature. The ratio would tend to, generally speaking, come down on the literature side in just pure time spent. But my English teacher, Olive McKee, at Princeton High School—she was my teacher for three of the four years—was also the drama teacher, and that's not unrelevant because she had a flair for a lot of things. She assigned us three compositions a week—not absolutely every week, but most weeks—all through the school year for three long years. They were short and they could be anything—poems, factual pieces of writing, fiction—but each and every one had to be defended with a separate piece of paper that showed its architecture, its structure. You didn't have to do it Roman numeral I, II, III if you didn't want to, but you had to show that you started somewhere, ended somewhere, knew what you were doing in between, and had a rationale for the piece. That, of course, started us thinking about different ways to do things that make sense. Olive McKee's emphasis on that is directly reflected in my work, and here in my course at Princeton.

Finding that rationale for the piece is for me the most interesting part in the cycle of writing, when I've collected the material and I'm trying to figure out what to do with it. It's like cooking. You've been to the market and you've got your stuff, but you can't make a soufflé out of a red pepper. You can, however, cook the red pepper in various ways. This is sort of what happened in her class. Also she encouraged students to get up and read to the other students. The other students would hiss and boo or whatever, and it was fun. I would say I learned a lot from her. Fortunately she lived long enough for me to have many a talk with her after I'd become a professional writer. She's no longer alive, but she lived a few years after I joined the *New Yorker,* and I was able to take to her three or four books.

In college here at Princeton, I majored in English. There was a creative writing program here, run by Richard Blackmur. You had to apply to get into it and get accepted, and, if you kept getting accepted and you wanted to stay on, you were in it for four semesters, ideally during sophomore and junior years because everybody here writes a senior thesis. I was in it and had instructors like Randall Jarrell and Tom Riggs. You produced a piece of writing each week. This program was not in your major; it was an elective. And I was involved in every extracurricular undergraduate publication—including the alumni magazine, which was probably the best thing from the point of view of learning. I wrote a column in it every week for a year. And I wrote a creative thesis, a novel for a thesis. Take all that together—writing begets writing, writing teaches writing. That's how I learned how to write.

Haynes: Does that constant involvement in writing make it less daunting to start a new piece?

McPhee: Maybe when you're young. I didn't think about the dauntingness as much then, particularly when I was in college. But the daunting aspect of approaching a piece of writing is eternal. It's there now, it's been there all through my professional life. My confidence about approaching a piece of writing has not risen over all the years, ever. Right now, I'm at the place where I'm getting near starting something. It's not going to be a very long piece, but I'm not exactly swaggering around thinking it's going to work out. Just the reverse.

Haynes: How do you get through those periods? Do you say, "I've done this before, I can do this now"?

McPhee: I wish that helped more than it does, but it doesn't help much at all. What helps is routine. What causes a piece of writing to be done is just being there, over and over and over again. I sit alone—I would say here in this room, but I've just changed offices, my late office has become a women's toilet—I sit alone doing nothing most of the time. I know what it is I want to write, I know where I am in a piece of writing, and I know what I want to accomplish right at the moment, where the front edge of the thing is. But the day goes along and the clock ticks. A certain apprehension rises. The largest fear is that I'll go home without having done anything. If I do, I go home depressed, with a sense that things are really falling apart. With that sitting as a possibility at the end of the day, there's a certain compression as time moves along. I don't get anything done in the morning. I don't get anything done at two o'-clock, at three o'clock. Somewhere around three-thirty or four o'clock, this panic has risen to a sufficient level that I get myself going. Something kicks over and I get to it physically. I'm actually putting words down. Then I work until eight, every day. My wife, Yolanda, who's a horticulturist, works until eight every day. So it's all compatible. I go home and cook dinner or she cooks dinner and we eat late. And then the next day is just exactly like the one I just described.

Haynes: So it's not just when you're beginning to write; it's all the way through.

McPhee: Oh, yes. Absolutely. All the way through, especially the first draft. The first draft of *Assembling California* took two years. There were many days during those two years when I thought the thing would never, ever be written.

But when you get into the second draft, which in that case took six months, a different person is working on that manuscript. That panic building up slowly over the day isn't there. Now I've got something in my hand to deal with. The six months were very pleasant. Then the third journey through the piece only takes about a month and the fourth about a week. That was a long project, but that's a typical set of ratios. In a short piece, the same ratios would occur—some months to do a first draft and weeks to do a second draft.

Haynes: All you've ever wanted to do is to be a writer, yet when you talk about writing, some parts of it seem to be such agony.

McPhee: It's a paradox, all right.

Haynes: What pieces have you written that have given you the greatest anguish?

McPhee: They all do that. In the first draft period, there's always a great deal of anguish. But *The Survival of the Bark Canoe*—you would have thought I would have written that fairly easily because you'd imagine that since I'd been riding around in canoes all my life the material would be very familiar to me. But for some reason I found that awfully difficult. It was painful. I've been accused of writing too positively about the people I write about. It's not true of that piece. I was committed to the piece of writing and the piece of writing had to be honest. If I had sketched Henri Vaillancourt differently, I would have sketched him as I didn't see him. I felt the weight of it.

Haynes: About halfway through that piece, you're thinking Henri is really a great guy; he is a master at crafting bark canoes, and he's learned this craft virtually on his own. And then you begin to discover that he doesn't really know much about the backwoods and that he's petty and imperious.

McPhee: That latter part had a profound influence on the structure of the story. He was what an English professor might call an unsympathetic character. I developed a structure different from the one I would have chosen had he been more sympathetic. The first seven thousand words of it—it's about forty thousand words in all—describes him in his shop in Greenville, the person I got interested in, the person I went up there to watch making things. And then comes the canoe trip in chronological sequence. If I hadn't had any special problems with that piece of writing, I probably would have begun it with the canoe trip or in the trip. I mean, look at other pieces of mine that involve journeys. They begin in the middle, they flash back. They start in some place and they go back and they go here and there, because I've got some thematic or whatever reason for doing these chronological shifts.

If I'd done this story the same way, I would have started somewhere on the trip. The pictures and scenes of him in Greenville making ribs and thwarts in his shop—all that material that's up front now—would have been in the form of a flashback, remembering when I first met him. So why is this seven thousand words first? Because a reader goes through a process of learning about a character, and I wanted the reader to appreciate Henri's skills without being prejudiced by a description of his behavior on the canoe trip.

But all pieces cause anguish. The geology pieces were really, really difficult. *Basin and Range* was the hardest of all because it was the first of those geology pieces. I was in over my head and I kept saying, "What am I doing? Why am I doing this? How did I get into this?" more intensely than I had done with anything else. With the geology, I made the unhappy discovery that you couldn't just learn a little corner of it, use it for journalistic purposes, and then go on. The stuff is just too much this-related-to-that-related-to-the-other-thing. You had to know it. And I didn't know it, so I said to myself, very reasonably, "Who are you to be doing this? You're not a geologist." It took me five to ten years to get past that.

Haynes: What kept you going?

McPhee: What kept me going was that I bit off more than I could chew. I started that piece as a two-day project for an unsigned *New Yorker* piece for "The Talk of the Town." I was going to go up to a roadcut outside New York City and describe its origins and be done with it. And I asked Ken Deffeyes if he'd go do that. He said yes, he would. Then I said to him before we went, "You know, it's a pretty good idea. What if, instead of just that one roadcut there, we were to go up the beautiful Adirondack northway, past all that rock, and have a larger piece." And he says, "Not on this continent. If you want to do something like that on this continent, go west. Go across the structure." North-south is the wrong direction. So I inflicted this on myself. I decided, why not go all the way? All this happened before I did any writing. I didn't even go write the short piece. This expanding idea occurred over two or three weeks. I said to Ken, "What if I went with different geologists and spent the better part of this year just going right across the whole thing? Would you do the Great Basin with me?" I thought I was doing a single piece of writing, and in fact I was. Those four books are really one book. So I traveled for a little over a year and I came back and typed up all the notes and I realized it was much too much for one project. Over time, if I did nothing else, it would take me ten years to do. As it turned out, it took fifteen.

By the time I'd made that decision, I'd not only typed up all the notes, I'd also made up a structure. And I followed that structure from 1979 until 1993, with some alterations, some changes, incorporating things like the 1992 earthquakes. The piece was essentially written when they occurred, so they were written into it, but that's small. Of course, the 1989 earthquake provided a rather large dimension that I hadn't anticipated.

Haynes: At the point where you saw this was going to be ten or fifteen years of work, what kept you from saying, "Maybe I'll just go back and do the short piece"?

McPhee: Well, I'd already traveled for a year at that point and I still saw it as one piece. I went to Nevada in 1978 with Ken Deffeyes, and then we went to Mussel Rock. I took him to the airport in San Francisco, and then by myself I drove the pickup we had rented back to Salt Lake. Along the way, I went to Davis to meet Eldridge Moores because Ken had set up the whole thing. He'd called Dave Love and he'd called Anita Harris. I was going to be spending time with these geologists because it was a single piece. I wasn't going to be doing them one at a time. I went up into the Sierra with Eldridge in December of '78, and I kept going and met Dave Love up in Wyoming right before Christmas, and then when April came Anita and I went up to the Delaware Water Gap and kept on going.

But I was so at sea. I could feel my neck turning red as Anita would talk in front of the outcrops at the Delaware Water Gap. I didn't understand one word. I was scribbling everything down and I understood nothing. At one point, when I was scribbling those notes and feeling so nervous that I almost collapsed, with Anita telling me about this Silurian rock in the Water Gap, I said to her, "Do you do this often?" She said, "I haven't worked at this level since I don't know when!" This was about as low as it got for her. One of the strangest experiences I had was reading those notes two years later and understanding them clearly, long before I wrote the book. When I look at them now, they look like a map of my hometown. But when I scribbled those notes down and typed them up, I had no idea what they meant.

I just had the concept that I would go along talking to geologists and do a piece about the United States—a verbal cross-section of North America—without realizing what it was I was undertaking. It was a to-tally naïve thing to get into, and the next thing I know I'm traveling around scribbling these notes about Anita Harris and wishing I had some way to back out of the overall project because I felt so inadequate. But there's a kind of a vortex, and you're gone. I can't tell you how many times in those fifteen years I wondered if the whole thing was going to collapse. I thought *Assembling California* would never get written. I really did. Probably that ended somewhere in 1991, thank heaven. I don't think about it not getting written anymore because it is written. From my point of view, that's really the single best thing about a piece of writing: it's done and can never be undone. It's over.

Haynes: One of the geologists in *Assembling California* said that it's hard to make sense of the geology of California. Did the jumbled nature of the geology make it difficult to put the piece together?

McPhee: That's where this preoccupation of mine with the structure of the piece of writing and the planning of it beforehand makes the differ-ence between the thing being done or not. When I started to write, I saw the book whole, because it had been figured out. Actually, it has one of the simplest structures of all the pieces of writing I've ever done. The structure of all four books of geology [*Basin and Range, In Suspect Terrain, Rising from the Plains,* and *Assembling California*] is a single structure—I've got it in a drawer here somewhere. These books span the continent, more or less adhering to the region of the fortieth paral-lel, which is more or less traced by Interstate 80. So I knew that one component of the narrative was going to be an east-west journey across the nation. Of course, it doesn't have to be consecutive. It flashes back and it flashes forward. And when you reach a certain point, like the ophiolites at Auburn, that being Eldridge Moores's specialty, it's an obvious place to depart, first from the interstate and then from California, to sketch in his life and work. Then you come back to Davis, where his life has brought him to teach, and Davis is in the valley, so I talk about the valley and keep going to San Francisco and back to Mussel Rock where the thing started. As structures go, that structure is very plain.

Haynes: How about *Looking for a Ship?* That seems as if it would be very simple to structure.

McPhee: Just the opposite. It's the most complicated structure that I ever got into. The ship's itinerary is from New York to Valparaiso and back with intermediate stops, going, in both directions, through the canal and along the coast of South America. Well, that's simple. But it was important to communicate to the reader the fact that the ship and the journey were completely randomly arrived at. It wasn't planned through a company, with the president of Lykes Brothers giving a stamp of approval. It was just me and Andy Chase going to a union hall. Andy was just another mate. He didn't know what ship he was going to get, if any, or with what company. This is typical of the Merchant Marine. So the beginning in Charleston was there for the purpose of making that point. It was a total spin of the roulette wheel what would happen. And we end up on this ship—with Paul Washburn, of all people—and go to South America.

Once Andy gets the ship, it would be tedious, I thought, to get on the ship when the ship arrives and then write about the whole process of how you get to know people. If, instead, you leap forward from the union hall scene to a point way down the line, it's a given that the author has been on this ship for some time and knows these people. It's a whole lot more interesting. All you're doing is jumping forward in time, and jumping forward in time is not an illegitimate thing for a nonfiction writer to do. So that's why the next scene is on the bridge of the ship off Chile, where it's dark, and the sun comes up and reveals the people, including the central figure: Washburn. It's exciting to get an idea like that and then bring a scene like that off, all in terms of facts as they happen. You introduce your people that way, but, of course, you've left out a lot of stuff that needs filling in. You flash back.

Notice, too, the tenses. The scene in Charleston is in the past tense, but the author elects, for his own capricious reasons, to tell the Valparaiso approach in the historical present. That establishes the approach to Valparaiso as the time fix of the overall piece. That's where we really are, and Charleston is a flashback, even though it came first. After that, tenses have to relate to Valparaiso. So when you narrate events in Colombian waters going south, they're in past tense. Then I have another problem. I want the book to end with the ship dead in the water and its black flag flying; it was a gift of an ending for this to have happened to the ship, and it's a good ending from a literary point of view. But you have to contrive a way to include in the text before that ending things that happened after it—what happened to the stowaways in Panama, what happened to the ship in New York when they discovered what was wrong with it. So the ending is also a flashback.

Haynes: How long did it take you to make the decision that the focal point would be off Valparaiso and that those events would be in present tense?

McPhee: A while. You see, you've been on the ship, you've got all your notes, you've typed them up, you've got them to study, you've read whatever books you're going to read, you've done whatever peripheral interviewing you're going to do, and now you've got everything in one big pile. And you're thinking about it. The duality of that structure must have occurred to me over several weeks of thinking about it.

Having figured it out that far, with Andy looking for the ship in Charleston and then the cut to the ship off Valparaiso, without going any farther into the pile of material you would write a beginning, a lead. You don't even need to refer to any notes or to anything else. You just want to make sure that you have a lead that will work. The same with *Assembling California*. I wrote the passage about Mussel Rock, and I rewrote it and I rewrote it and I rewrote it, as if it were a piece of writing in itself. I carried it through many drafts, sent it to Sara Lippincott, who was an editor of science pieces at the time at the *New Yorker,* and asked her what she thought of it. I was seeing whether I could get a thing going that gave me a sense that I had a beginning that would work. That's the case with every piece. And then, when you have that in hand, some little lead (it could be only two paragraphs or it might be two thousand words: something that is the beginning of a piece and makes you think, "That's where I'm going to start"), you pause and go back for whatever length of time it takes—hours, days, weeks, depending on the piece—to go through all your material and get a sense of an overall structure and an ending. I always know the ending before I start the first draft. Then you build up the structure and subdivide all the material into the appropriate places, where they're going to be. In other words, if you've got a great big pile, you divide it all up and now you've got seventeen piles and one comes after the next, because you've figured this all out.

If that sounds ultimately mechanistic, what it does is free the writer to write. Once you've got that structure figured out, then writing, pure and simple, is what you have left to do. When I come in here in the morning, I don't have to figure out what it is I'm trying to do, I just have to try to do it.

Haynes: So generally you have to write that lead before you figure out the details of the structure?

McPhee: I used to say generally. Now I'd say always. I just think it's such a good idea. I would tell anybody just to write something—don't worry about hunting around in your notes, wasting time, figuring you have to cross the last "t"—just write something that starts the piece, and if you can feel comfortable that that lead is appropriate, sound, and not meretricious, then you can turn around and figure out where you're going to go from there. Go back and look at materials and study them and all that.

Haynes: When do you decide what exactly you want the piece to do?

McPhee: It's at this phase that you are figuring that out. You didn't know before you started the research, because it's obviously terribly inconvenient to begin a piece thinking you know what it's going to say. You go out and have the experience of being at sea with Andy Chase and Paul Washburn and things change every day. Then you've got this net experience and the reading that goes with it and other things that you take home. You've been thinking all these months about the ultimate product, you've gone over it in your mind many, many times, and then you sit down and write that lead, and you try to see the span of the piece. It's at that point that you make semi-firm what you're doing and where you're going. But it isn't written in stone at all.

Haynes: Where do the ideas for pieces come from?

McPhee: Ideas stream by by the millions. What makes me fasten onto a given thing? I once thought that out long enough to realize that well above ninety percent of the projects I've gotten into over the years relate to things that I was interested in when I was young, before I was twenty-one, many of them before I was sixteen. For example, I played on my high school basketball and tennis teams, and those are the two sports I've written about. And when I was under ten, when I was six or seven years old, I started going to the summer camp where my father was a doctor. This place specialized in backpacking trips and canoe trips and taught a lot about what we now call ecology. They didn't use that word, but that camp taught me all about the outdoors and the inter-dependence of things in nature. I was out there every summer from one-digit years until I was twenty or so, when I was leading those trips. That had a tremendous influence on my later work.

Haynes: When you have some idea of a project you want to work on, what do you do first?

McPhee: When I first get the idea, I go interview somebody. Usually you're talking to someone, trying to have some kind of experience. It varies a great deal with the piece. If you wanted to do something about a region or a landscape, you would just go there and hang around until you started meeting people, as I did for *The Pine Barrens*. It's pointless to go into one piece, though, approaching it as you did another piece. Something is going to be very different. So I guess I can't generalize about it.

Haynes: Once you've gotten one of these ideas for a piece and you head out to do the first interview or beginning research, how do you pro-ceed? Do you take notes?

McPhee: All the time. I scribble constantly in a notebook. Fundamen-tally, when I scribble notes, I am writing. Writing is selection, by defini-tion. You're choosing what you're going to put on the paper. When I crossed the Cascades with David Brower and Charles Park (the explo-ration geologist), I was behind them, hiking with my pack on, scribbling away. I put down anything that I want to remember, including sketches of people, what they're wearing, what they're saying, how they look, whether they're sunburned—whatever it is I want to remember it. The notebooks contain a great deal more than answers to the questions I ask.

If I lose a notebook, I am dead. I've never lost one, though I've come near it.

Haynes: How many notebooks' worth of notes would you take for something like *Coming into the Country* or *Looking for a Ship* or any book-length piece?

McPhee: There may be several dozen of them—little spiral notebooks that are four by six inches.

Haynes: How close do you try to get to the exact words of the people you interview?

McPhee: As close as I can. I use a shorthand. It's not a formal shorthand, but the kind of shorthand you evolve by just having to write fast. I try to get the words the way they say them. Sometimes I check back with them, particularly if they say something that's incomplete or isn't clear. I'll run it past them and say, "Do you want to patch that up?" and they do. But not all that much.

Haynes: Do you have any particular techniques for asking questions and getting information out of people?

McPhee: One thing I've never had is a prepared list of questions, unless I'm going over something with someone. I learn a lot on the job. So I really dread the beginnings of things. My goal is to get into a situation with the people where I can go along with them and watch them do what they do. I've spent a lot of time in pickups. I just want to get to know a person and let him or her know what I'm trying to do. The person is going out to inspect a bunch of cattle somewhere and I go along and watch. I talk and ask questions, when I'm not interrupting the work, and also on the way home. That's the way it goes. To sit down with someone you've never met before and say "Mr. Jones, tell me about your work" is pretty difficult. I do think you owe it to the person you're interviewing to prepare so that you're not wasting that person's time, but I've never been so prepared beforehand that I could walk right in and ask somebody everything I wanted to know. So I really drag my feet at the start, because taking the plunge into it is not comfortable.

Most of the reading I do is afterward, not beforehand, when I know what I want to read.

Haynes: Do you write up your notes every night?

McPhee: No. I write them up once I get home to Princeton. I can read my notes a long time later, I've found, but usually I get to them right away once I've gone home.

Haynes: Do you ever use a tape recorder?

McPhee: I'm not too fond of using tape, but I use tape when I have to. When sixteen geologists in Vermont are arguing over an outcrop, you cannot get all that down, so you stick the tape recorder on the outcrop, and let them argue, and listen to it later.

I tape-recorded a lot of stuff on the ship to South America. You had to record the captain. He spoke rapidly and unself-consciously. Those are two criteria that would make you use a tape recorder. He didn't care whether it was a tape machine or a man from New Jersey—it didn't bother him. I tape-recorded a lot of stuff from Captain Washburn.

But mostly I was going around the ship with my notebook. Something would happen and I'd write it down. Remember that the working span was from ten minutes to four in the morning until eight fifteen in the evening, every day. I'd never been in any situation like this. It's all day, every day, and I was on the bridge every morning at four, just talking to Mac and Andy and so on. There's a lot of osmosis in something like that. It was a very pleasant experience. I wanted to get home and I missed home, but I really loved being out there. I understand those people and why they're in the Merchant Marine. And Washburn's philosophical remarks were not wasted on me.

For *Assembling California*, I almost entirely used notebooks. I mean, a tape recorder is ridiculous when you're on twelve-hour field days, day after day, out in the mountains doing geology. But later, when there were a couple of things I wanted to get Eldridge to articulate that had to do with ophiolites around the world or tectonic theories, I'd sit in his office at UC Davis and record it all, just as we're doing in Princeton right now. That was very useful, because I learned a lot from listening to those tapes over and over again, and transcribing them; there was some pretty hard-core geology there.

The notebook is the natural medium in the interview process, in my view. The tape recorder is unselective. It just soaks up everything. There's a lot to be said about not having a machine between me and a person I'm dealing with.

Haynes: How do you deal with the mass of notes once you get back home?

McPhee: I type it all up. I just work my way through it. It's almost mindless, but not totally. You can't help but think, and so if I think about ideas for the structure I'll throw them into the pie there, and I'll throw in thoughts, of all kinds, that occur to me, including phrases. The notes swell a bit as I'm getting ideas on what I might write, so there's some expansion, but not a whole lot. Basically I'm just copying the notes.

Before I had a computer, I used to cut those notes up with a pair of scissors and sort them all into appropriate folders so that when I was writing a given chapter I would be dealing only with the material that related to that chapter. But I don't do that anymore, because my computer does it. Howard Strauss, a friend of mine here at the university, wrote two computer programs for me imitating the methods I used before I had a computer. As a result, my computer knows how to go into the typed-up notes—they might be fifty thousand words long—and take them all apart, and spread them out into fifteen or twenty different places, and name each of those places, and preserve the original, so that I end up with, say, seventeen files where I started with one. Each of those files will still contain a huge body of notes. And so, as I approach a given segment, I develop its structure, *ad hoc,* recapitulating the larger process. As I approach chapter four or section six, it too has to have a beginning, a middle, and an end, none of which has been worked out in advance. I need to break apart the notes for that segment. But if I broke them apart with the same program that broke the total set of notes I would be in chaos that would be comparable to the process of fissioning uranium. I'd have a zillion little files. So after I've studied the material in a given segment, another program takes it and churns it all up but keeps it one file. It chews it all up and rearranges it until the notes are in the approximate order in which I want to tell the story. It's just a way of looking at my notes in the order in which I want to write.

Haynes: How do you know when you've done enough research and you're ready to start writing?

McPhee: That's a very tough decision. A lot of people founder on it, because it's obviously easier to research than it is to write. Something just shoves you across the line. A friend of mine once told me that you know you're ready to write when you meet yourself coming the other way. I think he was talking about the process of interviewing. If you keep interviewing different people about the same subject, pretty soon you'll find that everything you're hearing you've heard before. I think that's what he meant. Something or other kicks you into starting writing. Fatigue or whatever. For the piece I'm working on now, I've talked enough to the main figure, but I want to talk to a couple of dozen people that he and others have mentioned. Then maybe I'll be ready to write. But you always have a sense of incompletion about it. There's always a little more you could do. Always.

Haynes: But you don't hesitate to go back and do a little more research if you need it?

McPhee: I really prefer, ideally, to have everything separate. You collect your material, you develop your structure, then you write your piece. It's a little awkward to open it up and do a whole lot of new stuff. If necessary, you do that, but it works out best if it is only for a specific set section within the overall piece. Let's say you're writing about somebody who is developing an experimental aircraft and there's a historical something that's relevant. You know in your structure when that's coming up, and you know that what you need to do is go to the microfiche and read 1860s newspapers in order to be able to tell it. That's all very contained. I wait until that point. I'm sitting right here, and when I get to that point I get up and go over to the library and do it.

Haynes: When you're ready to spend the months or years writing the first draft, how do you set up your work space?

McPhee: The working space you're in is really important. You've got to be really familiar with it. You've got to get rid of any sense of novelty. Long ago I had the idea that there was an ideal room to work in if you were doing a piece of writing that depended on research, factual research. There wouldn't be anything in the room except stuff that related to that piece. This was absolutely true in *Coming into the Country*, because I had only recently started working in that particular room. I covered the walls with bulletin boards and I started sticking up stuff about Alaska—maps and who knows what. The bulletin boards are part of the writing process. The structure of the piece will be sitting right in front of me so that I can just look up and see it. Invariably, though, bulletin boards get cluttered with souvenirs and pictures of daughters. It's probably a good idea to move every once in a while, as I've just done.

I always have in the room where I work a place where I can sleep. When I'm trying to write, I react by getting sleepy, which I think is a psychological reaction to the fears and the doubts—the whole business which, taken together and stretched out over enough time, is known as "writer's block." When I'm confronted with the fact that I've come to the moment where I have to write, my head starts to droop. I don't fight it. I lie down. I don't sleep long—ten minutes later I'm up and alert. So I really need a place where I can just flip over. Sometimes when it's not going well and I can't think of what to say—how to work something out or how to begin something—I lie down until I have figured it out. I tend to be able to figure it out better horizontally. I'll lie down with a yellow pad and write it out by hand, and somehow that works better. Then I'll transfer that into the computer.

Haynes: Once you have the structure and you're going through it, do you ever skip ahead and write a part out of sequence?

McPhee: No. I go through it in order. I do some things more thoroughly than others, in a more polished way. But I follow the structure. I don't write part seven before part two.

Haynes: Could you be halfway through a piece and decide to change the structure?

McPhee: Rarely. I might change the structure a little bit, but not much.

Haynes: Is it possible to imagine a different structure for a piece? Is there only one best structure?

McPhee: There's one you're going to arrive at that feels sound and works. If you want to be tricky, you'd think up any number, but that's not the point. The structure is not the message; it is the pattern of the piece as you see it. The point is to find the simplest and soundest way to accomplish what you want to do. I always have a sense that there's another way to do it, and the other way may make sense. But so does this one.

Haynes: When you've the typed first draft and you're ready to revise, how do you proceed?

McPhee: I print it out, and then I work on a clipboard with a pencil, a page at a time, triple-spaced, about nineteen lines on a page. This is largely done lying down or sitting in a chair, but away from the computer. Very often, I write so much on that page that the original stuff is almost obscured. That's the way I go through the whole second draft. For *Assembling California,* that process took six months, with the computer off except at the end of each day, when I'd put in what I'd done.

On a first draft, I've rearranged my notes and done some writing, but it's awful. It really is awful. I've got some standards of judgment as a writer. I know what I want it to look like, and this terrible stuff is sitting there. Yet this is the only way to get it down, to get it onto the paper, to get started. Then if something worthwhile is going to happen, if this piece of writing is going to look like a piece of writing that I'd like to publish, it happens there with the pencil in the second draft. That's when I'm altering the first draft toward reasonable prose. And the third polishes that up and the fourth chooses some words. Those are also done in pencil. There's a lot of work with the pencil, a page at a time.

Haynes: Why the pencil and not the computer?

McPhee: That's a whole theme in itself—about the computer and composition. I always tell my students, "Don't trust that thing. It all looks so neat when it's printed out, but take a look at what you've written." It looks finished and it's beguiling, but it could be misleading. The evidence is absolutely clear that certain of my students from time to time do not proofread their printouts. When you look at something that seemed all right when it was in the computer, and then look at it on a piece of paper, you may realize that you're not there yet. It's that factor, whatever its cause, which determines that there will be no finished product from me that hasn't been looked at on a piece of paper. For me, it is a vital stage. It could be explained by my having learned to write on a typewriter and not having acquired a computer until 1984. But I don't think so. There's no way I'll ever know, but I don't think so. I think that the computer is the greatest device that has come along, the single most wonderful toy I have ever had in my life, but it has to be used in conjunction with other methods. If you use it alone, I don't think that you will get as much out of it. My computer guru, the one who wrote the programs for me, agrees with that.

Haynes: Was the transition from typewriter to computer difficult?

McPhee: Same day. I was writing *Rising from the Plains,* which has a lot of stuff from Ethel Waxham's journal that she wrote when she was a young woman in Wyoming. I was using the typewriter and I was looking at these long quotes from her. There's nothing else like it in my writing—where there's that much stuff quoted from something. I was in a kind of duet with her. I thought, Am I going to type these things over and over and over and over again? That's what sprang me into getting a computer. When the computer arrived, I started writing on it that afternoon. Fortunately I had a person who shepherded me through it, and if I had a question I picked up the phone and asked him. I still do, but not very often.

Haynes: Do you get any editorial advice or feedback from people at the *New Yorker* or from other people who read your drafts?

McPhee: I don't depend on feedback. I think the most important thing an editor does is to talk things over with you beforehand and to let you know, because you're in the dark, that some idea seems workable. You need that dialogue with other people. I certainly need it and talk to people a lot. In a way that isn't feedback. Feedback applies to pieces of writing that have been written. At that point, there isn't much that will alter what I do.

Haynes: When you turn a piece in to the *New Yorker,* do they ever say, "We'd like you to rearrange this," or "This particular paragraph doesn't seem to be working"?

McPhee: Sure. That kind of thing comes up in various ways. I had an editor there for many years who wasn't trying to "fix" my pieces, but if he had a question or if he thought something was opaque, he'd stick a little bracket in the piece with a letter in it—A or B or C. He had these things to ask me, like, "You know, I really don't get that. I don't think you're clear there. I really think you ought to go back to the drawing board and do it over again." So on and so forth, all the way down the piece. Sara Lippincott, the editor of the geology pieces, would just about damn near ask me about every sentence: "Do you think people will understand this?"

Editors have their own styles. Pat Crow, who is my principal editor at the *New Yorker* now, is a very good editor. You get the sense that the whole thing is going by him—that he is fly fishing in his imagination—but then he pounces. You think he's asleep, but he wakes up and "Bang!" He really hits the places that don't work well. But mostly I call him up and ask, "Do you think this piece will work? Does this sound like something I can make something out of?"

Haynes: What about reading your work out loud?

McPhee: Reading the stuff out loud is a part of the composition of every piece. It comes after the second draft. I say these things so clearly—first draft, second draft. It's the computer that's done that. The computer has caused these levels to be very clear. When I finish the first draft, there may be areas of it that are never going to change, because they've been written five times as I've paused over them. But when I finally get out to the end of the thing for the first time, even though there are some places where I've gone through multiple drafts I'm looking back through material that is largely terrible.

When I have gone through that with the pencil and cleaned it all up, and when I get to the end of a section or a segment that isn't too long, I'll take it home and before dinner I'll read it to Yolanda. I call her up and warn her first, ask if she can handle it. But it's never longer than fifteen or twenty minutes. Before I'm done, I've read the whole thing to her. Then I have heard it on my own tongue and I have made little quick pencil jots about this or that as I read it. She'll comment, or not. There have been times when she really threw up her hands and said, "That doesn't work at all." For example, the section in *Coming into the Country* about the Indians. I made the great mistake of trying to do that by relying too heavily on the dialogue I'd collected. I think I was tired, and instead of doing descriptions with dialogue sprinkled through it I just sort of said, "Joe said," and quoted what he said. Yolanda said, "That's terrible. I'm totally uninterested in it." And she was right. So after a night's sleep, I started over again. I told the story myself and used the dialogue sparingly.

Writers can be tempted to depend too much on others' speaking for them. If you tape-record something and make a transcription, it's a lot easier just to print that than to write something. A lot of books smell of tape.

Hearing it on my own tongue is really important, and I can't do it alone. The idea that someone is listening—that it will be interesting and entertaining, and that it will work for that person—is important.

Haynes: Do you think about the readers when you're sitting alone and writing?

McPhee: In a certain way I do. I think that it's unarguable that there are numerous people out there who are going to read this piece of writing and who are smarter, better educated, more sensitive, and swifter than I am. There has to be a large body of people of whom that's true. And I'm aware of that when I'm doing a piece of writing. I try to make it work for them. Beyond that, you can't be thinking that you are writing for a certain kind of group. You're not, for example, writing for an audience of geologists. Those people I was describing are not geologists and may never have read anything about geology.

But then comes the interesting problem. What do you do when you want to explain very elemental geologic matters, but you know there will also be geologists who will read it? You want them to read it, but that's not who you're writing for. You find a way to do that so the layperson is going to get it, but also so the geologist is not going to be put off by having this stuff presented in an introductory way. The best way to do that is through children. Here are two examples. In *Assembling California,* early in the piece, there's a little scene describing something Judy Moores did. She teaches science in the Davis Science Center. Very early on in knowing her, I had seen her go through some hand motions in showing kids how plate tectonics work. So a geologist might be charmed to read about that, because it's a little different from saying, "Now we're going to discuss plate tectonics, which is a theory that was evolved . . ." You find these things as you go along. In that case it was fortuitous that Judy did that. The same with Ted Taylor, the physicist in *The Curve of Binding Energy.* He'd had a chemistry set at home in Mexico City, and then he went to Exeter and took his first physics course there. He told me about learning physics. So I described Ted's introduction to physics. I'm free at that point to speak generally. I'm not using dialogue or quoting him. I'm just saying what he was learning about electrons and neutrons and protons in atoms, basically, and how one electron and one proton together are hydrogen, and two electrons and two protons and some neutrons are helium, and then run it on up. What you're doing is laying out the periodic table, because you are aiming toward a discussion of fusion and fission. You can approach it in a way that serves a purpose. Through early youth is one good way to do it. In any case, you find a way that's consistent with the nonfiction patterns of what you're doing. It'll be there somewhere.

Haynes: Do you get any complaints that the geology books are too technical?

McPhee: People write to me and say they wish there was a glossary for *Assembling California.* That's a little disappointing, because I try to incorporate into the text the definitions of the words I'm using where I feel that's necessary. Somewhere nearby, probably a little bit before, you'll find the definition of the word. But because there isn't a glossary to look it up in the person doesn't bother to notice it in the fabric of the piece. Often it's a word that's in the dictionary, so I'm not going to belabor it. There probably are also a few places in *Assembling California* where I didn't define something because it is defined in earlier geology books of mine. Mea culpa.

Haynes: You occasionally take a calculated risk in not defining a word. I remember a piece of equipment, some specialized type of crane, in *Looking for a Ship,* that you tossed in without explanation, perhaps for the flavor of the words.

McPhee: That's right, that's a conscious decision. It's there for the interest of the word, for the verisimilitude, the texture of the language, but to tell what that crane was all about would be tedious beyond belief.

I'll tell you a great device that Evan S. Connell uses in *Son of the Morning Star.* He mentions something. This isn't just a word, it could be a person. But he doesn't tell you who it is. Then you go along and he brings it up again. For example, he mentions Gall, and then later he says "Gall said" and Gall is saying something really interesting. And you say to yourself, "Who is Gall?" and he doesn't tell you. Then five pages later, ten, fifteen pages later, Gall returns. Some great scene has just happened, and then comes "Gall said." And Gall's comment is even more interesting than what Gall said before. Who the hell is Gall? And you begin to get slightly irritated. And then twenty pages further on, Gall appears again. Remember that that book warps and woofs its way back and forth through June 25, 1876, so he's always coming back to the moment. Gall gets more and more interesting and you get more and more curious and a little angry at Connell because he's not telling you enough about Gall. You are ready to kill the author, and just about the time you are ready to choke him, you turn the page and there sits a beautiful two- or three-page, fifteen-hundred–word, two-thousand–word portrait of Gall. You're ready for it now and you'll never forget it as you would have if he'd pedantically told you all about Gall when he first mentioned him. He does that with numerous things. He does it with the song "Garry Owen." How boring would it be to tell you, when he first mentions it, all about the song and who wrote it, but by the time you're ready to kill him, he tells you. I think that's wonderful stuff.

Sometimes you plant something, so that when the reader comes to it the reader knows about it. Let's say that in a quote somebody is going to refer to Branch Rickey. You cannot break into this person's quote and have the person define or describe what he's referring to. And it's extremely lame to do it in a parenthesis after the quotation. But suppose five pages before it, in a totally different context, you just happen to have inserted enough about Rickey so that when the readers reach this quotation they're prepared for it.

That's with references. Definitions are likely to lie a little closer in the text—nearby.

Haynes: Has your style changed over the years?

McPhee: I don't know. I don't feel so, but I don't know. I don't go back and read the things that I wrote before, not at great length unless I need to—if I need to get a reading together, for example—but sometimes I just grab one off the shelf and read two pages of it. It's just a strange little habit. And then I put it back. I've done that over the years, now and again. And I don't get a sense from those little jaunts that there was a different me there that doesn't exist now. It's as if I wrote it yesterday.

Haynes: Do you feel any pressure from your own reputation when you're writing? Does your reputation get in the way at all?

McPhee: It's a component that obviously wasn't there when I had no reputation. It's grown over the years. If you've done one piece, and people have liked it and told you so, then that sort of pressure would start right there. You don't have to write nine books for it to start up. It's a factor; it's not too big a one because I tend to have so many things to worry about anyway that that one gets obscured. If I were worried about nothing else, I think I'd probably be worried about that. It hasn't been a big problem so far.

In terms of going out into the field, sometimes my reputation is a considerable inconvenience and sometimes it's a help. There are times when doors open to me because of the work I've done before, and that makes things a lot easier for me. Then there are situations where I just totally want to be a fly on the wall, but I suddenly become a person people want to talk to because I wrote some book sometime, and I'm really inconvenienced. It can go both ways.

Haynes: Have you ever abandoned a piece?

McPhee: I'd be scared to abandon a piece just because I thought that I'd lost confidence in it, that nobody would be interested in it. If I abandoned it for that reason, then I'd abandon everything. Once I've started writing, I've never quit. At that point, you just lower your head and go for it. I can't stop there, because then I'd never know whether I was right or wrong.

I have given up pieces when the research was fairly well along. In one case, some other writer was working on something very close and Shawn asked me not to do it. In other cases, something won't gel. You're looking for a good central story to hang everything on and you don't have that. There haven't been too many of those, maybe half a dozen. Not too many, because usually, things go along, they are never quite what you anticipated when you first got the idea. The piece is not going to turn out exactly as you first imagined it might. So you just sort of adapt to what's happening as you go along and you follow your interests until you find something. I'm always amazed at my incredible luck. It was an amazing piece of luck to be on a ship with Paul Washburn. The ship was totally random and he was one of two alternating captains that ship had. The other captain would have been a very different person.

Haynes: When you think back over your work as a writer, do you have any particular pieces of yours that are favorites, that you look back on with particular fondness?

McPhee: No. Absolutely no favorites among my pieces of writing.

Haynes: Or ones where you particularly enjoyed the research?

McPhee: Oh, yes. I look back with great nostalgia on all kinds of them in terms of the experiences that went into the making of them. Those things vary a lot. If you really get to care about Alaska, it's possible to feel guilty that you're not there. I've gotten over that, but I've certainly felt it.

Haynes: Some of your critics have said that they'd like you to be a little less objective in your writing, to take sides on some of the environmental issues and put more of yourself in there.

McPhee: It's not difficult to ignore that. There are a lot of journalists and writers who have a whole lot of themselves in their pieces, and then the reviewer says there's too much of this writer in here. A reviewer has to say something. Nothing like that could cause me to put more or less of myself in a piece. I have some pretty clear feelings about how much of me belongs in a piece.

Also, I'm not going to tell the reader how to think. I don't care how many people who write book reviews make the point that they wish I would. I'm not a writer of sermons. I also have extremely strong feelings that if a point is to be carried somewhere, it's going to work best in the eye of the reader, in the judgment of the reader. You can lay stuff out there for a reader to form a judgment about, and once that judgment is formed, it's a thousand times more firm than the one the critics are talking about, which is the editorial writer telling somebody how to vote. Those things sort of irritate me when I read them. But not too much. I have a very different goal and I have no difficulty sensing what that goal is. When I read a criticism of that in a review, I think, "Well, basically that person is telling me about another book they think I ought to write."

You can't help subconsciously nudging a reader, but that's all right. I mean, why am I called an environmental writer? It's the topics I pick. Clearly I care about the outdoors, and I'm sure a reader can sense that. But my mission is not to do "op ed" pieces about it. I'm trying to do something different from that.

It seems to me that life is not simple, it's complex. There are always many factors. In some instances, you have to pull a lever and vote, but there's always something to be said on the various sides. For example, in *Coming into the Country,* I wanted to show what Alaska in that era was like, what the people thought. I was not up there to say what I thought about the issues—to say, "Feel *this* way." There were people coming at all kinds of issues from countless vectors. My goal was to show that against the background of the wild places, because that was the size and shape of the canvas. I wasn't going to get caught up in worrying about just one environmental issue. My goal is life in the round, not instructions on what lever to pull. I don't have any trouble with that goal at all.

Barbara Lounsberry

Pieces and the Frame

McPhee and Portraiture

My deepest goals are aesthetic.
                    John McPhee, 1978

J ohn McPhee is most widely recognized as a nature writer, as an artist
   acutely aware of environmental issues who inclines toward geology, to
limning the (literal) levels of the earth. As a painter of natural landscapes
he might be likened to George Inness, the New Jersey–born nineteenth-
century son of a Scotsman, who brought the Hudson River School to
national and international prominence.[1] Yet McPhee has always been
more than a deft landscape painter. He is an extraordinary portrait
painter as well. Readers too often take for granted McPhee's portraiture, forgetting that his first impulse, as well as a co-equal portion of his
legacy, has been as an American portrait painter, one who has taken the
New Yorker "Profile" and turned it frontal, indeed, made it three-di-
mensional, multiradial, and panoptic.[2]

Alva Johnston and 1952: "I had the feeling I could do it"

The roots of McPhee's portraiture can be traced to his twenty-first year
and a train ride home to Princeton from the New York City radio and
television program *Twenty Questions,* on which he exhibited his knowledge of animals, vegetables, and minerals. On that serendipitous day
McPhee read Alva Johnston's *New Yorker* "Profile" of colorful Palm
Beach architect Addison Mizner and felt immediately drawn to Johnston's enterprise. "The material was rich," he recalled nearly a quarter of
a century later. "The writing was light, skillful, funny, adroit. It had the
right timbre to it. I remember thinking it was something I'd like to do.
I had the feeling I could do it" (Shenker, NJ20).[3]

More than a half-century and thirty-plus McPhee *New Yorker* "Profiles" later, his assessment of Johnston's portraiture remains astute, and
one can locate in Johnston's profile elements McPhee would draw upon
and extend in his own portraits. Addison Mizner, as it happened, was a
quintessential McPhee subject. Johnston portrays him as a multifaceted
figure—an early model, perhaps, for McPhee's "A Roomful of Hovings" (1967). Mizner was more than Florida's premier society architect
of the 1920s and early 1930s; in Johnston's portrait he is a painter, interior decorator, landscape designer, antiquarian, curio peddler, chow
raiser, and society wit as well (I, 50, 64). Like McPhee himself (and David
Brower, the subject of McPhee's 1971 *Encounters with the Archdruid*),
Mizner possessed "a great sense of beauty" (I, 46). His goals, too, were
aesthetic. Paris Singer, the sewing machine heir who bankrolled Mizner,
waited to acquire the last of Mizner's homes, for he declared: "Each
house that Addison builds is more beautiful than the one before" (I, 46).

I have written elsewhere that McPhee preserves the nineteenth-century values of Emerson and Thoreau for the twentieth and twenty-first
centuries.[4] McPhee's portraiture is *prima facie* evidence. McPhee gravi-
tates for his portraits to Emerson's "representative men." He frames his
figures as templates of their fields, as epitomizing the highest levels
of excellence in a given endeavor. Emerson was fond of saying that
"[c]haracter is higher than intellect" (1108), and McPhee follows this
lead as well in choosing for his portraits individuals who scorn traditional education to pursue their own intuitive genius. Addison Mizner
was just such a figure. Johnston writes that "Addison was not a regular
architect. He never attended a professional school or even took a correspondence course in architecture. . . . The great man had dotted the enchanted island of Palm Beach with masterpieces, but he couldn't pass
the most elementary examination in his profession. Although cultured
to his fingertips, he couldn't compete with a seven-year-old schoolboy
on any academic topic" (I, 46, 58).[5] Like McPhee's *Archdruid* David
Brower, Mizner refuses to be tethered to facts: "Distrusting blueprints,
preferring metaphors to diagrams," Johnston writes, "[Mizner] would
explain and reexplain the effects he was seeking to his aides. He liked
phrases such as 'about so high' or 'right about here,' rather than exact
measurements. . . . He wanted his structures to give the impression that
they had evolved from century to century, not that they had sprung
ready-made from a blueprint" (I, 52, 54).

As congenial as Johnston's subject was to McPhee's emerging sensibility, Johnston's "light . . . funny [and] adroit" brushstrokes were equally appealing. It does no dishonor to McPhee to note that he found in Johnston a model of the fresh and wry good humor he could summon in abundance for his own portraits. Johnston offered stylish aphorisms. Of Wilson Mizner, Addison's ne'er-do-well brother, he would observe, "Wilson never believed in doing anything by violence that could be done by knavery" (IV, 51); and again: "[Wilson] had always regarded a lawsuit as a contest in which rival raconteurs took the witness stand and tried to outnarrate one another" (IV, 85).

McPhee also seems to have grasped Johnston's habit of switching fields unexpectedly within a sentence to achieve depth, surprise—and delight. Johnston particularly enjoyed inserting psychological drives into concrete contexts. "Architecture has been described as frozen music," he wrote. "[M]uch of Addison's architecture was solidified social ambition" (I, 61). Fashion arbitrator Ned Greenway "could put on the black cap and sentence a man to be hanged by his exclusive neck until he was socially dead" (I, 78). McPhee draws on this technique in many of his portraits—for example, this surprise turn in his 1984 portrait of the Swiss Army, *La Place de la Concorde Suisse:* "We have inched our way down the valleyside and taken the Nussbaum bridge—that is, taken notes on its width, its tonnage, its lack of prepared demolition" (124). In truth, McPhee's early cover subtitle for *Encounters with the Archdruid*, "[Narratives about a Conservationist and Three of His Natural Enemies]," may have come directly from Johnston's equally droll reference to the architect's "natural enemy, the husband" (I, 61).

One can even note in Johnston's deeply researched, four-part Mizner "Profile" the seeds of McPhee's gradient way of seeing. "[Addison] knew his profession at the top and at the bottom but not in the middle," Johnston observed. "At the high level, he had an imagination that teemed with beautiful facades and interiors, with striking vistas and splendid theatrical effects. At the low level, he was a master artisan, skilled in nearly all the building trades from carpentry and cabinetmaking to ironwork and plastering. About the middle, or technical, part of his profession, he was strangely defective" (I, 50). In what seems today like a quintessential McPhee line, Johnston in 1952 wrote of Palm Beach socialite Mrs. E. T. Stotesbury: "Her nickname was Queen Eva, and gossip writers of forty years ago said that being able to address her as Eva was enough to raise a woman socially from sea level to a moderate elevation" (II, 64).[6]

Time and the Early 1960s:
"They always had you on the defensive"

Those who revere McPhee the nature writer find it hard to fathom him as a "Show Business" reporter. Nevertheless, McPhee's first portraits can be found in *Time* magazine, where he worked from 1957 to 1964. "I worked at *Time* for seven years," he told the *New York Times Book Review* in 1977. "It was like mowing the lawn: once a week, you had to do it. Editors would come in and say, 'How would you like to write 5,000 words on Barbra Streisand' and I would wince.[7] They always had you on the defensive" (Singular, 1).

The eight *Time* cover stories McPhee crafted from 1960 to 1964—profiles of Mort Sahl ("Comedians"), Broadway musical composers Alan Jay Lerner and Frederick Loewe ("Two Parfit Broadway Knyghts"), humorist Jean Kerr ("Children Run Longer Than Plays"), Jackie Gleason ("The Big Hustler"), Sophia Loren ("Much Woman"), Joan Baez ("Folk Singing: Sibyl with Guitar"), Richard Burton ("The Man on the Billboard"), and Barbra Streisand ("The Girl")[8]—can be understood as McPhee's miniaturist phase. Most of the hallmarks of his later and more elaborate *New Yorker* portraits are present—but compressed and in miniature in the constricting space of *Time*. A *Time* cover is literally a portrait, and McPhee makes clear through humorous asides that he is aware he is working in the tradition of portraiture. Falling back for a metaphor on his *Twenty Questions* mineral expertise, he declares: "Spelunkers of the writer's mind will find no dark pockets in Jean Kerr's memories of her girlhood. Norman Rockwell might have painted it" ("Children," 83). Burl Ives, he tells us, has been "dipped in taint" ("Folk Singing," 59). More seriously he reports that composer Frederick Loewe "thinks of music in terms of color [and] once turned out compositions that reflected what he saw on an artist's canvases" ("Broadway Knyghts," 72). Michael Pearson has observed that the underlying text of many of McPhee's portraits is "the tale of a craftsman or artist" (*John McPhee*, 33). Say what one will, *Time*'s "Show Business" desk allowed McPhee to write about artists. His appreciation of Loewe's musical colors offers an early sign of his interest in craft, as does his revealing assertion in his Jean Kerr profile that "[a]ll situation comedy is clockwork; what matters is who makes the clock" (82).

In "making" these eight *Time* cover stories, McPhee offers the first signs of his penchant for framing his subjects as representative figures, as models of human achievement. In the postage-stamp confines of 5,000 words, he forges the template swiftly by stamping superlatives on precision-fine (often capitalized) delineations of fields. Mort Sahl is "the freshest comedian around. . . . The best of the New Comedians" ("Comedians," 42), while Jean Kerr is "one of the pleasantest humorists now working" ("Children," 82) and Jackie Gleason "the most celebrated buffoon ever to rise through U.S. television" ("Big Hustler," 34). Lerner and Loewe are "now the best writer-composer team in the American musical theatre" and their forthcoming musical *Camelot* is "probably the biggest, most beautifully set, and most complex musical play yet attempted" ("Broadway Knyghts," 64). In his portrait of Sophia Loren, McPhee goes so far as to employ "New Template" as a subhead and writes: "Loren sets the template [for women] now" ("Much Woman," 78). That he was thinking in "types" is clear from this witty depiction of Alan Jay Lerner's (many) wives: "Ruth Boyd (1940–47) was *Social Register,* Marion Bell (1947–49) was his Leading Lady, as she was in *Brigadoon.* . . . Actress Nancy Olson (1950–57) was the Upper-Middle-Class-All-American Girl. . . . Micheline Muselli Pozzo di Borgo (1957–), a slim, blonde, Corsican beauty equipped with a law degree and a fine record at the French bar, is Sophisticated European Woman" ("Broadway Knyghts," 69).

Of the eight small portraits for *Time,* the profile of Jackie Gleason best anticipates McPhee's later full-blown *New Yorker* portraiture. Like Johnston's Addison Mizner, Jackie Gleason was multifaceted. "[T]he storied comedian, egotist, golfer, and gourmand, mystic, hypnotist, boozer and bull slinger, is now emerging as a first-rank star of motion pictures," McPhee declares ("Big Hustler," 34). Even more clearly than Thomas Hoving (of "A Roomful of Hovings" to come), Gleason was a union of many personas. "Reggie Van Gleason, the patrician sot; Charlie Bratton, the loudmouth; the Poor Soul, who always got into trouble trying to do things for other people; Joe the Bartender, the 3 cent philosopher—all [are] played by Gleason," McPhee notes, "and all represent . . . some aspect of Gleason himself" (36). And Gleason unquestionably was one of Emerson's rough geniuses, having dropped out of school at eighth grade. "Largely self-educated," McPhee affirms, "he is forever apologizing for his lack of education, but he has no need to: he is informed and knowledgeable" (36).

A special charm of the Gleason profile is that it foreshadows McPhee's fascination with circles and spheres, which he would soon unfold at great length in his first *New Yorker* portrait, "A Sense of Where You Are" (1965), on basketball's Bill Bradley. Gleason's own obsession with circles must have been particularly appealing to McPhee the aesthete, alert to natural forms. Perhaps only McPhee would portray Round Rock, Gleason's home, as "basically an immense rotunda, with circular rooms, circular terraces, circular shower baths, and a circular sky-dome" ("Big Hustler," 37). Beyond mutual appreciation of circles, Gleason also shared McPhee's attraction to the aesthete's essential descriptor: "beautiful."[9] "[Gleason's] favorite adjective is 'beautiful,' " McPhee notes, "his favorite noun is 'pal,' and his favorite phrase is 'beautiful, pal, beautiful' " (35). McPhee knew he was painting an artist's portrait, for he quotes not only John O'Hara's assertion that "Jackie Gleason is an artist of the first rank" but also the novelist's explanation that "[a]n artist puts his own personal stamp on all of his mature work, making his handling of his material uniquely his own. Millions of people who don't give a damn about art have been quick to recognize a creation" (36). And as with later portraits of David Brower (*Encounters with the Archdruid*) and David Love (*Rising from the Plains*), McPhee makes it clear Gleason may be an endangered species. "He is a thundering talent," he quotes David Susskind as asserting, "the kind of raw, brilliant talent that has gone out of style" (34).

Signs of the exhaustive research McPhee expends on his portraits are present in abundance in the *Time* miniatures. The Mort Sahl profile offers the history of American satire from Thomas Morton in colonial times through Artemis Ward, Mark Twain, and Will Rogers ("Comedians," 42). The maddening need to compress such research can be seen in McPhee's similar effort to place Jean Kerr in her rightful tradition: "From Piltdown man to Perelman, the history of humor is overwhelmingly male and only a few representative female names present themselves for comparison with Jean Kerr" ("Children," 83). And McPhee can draw from literature as well as from history. He can evoke Chaucer's famous road story to dub Lerner and Loewe "Two Parfit Broadway Knyghts"; and who else could offer this appreciation of the source of *Camelot?:* "In adapting T. H. White's *The Once and Future King*—the whole glorious frieze of Arthurian legend and the Middle Ages spread by a writer with the rarely combined gifts of levity, scholarship and poetry—Lerner and Loewe have unquestionably taken on the greatest and heaviest theme that has ever been attempted in the field of musical comedy" (72). To compress "the whole glorious frieze" must have been frustrating for McPhee.

Equally disconcerting must have been the need to reduce character and visage (when brushstrokes could be added at leisure and in context in a multipart *New Yorker* "Profile") into single-sentence portraits such as this extraordinary turn on Mort Sahl: "Bright and nervous, frenetic, full of quick smiles and dark moods, shouting 'Onward, onward' between laughs, performing in a cashmere sweater, always tieless, he manages to suggest barbecue pits on the brink of doom" ("Comedians," 43).

A Larger Canvas

Time's canvas was small, and its time-frame for composition narrow. Bernhard M. Auer, the magazine's publisher, bragged that McPhee turned out the Lerner and Loewe profile in "a 61-hour, mostly sleepless writing stint" (17). McPhee was further compromised in that he was forced to use others' research—a common practice at *Time*. He has yet to speak with relish of his apprenticeship in "show business."[10] There is little doubt that from 1952 on he recognized that the larger canvas of the multipart *New Yorker* "Profile," as well as the unlimited time given *New Yorker* writers, better fit the multiradial and comprehensive portraits he wished to paint.

What do we ask of a portrait? In his volume *Problems of Portraiture,* E. M. Benson offers a useful answer: "That it be a work of art achieved not by the substitution of esoteric symbols for a person . . . or by the deadening process of duplication, as in the case of Madame Tussaud's effigies, but by an act of mature creation: that is to say, a successful (good intentions are not enough) attempt to translate the image and character—the essence of a person from Nature's medium of flesh and blood into art's medium of paint, sculpture, mosaic, black and white, or celluloid" (3). Or words, one might add. McPhee's rich legacy of portraiture reveals that his nineteenth-century allegiance extends beyond his affinity with Inness, Emerson, and Thoreau: the nineteenth century was also the era of American portraiture. As early as the 1840s art historian William Dunlap was observing that "[b]y and by you will not by chance kick your foot against a dog kennel but out will start a portrait painter" (Benson, 21). Folk art portraits painted by itinerant nineteenth-century painters as well as the large number of portraits by professional artists painting oils and miniatures "swelled the production of portraiture in America," according to Benson, "to a point exceeding that of any single European country" (20–21).

The word "portrait" derives from the Old French *portraire*—meaning to draw (*traire*) forth (*por*). A McPhee *New Yorker* portrait is easily distinguishable from the portraits of the other well-known literary journalists of the 1960s—Joan Didion, Tom Wolfe, Norman Mailer, and Gay Talese. Joan Didion stays aloof from her subjects, the better to puncture their fantasies. Tom Wolfe also keeps his distance. A brilliant satirist and social critic, he employs comic exaggeration in his portraits to expose human vice and folly for our moral edification.[11] Wolfe's gift in portraiture is for humiliation. His gleeful reproductions of human embarrassment—the humiliation of the astronauts by the chimpanzees or the "Flak Catcher" by the "Mau-Mauers"—require a cool gaze and, as with Didion, a comparatively short haul. Norman Mailer's nonfiction portraits are fascinating, for he employs metaphors as probes of human character. Still, Mailer's gift is for self-portraiture. He is our comic Rembrandt and his own most interesting subject.

McPhee's portraiture shares more traits with that of his fellow New Jerseyan, journalist/artist Gay Talese, than it does with the others; yet even here each artist's portraits are distinctive. Much more than Didion, Wolfe, or Mailer, McPhee and Talese choose to spend extensive time, even live, with their subjects in order to present detailed and thorough portraits. Their general aim, moreover, is not to skewer or satirize but to provide portraits of individuals they feel drawn to—by admiration, sympathy, or empathy. McPhee and Talese are sports enthusiasts, and each has painted enduring portraits of sports figures (McPhee of Bill Bradley and Arthur Ashe; Talese of Floyd Patterson, Joe DiMaggio, and Muhammad Ali). Each artist, in addition, has moved away from celebrity portraiture toward portraits of individuals more obscure.

In spite of these many similarities, a McPhee portrait would never be taken for a Talese portrait—or vice versa—for the writers are attracted to different subjects. Talese, the son of an immigrant Italian tailor, is drawn to outsiders, to the unnoticed, and to losers, with whom he profoundly identifies. McPhee, the son of the physician to the U.S. Olympic team, is drawn, as I have noted, to individuals who represent high achievement in a given field, craft, or art, individuals with whom he, too, identifies. While McPhee and Talese both seek to extend the "frontal" and "profile" views of historical Western portraiture, Talese's inclination is to go behind the façade. "I am a fractured person, prismatic," he told me in a 1984 interview. "You turn me around, you get other colors. That is the way I think people are, but you have to turn them around.

You have to see them from different angles, so I do not come on one-dimensionally and see people from a frontal position as they might wish to project themselves, showing their best profile. I turn them around, or I turn myself around, so I can see them from different perspectives" (personal interview, 18 August 1984).

McPhee also seeks different perspectives and to come at his subjects from many angles. He does this, however, not with Talese's goal of discovering the reality behind the appearance (the truth behind the façade) but in order to achieve a complete view. McPhee is not so much in search of what is *hidden* (the essential Talese assumption); rather, he is always angling to get it all. His goal in portraiture, as in his landscape painting, is to achieve the panoramic view. One might even say he seeks to treat portraiture *as* landscape painting. The word "panoramic" stems from the Greek words *pan* (meaning "all") and *horama* (meaning "sight"). Here is the tie between McPhee's portraiture and his environmentalism, for his effort in both is to bring everything into view: to provide a comprehensive view of the individual or ecosystem.

McPhee's drive for the panoptic portrait spurs his conceptual ingenuity: he seeks imaginative ways to showcase his subjects—to suggest their range and dimension. To provide a comprehensive portrait of "Forager" Euell Gibbons (1968), McPhee arranged a one-week foraging expedition in Pennsylvania, with Gibbons adding a new wild ingredient at each meal. To showcase conservationist David Brower (1971), he arranged "encounters" for his *Archdruid* in three threatened terrains. To explore excellence in tennis in *Levels of the Game* (1969), McPhee chose one semifinal tennis match as his centerpiece from which could radiate, point by point, a veritable pointillist record of contributing elements.

"My deepest goals are aesthetic," McPhee has insisted (Drabelle, 62), and it seems clear he has brought his interest in forms to the challenge of human portraiture. During a telephone interview in 1987, McPhee told me he believes that form should emerge from the subject; it should not be imposed artificially from without. He said he dislikes structures that are "obvious." However, because McPhee seeks the panoptic view, a natural form that tends to emerge frequently in his portraits and appears to be highly congenial is that of the multiradial sun. As landscape, McPhee described this form as his *Place de la Concorde Suisse:* the supreme glacier of Europe has "avenues of ice coming from six or eight directions to conjoin in frozen intersection" (11).[12] This multiradial form places the subject of the portrait in the center, the circle if you will, but insists on the many "avenues" that contribute to the portrait.

"A Roomful of Hovings," McPhee's 1967 portrait of art connoisseur and Metropolitan Museum director Thomas Hoving, offers a particularly appropriate as well as straightforward illustration of this favored McPhee portrait structure. McPhee's title and central conceit, "A Roomful of Hovings," arises from the tenth of eleven "sections" of the portrait: from the literal fact that Hoving's New York City apartment contains a room full of Hoving portraits. "Framed and under glass," McPhee writes, "is a large sketched composition by Knud Nielsen that consists of fragments of Hoving: several aspects of his head, and a study of his hands—tapered, talon fingers holding the head of a griffin. On a freestanding set of shelves is a Basen head of Hoving, made from blocks and chips of wood that Basen nailed together, partly wrapped in strips of canvas, and daubed with paint. The likeness is remarkable" (51). And, of course, Hoving himself is in the room as well. It could hardly have been lost on McPhee that his own portrait of his Princeton classmate would be composed inescapably of "fragments of Hoving," so he foregrounds that truth by framing (and labeling) each section as a specific aspect of Hoving's life. Put another way: if Hoving himself were the Metropolitan Museum, the eleven sections would be its labeled rooms.[13]

The beauty of the multiradial form—many roads leading to Thomas Hoving—is that it provides a portrait structure that is accurate and comprehensive (we are wholes comprised of many contributing parts), yet it allows for considerable artistic freedom (in the ordering of the avenues or segments), resulting in a final product whose form is not "obvious." McPhee's "sections" consist of six places ("Fifth Avenue," "Edgartown," "Parks," "Princeton," "Seventy-third Street," and "Eighty-second and Fifth"), four people or roles ("Rorimer," "Schoolboy," "Father and Son," and "Curator"), and one topic ("Art and Forgery")—an indication that, for McPhee, human beings are shaped not only by places but also by individuals and ideas. His artistry can be grasped by comparing the chronological sequence of the eleven Hoving parts (on the left) with McPhee's re-presentation to achieve a deeper and more dramatic portrait:

Hoving in Actual Time   McPhee's Portrait of Hoving

Father and Son   Fifth Avenue
                          [Hoving as 19-year-old floorwalker]

Schoolboy	Edgartown
	[Hoving's adolescence]
Edgartown	[James] Rorimer
	[who hired Hoving for the Met]
Fifth Avenue	Schoolboy
	[fourth grade through prep school]
Princeton	Art and Forgery
	[Hoving's work at the Met]
Rorimer	Father and Son
	[Hoving's birth and early life]
Curator	Parks
	[Hoving as New York park commissioner]
Parks	Curator
	[Hoving as Met curatorial assistant]
Eighty-second and Fifth	Princeton
	[Hoving at college]
Art and Forgery	Seventy-third Street
	[Hoving's apartment]
Seventy-third Street	Eighty-second and Fifth
	[Metropolitan Museum]

In comparing Hoving's "as it happened" biography with McPhee's re-presentation for this portrait, one immediately notes that McPhee leaps backward and forward in time in order to present Hoving's passion for art as the central and recurring theme (or color) of the portrait. The flashbacks to his early days as a "Schoolboy," to his youthful "Father and Son" conflicts, and even to his short term as Mayor John Lindsay's flamboyant park commissioner function as both digression from and background for the portrait of Hoving as art curator and museum director. Had McPhee waited to introduce James Rorimer and the Metropolitan Museum until they actually arose on Hoving's horizon, the resulting portrait would not only be ordinary (Everyboy's growing pains) but would be unbalanced as well. McPhee's artful re-presentation also subtly suggests that the past is with us in present glories, lending lights and shadows to the portrait.

Thomas Hoving offered McPhee more, however, than just a multi-faceted subject. In this portrait Hoving's aesthetics and approach to museum collection resonate with McPhee's own developing sense of portraiture. "The notion that we're supposed to collect only masterpieces is a little bit false," Hoving states (57), endorsing, perhaps, McPhee's own penchant for what have been called obscure or "unpromising" subjects. "Concepts of masterpieces change," Hoving declares. "We're collecting for 500 years from now. We're after the top quality, but since the Museum is a great encyclopedia of man's achievement, we also collect backup material—footnotes and appendices to great chapters in art history" (57). "We collect, preserve, exhibit, educate," Hoving explains (60), each word capturing McPhee's own endeavor. Hoving also endorses the "representative man" aesthetic, the drive to portray the highest standards of achievement. "In collecting modern paintings, we try to decide what are the best pieces that a man has done," Hoving tells McPhee. "Then we try to get the absolute best one—the best, without any question, that he has ever done. That's what it's all about. . . . [M]y only standard will have to be over-all quality. I'll have to think very deeply about what the work of art does, not only in its aesthetic nature but in its historical and humanistic nature—how it sums up its time, how it expresses its creator" (64, 61).

The multiradial form undergirds most of McPhee's portraits and interfaces effectively with what at first might seem like a competing structuring principle: rising levels. In both *A Sense of Where You Are* and *Levels of the Game,* for example, the rising levels of the basketball tournament and tennis match supply dramatic tension as the portraits unfold. While the level of play rises, however, McPhee is painting the many planes and avenues of the portrait. The reality of McPhee's vision is this: his eye is as obsessively drawn to levels of human attainment as it is to the geological levels of the earth because, for him, it is essential to have "a sense of where you are," to quote the title of his first book. Forever seeking the panoptic perspective, McPhee would have us be aware, simultaneously, of heights of representative achievement; the many levels—like Oliver Wendell Holmes's chambered nautilus—to reach that height; and our locations on this grid. When a representative type is endangered or passing (David Brower, Henri Vaillancourt of *The Survival of the Bark Canoe,* David Love, and many others) McPhee captures its plight in portraits that are themselves preservative measures. While some might regard his pursuit of the panoptic perspective as a drive to achieve authority and exert power (as described in Albert Boime's *The Magisterial Gaze*), I resist this view and suggest instead that McPhee seeks to empower (rather than to exert power) by providing a comprehensive view.

Negotiating Postmodern Snares:
The Portrait Painter as Judas

McPhee's allegiance to nineteenth-century values and his sense of himself as a working journalist crafting his portraits within the established *New Yorker* "Profile" tradition have enabled him to remain, by and large, aloof from postmodern self-consciousness and its touching anxiety regarding human portraiture.[14] In both his work and his words McPhee has challenged the seemingly sophisticated and distractingly confessional postmodern view of fellow portraitists Joan Didion and Janet Malcolm that the portrait painter always "betrays" the subject. In the famous closing salvo to her "Preface" to her first nonfiction collection, *Slouching towards Bethlehem* (1968), Didion warned her readers that "people tend to forget that my presence runs counter to their best interests. And it always does. That is one last thing to remember: *writers are always selling somebody out*" (xvi).

Twenty-two years later Janet Malcolm elaborated this theme across an entire book titled *The Journalist and the Murderer* (1990), a volume of relentless charges launched with this grenade: "Every journalist who is not too stupid or too full of himself to notice what is going on knows that what he does is morally indefensible. He is a kind of confidence man, preying on people's vanity, ignorance, or loneliness, gaining their trust and betraying them without remorse" (3). For Malcolm and Didion, the artist/subject relationship is a limited and dangerous encounter, "the old game of Confession," Malcolm writes, "by which journalists earn their bread and subjects indulge their masochism" (8). For Malcolm, the portraitist is a kind of "enemy infiltrator" (24) who engages in "perfidy" (5), "bad faith" (9), and "a kind of soul murder" (21). McPhee challenged this narrow thinking in a 1978 interview: "Joan Didion says . . . that you always betray the people you write about, but I don't agree. If anything, I've been too careful when there have been negative aspects to a portrait. Praise comes easily, and if I have any regrets about my writing as a whole, it's about one or two people I've lionized. I could have toned down the portraits in a couple of my books" (Drabelle, 63).

Portrait painters can enhance a likeness, and they can caricature and degrade. A full range of aspects is open to any portraitist, just as an extraordinary variety of relationships can arise between artists and their subjects. Betrayal is one possibility, of course, but it is hardly the only outcome. McPhee's interaction with his subjects might be offered as a model of principled behavior, as evidence that, contrary to Malcolm's claim, portraiture can be morally defensible. McPhee's portraits, one can argue, serve educational and preservative as well as aesthetic goals. "When McPhee conducts an interview," William Howarth has reported, "he tries to be as blank as his notebook pages, totally devoid of preconceptions, equipped with only the most elementary knowledge. He has found that imagining he knows a subject is a disadvantage, for that prejudice will limit his freedom to ask, to learn, to be surprised by unfolding evidence. . . . In an ideal interview he listens without interrupting, at liberty to take notes without framing repartee or otherwise entering the conversation" (xv, xvi). McPhee asserts he has inviolable criteria: "One is that if I'm doing a piece of writing about somebody, they know what I'm doing to the extent that I can make it known to them. The thing is, your notebook's always out. There's no subterfuge in what you're doing. I don't think that you run into a bathroom and scribble notes that you didn't want the person to know you were taking down" (Dunkel, 45–46). McPhee will even protect a subject's private life. "A perfectly artistic, excellent portrait of somebody can be done that does not include everything about them," he reminds us. "If some journalists think that that's what journalism is all about, they ought to go back to square one and learn over again" (Dunkel, 46).

McPhee has painted negative portraits. "I have a total inability to conceal my mood," he told the *New York Times* in 1976. "If I'm annoyed at something I have no poker face. Zero" (Shenker, NJ20). McPhee's portrait of bark canoe maker Henri Vaillancourt in *The Survival of the Bark Canoe* (1975) is his most overtly unflattering character study. McPhee was likely thinking of Vaillancourt when he chided himself in 1978 for being "too careful when there have been negative aspects to a portrait" (Drabelle, 63), for in 1994 he told Jared Haynes that he "developed a structure different from the one I would have chosen [for *The Survival of the Bark Canoe*] had [Vaillancourt] been more sympathetic" (I, 113). Facing a more attractive sitter, McPhee would have started the volume with the canoe trip and then flashed back to his first meeting with Vaillancourt. Instead, the first 7,000 words of the 40,000-word "Profile" describe Vaillancourt in his shop in Grenville, describe "the person I got interested in, the person I went up there to watch making things. And then comes the canoe trip in chronological sequence. . . . So why are these seven thousand words first? Because a reader goes through a process of learning about a character, and I wanted the reader to appreciate Henri's skills without being prejudiced by a description of his behavior on the canoe trip" (I, 113, 114).

The classical flaw of hubris (arrogance, presumption, or overweening pride) stands out in McPhee's portraiture as the most damaging of human weaknesses. Regrettably, young Henri Vaillancourt possessed this quality in abundance. While McPhee admires the fact that Vaillancourt "has appointed himself the keeper of this art" (5), he exposes the canoe maker's failings through the eyes of Vaillancourt's lifelong friend, Rick Blanchette: "Rick is sensitive to Henri's insensitivities—to his opinionated arrogance, to his inconsiderate manner, to his platoon-leading orders" (86).

It also comes to pass that Vaillancourt lacks the broad vision (with its incumbent humility and generosity) so often present in McPhee's other "representative men." Narrow range is as large a failing for McPhee as hubris (hubris, in fact, may be viewed as tragic narrowness), and it must have been incredibly disappointing for him to learn that "Henri's expertise stopped at 'the yard'; out here [on the lakes and rivers of Maine] he is as green as his jerky" (85). Vaillancourt's narrowness is reflected in his language—experience reduced to the word "bummer"—as well as in his limited knowledge of the wild. His aesthetics turn out to be narrow as well. Vaillancourt has only one criterion for a canoe: "It looks good." Yet the artist who finds supreme beauty in the bark canoe fails to appreciate nature's grandeur. "The great beauty of this lake apparently means nothing to him," McPhee laments. "He has worked for two days to get to it, and now wants to rush across it and portage away from it in the dusk and dark" (106). McPhee is aware that he has "been accused of writing too positively" about his subjects but insists that this is not true of Henri Vaillancourt (Haynes, I, 113). "I was committed to the piece of writing and the piece of writing had to be honest," he says. "If I had sketched Henri Vaillancourt differently, I would have sketched him as I didn't see him. I felt the weight of it" (I, 113).

Tennis player Clark Graebner, in an earlier McPhee portrait, exhibits weaknesses similar to Vaillancourt's. After painting his *Time* miniatures and the portraits of Bill Bradley (*A Sense of Where You Are*), Frank Boyden (*Headmaster*), Thomas Hoving ("A Roomful of Hovings") and others, McPhee confessed he felt "a little jaded" (Haynes, I, 123). He wished to challenge himself as a portraitist. "It occurred to me," he told Jared Haynes, "that if you wrote about two people who related in some way, did two profiles, wouldn't they be inter-reflective, wouldn't one plus one add up to more than two?" (I, 123). The result was the ingenious *Levels of the Game* (1969), McPhee's portrait of a National Open semifinal tennis match between Graebner and Arthur Ashe. McPhee had proven himself master of small group portraits in such early *Time* pieces as "Comedians" and "Folk Singing"; however, in both *Levels of the Game* and the even more complex *Encounters with the Archdruid,* his goal is to contrast his "sitters" and their values, and this results in more subtle negative portraits than Vaillancourt's forthright depiction. In both *Levels* and *Encounters,* McPhee strives mightily to give each major figure his due. Nevertheless, through subtle undermining brushstrokes he creates complex yet real villains in these portraits and communicates the values he most admires.

"A person's tennis game begins with his nature and background and comes out through his motor mechanisms into shot patterns and characteristics of play," McPhee writes at the beginning of *Levels of the Game,* setting up the unfolding match as a contrast of backgrounds and character—which he then supplies (6). He notes that Clark Graebner has "a facial bone structure that suggests heroic possibilities" (31) and later stresses that "[i]t is doubtful whether a trimmer, healthier, better-built, or more powerful human being than Graebner has ever stood on a tennis court" (119). McPhee goes to great length both to build sympathy for and to defend Graebner from charges of "cockiness," assigning the cause of some of his court strutting to the osteochondrosis Graebner suffered in his teens.

Yet despite his present physical superiority and his more advantaged upbringing—or, one might argue, *because* of them—Graebner's range is much narrower than Ashe's. On the court, McPhee writes, "Graebner is a deft volleyer, reacting quickly and dangerously at the net, but in general—although the two players technically have the same sort of game—Graebner does not have the variety of shots or the versatility that Ashe has. Ashe says that Graebner 'could use a little more junk in his game'" (22). Off the court, this narrower prospect is replicated. While Ashe knows well his ancestry, "Graebner has no idea whatever when his forebears first came to this country" (13); and his limited historical range extends to geography as well. Graebner is "not interested in sightseeing," while Ashe is "an aggressive tourist" (120). Like Henri Vaillancourt's, Graebner's vocabulary is also impoverished. He is "less verbal than Ashe," who is "meticulous" about language (110). Most sobering, however, is the narrow and arrogant certainty Graebner exudes, not only regarding his own place in the world—he expects to be a millionaire before the age of forty—but also regarding Ashe's place as well ($50,000–$60,000 a year), while Ashe possesses no such certainty (104).

Clark Graebner thus anticipates Henri Vaillancourt in exuding arrogance as well as narrowness. In McPhee's telling, even the Graebner home is overweening: "The houses of Wimbledon Road appear to be . . . almost too big for the parcels of land allotted to them" (59). Clark's signature is "pi Hancock squared," and he is "aggressively vain about his tan. . . . When he is sunbathing, he will snap at anyone who stands between him and direct sunlight for as much as three seconds" (119, 31). In a contrasting character study such as this one, even a small unflattering detail casts a shadow on the sitter's character, and it is not too much to say that *Levels of the Game* is rife with these darker Graebner colors. That McPhee views Graebner's character flaws in classical Greek terms can be seen in his inclusion of this comment from Davis Cup captain Donald Dell as the level of Ashe's game rises above Graebner's: "Look at him [Graebner]—the Greek tragic hero always getting pushed around by the gods. He really sees himself that way, and it's his greatest weakness" (95). Once we begin to see the match in Aristotelian terms, McPhee's fourth set line, "Graebner is broken," is rich in ironic meaning (143).

In our first view of Clark Graebner, McPhee tells us that "Graebner has a plan for this match" (4). Graebner's greatest misfortune, however, may have been to be matched against one of Emerson's "representative men"—one of the rough, intuitive geniuses McPhee adores. Arthur Ashe's father speaks in Emersonian maxims—as does Arthur Jr. himself, who acknowledges that he behaves "instinctively" rather than following a Graebner plan (63, 124, 88). McPhee suggests that Ashe's ability to elevate his game stems not only from his trust in his intuition but also from his wider perspective. Ashe tells McPhee that he can do three things at once (123), and McPhee tells us that "[o]f the six young men on the United States Davis Cup Team, [Ashe] seems to have the widest range of interests" (124). Ashe's broader vision allows him to view himself in proper perspective. "His summary of his own life is that it has been 'a succession of fortunate circumstances,'" McPhee tells us. "He has seen them in perspective" (125).

Of the 242 paragraphs in *Levels of the Game*, 82 limn Ashe's portrait; 68 paint Graebner's, while 92 move between them like the tennis ball itself. Advantage Ashe, we must say; for in this dual portrait, broad vision and intuitive genius outshine a more powerful and scripted nature—yet one, ultimately, of flawed and narrower range. Comparatively, Graebner's is a negative portrait, and readers are led to root for Arthur Ashe and to admire the values he exemplifies. The same might be said for David Brower, the archdruid of McPhee's *Encounters with the Archdruid*. "*Levels of the Game* worked out," McPhee told Jared Haynes in 1994. "But then I developed a weird ambition. If two people had worked out, what about more? I had the notion of relating three people separately to a fourth. . . . The whole notion was that these had to be four working, successful profiles. I shouldn't just set people up for the environmentalist to knock off. That would be a failure" (I, 123, 124).

Archdruid does not fail as complex portraiture. As in *Levels,* its villains are admirably complex and human.[15] McPhee frames each subject as a noteworthy representative figure of his particular field: mineralogy, real estate development, dam construction, and conservation. In addition, in each of the work's three *Encounters* he strives conscientiously to capture the strengths of each Brower antagonist. In part I, mineralogist Charles Park is portrayed as "a man who knows what he is looking at in wild country" (67). McPhee asserts that he has never spent time with anyone who is more aware of the natural world—including David Brower. In part II, McPhee's fellow Scotsman Charles Fraser is recognized as representing the highest levels of enlightened real estate development; and in his final section, McPhee devotes early (Vaillancourt-like) time to establishing the challenging conditions of Floyd Dominy's western water-starved childhood to encourage reader appreciation of his motives for building dams.

Despite these generous highlights, however, the four remain comparative portraits; and through use of revealing gestures and juxtapositions, levels, and religious allusion, McPhee makes clear which figure is most admirable. Persons who define themselves through repeated gestures or revealing phrases lend themselves to easy portraiture. Mineralogist Charles Park offers McPhee a vivid defining gesture in part I, "The Mountain": his obsessive striking at mountain outcroppings with his pickaxe. When McPhee asks Park why he persists in this indiscriminate undermining, Park replies only "I just haven't hit one in a long time" (18). In a text where David Brower is equated with the mountain, Park's behavior takes on symbolic (and sinister) nuance. McPhee's attitude toward Park is also subtly conveyed in his portrayal of the mineralogist at lower levels of elevation than Brower throughout the section.

McPhee's religious allusions in *Archdruid* are so rich—beginning with the pagan image of the title and including touches of Greek mythology and a broader Christian typology as well—that they at first almost seem to confuse his canvas. Charles Fraser casts David Brower in the role of a tree-worshipping archdruid (II, 95–96), but McPhee himself more often equates Brower with Christ. "They are crucifying him, and they are self-congratulating bourgeoisie," McPhee quotes an unnamed Sierra Club member as stating at the climactic moment in part III when Brower is ousted from that organization (209). In part I, McPhee presents Brower as reenacting the Sermon on the Mount, generously sharing his berries with Park and others; in part II, he depicts Brower enlisting Charles Fraser into discipleship; and earlier in part III—in a moment contrasted with Floyd Dominy's satanic hubris—he paints a scene in which two young hikers fail to recognize Dominy yet act as if they wish to "draw a picture of a fish in the sand" when they are introduced to David Brower (207).

In McPhee's Christian typology all three of his Christ figure's "natural enemies" are depicted as devils. In part I, McPhee links Park's mining enterprise both to hell and to the fall of Adam and Eve. The concentric circles of a mine, to David Brower, are the circles of hell; he says any mine would "puncture" the wilderness "like a worm penetrating an apple" (39). Charles Fraser, the enlightened real-estate developer of part II, is depicted as an overbearing landlord of his Hilton Head and Sea Pines Plantation estates. On Cumberland Island, his major failing is that of Henri Vaillancourt in Maine: his wish to race across the landscape rather than to savor its natural beauty. Satanic reference exists here as well, for McPhee quotes an old expression now rising again: "The Devil has his tail wrapped around Cumberland Island" (99).

In part III, McPhee locates dams at "the absolute epicenter of Hell on earth" for conservationists and reveals Floyd Dominy's satanic pride to be of such dimension that he assumes the role of supreme deity. When a New Yorker says of Lake Powell, "I see God has given us good water here this morning," Dominy replies, "Thank you"—an overweening moment repeated three times in the section (190). The conclusion of *Encounters* is particularly adroit, for it provides a triumph of vision for Brower over Dominy, conveys McPhee's own view in the complex environmental debate, and hints ominously at future peril. If reading a river provides one index of proper appreciation of nature, then the contest over Lava Falls provides a test of Brower's and Dominy's vision. In this debate, Brower reads the river better (244); and immediately afterward McPhee himself sides with nature and the long view over Dominy's short-term dams: "My own view was that the river would make all the decisions" (244). But McPhee does not give himself the final word in this volume. Man and his satanic hubris—his narrow arrogance and pride—remain alarming forces, McPhee seems to imply, for he ends his volume not with David Brower's triumph, or with nature's final sway, but with the devil, Floyd Dominy, striking a match and lighting his cigar again (245).

Avoiding Postmodern Snares II: Balance and Self-Portraiture

If McPhee rejects the notion of inescapable betrayal of subjects—offering himself as a portraitist appreciative of human gifts yet conscious of human weaknesses as well—he has also resisted the postmodern temptation to make the artist's presence a major portion of the portrait. "The only portraits in which one believes are portraits where there is very little of the sitter, and a very great deal of the artist," Oscar Wilde famously said (Nadel, 24). The risk for postmodern portrait painters willing to acknowledge their own presence in the scene, however, is at least as old as Boswell: the danger of competition with the primary subject—as many have noted of Boswell's frequent overshadowing of Dr. Johnson. Ira B. Nadel has suggested that "the presence of the biographer in the biography marks a new maturity in biographical form" (27). McPhee, however, seems able to keep the proportions in balance. Focus is always on his subjects; he exists in his texts only to the degree necessary to the context: observing, framing, paddling a canoe. As Ronald Weber has noted of *Coming into the Country* (1977), McPhee's references to himself "are usually fleeting and often amused, as when after eating the flesh of a grizzly he remarks, 'In strange communion, I had chewed the flag, consumed the symbol of the total wild, and, from that meal forward, if a bear should ever wish to reciprocate, it would only be what I deserve'" (120).

McPhee's response to postmodernism, in sum, has been light, adroit, and funny. He wittily reminds us of his presence (and his enterprise) through titles such as *A Roomful of Hovings and Other Profiles* and *Pieces of the Frame*. His most elaborate and charming bow to self-portraiture, however, is his engaging tribute to his "other self," John McPhee the Maine woods game-warden pilot, in "North of the C. P. [Canadian Pacific] Line." In this moving double portrait, McPhee captures his own life as an American portrait painter and acknowledges its sacred trust: "There is a lot of identification, even transformation, in the work I do—moving along from place to place, person to person, as a reporter, a writer, repeatedly trying to sense another existence and in some ways to share it. Never had that been more true than now, in part because he was sitting there with my life in his hands while placing (in another way) his life in mine" (249).

Yet even in this moment so evocative of Joseph Conrad's "Secret Sharer," McPhee retains his perfect balance: "We are not altogether the same," he reminds us:

> He is John Malcolm, son of Malcolm, son of John. I am John Angus, son of Harry, son of Angus. He is a pragmatist of the north woods. I am a landscapist of the Suppressed Mudjekeewis and Muttering Hemlock School. I have seen him carry briquettes into First Currier Pond. I have seen him start a campfire with gasoline from the wing of his airplane. . . . Whenever I think of him, however, I feel such a strong sense of identification that I wonder if it is not a touch of envy—an ancestral form of envy, a benign and wistful envy, innocent of chagrin. As anyone might, I wish I knew what he knows—and wish not merely for his knowledge but for his compatibility with the back-country and everything that lives there. I envy him his world, I suppose, in the way that one is sometimes drawn to be another person or live the life of a character encountered in a fiction. Time and again, when I think of him, and such thoughts start running through my mind, I invariably find myself wishing that I were John McPhee. (292–93)

Pieces and the Frame

John Angus McPhee is a major figure in American literary portraiture. His portraits of "representative men" carry forward the nineteenth-century "great man" tradition of Ralph Waldo Emerson and Thomas Carlyle; yet his choice of less famous figures and his ingenuity in showcasing his "sitters"—in truth, for animating his sitters (for depicting them in action)—make McPhee's portraits contemporary, fresh, and engaging. McPhee is drawn to figures who exhibit the highest levels of excellence in their fields. These tend to be Emerson's intuitive geniuses: subjects exuding individualism, broad vision, and an appreciation of beauty. Their individuality ensures distinctive and memorable portraits: their broad vision brings range, depth, and elevation to the portrait, and their aesthetic sense asserts the importance of aesthetics in contemporary life.

That McPhee is drawn to multifaceted subjects reflects his own wide-ranging mind; however, he may recognize as well that a multidimensional "sitter" helps ensure the rich texture he desires in his portraits. McPhee told Michael Pearson that "[n]onfiction writers go out not knowing what to expect. In a way you're like a cook foraging for materials, and in many ways, like a cook, you're only as good as your materials. You go out looking for characters to sketch, arresting places to describe, dialogue to capture—the way you would gather berries. You hope for the greatest variety" ("Twenty Questions," 107–8).

When he comes in from the field, the form of a multiradial sun helps McPhee draw forth (*por traire*) this variety. The sun is a natural form, one that projects an individual as a union of many (radiating) attributes. Symbolically this structure also underscores McPhee's enterprise, for in theogony the sun represents the moment when the heroic principle shines at its brightest. In many cultures the sun is a symbol of the "higher self" and serves as a means by which the lower consciousness can rise to union with the higher. In fact, in many Western and Eastern cultures the sun inherits one of the most notable attributes of deities: it sees all and, consequently, knows all. In that respect the multiradial sun reinforces the comprehensiveness that McPhee hopes to achieve in his portraits. Carl Jung said the sun is a symbol of the source of life and of the ultimate wholeness of man and woman (Jung et al., 32). McPhee's use of the multiradial sun gives him a structure for his portraits that allows him to be thorough and comprehensive, free to move creatively among the facets in a manner natural yet not obvious and also subtly to offer, through its very form, reinforcing symbolism.

The risk of McPhee's solar ambition, his penchant for panorama, his drive for comprehension, is, of course, superficiality: portraits capturing surface but not depth. His "light . . . funny [and] adroit" brushstrokes may also lead readers to believe, mistakenly, that he offers shallow rather than profound likenesses. The many vectors of McPhee's "suns" address this persistent danger, providing him avenues for limning depth as well as range—giving him the rich texture he desires. Similarly, his classical balance and Montaignian equanimity of temperament should not distract us from the thread of elegy lending somber tones to many of his portraits, which are simultaneously celebrations of and elegies for endangered values and arts. McPhee's radiant way of seeing may be his supreme contribution to literary portraiture. The sun's cultural history, J. E. Cirlot reminds us, is as "an heroic and courageous force, creative and guiding" (317). McPhee's portraiture constitutes an heroic aesthetic religion complete in itself.

Notes

1. McPhee celebrates Inness in *In Suspect Terrain* (1983), noting that "in the eighteen-fifties George Inness came to the Water Gap and set up his easel in sight of the trains. The canvases would eventually hang in the Metropolitan Museum, the Tate Gallery, the National Gallery (London). Meanwhile, in 1860, Currier & Ives made a lithograph from one of them and published it far and wide" (98). Inness's memory was "stored with beautiful forms," Frank Jewett Mather, Jr., tells us (55). "Certainly none of our landscapists was more various and skillful" (67). Mather could have been referring to McPhee when he noted that "it was the variety of Inness that bothered his contemporaries to the very end" (53).

2. In *John McPhee*, Michael Pearson reports that across its first decades, *New Yorker* "Profiles" were "slight sketches" (32); however, later writers like St. Clair McKelway, A. J. Liebling, Joseph Mitchell, and Alva Johnston added depth and dimension to the "profile." McPhee is working in this latter tradition.

3. Almost two years later, McPhee again acknowledged the influence of this Johnston "Profile" during an interview with the *New York Times Book Review* (Singular, 51).

4. "John McPhee's Levels of the Earth," in *The Art of Fact: Contemporary Artists of Nonfiction*, 65–106.

5. Mizner is a precursor of Theodore Taylor in McPhee's *The Curve of Binding Energy* (1974). Taylor barely noticed the "D" he received in his Modern Physics course at Exeter, for he "was getting a look for the first time . . . at what he would call 'submicroscopic solar systems' and he found that they had for him enormous appeal" (29).

6. In a telephone interview on 22 June 1987, I asked McPhee if he was drawn to natural forms, such as circles and levels. He first encouraged me by recalling that he had told a friend early in his career that "[e]verything I write about is round," but then he disavowed any attraction to circles and spheres. "You are batting .500," he countered. "Levels, yes; circles no." Within a few years, however, the *New Yorker* published "Duty of Care," McPhee's article on tires (28 June 1993, 72–80).

7. In 1977 John Baker wrote in *Publishers Weekly* that McPhee "seems happiest at about the length of what in fiction would be called a novella, averaging around 50,000 words, with 65,000 ('The Deltoid Pumpkin Seed') the longest to

date. That length divides into two or three *New Yorker* installments, and makes a slim Farrar, Straus, and Giroux book" (13).

8. "Comedians: The Third Campaign," *Time* (15 August 1960): 42–44, 47–48; "The Road: Two Parfit Broadway Knyghts," *Time* (14 November 1960): 64–66, 69–70, 72; "Broadway: Children Run Longer Than Plays," *Time* (14 April 1961): 82–86; "Movies: The Big Hustler," *Time* (29 December 1961): 34–38; "Movies Abroad: Much Woman," *Time* (6 April 1962): 78–82; "Folk Singing: Sibyl with Guitar," *Time* (23 November 1962): 54–56, 59–60; "Actors: The Man on the Billboard," *Time* (26 April 1963): 70–74; "Broadway: The Girl," *Time* (10 April 1964): 62–67.

9. "Beautiful" is McPhee's own most frequent adjective.

10. In 1994 McPhee granted this much to Jared Haynes regarding his years at *Time:* "You do four or five stories per week, each with a beginning, a middle, and an end, based on a set of facts; it was a very good training ground in that way. You were exhausted at the end of one week, and a little more at the end of the next week, but after three or four years there I think I learned quite a bit" (I, 110).

11. Wolfe sketches as well as writes and has published and exhibited his caricatures of dandies and other types.

12. Oranges, with their radiating segments, are a similar natural image; indeed, fascination with the form may explain McPhee's 1967 book *Oranges.*

13. A "museum" is an apt metaphor for McPhee as well as for Hoving, for the word derives from a Greek root meaning a seat or home of the muses. A museum is literally a repository for the preservation and exhibition of objects illustrative of natural history, fine arts, and industrial arts as well as antiquities, and thus its purpose resonates with McPhee's.

14. In 1977 McPhee told the *New York Times Book Review:* "[F]undamentally, I'm a working journalist and I've got to go out and work. . . . I feel that I've wandered into a large room [the *New Yorker*] that was set up before I knew the difference between a grapefruit and a softball. And since I've been inside the room I've thrown around a few bricks. I've found my place in it; but I haven't built it" (Singular, 50, 51).

15. Perhaps it was to reinforce this point that McPhee removed his subtitle, *Narratives about a Conservationist and Three of His Natural Enemies,* from later editions of the volume.

Works Cited

Auer, Bernhard M. "A Letter from the Publisher." *Time* (14 November 1960): 17.

Baker, John F. "John McPhee." *Publishers Weekly* (3 January 1977): 12–13.

Benson, E. M. *Problems of Portraiture.* Washington, D.C.: American Federation of Arts, 1937.

Boime, Albert. *The Magisterial Gaze: Manifest Destiny and American Landscape Painting, 1830–1865.* Washington D.C.: Smithsonian Institute Press, 1991.

Cirlot, J. E. "Sun." In *A Dictionary of Symbols*, 2nd ed., trans. Jack Sage, 317–21. London: Routledge & Kegan Paul, 1962.

Didion, Joan. "A Preface." In *Slouching towards Bethlehem*. New York: Farrar, Straus & Giroux, 1968.

Drabelle, Dennis. "A Conversation with John McPhee." *Sierra* (October–November–December 1978): 61–63.

Dunkel, Tom. "Pieces of McPhee." *New Jersey Monthly* (August 1986): 37–51.

Emerson, Ralph Waldo. "The American Scholar." In *The Norton Anthology of American Literature*. 5th ed. Nina Baym, gen. ed. Vol. 1. New York: W. W. Norton, 1998.

Haynes, Jaynes. " 'The Size and Shape of the Canvas': An Interview with John McPhee: Part I." *Writing on the Edge* 5(2) (Spring 1994): 109–25.

———. " 'The Size and Shape of the Canvas': An Interview with John McPhee: Part II." *Writing on the Edge* 6(1) (Fall 1994): 109–25.

Howarth, William. L. "Introduction." In *The John McPhee Reader*, ed. William L. Howarth, vii–xxxiii. New York: Vintage Books, 1978.

Johnston, Alva. "The Palm Beach Architect": "Part I: Construction First, Blueprints Afterward," *New Yorker* (22 November 1952): 46–93; "Part II: The Boom," *New Yorker* (29 November 1952): 46–94; "Part III: Vision and Subdivision," *New Yorker* (6 December 1952): 48–64; "Part IV: When Fish Became Birds," *New Yorker* (13 December 1952): 42–85.

Jung, Carl, Joseph L. Henderson, Marie-Louise von Franz, and Aniela Jaffe. *Man and His Symbols*. New York: Doubleday, 1964.

Lounsberry, Barbara. "John McPhee's Levels of the Earth." In *The Art of Fact: Contemporary Artists of Nonfiction*, 65–106. New York: Greenwood Press, 1990.

Malcolm, Janet. *The Journalist and the Murderer*. New York: Vintage Books, 1990.

Mather, Frank Jewett, Jr. "George Inness." In *Estimates in Art: Sixteen Essays on American Painters of the Nineteenth Century*. Series II. New York: Henry Holt & Company, 1931.

McPhee, John. *Coming into the Country*. New York: Farrar, Straus, & Giroux, 1977.

———. *The Curve of Binding Energy*. New York: Ballantine Books, 1974.

———. *Encounters with the Archdruid*. New York: Farrar, Straus & Giroux, 1971.

———. "A Forager." In *A Roomful of Hovings and Other Profiles*, 65–118. New York: Farrar, Straus & Giroux, 1968.

———. *The Headmaster: Frank L. Boden, of Deerfield*. New York: Farrar, Straus & Giroux, 1966.

———. *In Suspect Terrain*. New York: Farrar, Straus & Giroux, 1983.

———. *La Place de la Concorde Suisse*. New York: Farrar, Straus & Giroux, 1984.

———. *Levels of the Game*. New York: Farrar, Straus & Giroux, 1969.

———. "North of the C. P. Line." In *Table of Contents*, 249–93. New York: Farrar, Straus & Giroux, 1985.

———. *Oranges.* New York: Farrar, Straus & Giroux, 1967.

———. *Pieces of the Frame.* New York: Farrar, Straus & Giroux, 1975.

———. *Rising from the Plains.* New York: Farrar, Straus & Giroux, 1986.

———. *A Roomful of Hovings and Other Profiles.* New York: Farrar, Straus & Giroux, 1968.

———. *A Sense of Where You Are: A Profile of William Warren Bradley.* New York: Farrar, Straus & Giroux, 1965.

———. *The Survival of the Bark Canoe.* New York: Farrar, Straus & Giroux, 1975.

Nadel, Ira B. "The Biographer's Secret." In *Studies in Autobiography,* ed. James Olney. 24–31. New York and Oxford: Oxford University Press, 1988.

Pearson, Michael. *John McPhee.* New York: Twayne Publishers, 1997.

———. "Twenty Questions: A Conversation with John McPhee." *Creative Nonfiction* 6 (1996): 103–15.

Shenker, Israel. "The Annals of McPhee." *New York Times,* 11 January 1976, NJ20–21.

Singular, Stephen. "Talk with John McPhee." *New York Times Book Review,* 27 November 1977, 1, 50–51.

Talese, Gay. Personal interview. 18 August 1984.

Weber, Ronald. "Letting Subjects Grow." In *The Literature of Fact: Literary Nonfiction in American Writing,* 111–22. Athens: Ohio University Press, 1980.

Norman Sims

"Essence of Writer"

John McPhee's Early Training

The range of subjects that John McPhee has taken on—a portrait of a man who creates birchbark canoes, profiles of people living in primitive conditions in New Jersey and in Alaska, and scientists arguing about the revolution that transformed geology—always makes me consider his intellectual preparation. Writers are made, not born. What prepared him to create an elaborate and effective architecture in his writing? What interested him enough to write about people building airplanes, examining rocks, paddling canoes, playing basketball and tennis, living on an isolated Scottish island, and trying to hold back the Mississippi River? What life trajectory permitted him to become a writer, achieving his early ambition? Any reasonable answer reaches back into McPhee's childhood.

The story begins with his parents. His father, Harry McPhee, a doctor with a specialty in sports medicine, served as the U.S. physician at the Pan-American Games and the winter and summer Olympics for twenty years. McPhee's mother, Mary Ziegler, had taught French in Cleveland before their marriage, and her father had been a publisher in Philadelphia. McPhee's brother, Roemer, and his sister, Laura Anne, were born while Harry was a physician at Iowa State University. The family moved in 1928 to Princeton, New Jersey, where Harry became the physician for the Princeton University athletic teams and a member of the faculty.

John Angus McPhee was born 8 March 1931. The family house stood on the edge of town with fields and woods beyond it, but the family soon moved to a little street right next to the campus. The Princeton campus was an open playground for McPhee as a child. His interest in writing could have been absorbed by osmosis from Princeton or inherited from his maternal grandfather, the publisher. But McPhee thinks it

derived from his father's Scottish heritage. "There's not so much difference between the Scots and the Irish," McPhee said, referring to the
Celtic verbality of both people, "except that the Scots are responsible."[1]
Genetics aside, growing up in a household and on a campus where conversation was valued contributed a lot to McPhee's later career.

McPhee and his father had a close relationship. They attended football and basketball practices together. For several years as a child
McPhee served as team mascot and retrieved the ball after extra points
at football games. In the summer, his father drove him to the Keewaydin canoe camp in Vermont. "I fished a great deal for ten or fifteen years
with my father, starting when I was about five," McPhee said. He grew
up among college sports at Princeton and water sports in Vermont.
"That's all I cared about until I finished high school," he told me.

> I grew up with this great affection for Princeton athletes that went on
> through my father and the fun of it. I knew those guys. I wasn't just
> sitting there, looking at them. I played basketball with them, in a way,
> always throwing a ball through the hoop at practice and joking with
> these guys. I developed a lot of affection for Princeton through this
> milieu when I was a kid. I never thought of going to another school.
> It never crossed my mind. I never applied to another school. I just
> went to Princeton in the way you'd go to your elementary school. I
> never thought a whole lot about it until I was thirty or beyond.

During this conversation we were sitting on couches in McPhee's living room. He built the house in the 1960s and except for a period during his divorce has lived there ever since. Through the windows in the
living room we could look out over his back yard, where deer wander
through and a picnic table sits under a shade tree. I was visiting to ask
for McPhee's reading on the origins of his work.

"All I ever wanted to do was be a writer," McPhee said, "from way
back as a child":

> Not that I did a whole lot about it when I was thirteen years old, but
> I definitely had that feeling then. I tell a story about how I'm down
> there on the football sideline, nine years old, and here are these people
> who show up for the football game. They sit up there in a sheltered
> place, the press box, and they got to watch all the football games.
> Then, talking through their fingers into a typewriter, they would write
> a story about the game. That's what they were paid for. I thought that

looked like a pretty good way to go to a football game and a pretty interesting thing to do. Above all, it looked easy. I thought it was easy, and that's the biggest mistake I ever made in this world.

An inherent disposition to become a writer—assuming such a thing exists—would probably be expressed first as a love of language rather than as an admiration for sports writers. McPhee said when he was a child he was forever saying words just because they sounded good. "Even the name of a commercial product, a proper name, if it had some flavor that appealed to me, I'd repeat it over and over again, *ad infinitum,* sometimes out loud. My brother and sister would make fun of me for that." In 1998, explaining why an English major would write about geology, McPhee wrote:

> I used to sit in class and listen to the terms come floating down the room like paper airplanes. Geology was called a descriptive science, and with its pitted outwash plains and drowned rivers, its hanging tributaries and starved coastlines, it was nothing if not descriptive. It was a fountain of metaphor—of isostatic adjustments and degraded channels, of angular unconformities and shifting divides, of rootless mountains and bitter lakes. Streams eroded headward, digging from two sides into mountain or hill, avidly struggling toward each other until the divide between them broke down, and the two rivers that did the breaking now became confluent (one yielding to the other, giving up its direction of flow and going the opposite way) to become a single stream. Stream capture. . . . There seemed, indeed, to be more than a little of the humanities in this subject. Geologists communicated in English; and they could name things in a manner that sent shivers through the bones.[2]

It has always puzzled me that a writer with McPhee's love of strong, expressive characters and intelligent action would take on a subject that moves as slowly as a glacier and whose brute actions took place generally before humans were present on the planet. The answer may involve the language with which clever geologists describe the wandering of the poles and the continents floating like ships on the ocean.

McPhee's formal education began with two years in kindergarten— his parents decided that he was too young and too shy for first grade— but then he did the second and third grades in one year. "There was a lot of backing and filling in there like freight cars hitting. I did the first six grades in five years. I got a lot more playschool or jungle gym than I got primary education," he said.

The attack on Pearl Harbor brought the United States into World War II when McPhee was ten years old. He contributed by spotting aircraft from a little hut on the high ground of Rocky Hill:

> I knew every airplane that flew in anybody's sky in the world. It wasn't difficult to know that then. I went over to the university and was trained. They would flash silhouettes on a big screen for one second, and then you had to write down what the plane was. I knew them all. I was twelve years old and it was like some kid with cars. With me it was airplanes. You had binoculars and you spotted every plane that went over and you phoned it into New York. You rattled them off in shorthand to somebody there. You went with an older person. I knew the planes and the older person, I suppose, was responsible. I had a little armband and I did that all through the war.

While praising his elementary, junior, and high school teachers in Princeton, McPhee specifically mentioned only one. He was not, apparently, a dedicated student:

> I took the books home, threw them under the bed and got into the bed. When I played basketball, I went to practice and got out of there at six o'clock. I went home and ate my dinner. I flicked on the lights that I had arranged around the trees in the back yard, and I shoveled the snow away if it was there, and shot baskets until nine-thirty. Why? Because I wanted to be a basketball player? No. Because I loved doing it. It's a narcotic. I went out there for the sheer love of it. What happened to my books? Well, I did the homework in school and my mother would jump all over me. I was getting good grades—A's—and she said, "But you're not doing any work." In a way, she was right.

Olive McKee was another matter. She taught McPhee's English class for three out of four years in high school. McKee, the school's drama teacher, emphasized writing above literature in her English classes. "Not that we didn't read *David Copperfield*, but she assigned on most weeks of the year three pieces of writing, and I had this teacher for three years. The piece of writing could be anything you wanted—fiction, poetry, essay—it didn't matter. Every piece of writing you turned in had to have a piece of paper on top of it showing the structure. In her case it was Roman numerals and that kind of thing." McPhee, who now teaches in the Humanities Council at Princeton, requires his writing students to turn in a similar page with each assignment. "It doesn't have to be Roman numerals," he said. "It can be a drawing, but they have to show that they have an idea of the internal structure of their piece." He follows his own advice, spending weeks planning the structure of a book before he begins the formal process of putting words on paper. He says he knows the first and last sentence of a piece and his structural outline before he begins.

Olive McKee also required her students to read their compositions to the rest of the class. "You got a sense of the oral tradition involved in writing," McPhee said. "I never publish a word, never have, in the *New Yorker* magazine or anywhere else, that wasn't at a given point in the course of the composition read aloud." Today he generally reads to his wife, Yolanda:

> In hearing that come across my tongue, I not only pick up her reaction but I pick up my own reaction—how it feels. I don't know if I picked that up in Olive McKee's class but I remember reading things all the time and being conscious, when I was writing the piece, that I might be reading it to the class. I think it conditions you. You start listening more. I liked doing that. Some of the things were entertaining, maybe, and you wanted to get up and hear the other kids laugh or jeer or whatever. I feel a large and considerable debt to her.

▲

Structure has been an important tool in McPhee's hands. It leads the list of distinguishing characteristics of his literary journalism. He works with graphic internal structures in mind—a lowercase *e* in "Travels in Georgia," an articulated *Υ* in "A Roomful of Hovings," and other drawings that have been pinned to his bulletin board during composition. These planned patterns help solve the problems that any nonfiction writing project can encounter.

McPhee's literary journalism began with a profile of Bill Bradley in *A Sense of Where You Are* (1965), a story based on a single individual. Similar profiles followed—*The Headmaster* (1966), "A Roomful of

Hovings" (1967), and portraits of Euell Gibbons (an expert on edible wild foods) and Robert Twynam (who grew the grass on Wimbledon's tennis courts). Then came a moment of decision.

Several years ago, sitting at his desk in the East Pyne Building at Princeton, McPhee explained that decision. He had started to think about a new structure. On a blank piece of paper he drew a structural pattern he was thinking about after he completed those single profiles. "What developed in my mind for a long while was: 'What if you did the same thing with two people?' If you found two people and did all that for each of them, then things would start going back and forth in there. One plus one just might add up to more than two." On the paper he drew the two individuals, each surrounded by dots representing the satellite figures in their lives. Lines rebounded back and forth among the dots. He said this structure was "the single most important thing for me, other than the final writing itself." When he created the structure, he had no idea who the two individuals might be. They turned out to be Arthur Ashe and Clark Graebner playing in the semifinals of the first U.S. Open Tennis Championship at Forest Hills, and his book was called *Levels of the Game* (1969).

"When *Levels of the Game* worked out," McPhee said, "I got ambitious and thought, 'Well, if it works for two, how about more?'" On his bulletin board he pinned a diagram that looked like this:

$$\underline{ABC}$$
$$D$$

"This is a weird way to go about something," McPhee said. "I haven't done that since. It was a totally abstract concept." The four people could have come from baseball, medicine, or golf, but at the time McPhee began to focus on the environmental movement. Ultimately, the diagram on his bulletin board became the structural plan for *Encounters with the Archdruid* (1971). One person, environmentalist David Brower, would relate to three "natural enemies"—Charles Park, a geologist and mineral engineer who wanted to dig an open-pit copper mine in the Glacier Peak Wilderness; Charles Fraser, a land developer with plans for a resort on Cumberland Island, Georgia; and Floyd Dominy, commissioner of reclamation, who wanted dams built in Grand Canyon National Park.

McPhee first imagined the structure then went out and found Graebner and Ashe and later Brower and his "natural enemies." He expanded the single profile structurally into two portraits then four interlocking relationships. Of all the "absolutely legitimate" tools a nonfiction writer can use, including narrative, dialogue, character sketching, and metaphor, McPhee emphasizes structural innovation. He is writing about "real people in real places," as he always reminds interviewers. Limited by the requirements of nonfiction, he selects the events he writes about and sometimes, as in sending David Brower rafting on the Colorado River with Floyd Dominy, he creates the events as well.

While the real people and real places are out there, it is a long way from "out there" to "literature." Any writer facing a blank page understands that nothing appears there naturally or on its own. McPhee's early structural innovations gave support for tons of information in his work and became a defining quality of his literary journalism. The structures owe a great deal to Olive McKee.

▲

When McPhee graduated from high school, he was admitted to Princeton University. But he was only seventeen years old, and for the second time his parents thought it would be a good idea if he repeated a year of school before moving on. This time he went to Deerfield Academy in rural western Massachusetts for a postgraduate year. "At Deerfield Academy," McPhee recalled, "I did every last assignment. I got some kind of education." He mentioned by name several teachers who put more education into him than he actually worked to acquire. He took English from Richard Hatch, a novelist. European history was Russ Miller's domain; and the headmaster's wife, Helen Boyden, taught chemistry. McPhee did not take chemistry at Princeton High School because he wanted to take Mrs. Boyden's legendary chemistry class at Deerfield.

McPhee said he had a "first-rate full-year" geology course with Frank Conklin. "Even then, I was an English-major designate, but in the decades of writing that followed—highly varied non-fiction writing, often involving natural scenes—the geology lay there to be tapped."[3] Conklin devoted his course largely to geomorphology, the sculpture of the surface of the earth. "If you want to know why things look the way they do, geomorphology is what tells you. The river cuts, continental glaciation, young valleys, the Grand Canyon. But geomorphology will not tell you the whole story. Geomorphology tells you how the Colorado River cut this canyon, but it doesn't tell you where the river got the energy to do that. It doesn't tell you about the uplift of the Colorado Plateau which produced the energy that cut the canyon. The uplift is tectonics." In 1949 "continental drift" (as it was then called) or plate tectonics was not an explanation for canyons and mountain ranges; that had to wait for fifteen scientific papers published during a scientific revolution that eventually triumphed around 1968, according to McPhee.

In comparison to Princeton High School, McPhee wrote in 1997,

> Deerfield was—to understate the case—novel. Attendance was taken exactly seventeen times a day. You surely had a sense that you belonged. In all kinds of ways, actually, the school was abundantly welcoming, and soon made this new-boy senior feel as if he'd been a part of it for the three previous years. In fall, attendance was taken on the Lower Level by Robert McGlynn with a clipboard. Relying on recognition alone, he checked off names. In the ranks and files of lightweight-football calisthenics, he failed to see me. He walked around behind my jumping and flapping teammates, and found me lying on the ground looking at the sky. He liked that. He checked me off. In the extended indolence on the grass, he recognized essence of writer.[4]

McGlynn—a voracious reader with an Irish background and a babbling, fluid way of talking—got McPhee excited about literature in a way Olive McKee did not. One day he would hand McPhee a book, and later McPhee would go back and discuss it with him. "He was willing to talk about them, that was the thing. Like the students, he lived there the whole time and the school was his life," McPhee said. Deerfield Academy has a special collection of Robert McGlynn's library that contains every one of McPhee's books. In a foreword to a McGlynn novel, McPhee wrote that McGlynn "became, among other things, a student of his students, exposing their innards with rays of humor that went to the bone but cut nothing. He led us up the hill to Joyce and Conrad, and down the other side to meet ourselves. He was prodigal with his talent—that brook he was babbling wherever he might be. It was for anyone. It was for me. As a writer now, I am forever grateful to him. And, as it happens, I was never in his class."[5]

As the scenes in McPhee's books testify, he has a fondness for the outdoors. Talking to me on his living room couch, he wore a sling on an arm dislocated during a cross-country skiing mishap in the mountains of

California. He has a short, trim, and muscular frame. For the athlete in McPhee, Deerfield was paradise. Every student had to participate in a sport. He played lightweight football and basketball, and one day the lacrosse coach recruited him even though he had never picked up a lacrosse stick in his life. As a short forward on the basketball team, McPhee led the team in scoring, according to longtime Deerfield faculty. He would never mention such a thing himself. More importantly, the basketball coach was Frank L. Boyden, headmaster of Deerfield Academy.

McPhee and Mr. Boyden, the shortest two on the team, rode together in the middle jump seats of a Cadillac that served as a team bus for away games. "He had almost nothing to say about basketball beyond a few remarks about the coming game," McPhee explained. "He talked about his school. There was never a need to ask him to do that. For my part, because I had come from a public high school I was especially interested in what made Deerfield work, and what made Deerfield work was sitting on the other jump seat." Sixteen years later, encouraged by Conklin and McGlynn, McPhee started work on a profile of Mr. Boyden, who was entering his sixty-fourth year as headmaster at Deerfield. McPhee spent the fall in the Boydens' house, immersing himself once again in his subject matter. Before he went home, Mrs. Boyden and her son John both warned McPhee not to show the piece to the headmaster

John McPhee sits in front of headmaster Frank L. Boyden in the 1948–49 Deerfield Academy Varsity Basketball team photo. Photo credit: Deerfield Academy Archives, 1949 *Pocumtuck* yearbook.

before publication. When the profile came out in two issues of the *New Yorker*, there was no way to keep it from Mr. Boyden. "When the first part appeared," McPhee wrote in 1997, "the headmaster happened to be in Los Angeles for a Deerfield gathering. John Boyden was there, too, and later described to me the following scene: The headmaster, in a hotel room, picked up *The New Yorker*. He read it for a time and then stood up and sent *The New Yorker* flying through the air and into a wall. It fell behind a couch. Time passed. Eventually, he reached down behind the couch and retrieved the magazine. He read for a time. Then he sent it fluttering into another wall." McPhee was summoned to Deerfield for a chat. He went.

> I found him in the front room of his house enjoying a steaming cup of hot water. He was looking through a neatly assembled, handmade book that consisted of cut-out *New Yorker* columns absolved from their flanking ads and mounted on white paper. As we turned the pages, sitting side by side on two small chairs, he was amiable, anecdotal, and matter-of-fact. Wherever there was something that troubled him, he stopped to tell me what it was. He stopped nowhere near as often as I had thought he would. He told me he had no desire to diminish my piece of writing but there were some things he wanted me to understand. One at a time, without hurry, he went through them.
>
> I was tense all the way, but then, at the end, felt suddenly relaxed. After I went home, I changed some things and left others as they had been. From beginning to end, the points he had raised had to do with others—with the sensitivities of townspeople, teachers, and students, and of their families and descendants. Not one of his objections had to do with himself.[6]

▲

Concerning his following four years at Princeton University, McPhee mentioned only a few faculty members. First was his advisor, Larry Thompson, who "managed to get me quite excited about the possibilities for five or six things to be going on in a piece of writing at one time. If you didn't get that idea out of the Princeton English Department, you weren't there."

Another was Richard Blackmur. McPhee explained that Blackmur was a different sort of college English professor. He had attended

Boston Latin—a top-quality high school—and dropped out, but he kept going to classes. He went to Harvard but did not enroll or apply. "Blackmur was a very well-educated man," McPhee said. "He just didn't happen to be officially involved in any of those things. The story that Blackmur didn't have a high school degree needs to be qualified. He was a critic. He was hard to read, a match for Derrida in the difficulty of approaching him." Blackmur organized the Creative Writing Program that enrolled McPhee—it is now housed in a university building at 185 Nassau Street where McPhee went to elementary school. For his thesis, McPhee wrote a novel, which was a new idea at the time.

Perhaps more importantly for his later career as a journalist, McPhee also worked for the *Nassau Sovereign,* the *Daily Princetonian,* the *Princeton Tiger,* and the *Nassau Literary Magazine.* After graduation he spent a year in England as a postgraduate at Cambridge University, during which time he played basketball and studied.

McPhee said he developed a desire to write for the *New Yorker* at the age of eighteen, well before he knew anything about its editors Harold Ross and William Shawn. "I was drawn to the pieces that were in the same vein that I do now, the so-called long fact pieces. I liked the fiction, too." After graduation from Princeton, his goal seemed a long way off. He steadily submitted articles to the *New Yorker,* but they were all rejected. He wrote trial pieces for "Talk of the Town" but heard nothing in response.

Becoming a writer was a bewildering business. "Saying you want to do that isn't the same as being in a training program somewhere, being trained as an investment broker or something tangible you could do. How the hell do you become a writer? What do you do?" He took a job at Time-Life and eventually spent seven years writing features for *Time* magazine about people, art, show business, religion, education, and books. He wrote articles, poetry, and short stories in his spare time. He wrote television plays for *Robert Montgomery Presents,* two of which were produced. Harold Hayes, the great editor at *Esquire,* commissioned McPhee to write about his year playing basketball at Cambridge. When he finished the article, Hayes no longer wanted it. But on the rebound the *New Yorker* bought "Basketball and Beefeaters" (1963), McPhee's first published piece in the magazine. It made no difference. He continued working at *Time.* Two years later his profile of Bill Bradley, "A Sense of Where You Are," won him a position at the *New Yorker.*

▲

In John McPhee's substantial body of work, three enduring patterns had formed by 1978. First, he had written profiles of strong, independent, craftsmanlike characters such as Bill Bradley, Thomas Hoving, and David Brower. Second, he had created regional profiles of distinctive places such as the New Jersey Pine Barrens and Alaska. Third, he had begun a series of books on scientific themes that started with *Oranges* and would eventually culminate in five volumes on the geology of North America. Within these patterns, the subjects of his journalism ranged widely.

"If you make a list of all the work I've ever done," McPhee told me, "and put a little mark beside things that relate to activities and interests I had before I was twenty, you'd have a little mark beside well over 90 percent of the pieces of writing. That is no accident."

We have already seen some of the obvious connections. "Basketball and Beefeaters" and *A Sense of Where You Are* about Bill Bradley came from a longstanding personal interest in basketball. *Levels of the Game* tapped his love of tennis in high school. *The Deltoid Pumpkin Seed* (1973), about the creation of a new airplane, is linked to his plane spotting during World War II. His family heritage and his education from Deerfield Academy and Princeton University can be seen in works such as *The Headmaster* (1966), *The Crofter and the Laird* (1970), *The Curve of Binding Energy* (1974), and all of his books on geology. The Keewaydin canoe camp in Vermont gave him a lifelong love of paddling, and references to canoeing wander throughout his work, including most prominently "Reading the River" (1970), "Travels in Georgia" (1973), *The Survival of the Bark Canoe* (1975), *Coming into the Country* (1977), and *The Control of Nature* (1989). An interest in fishing formed early through his relationship with his father, then after a long hiatus returned and became *The Founding Fish* (2002). McPhee said that working on *Coming into the Country* deepened his interest in geology, which had originated in Frank Conklin's classroom at Deerfield. "I was writing about the gold fields of Alaska up there near the Klondike strike. It suddenly occurred to me: I had no idea how the gold got there. I well understood why it was in the streams. The mountains break apart and there's the gold. Geomorphology, right? But how did the gold get into the mountains in the first place?" McPhee called a Princeton geologist, Ken Deffeyes, and shortly a new set of books was launched, culminating in *Annals of the Former World* (1998), which won him the Pulitzer Prize.

"Why did I write about tennis players? Why did I write about a basketball player? Why hold this person up for scrutiny and not that one? Because you've got some sort of personal interest that relates to your own life. It's an important theme about anybody's writing," McPhee said.

While that list only scratches the surface of McPhee's interests and their origins, it may be overstated. The connection between an author's books and the biography that stands behind the books can be a tenuous matter, the subject of great speculation. It seems remarkable that McPhee draws a connection between his interests developed before the age of twenty and his subsequent twenty-seven books and fifty years—or perhaps not.

Beyond the obvious connections, the more subtle and psychological links to events and interests before the age of twenty are harder to specify. Relationships with parents and teachers create layers and layers beneath the surface that last a lifetime. McPhee said he settled into his own distinctive style of nonfiction, as opposed to all the other opportunities for a writer, because it has so many interesting possibilities. "Remember the possibilities in nonfiction writing," he said:

> The character sketching that stops well short of illegitimate invention. There's plenty of room for invention, for "creativity," and so forth in this field. Lots of it. These possibilities, stopping well short of invading a number of things that only fiction can do. You can use fictional techniques—narrative, dialogue, character sketching—absolutely legitimate. Why do I make those trips with those people participating? I make them so I'll have something to describe. Sitting here like this, you don't have the matrix of a narrative. Sitting in a canoe for two weeks, you've got the narrative.

We came back again to why one topic would appeal more than another. "When an idea comes along—there are tens of thousands of ideas coming along all the time, just swarms of them—for some reason or another something sticks, and then you start to live with it and develop it." McPhee collects material for a piece of writing using the same filtering mechanism—"because something or other made you more interested in that subject than any of the thousands of others lying around at the same time." And then the voice and the architecture of the piece start to take shape. He looks for "a structure that rises organically from the material as collected, not something imposed from the outside."

Writing in *Natural Acts*, David Quammen noted that certain writers on the natural world are actually scientists. Quammen lamented that he does not have even a toehold in their world. "What I am," he said, "is a dilettante and a haunter of libraries and a snoop. The sort of person who has his nose in the way constantly during other people's field trips, asking too many foolish questions and occasionally scribbling notes. My own formal scientific training has been minuscule. . . ."[7] The same is true of McPhee, who, although he took a few science courses in high school and college, has no advanced training in it. Yet his books on geology are read in hundreds of college geology courses every year, and the natural worlds portrayed in *Coming into the Country, Encounters with the Archdruid,* and *The Control of Nature* are the envy of every writer I have met. Of course, anyone can write about the natural world, but to do it as effectively as McPhee does demands a literary quality in his journalism. He immerses himself in his topics, sometimes for months or years at a time, and prides himself on the extraordinary accuracy of his reporting. McPhee employs the techniques of good writing in creating scenes that advance a narrative, in bringing characters to life, and in developing complicated ideas. His literary journalism depends on the creation of a distinctive voice and an effective architecture, qualities that enliven our interest no matter what subject he takes on. He is one of the great literary journalists of the twentieth century.

But ultimately, McPhee said, making sure that our view of him does not get obscured by the topics he has chosen, "I'm not writing about subjects—oranges and agriculture and so on—I'm writing about the people who do it. The common thread in all the work I've done from scratch is people, their natures, their reactions, their expertise, whatever they're up to, and how that expresses their characters."

Notes

1. Except where otherwise noted, all quotations from McPhee came from personal interviews.

2. John McPhee, *Annals of the Former World* (New York: Farrar, Straus & Giroux, 1998), 31.

3. McPhee, *Annals of the Former World*, 8.

4. John McPhee, "Warming the Jump Seat," *Deerfield* magazine, vol. 54, no. 3 (Summer 1997): 20.

5. Robert McGlynn, *10 Trial Street* (Deerfield: Gallery Press, 1979) (foreword by John McPhee).

6. McPhee, "Warming the Jump Seat," 22–23.

7. David Quammen, *Natural Acts: A Sidelong View of Science and Nature* (New York: Schocken Books, 1985), xiii–xiv.

II

McPhee and the Natural World

For many McPhee readers, his writing about the natural world is simply his best and most enduring. From his early work *The Pine Barrens* through his *Irons in the Fire* collection, McPhee takes us on the road, off the trail, or down the river as we poke around, usually in the company of a local resident or field guide. The themes that arise from these journeys near and far, particularly his commitment to preservation and his celebration of local human habitation in out-of-the-way places, endear him to a wide range of readers. O. Alan Weltzien's essay addresses these themes and tries to resolve the issue—annoying for some types of environmentalists—of McPhee's environmental advocacy. Weltzien concludes that McPhee, though quieter than some would like, is clearly committed to environmental preservation. Michael Pearson's essay studies one of McPhee's two biggest projects, *Coming into the Country,* which is central both to his oeuvre and to his moderate environmentalism. Pearson locates McPhee's longest single book in a broad tradition within American literary history. Brian Turner's essay provides a rhetorical analysis of McPhee's environmental appeals and thereby explains why his moderate, self-effacing persona (coupled with his exemplary guides) effectively persuades a wide range of readers, particularly those who might judge McPhee insufficiently partisan. McPhee's oldest, and perhaps favorite, mode of travel in the woods is canoeing; Theodore Humphrey's essay follows him down many drainages, in the process defining his "immersion journalism." The final two essays in part two both address McPhee's masterwork, the tetralogy *Annals of the Former World*. Rick Van Noy's and Barbara Stevens's essays probe the relation of geology to language and propose ways of reading McPhee's translation of geology's expository complexity into artful narrative. McPhee has been called a "rhapsode of deep time," and perhaps no other writer has explained plate tectonics in terms of one swath of the North American continent more ably to more readers than he has. McPhee braids geologic and human history as have few others.

O. Alan Weltzien

John McPhee and the Question of Environmental Advocacy

I

At the beginning of *Voices in the Wilderness: American Nature Writing and Environmental Politics,* Daniel G. Payne makes an unsurprising concession. Though he claims that "Edward Abbey may be justified in his assertion that it isn't enough merely to write about nature any more—now one must take direct action to protect it," he also grants that "there is something to be said, even from a modern political perspective, for a writer who can simply convey a love of nature to others" (3). I heartily sympathize with Abbey's belief yet recognize in Payne's concession the history of American nature writing. Given that history, particularly its increasing range and sophistication by the late twentieth century, I read Payne's "simply" ironically. Certainly there is nothing simple about the relationship of environmental knowledge to politics, particularly the dependency of the latter upon the former, suggested by Scott Slovic in "Politics in American Nature Writing." Nor is there anything simple about John McPhee's environmentalism—a term he resists with some annoyance and discomfort. Writers as diverse as Abbey and McPhee both protest the "nature writing" label, McPhee because he associates it with the polemicism typical of an Abbey (Pearson, 100). While McPhee assiduously avoids polemics, I want to situate him as an environmental writer by sorting through the charges and counter-charges then taking another look at some of his environmental books, above all *The Control of Nature* (1989). In his rhetorical reading of McPhee, Brian Turner concludes, "McPhee recommends a moderate pro-environmental stance" and "quietly encourages a cooperative pluralism" (180–81). While the "moderate" voice has discouraged some readers and protégés, I judge it paradoxically as potent as polemical environmental voices.

McPhee's career stretches longer than the modern environmental movement if one marks the latter's genesis by the first Earth Day in April 1970. By that time he had published *The Pine Barrens* (1968), his first clearly environmental book, and was poised to publish *Encounters with the Archdruid* (1971), one of his most important. McPhee regards Camp Keewaydin as his most important educational setting; he calls all his outdoors books his "Keewaydin Stories," and for many readers these remain his best. Environmental writing has flowered in the intervening decades and, in some hands, taken on a new urgency, sharper edges. In many cases louder voices have obscured moderate ones such as McPhee's. If McPhee represents a muted advocacy, Michael Pearson explains, as well as anyone, its source in his ongoing balancing act. In regard to *The Control of Nature*, Pearson concludes that the writer "strives to write . . . with equal respect and attention about Nature and human nature as well" (108). This balancing, however, does not preclude the reader from drawing conclusions about anthropocentric arrogance and myopia. In fact McPhee's deep respect for his subjects, major and minor, renders those conclusions all the more persuasive. A muted environmental advocacy, a voice urging moderation, should never be mistaken for an absent environmentalism. Some environmental writers, however, perhaps an increasing number, bridle at the sound of moderation as though our enlarging understanding of more environmental crises warrants calls to arms, expressions of sorrow or anger, not moderation. Yet McPhee, a giant in American literary nonfiction of the past two generations, is also an environmental writer if the genre is defined generously enough.

Prominent among those castigating McPhee's lack of activism is David Quammen, an impressive writer whose impatience with McPhee's self-effacement has grown over many years. He disliked the apparent lack of commitment in *Control* and years later famously took *Annals of the Former World* to task in his *New York Times Book Review* (5 July 1998). Quammen accuses McPhee of "adamantine reserve" and making the "elemental" "mistake of impeccable caution" (9–10). For people like Quammen, McPhee's masterwork is fundamentally flawed because he fails to "write with his whole person and not just with his brain." These are serious charges with which I sympathize, but I finally judge them inaccurate, even unfair. One should not confuse McPhee's assiduous balancing of points of view with terminal caution; nor is his rhetorical appeal solely or even primarily cerebral. Yet other critics echo

Quammen's impatience if not anger. In her *Sierra* profile, Joan Hamilton judges McPhee "a closet conservationist at best": "Conclusions are indeed rare in McPhee's work, and where they do occur the author seems embarrassed by them" (54). If McPhee is as terminally cautious and evasive as these critics claim, how then does one explain his power and influence across a wide and diverse readership, some of whom do not count themselves environmentalists?

On the other end of the spectrum one finds such admiration as William Howarth's, who praises McPhee for his "scrupulous nonfiction"; and that sense of thoroughness, care, and fairness conveys not only McPhee's balance but his power. In his "Introduction" to *The Second John McPhee Reader,* David Remnick overstates the case in an opposite way from Quammen, deeming McPhee "the most effective literary advocate for environmentalism." I certainly would not push McPhee onto that pedestal, and presume he would shy away from such puffery. Remnick, however, suggests a way to define McPhee's environmentalism when he reminds us that he "tells stories—stories that, in the margins, fairly bark the most important ecological questions" (xiii). While McPhee himself hides, his indirect presence "in the margins"—through character and every other familiar novelistic device—makes itself felt continuously though never noisily. That presence works contextually, multivocally; and the reader sifts between positions, like any good reader of novels, to intuit the writer's own, whether conflicted or not. In his reading of McPhee's oeuvre as pastoral allegory, James N. Stull claims that, through his subjects, McPhee "acknowledges the ideological nature of his enterprise"; he "established a rhetoric of certainty by creating an illusion of completeness" (13, 21). Such a "rhetoric of certainty" does not exclude the articulation and treatment of "ecological questions" intuited "in the margins." Admirers such as Stull approvingly cite McPhee's "own place in the world: in the background" (27); detractors such as Quammen criticize McPhee for remaining there. Yet such a background presence orchestrates the foreground so that readers discern the former as clearly as the latter; like a fictionist, McPhee typically speaks through his characters rather than standing aside from them. Let us examine conclusions from a couple of his "Keewaydin Stories" to begin plotting his environmental stance.

McPhee titles the final chapter of *The Pine Barrens,* his fourth book, "Vision"; and in it he traces the recent history of bogus land development schemes and pressures in that forested section of New Jersey, including Herbert Smith's (1964) jetport proposal. Leaving aside the ironic scrutiny of this flight of fancy, McPhee concludes,

> [the Pine Barrens] seem to be headed slowly toward extinction. In retrospect, people may one day look back upon the final stages of the development of the great unbroken Eastern city and be able to say at what moment all remaining undeveloped land should have been considered no longer a potential asset to individuals but an asset of the society at large—perhaps a social necessity. Meanwhile, up goes a sign. . . . At the rate of a few hundred yards or even a mile or so each year, the perimeter of the pines contracts. (156–57)

This gloomy assessment locates McPhee in a familiar contemporary rhetoric of environmental elegy. It is hard not to see him as wholly pro-preservationist and anti-development in his first Keewaydin book. Having surveyed the Fred Browns and other Pineys and traced a lengthy social ecology and natural history in this sparsely populated area of our most densely populated state—his own—McPhee waxes prophetic as he worries about its future. His evocation of "social necessity" places limits on the sacrosanct value of private property in this futuristic glance at an all-urban New Jersey. *The Pine Barrens* does not close with the writer "in the background"; McPhee does not veil his admiration for this place and its scattered inhabitants. In saluting this wooded tract trembling with water, he sounds alarms in 1968 that since then have grown increasingly commonplace. As Kent Ryden concludes, it "demands that we refine our understanding of exactly what makes up the environment," as it presents "a forest filtered and given meaning through human lives, and through which those lives have been filtered and given meaning at the same time in an endless reciprocal process" (60, 59). In another New Jersey piece written more than a dozen years later, "A Textbook Place for Bears," McPhee admits his dire prognostications were wrong. He does not admit that his eloquent book may have contributed to the preservationist success story: "The Pine Barrens . . . had recently been preserved and protected by state and federal legislation . . ." (*Table of Contents,* 48). Early in his career, McPhee sounds neither cautious nor evasive; subsequently, his environmental advocacy grows more muted because of his philosophical and formal (e.g., structural) commitment to moderation, but it does not lose its essential grain.

By the time he published *Coming into the Country* (1977), McPhee was a widely known writer; and for some readers this long book, at the literal center of his oeuvre, remains his single best. Like *Encounters* and *Control,* it is a triptych, although in this case an uneven one, since book III, "In the Bush" (which also carries the book title), occupies more than the second half. Near its end, McPhee comes forward with one of those rare, embarrassing conclusions cited by Joan Hamilton—except that I find not embarrassment but an alignment of opposing opinions from which his own emerges. McPhee has been admiring Ed and Stanley Gelvin for many pages; and after sketching their back-country gold mining operation as yet another story of waste and degradation—which might fit into the closing of *The Pine Barrens*—he catches us off-guard:

> Am I disgusted? Manifestly not. Not from here, from now, from this perspective. I am too warmly, too subjectively caught up in what the Gelvins are doing. In the ecomilitia, bust me to private. This mine is a cork on the sea. Meanwhile (and, possibly, more seriously), the relationship between this father and son is as attractive as anything I have seen in Alaska. (430)

Instead of that increasingly predictable, and usually laudable, environmental elegy or anger, McPhee inverts our expectations by foregrounding human nature rather than nature. As Brian Turner remarks, "McPhee's *ethos* seems sane and balanced. . . . His love of nature never overwhelms his love of people" (169). In Alaska's interior, this particular operation is a "cork," whereas McPhee believes this filial bond, their mode of self-sufficiency, is something like an endangered species. In the self-mockery of his military metaphor, he defuses some—but not all—of the animosity latent in "ecomilitia." He hastens to explain himself between the extremes:

> Only an easygoing extremist would preserve every bit of the country. And extremists alone would exploit it all. Everyone else has to think the matter through—choose a point of tolerance, however much the point might tend to one side. For myself, I am closer to the preserving side—that is, the side that would preserve the Gelvins. To be sure, I would preserve plenty of land as well. My own margin of tolerance would not include some faceless corporation "responsible" to a hundred thousand stockholders, making a crater you could see from the moon. Nor would it include visiting exploiters—here in the seventies, gone in the eighties—with some pipe and some skyscrapers left behind. But I, as noted, am out of sync with the day. (430–31)

The conclusion of *Coming into the Country* epitomizes McPhee's balancing act and hence his muted environmental advocacy. His dash again instructs through inverted expectations, since for him preservation includes such pioneers as the Gelvins, who exploit on a miniscule scale. If anything, that dash situates McPhee in American literary history, a descendant of James Fenimore Cooper with Natty Bumppo or A. B. Guthrie, Jr., in *The Big Sky* (1947): our allegories of frontier into which development inevitably hurries, forever changing the frontier and those scattered individuals at home in it. After the dash and surprise, McPhee spends the rest of the passage qualifying his "tolerance" for preservation that includes the occasional Gelvins—and occasional is the issue. In the process he sings a familiar chorus of environmentalism. I read his final confession about being "out of sync with the day" as a metaphor as much as a fact—his quick narrative exit from this key passage in his career. He probably suspects and fears that the Fred Browns and Gelvins are vanishing faster than undeveloped tracts in tiny New Jersey's Pine Barrens or gigantic Alaska—in many respects an extension of the nineteenth-century continental United States. I suspect he recognizes that this type he repeatedly showcases and lauds—his translation of Emerson's "representative men," avatars of Self-Reliance—grows increasingly rare and anachronistic in a culture defined by suburbs and late-stage capitalism. Also, in McPhee's "day" (1977) the environmental movement was still gathering headway and had not made itself felt as it had repeatedly by the 1990s.

McPhee's moderate voice, then, locates itself almost as far from the positions of Earth First! and deep ecology, for example, as it does from developers (the Gelvins en route to becoming multinational corporations)—almost, but not as far. His environmentalism rests upon a commonplace: human communities, however small or isolated, have their place in the woods or the bush. It is all a question of scale, and McPhee's reverence for the small scale, not his presentation and resolution of opposing points of view, makes him "out of sync with the day." How many of his urban and suburban readers share his reverence and worry? In "Los Angeles against the Mountains" in *Control,* for example, scale has run amok; yet even here, he dilutes satire with his usual human interest stories. His longer profiles, Brian Turner reminds us, embody his own predilections: they are both "expository tour guides" and "moral guides of a sort, implicitly appealing to us to take an involved yet balanced approach to environmental issues . . . [which requires] the kind of knowledge that can be derived only from a 'hands-on' familiarity with nature, as well as the ability to see both sides of the environmental debate" (178). McPhee's well-known obsession with structure reflects his epistemological and ethical commitment to what I have called his balancing act. Above all, the alignment of oppositions forces the reader's mediation between them, and that process of negotiating rebuttals and granting concessions typically moves the reader toward McPhee's moderate environmentalism. And with no disrespect to Quammen, this process involves much more than cerebration.

At the end of Jared Haynes's lengthy interview with McPhee, " 'The Size and Shape of the Canvas' " (1994; this volume), McPhee directly addresses the recurring demand sounded by Quammen and Hamilton that he should "take sides on some of the environmental issues and put more of [him]self in there." The writer has, I presume, grown tired of the accusation of self-effacement:

> I'm not going to tell the reader how to think. . . . I'm not a writer of sermons. I also have extremely strong feelings that if a point is to be carried somewhere, it's going to work best in the eye of the reader, in the judgment of the reader. You can lay stuff out there for a reader to form a judgment about, and once that judgment is formed, it's a thousand times more firm than the one the critics are talking about, which is the editorial writer telling somebody how to vote. Those things sort of irritate me when I read them. But not too much. I have a very different goal and I have no difficulty sensing what that goal is. . . . [Re *Coming into the Country*] I wasn't going to get caught up in worrying about just one environmental issue. My goal is life in the round, not instructions on what lever to pull. (Haynes, 25)

In distinguishing himself from the preacher and the editorialist, McPhee rehearses an old argument familiar to novelists—"life in the round" reminding us of E. M. Forster's famous discussion of character in *Aspects of the Novel*—but less common in literary journalism. For McPhee, the disclaimer is all the more ironic and striking, given his steady stream of instruction. In his virtuosic arrangement of what we should *know* about the natural world he implies, probably more than he would care to admit, what we should *believe*. McPhee tacitly acknowledges the ancient dichotomy between fact and value, what is and what ought to be, even as he elides it. To know the meaning of deep time from *Annals*, for instance, is to accept geology's radical lessons in humility. *Basin and Range* (1981) makes clear that these lessons have begun, Quammen's accusation of "impeccable caution" notwithstanding. Obviously, environmental writers fill the space between knowledge and belief in a range of ways. McPhee pledges allegiance to the novelist's creed of working behind the scenes and creating truth through implication rather than through statement or homily—though his primary domain is the factual.

The writer's distance from the editorial, whether concerning an environmental topic or not, sounds loud and clear even though, in his Keewaydin Stories, he occasionally resorts to it. McPhee makes the same claim speaking about *The Control of Nature,* according to Philip Shabecoff: " 'My book is not an editorial. It is a description of people defying nature. They may have no choice' " (22). Given the foregone conclusion of his announced theme—that " 'nature is going to win these battles' "—McPhee's narrative tends toward the editorial, his protest notwithstanding. While his final judgment reveals his deep sympathy for his countless anonymous subjects, its fatalism (i.e., " 'no choice' ") does not preclude his satiric verdict, however muted or plainly voiced.

McPhee's interview statement is disingenuous in its modesty. I have shown that his conclusions in *Pine Barrens* and *Coming into the Country* unveil his environmentalism, and I argue that *The Control of Nature* suggests to—not "tell[s]"—"the reader how to think." That makes all the difference. In the past few decades increasing numbers of environmental writers have been telling us how to feel if not think; and whatever their brand of lament or wrath or lyric celebration, their eloquence often prompts my happy accession to their homilies. I like polemical writing sometimes, though it runs the risk of making no net change in sentiment, since it typically preaches to the choir or goes unheard. Daniel G. Payne reminds us that

> if nature writers are to influence the debate over the environment in a meaningful way, they must continue to expand their audience, to reach out beyond the committed core of sympathizers who are already predisposed to nature writing and environmental reform. . . . it is in the mainstream of American culture that today's nature writers will find the greatest rhetorical challenges and opportunities. (174)

From a political or reformist point of view such as Payne's, there is little to argue with. And who is to say *The Pine Barrens* (1968), for example, did not influence subsequent preservationist legislation mentioned in passing in "A Textbook Place for Bears" (1985)? Yet from an aesthetic perspective, McPhee belongs in the ever-broadening genre of environmental writing at least as much as do louder voices of advocacy. If one construes environmental writing along a continuum running from "no implicit advocacy" to "heavily explicit advocacy," I would not place McPhee at the former pole any more than I would place David Quammen at the latter. Clearly, *Annals* exists closer to the left end than *Song of the Dodo,* for instance, but these masterworks instruct in many similar ways. The alarm calls resonating through *Song,* however, should not obscure what I have called the crash course in humility implicit in *Annals.*

II

In labeling John McPhee a "meta-naturalist," Thomas Bailey stresses the consequences of McPhee's increasing attention to nature as system: "nature's system is inherently in conflict with human culture, and . . . as these systems collide, the puny ones devised by human intelligence are doomed to defeat." Furthermore, nature proves "a violent system beyond our human capacity to be violent" (Bailey, 197, 210). As much as any of McPhee's books, *The Control of Nature* dramatizes this credo. Having touched on the climax of McPhee's longest triptych, *Coming into the Country,* I want to read the climax of his first, *Encounters with the Archdruid,* as a vehicle for assessing satire in *The Control of Nature.* In its satirical effect, "Los Angeles against the Mountains" particularly stands out in McPhee's oeuvre, as he infrequently uses satire to intimate his environmentalism. Yet his survey of chaparral fire ecology in the San Gabriels and his analysis of debris basins lead to a closing scene as close to barbed satire as any in his work. To reach this scene we must quit the country beyond Eagle, Alaska, as well as the Colorado River's deep crevice, for the Los Angeles basin—for more than three-quarters of a century probably America's most conspicuous alternative to natural environments. The initial set of triangulations in *Encounters* achieves a more literal cohesion than the later triptychs because of the continuing dominance of "archdruid" David Brower. In its "Narratives about a Conservationist and Three of His Natural Enemies"—to quote the bracketed subtitle on the cover—I read the second "natural enemy," developer Charles Fraser, as a foil to the first, mineral engineer Charles Park. This triptych's second panel works as a contrasting slow movement to the quicker, livelier first and third movements of a Baroque concerto, and Park's antagonism reappears, in distilled form, in dam builder Floyd Dominy.

More than the academic Park, Dominy represents Brower's arch-foe—particularly since years before this Colorado River trip Brower, as Sierra Club president, was known as the man who stopped the Echo Park dam proposal on the Green River as well as the man who endlessly regretted the building of Glen Canyon Dam. McPhee's success derives, among other reasons, from his steady respect for and criticism of both men. Yet his impressive balancing act notwithstanding, I have always found the scale tipping in favor of Brower, in part because his environmental advocacy exists closer to McPhee's Keewaydin essence than Dominy's credo that attempts to defy and dispel the arid truth beyond the hundredth meridian. More tellingly, there is more than a little swagger and bluster about Dominy, who cut his teeth in Nebraska and Wyoming and, through his tough-guy cursing, reveals himself a true son of the Rocky Mountain West. Dominy's cliched machismo, with its predictable flashes of gruff affection, had worn threadbare and found itself the subject of ironic revisionism by 1971, when *Encounters* was published. Consider McPhee's closing pages in *Encounters*, when the pair's evening respect for one another, a momentary truce (238–39), swiftly modulates into their chronic argument (240–41)—an argument that it is hard to believe Dominy wins. Mountaineer Brower has admitted his fear of Lava Falls and plan to walk that section of gorge somehow, but the next morning finds him in the raft after all. Just before, Dominy and Brower have both suggested the best route through: Brower turns out to be right and Dominy wrong (244). After running the falls, Brower speculates about its disappearance under "Lake Dominy," while Dominy "just sat there, drawing on a wet, dead cigar" (245). Though McPhee assures us that Dominy relit it ten minutes later, the cigar seems as out of place as some of his dam proposals; it functions as a novelistic symbol of the character's egotism and misplaced self-confidence.

Admittedly these are small narrative gestures, but cumulatively they weigh against the "natural enem[y]." Yet McPhee's myriad sympathetic gestures toward Dominy (as well as the two Charleses) and criticisms of Brower, who had just been ousted as Sierra Club president, serve to confirm rather than diffuse or efface his underlying advocacy. Though the "natural enemies" emerge as friendly and thoughtful, the net result of his triangulations clarifies his alliance with Brower's conservationism.

In McPhee's typical pattern, we read backward through framed narratives, inside the famed profiles, to intuit his own beliefs. Diana L. Ashe astutely assesses the foreground-background relationship when she writes, "David Brower functions as an idealized agent for John McPhee, representing the passionate advocate that McPhee the journalist chooses not to be himself" (144). In his *Sierra* eulogy following Brower's death, McPhee steps forward and makes explicit what, thirty years earlier, he kept implicit. "Farewell to the Archdruid," though a eulogy, forms an epilogue to *Encounters* that distills his admiration for Brower's leadership and unremitting environmental advocacy. He compares Brower to a Homeric protagonist, anecdotally describes his change of heart regarding protection for the Mojave Desert, and subordinates criticism to praise: "He was feisty, heaven knew. And arrogant, possibly. And relentless, certainly. And above all, effective—for he began his mission when ecology connoted the root and shoot relationships of communal plants, and he, as much or more than anyone in the midcentury, expanded its reach and inherent power until it became the environmental movement" ("Farewell," 8).

As McPhee and the environmental movement have both aged, he has zealously maintained his distance from most of its colorful manifestations even as his identity as an environmental writer has grown increasingly secure. For example, it is hard to misread McPhee's environmentalism in "The Keel of Lake Dickey" (in *Giving Good Weight,* 1979), which combines some of the effects of part III of *Encounters* with the Maine woods setting of *The Survival of the Bark Canoe* (1975). Its closing pages, climaxing an idyllic though wet canoe trip down Maine's St. John River, ironically depict the dimensions and transformations planned through a locally proposed "Dickey Dam" and another imagined reservoir lake beginning with "D." McPhee's opposition (*Giving Good Weight,* 173–77) emerges plainly; and in the later Maine profile of his namesake, "North of the C. P. Line" (1985), he judges it a "tirade . . . ranting against the people who wished to flood the North Maine Woods by building the twelfth-largest dam on earth," which embarrasses the other John McPhee, a state employee "under oath to be neutral on public issues" (*Table of Contents,* 251).

Yet McPhee's usual muted advocacy causes some to question his allegiance. Green writers of other stamps such as David Quammen repeatedly accuse McPhee of terminal fence sitting. Quammen's *Outside* review of *The Control of Nature,* "Muscling Nature" (1989), reads as a rough draft of his criticism of *Annals* published nine years later. He wrongly judges *Control* "not so much . . . a forceful book as . . . a loose pile," as McPhee "had seen much but . . . had refused to conclude anything," having "no evident thoughts or opinions of his own." Such points of view mistake self-effacement for no self. Quammen does concede the power of McPhee's title, which "speaks the name of the tortured idea that his three episodes variously exemplify, and which he remains shy about actively examining" ("Muscling," 30). Quammen's final judgment about McPhee's shyness does not account for the satiric energy of "Los Angeles against the Mountains" or the resonant irony of the triptych. Such irony constitutes a mode of "actively examining" environmental questions as potentially powerful as those more visible, homiletic modes that McPhee resists. Stephen J. Pyne, in the *New York Times Book Review* ("A War against the World"), gets it half right when he asserts: "Almost everyone is implicated, and nearly everything is diffused" (22). Like Quammen, Pyne faults the triptych for a teeming looseness, as "[t]he pressures against a smooth narrative are terrific"; but both ignore the book's cumulative, exegetical impact.

III

McPhee wrote *The Control of Nature* three-quarters of the way through his geology tetralogy; as is well known, he took his title from his travels with David Love, hero of *Rising from the Plains* (1986). Inscribed in a large, recessed stone panel above the entrance to the University of Wyoming's Engineering Building since 1926, in large block letters, is the motto: "STRIVE ON—THE CONTROL OF NATVRE IS WON. NOT GIVEN." The script style and spacing of letters match the handsome, ruggedly dressed sandstone facade surrounding the panel; the stone came from a quarry five miles northwest, in the Laramie Range, owned for almost a century by the university. The overall effect, monumental and potent as an incitement to action, underscores the dictate ("STRIVE ON") delivered *ex cathedra* like the stone tablets of laws given to Moses (Exodus 24). A cornerstone below, in identical script though much smaller, extends the credo: "THE CONTROL OF NATVRE FOR THE SERVICE OF MAN." It is hard to overestimate its range of unquestioned assumptions and hubris. The sense of contest perpetuates the Christian anthropocentrism of Genesis 1:26, 28 (i.e., "NOT GIVEN") and the American master narrative of conquest, and McPhee highlights that sense in each of his three panels. It is similarly hard to overestimate the range of irony with which he constructs his triptych—in formal design (e.g., pagination), the most perfectly formed of his three triptychs. For McPhee, the title forms an ongoing question, not a statement, let alone an exclamation. The phrase admits to some ambiguity, and the writer invites us into that space: a space that mutes, for some, his advocacy. We learn from Philip Shabecoff that the phrase's ambiguity appealed to McPhee, as "it could be read two different ways with diametrically opposite meanings" (20). Does it emphasize "control" as in the controlling hand of human agency or rather the second noun, "nature," as in nature's control, nature in charge? If the latter, then the notion of competition and winning is further mocked. The real issue, of course, is the extent of our ignoring the latter and, in the process, giving sustained credence to the former. In fact it is a hollow phrase, a false promise. As Thomas Bailey glosses the book, "there is no doubt in McPhee's mind who is going to win. He never lets the reader forget the ambiguities and ambivalences of the title" (213, n. 2).

In medieval and Renaissance art, triptychs usually carry a narrative burden as they present an allegorical sequence from Christian doctrine, for instance; we interpret an altar's right panel in light of the left and central panels. Similarly, "Los Angeles *against* the Mountains" (emphasis added) concentrates the battle metaphor central to his triptych. And given the metaphor, whether the rivers are water, lava, or a rock-and-dirt slurry, the conclusion—Genesis 1:26 notwithstanding—is foregone. If engineering goes up against gravity, sooner or later gravity will prevail; and in that respect all of *Control* accumulates like a river into its final scene above Los Angeles. Contrasting with McPhee's earlier triptychs, in this one acts of courage never emerge wholly from the suspicion of folly; "heroic or venal, rash or well advised" (69), they mix irrefutably, and that fatal mixture confirms the controlling hand of nature. Departing slightly from historical, exegetical order (i.e., left to right or front to back), let us glance briefly at the central panel, "Cooling the Lava," before studying the first, "Atchafalaya," en route to the third.

In *Encounters*, I have suggested, the second panel offsets the outer ones because developer Charles Frazier appears far more environmentally conscious and sympathetic than the other two "natural enemies": he represents a milder antagonism. Similarly, in *Control* the Icelanders on Heimaey Island come across less foolishly in their "encounters" with a 1973 lava flow than do the Louisianans and Angelinos in their respective "encounters." Even on remote, sparsely populated Heimaey Island, though, McPhee steps forward in his own voice and cautions: "The event had lost its status as a simple act of God. In making war with nature, there was a risk of loss in winning" (143). In "Cooling the Lava" he states that intervening in an "act of God" carries a price tag beyond our short-term imagining. The outer, American panels of *Control* provide stunning narrative commentaries on this scripture; and because the encounters of humans against nature involve far more time, money, and people, the scent of folly clings more closely to the Army Corps of Engineers and "Flood" (i.e., the Los Angeles County Flood Control District) and the interests supporting them. The structure also constitutes yet another variation on McPhee's home-away-home pattern traced by Michael Pearson in his critical biography, the variation grounding McPhee as an American writer emphasizing environmental problems on a systemic, American scale.

"STRIVE ON." The "Atchafalaya" panel establishes a subversive reading of this dictate that "Los Angeles" extends and sharpens, so we'll pause in the swamp before settling in the L.A. basin. McPhee's manifold novelistic gifts compete, in some respects, against his pervading irony. The Genofiles' story that opens "Los Angeles against the Mountains"— or the aura of Hans Brinker heroism in "Atchafalaya"—qualifies the resonating irony of human myopia but does not lessen it. After the second installment of the Genofiles' story, McPhee explains his lack of specificity about dates—his deliberate illusion about the present tenseness of debris flows—by commenting on "a great temporal disparity between the pace at which the mountains behave and the way people think" (202–3), one of those profound lessons in humility from *Annals*. The implication could not sound more clearly: "the way people think" fails them. In "Atchafalaya," McPhee gives the final word to district geologist Fred Smith, who, distinguishing his professional position from that of the Corps of Engineers, believes the Mississippi River will divert into the Atchafalaya Basin and abandon Baton Rouge and New Orleans (92).

However monumental the engineering at Old River, "Atchafalaya" never abandons the perfectly apt simile that McPhee assigns it early in the narrative. Summarizing its famed treachery as a navigable river, he places it far back in our imagination: "It lies there like a big alligator in a low slough, with time on its side, waiting—waiting to outwait the Corps of Engineers—and hunkering down ever lower in its bed and presenting a sort of maw to the Mississippi, into which the river could fall" (24).

McPhee distills the swamp basin and river into this primeval image—an archetype older than the history of human endeavor—and the narrative never escapes its influence. In his first panel, figurative language subverts his book title and renders Old River the cautionary tale of a geological nanosecond.

In McPhee's "suasive rhetoric" studied by Brian Turner and others, the writer-as-instructor typically stands as intermediary between the "expository tour guides" *cum* "moral guides" and the reader. Later in "Atchafalaya," McPhee mimics our self-education by confessing that the river and basin's name has become for him an extension of "Control of Nature" and that his green-and-white "Atchafalaya" window decal has been in his car "for many years, causing drivers on the New Jersey Turnpike to veer in close and crowd my lane while staring at a word that signifies collision" (69). But the passage's definition of the "collision" again gives the game away. The Corps of Engineers may have channeled the Atchafalaya; but when humanity seeks "to surround the base of Mt. Olympus demanding and expecting the surrender of the gods" (69), folly obscures courage and the writer's position could not be plainer. In fact, given this image from Greek mythology, there is no "collision," no contest. Similarly, the narrative stacks the deck in favor of the Atchafalaya basin, another Pine Barrens except more diverse in species and wetter, over the economic interests of those two downriver cities that receive only a token nod.

When McPhee turns, for his right panel, to the Los Angeles basin (for most environmentalists, one of America's preeminent nightmares), satire is probably unavoidable given that metropolis's imagery past and present, though he characteristically avoids most traces of sarcasm—most, but not all. If the first two panels of *Control* are primarily rural, the right one garishly flaunts its urban sprawl. For most of the twentieth century L.A. has been easy to mock, and McPhee acknowledges that tradition that extends through the present. Contrary to Morgan City and Heimaey Island, L.A. has accumulated layers of literary treatments, many overlapping in their satiric energy. McPhee's glance at Mike Rubel's castle in Glendora, "the Kingdom of Rubelia" (222–24), for instance, could come from the opening of Nathanael West's *The Day of the Locust* (1939) or countless movies such as Orson Welles's *Citizen Kane* (1941) or Billy Wilder's *Sunset Boulevard* (1950). His story of Flood pitting itself against the San Gabriels inevitably locates itself in a robust tradition recently summarized, in many respects, in Mike Davis's *Ecology of*

Fear (1998). Davis elaborates McPhee's ironic conclusions in "Los Angeles against the Mountains" through scrutiny of "the politics of environmental amnesia": "What is most distinctive about Los Angeles is not simply its conjugation of earthquakes, wildfires, and floods, but its uniquely explosive mixture of natural hazards and social contradictions" (160, 54).

McPhee paints his triptych as environmental allegory and occasionally, like a Nathaniel Hawthorne, provides the exegesis that the David Quammens find missing. He walks in front of his satiric curtain and warns in plain prophetic voice, though he prefers not to. For example, commenting upon the unsurprisingly steady failure of the debris-basin system, he points the finger at both the "calm and complacent" locals and "the politics of environmental amnesia" anywhere: "It appears that no amount of front-page or prime-time attention will ever prevent such people from masking out the problem" (245).

Given the panel's satirical thrust, we need to assess McPhee's balancing act, which begins with his title and ends with the scene in Burro Canyon above L.A., where we will end as well. The narrative often crystallizes in moments of contradiction that imply the foregone conclusion of "The Mountains" "against" "Los Angeles." At the conclusion of the Genofiles' story referred to earlier, we are told that they won a hefty lawsuit against Los Angeles County and their rebuilt home received a "Beautification Award for Best Home," one criterion of which includes " 'a sense of drama' " (202). That satiric mention pales before McPhee's preceding set-piece, as good a sequence from a disaster movie as his rendering of the 1989 Loma Prieta earthquake that climaxes *Assembling California* (1993) and, therefore, *Annals*. The Mountains moved against the Genofiles, but they take their stand in the same spot: the narrative carries the irony, and any additional comment would feel superfluous and detract from its effect. Yet here and elsewhere, true to his ethos, McPhee complicates our response by avoiding simple mockery of people. He exposes fundamental contradictions without derisively dismissing people, and that balancing qualifies the satire. We converse with "Cal Poly" geologists whose professional knowledge contradicts their personal lives—most of them live on the mountain front, on unstable fans next to faults. This crash course in the geology and fire ecology of the San Gabriels, "disintegrating at a rate that is also among the fastest in the world" (184) and "as rugged as any terrain in America" (205), puts the reader ahead of many Angelinos. As Mike Davis states, "Anglo-

Californians have always criminalized the problem of mountain wildfire. The majority have never accepted the natural role or inevitability of the chaparral fire cycle" (132). McPhee implies that they have done so out of either willful ignorance or apathy—yet we don't quite laugh at the Genofiles or the geologists.

The history of debris basins, which lags behind the surging demography of the Los Angeles basin, reads as a series of holding tanks that buy short, unpredictable amounts of time. And this rhapsodist of deep time does not mince words in his satire against human myopia: "In Los Angeles, even the Los Angeles time scale does not arouse general interest. . . . Mountain time and city time appear to be bifocal" (203). The writer's voice is not an angry one, but here and elsewhere the note of prophetic condemnation cannot escape notice. With increasing numbers bumping up into canyons, the debris basin system grows increasingly stressed like the Old River works in "Atchafalaya." Angelinos ranging from rich, eccentric Mike Rubel to those Cal Poly geologists and beyond enact McPhee's mythological scene climaxing "Atchafalaya," meeting the San Gabriels at their base and "demanding and expecting" control of geology and gravity. McPhee's satire pokes through any complacency felt by Angelinos or the reader with trenchant figurative language, similar to the prophetic Atchafalaya-as-alligator image. For example, after defining "dry ravel," McPhee remarks that "to live under one of those canyons is (as many have said) to look up the barrel of a gun" (212), even an "eighteenth-century muzzle-loader" (203). The escape of the wealthier onto geologic fans above smog layers is tantamount to suicide. He defines "dry ravel" and slurry before explaining San Gabriel rainfall cycles and "waterproof soil" and narrating occasional disaster anecdotes of canyon residents caught by debris flows. Or consider his pithy definition of the metropolis amidst his "tiptoeing h" icon and explanation of "Transverse Ranges," the "kink [that] conforms to a bend in the San Andreas Fault": "It resembles a prize-winning chair. Los Angeles is like a wad of gum stuck to the bottom of the chair" (226). The unflattering schoolroom image suggests McPhee invoking the cutting satire of a Jonathan Swift or the Mark Twain of *The Mysterious Stranger.* McPhee's profound kindness notwithstanding, as Stephen J. Pyne comments in his review of *Control,* "Irony edges into sarcasm" (22).

If the Mountains push Los Angeles, L.A. attempts to retaliate by moving their deposits. The final panel of McPhee's triptych explores the space between moving mountains as a figure of speech and moving mountains as fact "unexampled in heroic chutzpah" (265). The ironic commentary accompanying the latter leaches out any heroism implicit in the former. The narrative reads as a gloss on the myth of Sisyphus stripped of its idealistic, existential interpretation (e.g., Albert Camus, "The Myth of Sisyphus"). Its separate accounts of debris flows, its artful braids of word-slurry, snowball into a final series of unambiguous indictments that include "four cloud-seeding generators" capable of " 'enhancing the storm,' " the euphemistic move from debris basins to " 'sediment-placement sites,' " and the "elegant absurdity" of Burro Canyon above San Gabriel Dam, home of " 'fourteen million cubic yards' " transported uphill (268–71). McPhee compares this debris-filled tributary canyon to "an aircraft carrier in dry dock," complete with its own debris basins "along its upper flank, there to *protect* the man-made deposit" (271). His italics betray his own incredulity if not indignation.

McPhee closes *Control* sardonically, ridiculing L.A.'s attempt to best the Mountains, since this big flat grotesquerie forms "an edifice ten times as large as the largest pyramid at Giza" (272). The comparison with one of the Seven Wonders of the Ancient World exposes and belittles this act of human folly. McPhee had used this sardonic analogy earlier, when chronicling plans for a proposed floating nuclear power plant, the "Atlantic Generating Station," wherein "pharaoh" becomes "a collective name for people in New Jersey who pay electricity bills" (*Giving Good Weight,* 83–87). The fact that this "aircraft carrier" entombs a small canyon rather than a pharaoh does not lessen the snowballing moral. It is hard to miss and similarly hard to take seriously those who accuse McPhee of failure of nerve. Burro Canyon darkly parodies that eternal, whimsical dream of bright engineering majors to construct an elaborate apparatus that defies and reverses the flow of gravity. McPhee's history of L.A. debris basins reads like an example of chaos theory, and the image of basins upon/above basins suggests a willful, cumulative failure to understand the simplest principles of ecology, let alone local topography and geology and the law of gravity. As Ed Marston remarks in his review of *Control,* it is as if man has constructed "a kind of perpetual-motion rowing machine that makes him sweat harder than anything God ever dreamed up" (56).

Because of its distance from the Pine Barrens, the Alaskan bush, and the Colorado River canyon, for example, "Los Angeles against the Mountains" poses as McPhee's preeminent "anti-Keewaydin" parable. It belongs with all the Keewaydin Stories, including, more recently, the brief "In Virgin Forest," included in *Irons in the Fire* (1997). The remarkable unintended ironies of that big command above the keystone arch above the University of Wyoming's Engineering Building entrance eventuate in small Burro Canyon: a lunar, horizontal site that disguises the canyon's vertical *V.* " 'Fourteen million cubic yards,' " a parody of time-lapse erosion, obscure the canyon-as-canyon. Moving mountains means filling canyons. Again, the writer in the background strides forward to deliver the final judgment on his triptych's final panel, this "epic artifact" (271) looming larger and infinitely uglier than Mike Rubel's 22,000-square-foot Glendora castle, though not different in kind.

As suggested earlier, McPhee's judgment can be referenced in older L.A. literature than Mike Davis's recent apocalyptic environmental history. Writing a few years after McPhee, Davis echoes him in concluding that the metropolis has developed during a "most unusual episode of climatic and seismic benignity": "[it] has been capitalized on sheer gambler's luck" (37–38; cf. McPhee's opening note of deceptive serenity, 183). I wish to locate McPhee's environmental cautionary tale in one final textual example that punctures the "gambler's luck." I take it from a novel written half a century before *Control.* For in some respects Burro Canyon and Mike Rubel's castle work as synecdoche, signifying the whole place, and L.A. constitutes an "epic artifact" to the extent that Hollywood and Disneyland constitute our oldest homes of illusion and sites of hyperreality.

For me, one of the cardinal scenes in F. Scott Fitzgerald's *The Last Tycoon* (1940) occurs early in the novel, when an earthquake wreaks havoc off and on the studio back lot, which "looked like the torn picture books of childhood" (25). The novelist imagines the terror of his young narrator, Cecilia, in ways similar to the novelistic journalist's imagining of the Genofiles at the beginning of "Los Angeles": "for a full minute our bowels were one with the bowels of the earth—like some nightmare attempt to attach our navel cords again and jerk us back to the womb of creation" (23). Two visitors to theme park L.A. take an unexpected ride:

> On top of a huge head of the Goddess Siva, two women were flowing down the current of an impromptu river. The idol had come unloosed from a set of Burma, and it meandered earnestly on its way, stopping sometimes to waddle and bump in the shallows with the other debris of the tide. The two refugees had found sanctuary along a scroll of

curls on its bald forehead and seemed at first glance to be sightseers on
an interesting bus-ride through the scene of the flood. (25)

Impromptu "rivers" outnumber the mighty Mississippi and surge
through McPhee's triptych. His legions of characters struggle to contain or divert them, and perhaps Fitzgerald's anonymous pair of tourists
prefigures them all, riding a sudden river atop Siva the Destroyer, Hindu
god of destruction and regeneration. Siva controls, not us, as the cycles
he symbolizes stretch far beyond human endeavor.

IV

By the 1990s critical and popular attention to environmental writing had
grown by leaps and bounds from the preceding generation. A number
of indicators such as the appearance of *The Ecocriticism Reader* (1996)
mark this new quantity and range. Perhaps it comes as no surprise to
find no mention of John McPhee in its introduction's opening two sections, "Literary Studies in an Age of Environmental Crisis" and "Birth
of Environmental Literary Studies." McPhee wears too many hats. A
sense of cumulative crises dims the luster and place of moderate voices
such as McPhee's. But as all music lovers know, sometimes *piano* sounds
louder and carries further than *forte*. I have argued that his rhetorical
mode makes his voice as potentially effective an environmental voice as
polemical ones. Like many, I believe environmental writing must remain
an expanded, not restricted, genre capable of accommodating the
urban-wilderness allegory that is "Los Angeles against the Mountains,"
for example. It must include such sustained satire within which McPhee
occasionally waxes prophetic in the same way that marks Quammen's
Song of the Dodo like a chorus. As McPhee clarifies at the close of his interview with Jared Haynes quoted earlier, he insists upon the reader's
central place, but that view never masks his own environmental positions. Environmental crises, after all, undergird the battle metaphor driving *The Control of Nature;* and no doubt from the first occasion when
he raised his eyes to the big sandstone panel in Laramie, Wyoming,
McPhee knew what kinds of effects he intended to strike.

The first and oldest essay in *The Ecocriticism Reader,* Lynn White, Jr.'s
"The Historical Roots of Our Ecologic Crisis" (1967), was published one
year before *The Pine Barrens.* White's conclusion animates most of
McPhee's Keewaydin Stories because its credo is also McPhee's: "we

shall continue to have a worsening ecologic crisis until we reject the Christian axiom that nature has no reason for existence save to serve man" (14). Of course there are myriad ways to illustrate this biocentric truth, as the widening genre demonstrates. When McPhee spent time at the University of Wyoming with David Love, and subsequently spent two years researching and writing his third Keewaydin triptych, he knew how best to ironize that quasi-Mosaic law. And in "Los Angeles against the Mountains" McPhee's steady respect leavens his steady satire as it seeks to persuade, maybe even arouse, rather than offend. As more writers risk or court offense—Cactus Ed Abbey comes to mind—perhaps the difference between it and arousal grows elusive. Yet that difference makes all the difference, as McPhee's Keewaydin Stories consistently prove. If we accept Daniel G. Payne's reminder quoted earlier, then McPhee's muted advocacy may resonate loudest and prove most enduring.

Works Cited

Ashe, Diana L. "The Space between Text and Action: Redefining Nature Writing through the Work of Rick Bass and John McPhee." In *The Literary Art and Activism of Rick Bass,* ed. O. Alan Weltzien, 122–47. Salt Lake City: University of Utah Press, 2001.

Bailey, Thomas C. "John McPhee: The Making of a Meta-Naturalist." In *Earthly Words: Essays on Contemporary American Nature and Environmental Writers,* ed. John Cooley, 195–213. Ann Arbor: University of Michigan Press, 1994.

Davis, Mike. *Ecology of Fear: Los Angeles and the Imagination of Disaster.* New York: Metropolitan Books, 1998.

Fitzgerald, F. Scott. *The Last Tycoon.* New York: Charles Scribner's Sons, 1941.

Forster, E. M. *Aspects of the Novel.* New York: Harcourt, Brace Jovanovich, 1921.

Glotfelty, Cheryll, and Harold Fromm, eds. *The Ecocriticism Reader.* Athens: University of Georgia Press, 1996.

Hamilton, Joan. "An Encounter with John McPhee." *Sierra* 75(3) (May/June 1990): 50–55, 92, 96.

Haynes, Jared. " 'The Size and Shape of the Canvas': An Interview with John McPhee." *Writing on the Edge* 5(2) and 6(1) (Spring and Fall 1994): 109–25 (reprinted in edited form in the present volume).

Howarth, William. "Introduction." In *The John McPhee Reader,* vii–xxiii. New York: Farrar, Straus & Giroux, 1976.

Marston, Ed. "Morality without Moralism." *National Review* (2 June 1989): 54, 56.

McPhee, John. *Annals of the Former World.* New York: Farrar, Straus & Giroux, 1998.

———. *Assembling California*. New York: Farrar, Straus & Giroux, 1993.

———. *Basin and Range*. New York: Farrar, Straus & Giroux, 1981.

———. *Coming into the Country*. New York: Farrar, Straus & Giroux, 1977.

———. *The Control of Nature*. New York: Farrar, Straus & Giroux, 1989.

———. *Encounters with the Archdruid*. New York: Farrar, Straus & Giroux, 1971.

———. "Farewell to the Archdruid." *Sierra* (January/February 2001): 8–9.

———. *Giving Good Weight*. New York: Farrar, Straus & Giroux, 1979.

———. *Irons in the Fire*. New York: Farrar, Straus & Giroux, 1997.

———. *The Pine Barrens*. New York: Farrar, Straus & Giroux, 1968.

———. *Rising from the Plains*. New York: Farrar, Straus & Giroux, 1986.

———. *The Survival of the Bark Canoe*. New York: Farrar, Straus & Giroux, 1975.

———. *Table of Contents*. New York: Farrar, Straus & Giroux, 1985.

Payne, Daniel G. *Voices in the Wilderness: American Nature Writing and Environmental Politics*. Hanover: University Press of New England, 1996.

Pearson, Michael. *John McPhee*. New York: Twayne, 1998.

Pyne, Stephen J. "A War against the World." *New York Times Book Review* (6 August 1989): 1, 22.

Quammen, David. "Muscling Nature." *Outside* (December 1989): 29–32, 34, 36.

——— "Rocks of Age." *New York Times Book Review* (5 July 1998): 9–10.

———. *The Song of the Dodo: Island Biogeography in an Age of Extinction*. New York: Charles Scribner's Sons, 1996.

Remnick, David. "Introduction." In *The Second John McPhee Reader*, vii–xvii. New York: Farrar, Straus & Giroux, 1998.

Ryden, Kent. *Landscape* with *Figures: Nature and Culture in New England*. Iowa City: University of Iowa Press, 2001.

Shabecoff, Philip. "Defying Nature May Be the Only Choice." *New York Times Book Review* (6 August 1989): 20, 22.

Slovic, Scott. "Politics in American Nature Writing." In *Green Culture: Environmental Rhetoric in Contemporary America,* ed. Carl G. Herndl and Stuart C. Brown, 82–110. Madison: University of Wisconsin Press, 1996.

Stull, James N. *Literary Selves: Autobiography and Contemporary American Nonfiction*. Westport: Greenwood Press, 1993.

Turner, Brian. "Giving Good Reasons: Environmental Appeals in the Nonfiction of John McPhee." *Rhetoric Review* 13(1) (Fall 1994): 164–82.

White, Lynn, Jr. "The Historical Roots of Our Ecologic Crisis." In *The Ecocriticism Reader,* ed. Cheryll Glotfelty and Harold Fromm, 3–14. Athens: University of Georgia Press, 1996.

Michael Pearson

In the American Grain

John McPhee's *Coming into the Country*

Critics have always had trouble deciding where to place a certain kind of deep and artful nonfiction in their literary taxonomies. Even in the all-inclusiveness that seems to pervade the beginnings of the twenty-first century, nonfiction is often excluded. Most anthologies of American literature offer fiction, poetry, and drama, but few offer examples of literary nonfiction. How many include E. B. White, Joseph Mitchell, or John Hersey? No one would think of leaving Toni Morrison or Don DeLillo out of a gathering of work by contemporary American writers. But how many would automatically include John McPhee?

Scholars even appear to have trouble giving the form of nonfiction that McPhee and others write a name. Tom Wolfe has called the genre "the new journalism," and Norman Sims refers to it as literary journalism.[1] Some call it dramatic nonfiction and others narrative nonfiction or the literature of fact. Magazines have sprung up with titles like *Fourth Genre* and *Creative Nonfiction*. There is confusion in the critical ranks, opening up a gap that Barbara Lounsberry calls "the great unexplored territory of contemporary criticism."[2] William Howarth said in his introduction to *The John McPhee Reader:* "No one has a proper name for his [McPhee's] brand of factual writing."[3]

For many the form is unique, rising in the turbulence and disorientation of the 1960s as a literary challenge to consensual wisdom and accepted authority, a response to a new mass audience that needed a way of seeing and understanding reality that the postmodernist novel failed to give. Ronald Weber in *The Literature of Fact* interprets the situation this way: "With the new nonfiction, the audience received information but received it entertainingly, with familiar literary trimmings. It received an up-to-date factual fiction that abandoned the dreariness of day-to-day journalism yet did not fly off in the strange and complex

ways of Barth, Borges, Barthelme, and other fabulists."⁴ For many readers, the form defined itself in the fragmentation of the 1960s with books
like Truman Capote's *In Cold Blood* (1965), Tom Wolfe's *The Electric
Kool-Aid Acid Test* (1968), Norman Mailer's *Armies of the Night* (1968),
and Gay Talese's *Honor Thy Father* (1971). Each of these writers responded to the political and moral landscape of the times, and each ap-
proached his subject with novelistic vigor. They created what the critic
John Hellman described as a "contemporary genre in which journalistic
material is presented in the forms of fiction."⁵ This was a form of writing
that demanded the artistry of fiction and the gripping authority of actuality. It was a form that seemed to say "reality can be re-presented but
only by taking risks with scene and characterization and point of view."
The truth can be told, as Emily Dickinson suggested, but it can be discovered only through a slant. In David Lodge's analysis, such nonfiction
was as iconoclastic as the postmodern novel: "The nonfiction novel and
fabulation are radical forms which take their impetus from an extreme
reaction to the world we live in—*The Armies of the Night* and *Giles
Goat-Boy* are equally products of the apocalyptic imagination."⁶

So this "new" form blossomed in the late 1960s and spread in the
next few decades, perhaps helping shape the interest in memoir and the
fascination with reality television that for the time being seem to have
taken over American culture. In fact this type of nonfiction is not "new."
Literary nonfiction had a long and honorable tradition and did not
begin in the 1960s. After all, John Hersey had written *Hiroshima* in
1946, and James Agee had published *Let Us Now Praise Famous Men* in
1941. Lillian Ross had written her account of John Huston's film version
of *The Red Badge of Courage—Picture*—in 1952. And, of course, in the
1930s and 1940s there were A. J. Liebling's and E. B. White's reportage
and essays, as well as Joseph Mitchell's complex and darkly comic accounts of New York City. But nonfiction literature has a deeper heritage
still—back to Mark Twain in *Innocents Abroad, Roughing It,* and *Life on
the Mississippi,* Herman Melville in *Typee,* and others in the nineteenth
century.

Indeed, literary nonfiction has a history, although not as formal or
discernible as some forms of poetry and fiction, traceable back even before the nineteenth century. Augustine's *Confessions* in the fifth century
may lead us over a millennium and a half later to Frank McCourt's *An-
gela's Ashes*. Michel de Montaigne's essays may lead us to E. B. White's.
The periodical pieces by Joseph Addison and Richard Steele in the eigh-

teenth century foreshadow the *New Yorker*'s "Talk of the Town" pieces. Perhaps, as some literary critics suggest, literary nonfiction began to emerge with Daniel Defoe's *A Journal of the Plague Year,* which appeared in 1722. How much of the work is fiction and how much fact has not been fully established, but it is clear that Defoe wrote from a journalistic viewpoint. In writing about the great plague that struck London in 1665, Defoe could have pulled some of the information for the book from his memory (although he was only five years old at the time), and some could have been gleaned from interviews and books. *A Journal* has the feel and aura of history and memoir to it. It is filled with facts and statistics, but it is essentially a work of the imagination, a blend of fact and fiction that may preview some of the problems readers have confronted with contemporary works of narrative nonfiction.

As the novel rose in popularity in the eighteenth century with Henry Fielding, Samuel Richardson, and Defoe, so did the appeal of true narratives. Novelists created forms—the epistolary novel or the picaresque story—that imitated organic nonfiction patterns. Writers published their diaries and their accounts of voyage and adventure. Pedro de Castañeda, Richard Hakluyt, and John Smith were travel writers who opened literary paths for those who followed in their footsteps centuries later, like William Least Heat-Moon, Ian Frazier, and Bruce Chatwin. James Boswell's *Life of Samuel Johnson,* published in 1791, could have served as a model for much of the immersion reporting employed by Gay Talese and John McPhee.

The complex and long-established tradition of narrative nonfiction that John McPhee works in is part of a tradition of literature made of observation, verifiable fact, and research. The river of literary nonfiction has many tributaries—essays, reportage, travel narrative, memoir, biography—and McPhee maneuvers skillfully along every branch of the genre, shaping his work as both meticulous reporting and artful narrative. He re-creates memorable characters and settings along with conflicts and themes that hold us with the power of fiction. McPhee captures our attention, as well, with the distinctive American character of his voice and vision—in the lineage of Henry David Thoreau and Mark Twain, in a style and perspective that blend romanticism and realism patterned truly in the American grain.

Although it is difficult to choose which of McPhee's more than two dozen books seems most representative of American literary traditions, *Coming into the Country* might offer the most breathtaking canvas and the largest cast of characters of any of his works. More significantly, perhaps, it is a narrative that is characteristically American in its ability to balance the romantic and the realistic points of view. Similar to many of the great works of mid-nineteenth-century romanticism, *Coming into the Country* has, at its heart, a sense of the value of an independent, creative spirit, a cherishing of self-reliance and the iconoclastic instinct, a love of nature, a distrust of urbanization, and a belief in the spiritual necessity of the wild, for without the wilderness the individual's imagination loses the possibility of unfettered physical freedom and all that implies. *Coming into the Country* is also rooted in the tradition of American realism through its less sanguine vision of the social and natural worlds. As a work of nonfiction by one of the most meticulous reporters writing today, it is a book that first and foremost strives for fidelity to actuality. As with all realistic texts, it reaches for a truthful treatment of its materials. McPhee, like George Eliot, paints a picture of average experience and ordinary lives—at least the Alaskan version of such life.

Like a novel about ordinary heroes and heroines, characters living the unprincely, everyday lives of working-class citizens, McPhee's nonfiction narrative of Alaska depicts men and women in the hardscrabble reality of wilderness living. McPhee, like most realists, shows us individuals in action and sentimentally dramatizes the heroic and unpleasant in the typical lives of ordinary people. *Coming into the Country* scrupulously renders an American border life with a cast of characters at once unique and representative in a book that contains both romantic and realistic impulses. While he carefully records the skills necessary to survive in the Alaskan bush and the harsh realities of life in the wild, McPhee holds fast to a pastoral vision of the world he describes. Alaska is surely no Eden for him; but, to use Don Scheese's definition of the pastoral, McPhee does construct "nature as a retreat or sanctuary,"[7] even if that paradise comes with many dangers and is only for the tough-spirited and resilient. Scheese elaborates on his explanation of the pastoral tradition by saying: "Once the protagonist has completed the move from civilization to nature, pastoralist writing 'takes the form of an isolated moment, a kind of island in time, and one which gains its meaning and intensity through the tensions it creates with the historical world.' "[8] The dialectic that Scheese argues is central to American pastoralism—wilderness versus civilization, wildness versus culture, re-creation in opposition to recreation, Native American culture in contrast with Euroamerican culture—is a key theme in much of McPhee's work and central to *Coming into the Country.*

Many agree with Edward Hoagland's assessment of McPhee's accomplishment in *Coming into the Country:* it is a "long, permanent book . . . a species of masterpiece."[9] The book has a modern epic quality to it, with the requisite and often larger-than-life heroes, the vast setting, the deeds of great ability and courage, the simple yet literary style. Like most epics, the book begins *in medias res,* with McPhee in a canoe (the ideal vantage point for a man who loves rivers) as he journeys on the Salmon River of the Brooks Range, the most northern of Alaska's nineteen rivers carrying the name "Salmon." The watershed for this river is above the Arctic Circle, a place that probably seems as magical and faraway to most Americans as the dark side of the moon. McPhee recounts the stories of his Alaskan heroes and heroines with something close to the same balance and objectivity characteristic of epic poets. Like Homer in *The Iliad,* he employs his own type of catalogs—of people and equipment, of wild animals and mountain peaks. As much as Walt Whitman's *Leaves of Grass* is an epic describing the unique American—both singular and generic—McPhee's work is an account of a profound aspect of the American spirit on the verge of extinction. His characters in *Coming into the Country,* reminiscent of Bill Bradley in *A Sense of Where You Are,* Frank Boyden in *The Headmaster,* Andy Chase in *Looking for a Ship,* or so many others—Fred Brown or Carol Ruckdeschel or Otto the chef—are all individuals who seem anachronistic in their determined individualism and idiosyncrasy, particularly in a contemporary American society that seems always inclined toward homogeneity in its shaping of both people and landscapes. They all seem to be one of a kind and pushed (or propelled by their own instincts) into a corner of the world.

Coming into the Country may be McPhee's *Moby Dick* or *Adventures of Huckleberry Finn,* a work that strikes to the heart of American dreams and experience. Like these two works, *Coming into the Country* combines a sobering reality with a pastoral vision of escape and does so in a way that is simultaneously admiring and ironic. The Alaska that McPhee describes is essentially a separate country, as foreign to most of us as the islands off the coast of Scotland.[10] McPhee makes it clear that he considers Alaska a different kind of country, a separate land, one-sixth the size of the entire United States, essentially a wilderness where one can find "a life beyond community." But "ironic Alaska" is as American as the New Jersey Pine Barrens—in the sense of adventure it affords and the spirit of self-reliance it demands. As McPhee says, "Alaska is a foreign country significantly populated with Americans" (*Country,* 126). It is at once huge beyond the reach of the imagination and parochial in the strictest sense of the word:

> If Boston was once the most provincial place in America (the story goes that after a six-megaton bomb exploded in Times Square a headline in a Boston paper would say "Hub Man Killed in New York Blast"), Alaska, in this respect, may have replaced Boston. In Alaska, the conversation is Alaska. Alaskans, by and large, seem to know little and say less about what is going on outside. They talk about their land, their bears, their fish, their rivers. They talk about subsistence hunting, forbidden hunting, and living in trespass. They have their own lexicon. A senior citizen is a pioneer, snow is termination dust, and the N.B.A. is the National Bank of Alaska. (126)

"Alaska" is an Aleut word that means "the great land," a place that "runs off the edge of the imagination, with its tracklessness, its beyond-the-ridge-line surprises, its hundreds of millions of acres of wilderness" (133). It may be the last frontier for Americans. McPhee says that his pulse has quickened all of his life at the very sound of the word "wild," and in describing his journey down the Salmon River in book I of *Coming into the Country* he pictures for his readers the wildest river he had ever seen.

By the time *Coming into the Country* was published in 1977, McPhee had already written twelve books. Many of them—*The Crofter and the Laird, The Deltoid Pumpkin Seed, The Pine Barrens, The Headmaster, Levels of the Game, Encounters with the Archdruid,* and *The Survival of the Bark Canoe*—examined themes concerned with passionate individuality and escape from a deadening homogeneity. Most of McPhee's characters, as Barbara Lounsberry puts it, are "representative men," not only standing for the highest achievement in their fields but uniting the fields within themselves—"McPhee's representative men, like Emerson's, exert spiritual as well as physical or intellectual leadership. 'The world is upheld by the veracity of good men,' wrote Emerson in *Representative Men;* 'they make the earth wholesome.' "[11] Usually, the McPhee hero is an exemplum, an individual of hard-won skill, a resilient and resourceful person who cuts an energetic path through usually complex and challenging worlds.

The world of *Coming into the Country* is the landscape of the last frontier—an environment filled with ironies encountered on the political front and in the bush. In the first of the three sections that make up the narrative, "The Encircled River," McPhee introduces one of the major conflicts in the story—preservation versus development. "The Encircled River" is a story about circles, a tale with no conclusion and full of paradoxes. Alaska is a wilderness state, but few can get to the wilderness to enjoy it. It is too expensive and too difficult to reach the pristine wilds. To preserve the land means keeping it for the general public but also denying it to those who would enter it as pioneers. Even the Alaska Native Claims Settlement Act of 1971, which gave one billion dollars and forty million acres to the sixty thousand natives of the state, comes with an ironic price tag. As McPhee says:

> The sense of private property that has been jacketed upon them is uncomfortable, incompatible with subsistence harvesting and its changeful cycles. . . . Kobuk societies once functioned like the clans of Scotland. Terrain was common to all. Kinship patterned things; ownership did not. Use determined use. If you had been using a place—say, a fishing spot—it was respected as yours while you used it. Now the enforced drawing of lines on the land has created tensions among the Kobuk villages that did not exist before. (35)

In "The Encircled River," McPhee travels into the heart of the paradox with four men who are part of a state-federal study team trying to determine whether the Salmon should be included in a wild river proposal before Congress that would set aside the area as unalterable wild terrain. As McPhee says, the five of them are part of "perhaps a dozen outsiders [who] have traveled . . . in boats down the length of the river" (8). The river is part of what he realizes is, "in all likelihood, the most isolated wilderness I will ever see" (50). McPhee gets caught in his own circle, in the inherent contradictions of Alaska. It is open, inviting, threatening, beautiful, rugged, a place of Arctic sun and freezing temperatures, a land brimming with wealth and dense with dangers—simple and incongruous at the same time. McPhee's reaction to the wild landscape echoes Melville as much as it does Thoreau:

> What had struck me most in the isolation of the wilderness was an abiding sense of paradox. In its raw, convincing emphasis on the irrelevance of the visitor, it was forcefully, importantly repellent. It was no less strongly attractive—with a beauty of nowhere else, composed in

turning circles. If the wild was indifferent, it gave a sense of difference. If at moments it was frightening, requiring an effort to put down the conflagrationary imagination, it also augmented the touch of life. This was not a dare with nature. This was nature. (93)

The sense of place in Alaska comes from the spirit of the wilderness, and there is no more striking symbol of the country for McPhee than the grizzly bear. Bear stories inflame his imagination throughout the narrative. Bears are something to be contemplated with awe and respect. The grizzly implies a world—it is "an affirmation to the rest of the earth that this kind of place was extant" (63). McPhee admires its power, its dangerous wildness, its intelligence and independence. He dreams of the grizzly at night. The bear, in color, stands on the side of a hill. It is a vision of Alaska, of the contradictory place where beauty would not exist without danger, where the connection to nature means a difficult encounter with it. The bear suggests all that is dangerously alive and magnificent in the landscape and all that can be lost to greed and urbanization. The discovery of oil was like the discovery of gold: "Alaska suddenly had more development than it could absorb. It suddenly had manifold inflation and a glut of trailer parks. It had traffic jams. You could pick up a telephone and 'dial a date.' In the reasonably accessible bush, fishing and hunting—the sorts of things many people had long sought in Alaska—became crowded and poor" (84).

In section II, "What They Were Hunting For," McPhee describes a helicopter trip he took with a committee charged with selecting the site for a new Alaskan capital; an evangelical tone reminiscent of Thoreau in a virulent mood cracks the calm, often softly comic narrative voice: "Anchorage is not a frontier town. It is virtually unrelated to its environment. It has come in on the wind, an American spore. A large cookie cutter brought down on El Paso could lift something like Anchorage into the air. Anchorage is the northern rim of Trenton, the center of Oxnard, the ocean-blind precincts of Daytona Beach" (130). Many of the homes remind him of an architecture that he describes as American Dentist. The city is a "portable Passaic." Unlike the Alaskan wild, Anchorage is like much in the lower Forty-Eight. This is so disheartening to McPhee that he goes off on another uncharacteristic jeremiad: "Within such vastness, Anchorage is a mere pustule, a dot, a minum—a walled city, wild as Yonkers, with the wildlife riding in a hundred and ninety-three thousand trucks and cars" (133).

The question McPhee asks early in the first section—"what is to be the fate of all this land?"—haunts the entire narrative and implies others: what will be the fate of the people who go into the country if all they find are Anchorages? And what will become of the American dream of self-reliance and independence if there is no place left in the United States where the pioneer impulse can thrive? To take away the possibility and threat of the wilderness is to reduce our humanity, to diminish our imagination, McPhee implies. Late in the book he underscores this suggestion: "In the society as a whole, there is an elemental need for a frontier outlet, for a pioneer place to go—important even to those who do not go there" (436). This frontier outlet has been part of the American imagination from its very beginnings, expressed in American literature from Natty Bumppo's entering the woods to Huck Finn's dreaming of heading for the territories. It is this realm of possibility that F. Scott Fitzgerald celebrates at the conclusion of *The Great Gatsby:* "for a transitory enchanted moment man must have held his breath in the presence of this continent, compelled into an aesthetic contemplation he neither understood nor desired, face to face for the last time in history with something commensurate to his capacity to wonder." This is the story of Eugene Henderson in Newfoundland, Chief Bromden on his way to Canada, and John Grady Cole in Mexico. McPhee's story of Alaska is this same tale of contemplating something commensurate to our capacity to wonder.

McPhee compels the reader to feel the sense of wonder that Alaska is capable of evoking, but he also ironically suggests that the hunter may get caught in the trap, that civilization can be its own enemy. Caught between the conflicting notions of what the state should be, the natives and the settlers seem trapped. One of the primary images in the first section of the book is the image of the circle, McPhee's circular journey along the Salmon and Kobuk Rivers, the cycles inherent in Alaskan life, even the salmon he watches "circling, an endless attention of rings" (7). The Eskimos live in harmony with these cycles and are uncomfortable with the designs imposed upon them by politicians, lands divided and subdivided for political and economic purposes. Theirs is a true ecology, an accommodation with the cycles of fishing and hunting and gathering that the country and seasons demand. When the Kobuks hunt for caribou, for instance, they use the whole animal: "They eat the meat raw and in roasts and stews. They eat greens from the stomach, muscles from the jaw, fat from behind the eyes. The hide goes into certain winter clothing that nothing manufactured can equal" (33). The Kobuks have expanded and contracted along the river lands over the centuries in accordance with fluctuating caribou populations.

As McPhee describes his own river journey in book I, "closing a circuit, a hundred miles from the upper Salmon, where the helicopter took us, from Kiana, at the start" (40), he draws a picture of the natives that could have come from Paul Gauguin or Henri Rousseau. McPhee offers an idyllic miniature of the people of Kiana. While he waits for the plane to take him to Kotzebue, he falls asleep, only to be awakened a short time later by the voices of children. Three little girls who had been picking blueberries on the other side of the runway stood by McPhee, holding the berries along with hard candies and offering them to him.

> They asked for nothing. They were not shy. They were totally unself-conscious. . . . When they noticed my monocular, on a lanyard around my neck, they got down beside me, picked it off my chest, and spied on the town. They leaned over, one at a time, and put their noses against mine, draping around my head their soft black hair. They stared into my eyes. Their eyes were dark and northern, in beautiful almond faces, aripple with smiles. (41–42)

The scene is Edenic, the young girls more innocent and open than one can imagine their modern, media-saturated peers in most of the United States to be.

McPhee concludes "The Encircled River" by completing his own narrative circle: "We drifted to the rip, and down it past the mutilated salmon. Then we came to another long flat surface, spraying up the light of the sun. My bandanna, around my head, was nearly dry. I took it off and trailed it in the river" (95). Right before the final image of the bandanna, which closes the circle with the opening image of the section, McPhee describes sighting a grizzly that playfully tosses a ten-pound salmon into the air then, like the archetypal American cowboy, twirls it over his head, lariat fashion. It is an image that implies independence and power, the grizzly's brown fur rippling "like a field under wind" (95). McPhee suggests both the majesty and the threat: "If we were looking at something we had rarely seen before, God help him so was he" (95). The threat is not so much from the bear, it seems, but from humans. At the beginning of "The Encircled River," there is an image of circling salmon. At the end there is another—a mutilated corpse—as if to focus the reader's attention on humankind's entrance into paradise.

This section represents many of the most important themes in the book in general. As Philip Terrie points out in his essay "River of Paradox: John McPhee's 'The Encircled River' ":

> McPhee is constructing a narrative not only about nature but also about inner discovery. . . . Both "The Encircled River" and *Coming into the Country* are prime examples of one of American literature's most interesting and enduring genres, the wilderness travel narrative. And like the best of this tradition—from Thoreau's *The Maine Woods* to Abbey's *Desert Solitaire*—"The Encircled River" constitutes both a description of the wilderness and a tale of personal growth and discovery.[12]

Alaska may be free of snakes, but those who come into the country—into paradise—desiring to escape and carrying little more than a backpack and dreams of pioneering are due for an awakening. What McPhee learns, as Terrie points out, is that the wilderness demands an awareness of one's mortality, the inextricable link between the wilderness and death.[13] The last section, book III, "Coming into the Country," is longer than the first two sections combined and dramatizes many of the ideas and conflicts delineated earlier. The locus for McPhee's descriptions of Alaskan pioneers, and the center of his circle for explorations into the bush, is Eagle, a small town close to the Arctic Circle and near the Yukon River. As Ronald Weber notes, "In and around Eagle, McPhee finds characters of sufficient interest to populate a dozen novels."[14] In these people, McPhee finds and characterizes the American instinct for freedom and independence—and he examines the qualities of the individual who seeks such independence, the character of the place that permits (even requires) it, and the nature of the dream that is both true and false.

Barbara Lounsberry has aptly noticed that *Coming into the Country* is one of McPhee's most Thoreauvian volumes. McPhee, as she says, "goes to a cabin in the wilderness to confront the essential facts of Alaska."[15] And like Thoreau, McPhee spent approximately two years off and on at his Walden Pond. The bush seems truly to define Alaska; and the people who have "come into the country" define the bush. In a sense, the place illuminates the dream, and the dream shapes the character of the individuals attracted to the place. People in Eagle and the bush feel clannishly connected to Alaska; although they have many points of disagreement, there seems to be consensus about one thing—the importance of the wilderness in their lives. The majority of them want to live by the frontier code that emerges naturally in a land so wild and remote: "breathe free, do as you please, control your own destiny" (83). This is not the Los-Angelized lower Forty-Eight, but a country "so wild that valleys and mountains are without names" (89). It is a country imbued with dangers and surprises, a geography so unpeopled and mysterious that it both defines those who enter it or even contemplate it and eludes ready definition and understanding. It is not so much a place as a desire, an elemental impulse, a way of seeing ourselves and the world as Americans.

The people in book III of *Coming into the Country* are typical McPhee heroes. That is not to say that they are all attractive or unflawed characters; but they are all independent, skilled, passionate, brought to their lives as trappers or miners as one is called to a vocation. These characters—Donna Kneeland, Dick Cook, John Borg, Ed and Stanley Gelvin, Brad Snow, Lilly Allen, Mike Potts, Sarge Waller, and others— seem unlike anyone but themselves. They are not escapists but dreamers, coming into the country "for what is there" even though others "have come for what is not" (423). Like Gatsby they strive to spring from their own Platonic conceptions of themselves. Each of them, like Dick Cook, "has a certain picture of himself and he paints it every day-- another daub, another skill, becoming more and more of what he once only dreamed" (419).

All of the characters McPhee writes about, like Brad Snow and Lilly Allen, seek "terrain where the individual spirit might be confined only by the metes and bounds and rules of nature" (239–40). This is what Donna Kneeland seeks. Recently come into the country, she is the first profile McPhee offers in book III. Most of the McPhee heroes are men—from the early profiles of Bill Bradley, Frank L. Boyden, and Arthur Ashe to the stories of his museum directors, Merchant Marine sailors, and scientists—but Donna, like Carol Ruckdeschel in "Travels in Georgia," seems made to survive in such a lonely, difficult world as the Alaskan bush. At first glance, Kneeland would seem better suited to the world she came from—as an airline attendant—with her "criterion figure, dark-blond hair, and slate-blue, striking eyes" (186); but she is determined to live in the wild. She does not believe it would be prudent to live on her own in rural Alaska, but McPhee's description of her determination and strength of character suggests that she would be able to and may one day do so if or when she outgrows her companion, Dick Cook. Donna is a rarity in Alaska, a Euroamerican woman who grew up there. A short stay in Edmonton, Canada, left her with an undeniable yearning to live away from civilization. So she did what any practical young woman who wanted to learn how to live in and off the country might do—she hunted for a suitable trapper to share her life with in the wilderness. She stalked the meetings of the Interior Alaska Trappers Association and came upon Dick Cook, who had been in the country for the better part of a decade.

Cook, living in a cabin near a tributary of the Yukon River fifty miles into the wilderness from the town of Eagle, is a trapper by trade and, as McPhee suggests, a "sachem figure" by instinct. Cook is not afraid of hard work, "claiming that to lower his income and raise his independence he has worked twice as hard as most people" (186). One of his main precepts is that he tries not to make any more money than is absolutely necessary to live. In Cook, Kneeland found the ideal outdoorsman, part Kit Carson and part Daniel Boone. He is all pragmatist; there is nothing of the romantic about him. Cook is skilled in the many ways of surviving in the bush. McPhee catalogs his skills: he traps, hunts, gardens. He travels by canoe or dog sled. If his tooth needs to be pulled, he wraps a pair of channel-lock pliers with tape and attempts to do the job himself. He has an uncanny sense of where he is at all times. Although he has several hundred trap lines, he remembers where every one is "with no trouble." Cook is reminiscent of Henri Vaillancourt, the main character in *The Survival of the Bark Canoe,* in his admirable skillfulness but in his arrogance and pedantry as well. Sultan-like, Cook treats Donna Kneeland and others as if they were his inferiors. No one is to sit in his chair; no one is to talk while he is talking. He has the sort of pridefulness that makes him seem to be a perfect candidate for a character in a Flannery O'Connor short story. But he exists in the real world, one not for the weak or the meek, perhaps. In Cook's lexicon, the word "ecology" means "who's eating whom, and when" (417). Cook, who looks like "a scarecrow made of cables," is a survivor, essentially a lone wolf. Donna Kneeland is there with him, essentially follower with guru; and even though she knows how to tan hides, plant crops, and do an assortment of other tasks, she will always be a lesser being in his Darwinian universe. McPhee, like Walt Whitman in "Song of Myself," makes few judgments but instead presents the characters of Cook and others and lets the readers draw their own conclusions. With Cook, readers are left with contradictory views even from the residents of Eagle—he is "pontifical, messianic" or "a patient hunter . . . a wealth of information" (205).

Among the some two dozen characters that McPhee depicts in book III of *Coming into the Country,* most are spirited individualists, embodiments of a Thoreauvian ethic of simplifying one's life to confront the essentials of the world. Brad Snow and Lilly Allen come to the Alaskan frontier "to do without unnecessary things, to live out, to deal with the land in a more natural way" (241–42). To live in Alaska and have the chance of entering the world that borders his home, Jim Dungan is happy to live in an eight- by twelve-foot cabin—"not quite three steps by four" (218)—ironically bound in confined space in the boundless space around him. Viola Goggins, who came into the country with "a baby and a dime, and only the baby had substantially grown" (206), is content with the cost of her independence, it seems. Residents of Eagle become, by necessity, jacks of all trades. John Borg is a "one-man city," postmaster, president of the Eagle Historical Society, local reporter for the National Weather Service, and mayor. Those who are not self-sufficient don't last in Eagle or in the bush.

The Gelvin family—particularly the father and son, Ed and Stanley—epitomize all that is to be admired in the humble independence and self-reliance of those who come into the country and make their lives in it. They are men of meticulous practicality, the quintessential McPhee heroes—determined, unpretentious, superbly skilled, and self-trained. They have an artistic passion for what they do in the world, be it gold mining or repairing an airplane. Projects that would daunt most people, like dismantling a bulldozer and flying it piece by piece into a remote mountain location where they can reassemble it and use it to dig for gold, are for them like solving a difficult but manageable algebra problem. Like some of Willa Cather's pioneer heroes, the Gelvins are supremely capable, industrious, and inventive, a match for this place where civilization ends and only certain people are willing and able to go "deep into the roadless world."

The Gelvins are, among other things, gold miners, not members of the Sierra Club. They hunt wolves and dig deep into the beautiful mountains. For McPhee, the Gelvins symbolize what is best in the American spirit and, along with the land, must be kept intact. In speaking about the Gelvins' mining, he writes:

> This mine is a cork on the sea. Meanwhile (and, possibly, more seriously), the relationship between this father and son is as attractive as anything I have seen in Alaska—both of them self-reliant beyond the

usual reach of the term, the characteristic formed by this country. Whatever they are doing, whether it is mining or something else, they do for themselves what no one else is here to do for them. Their kind is more endangered every year. Balance that against the nick they are making in the land. Only an easygoing extremist would preserve every bit of the country. And extremists alone would exploit it all. Everyone else has to think the matter through—choose a point of tolerance, however much the point might tend to one side. For myself, I am closer to the preserving side—that is, the side that would preserve the Gelvins. To be sure, I would preserve plenty of land as well. (430)

The Gelvins fit into their environment as smoothly as the Eskimos do. The life in Alaska that attracts the Gelvins and people like them has "great liabilities . . . great possibilities" (229). It is a place for people like Eagle resident Jack Boone who are not impressed with "the advantages of modern civilization." People like the Gelvins, as Joe Vogler, another resident of the town, says, "would be misfits somewhere else. They're doers. They don't destroy. They build. They preserve" (317).

As in many of his other books that deal with human beings' relationship to the natural world—*The Pine Barrens, Encounters with the Archdruid,* and *The Control of Nature,* for example—in *Coming into the Country,* McPhee offers no simple solutions to the conflicts. He is like a novelist presenting us with the felt experience of living—a novelist of ideas, perhaps, preaching to us usually with grace and good humor about the value of preserving a way of life that is so inextricably tied to the American dream itself. He seems to call for a balance, a preserving of the land and the American character that is one and the same with the wilderness.

But for all his romantic leanings, his pastoral vision of the world, and, by omission and insinuation, his criticism of the meretricious urban landscape and the characterlessness of its inhabitants, McPhee is a cooleyed realist as well. The individuals who survive in the wild land are tough, skilled, and single-minded in their focus. In the final image of *Coming into the Country,* McPhee describes his meeting with a young man who has just come to Eagle, has stocked up with supplies at the general store, and is about to take off into the woods. The reader is left to decide whether the newcomer has what it takes to survive in the bush. McPhee shapes the conclusion this way: "I asked him where he meant to go. 'Down the river,' he said. 'I'll be living on the Yukon and getting my skills together.' I wished him heartfelt luck and felt in my heart he would need it. I said my name, and shook his hand, and he said his. He said, 'My name is River Wind'" (438). It is doubtful that the immense young man wearing the wide-brimmed hat and carrying the romantic but perhaps portentous name will make it in the country. The winter after McPhee meets him, no one in the town remembers or has heard of River Wind. He is just one of the dozens who tries his luck in the wilderness. But he is one more example of the need for the frontier, there for people to reimagine and, with the right sort of self-education, reinvent their own lives. It is there, as it has always seemed to be in America, for those with an adventurous instinct and a desire to seek a new life.

Like many of McPhee's other books, *Coming into the Country* is part of a long American tradition. There is a pastoral vision at the heart of his work. His America is populated with strong individuals, careful artisans, unrecognized adventurers, doers, builders, and makers. *Coming into the Country,* representative of his other books, is in the American grain— reminiscent of the values of Benjamin Franklin, Ralph Waldo Emerson, and Henry David Thoreau. The importance of independence, self-reliance, and respect for nature and the wild in us and around us and the necessity of a sovereignty of spirit are all essential aspects of his view of the world. Like Thoreau, he seems to cherish both the intellectual and the experiential, both the meditative and the participatory life.

Even McPhee's narrative voice is distinctively American, comic and self-deprecatory, clear and rhythmic. It is a poetry of epigrammatic description—characters are dissected in a phrase ("dour and apronly"), and features are captured with scientific succinctness ("dendritic streams" or "coleopteran eyes"). McPhee's humor typically has the American quality of understatement and irony and usually, echoing Mark Twain, points back at the narrator: "Tracks suggest that it is something of a trail. I am mildly nervous about that, but then I am mildly nervous about a lot of things" (13). When he does shine the light of satire on others, the wattage is generally mild: "Under the gin-clear water, his head, with its radical economy of hair, looked like an onion" (90) or ". . . because if their cabin was handsome, it was ten times as snug. A lighted match could make it warm" (339).

In all, McPhee is an original, but an American original for certain. The world he re-creates in *Coming into the Country* is American in its landscape and characters, in its blend of romanticism and realism, in its

self-deprecatory humor and its occasional bursts of righteous indignation. It is a book that demonstrates deep respect for individuals of practical abilities and large dreams. In it McPhee has created a nonfiction
narrative that is literature, as large and complex as its subject, which is
nothing less than the American wilderness, and American dream, itself.

Notes

1. See Tom Wolfe, introduction to *The New Journalists,* ed. Tom Wolfe
(New York: Harper and Row, 1973), 3–36; and Norman Sims, introduction to
The Literary Journalists (New York: Ballantine Books, 1984), 3–25.

2. Barbara Lounsberry, *The Art of Fact: Contemporary Artists of Nonfiction*
(Westport, Conn.: Greenwood Press, 1990), xi.

3. William Howarth, introduction to *The John McPhee Reader* (New York:
Farrar, Straus & Giroux, 1976), vi.

4. Ronald Weber, *The Literature of Fact* (Athens: Ohio University Press,
1980), 36.

5. John Hellman, *Fables of Fact: The New Journalism as New Fiction* (Ur-
bana: University of Illinois Press, 1981), 1.

6. David Lodge, *The Novelist at the Crossroads* (Ithaca, N.Y.: Cornell University Press, 1971), 33.

7. Don Scheese, *Nature Writing: The Pastoral Impulse in America* (New
York: Twayne Publishers, 1996), 4.

8. Scheese, *Nature Writing,* 4–5.

9. Edward Hoagland, "Where Life Begins," *New York Times Book Review*
(27 November 1977): 48.

10. It is interesting to note that McPhee draws analogies between Alaska and
Scotland, his ancestral home, a half-dozen times in the course of *Coming into
the Country*—as if he were implying even more of a personal connection to the
landscape than his journeys over a two-year period would suggest.

11. Lounsberry, *The Art of Fact,* 81.

12. Philip Terrie, "River of Paradox: John McPhee's 'The Encircled River,'"
Western American Literature 23(1): 4.

13. See Terrie, "River of Paradox," 5–8.

14. Weber, *The Literature of Fact,* 119.

15. Lounsberry, *The Art of Fact,* 68–69.

Brian Turner

Giving Good Reasons

*Environmental Appeals in the Nonfiction
of John McPhee*

Within his substantial body of nonfiction, there is, I think, no single metaphor that better describes John McPhee's relationship with his readers and his subjects than does the title of his third collection of essays. "Giving Good Weight," the lead essay in the collection of the same name, is an account of greenmarkets in New York in the 1970s. As one of McPhee's subjects tells us, the markets were planned mainly as "'a natural answer to a twofold problem': loss of farmland in the metropolitan area and a lack of 'fresh, decent food' in the city," but it was hoped that, with the right attitude and a little luck, they would also "start conversations, help resuscitate neighborhoods, brighten the aesthetic of the troubled town" (34). It is characteristic of McPhee and crucial to our reading of the essay that the perspective we are given on the interaction between buyers and sellers is both McPhee's own and, to a large extent, that of his principal subjects. McPhee consistently takes the side of subjects, and in this case he has done so quite literally: as the essay opens, the author is standing on the greenmarketers' side of the table, selling vegetables, discovering firsthand how it feels to face the urban hordes, who "slit the tomatoes with [their] fingernails," "excavate the cheese" with their thumbs, "pulp the nectarines and rape the sweet corn" (3). In taking the greenmarketers' perspective, McPhee establishes an identification that has important consequences for our reading of the entire essay. They are good people, these greenmarketers—honest, hardworking, and committed to what they do—and McPhee's ethos benefits from his respectful and respected association with them.

The governing metaphor captures the essence of the piece and of McPhee's ethos in almost all of his nonfiction. "Giving Good Weight":

apart from its prominence as the title of the title essay, this phrase is used only three times, yet it reverberates throughout one's reading. Indeed, it galvanizes all the unspoken responses one has to the varied themes that play across the essay. To "give good weight" means, literally, to be generous when selling produce, to give three and a quarter pounds of tomatoes for the price of three. But it also means, not only metaphorically but actually, the fostering of human fellowship and trust—the forging of an almost palpable bond through an act of commercial generosity. When customers find out that a young teacher selling produce in the Harlem Greenmarket will soon return to school, "they bring him things," for "he has always given [them] a little more than good weight" (129). A similar thing might be said about all of the greenmarketers. What they offer the city is much more than fresh, healthful, inexpensive produce; they offer warmth and vitality and, above all, an infectious feeling of community. Moreover, a similar thing might be said about the author himself. Let me push the comparison to its limits: when we come to the text to sample McPhee's reportage, we find not only fresh and healthful produce, a clear and reliable exposition, but something considerably more. As the alliance established early in the essay is reiterated and reinforced at every turn, we come to see that McPhee, too, arouses one's sense of community. He is no more a mere conduit for the exchange of information than the greenmarketers are conduits for monetary exchange: his very choice of subjects, his way of viewing them, their responses to his interest—all these are bound up in our assessment of what he gives us. What he gives us is good weight. And by doing so he elicits assent to the values for which he stands.

McPhee and the Rhetoric of Assent

Most of McPhee's nonfiction appeals in the way "Giving Good Weight" does. Rather than a disinterested observer, McPhee is an active participant in the events he reports, one who earns the approval of subjects and readers by combining a sympathetic imagination with an uncompromising commitment to journalistic accuracy. This attention to both fact and value makes his rhetoric a remarkable example of what Wayne Booth has called the "rhetoric of assent."

The rhetoric of assent is Booth's answer to the fact-value split, his attempt to bridge the gap between "the adherents of reason or knowledge or science and the adherents of values or faith or feeling or wisdom or 'true knowledge' " (*Modern Dogma,* 14). In retrospect, it can also be seen to bridge the gap between modern and postmodern definitions of rhetoric. When Booth was writing *Modern Dogma and the Rhetoric of Assent* in the late 1960s, rhetoric was generally understood in modernist terms, as a means of "making the truth effective" (Scott, 10)—in the best case, of winning arguments; in the worst, of duping audiences. Since its sole aim and function appeared to be persuasion, rhetoric was commonly viewed with suspicion. But the work of rhetorical theorists such as Booth and Robert Scott, building on postmodern reassessments of truth, alerted us to another function: rhetoric as epistemic, as a "way of knowing." The new function does much to redeem the old. When truth is understood to be contextual and socially constructed (rather than certain and absolute), rhetoric becomes a means by which individuals and communities can discover and build knowledge consensually; and persuasion, practiced in the spirit of collaborative inquiry, can expedite the process of knowing. Indeed, once truth is seen as consensual and at best partial—when even the self is seen to be constructed through symbolic interaction with others, as Booth contends—we all gain by arguing our positions as well and as openly as possible.

Accordingly, a key idea of *Modern Dogma and the Rhetoric of Assent* is that we ought to cultivate an attitude of "assent" or "benign acceptance" (40) toward others in any rhetorical exchange in order to elicit the fullest response from other rhetors, see for a moment as they see, and thus "expand" our selves and communal knowledge. Such assent will encourage, among other things, a more nuanced interpretation of arguments and a reevaluation of ethical and emotional appeals. There are many good reasons for being persuaded by others; when we assess truth and falsehood by an either/or scale and remain forever wary of arguments from the heart, we often waste ideas of great value. "All the art," says Booth, "lies in assessing degrees of reliability" (*Modern Dogma,* 157).

It is not hard to see how congenial Booth's rhetorical theory is to McPhee's rhetorical practice. Even a brief sample of McPhee's nonfiction suggests a willingness to see from his subjects' points of view, as well as an inclination to laud subjects whose conduct seems founded on an attitude of assent rather than one of distrust. All the more surprising, then, that these aspects of the author's rhetoric have been neglected almost entirely. The accepted critical view has been that McPhee is a "fact writer whose stock in trade is information" (Roundy, 75) and "one of the finest practitioners of aesthetic nonfictional prose in the twentieth century" (Schuster, 604). As far as they go, these assessments are accurate. But we need to recognize that McPhee's writing is also value laden and has a suasive function.

In an analysis of *Coming into the Country*, Elizabeth Giddens has shed light on functions other than the expository in McPhee's work. She sees McPhee as a kind of facilitator, someone who (in addition to providing information) "attempts to develop relationships among the people he writes about, himself, and his readers" (383) and thus provides us with "insights into the workings of an epistemic-rhetoric process" (379). From this point of view, McPhee never tries to persuade us of anything. By aiming for "mutual understanding" rather than "conversion on particular issues" and by acknowledging "others' lives, values, and opinions, granting them significance equal that accorded [his] own" (397), he promotes "honest inquiry, debate, and attitude change" (380) and opens the possibility of "communally constructed meaning" (379). While I find myself in agreement with many of the details of Giddens's assessment, as well as with her claims for McPhee's rhetoric as epistemic, I also find her unnecessarily restrictive in claiming that this rhetoric functions *only* to inform and to demonstrate a process of open inquiry. It is true that McPhee is not someone so convinced of his rightness that he will doggedly seek "conversion on particular issues" or "push for the reader to agree," but I doubt that he wants the reader only to "choose his or her own stance" (Giddens, 394). He implicitly and explicitly recommends stances, as "Giving Good Weight" reveals on a small scale. Not at random did McPhee choose to write about greenmarketers; nor is it because of a whim that he is on their side of the table rather than the other. As readers familiar with the full range of his nonfiction know, the choice and the stance are common. McPhee consistently writes about and sympathizes with those who respect nature.

This special interest of McPhee's is the focus of this essay. I consider not only the author's explicit statements on nature and environmental issues but also the implicit environmental appeals in his essays. As will become clear, my reading of McPhee's rhetoric is not entirely at odds with Giddens's reading of *Coming into the Country*. Since an important aspect of his position on environmental issues is that we must learn to trust one another and keep dialogue open, McPhee's rhetoric is indeed strongly epistemic. However, whereas Giddens sees the fostering of "honest inquiry" and "communally constructed meaning" as preeminent —the aim, I might say, as well as the means of McPhee's rhetoric— I see his concern for the environment as equally important. McPhee's exemplary epistemic-rhetorical conduct is from this perspective only one among several "good reasons," or warrants, for our assent. When readers enter the complicated minefield of modern environmentalism, they need an expository guide who is not only open-minded but also informative, discerning, and reliable. In McPhee we have this. He is the sort of man who secures confidence and trust, who demonstrates, in Aristotle's words, "good sense, good moral character, and goodwill" (1378a)—in short, a good man; and, as Aristotle says, "We believe good men more fully and more readily than others" (1356a). Moreover, the "believing" that McPhee's sympathetic ethos elicits for his position on the environment is intensified by the effect of his epideictic portraits. In this sense his subjects give us another good reason for assent. When we see McPhee moving comfortably amid praiseworthy people—when we see these people responding to him in person much as we respond to him through the printed word—we find by a kind of ethical feedback loop (much like the one at work in "Giving Good Weight") confirmation of our intuitions about the man. It is no accident, moreover, that these epideictic subjects consistently (though not exclusively) take environmental stances very like the author's own.

McPhee on People, Nature, and Technology: Ethical Appeals for Social Ecology

Although his substantial body of nonfiction deals with diverse topics, in the course of his career McPhee has focused on two with remarkable frequency. One of these is people or, more precisely, people living through the joys and frustrations of their jobs, using their expertise, solving workaday problems—people "engaged in their thing, their activity," as he himself puts it (quoted in Vipond and Hunt, 207). The other topic is nature. In *Oranges, The Pine Barrens, Encounters with the Archdruid, The Survival of the Bark Canoe, Coming into the Country, Basin and Range, In Suspect Terrain, Rising from the Plains, The Control of Nature, Assembling California,* and a number of essays from *Pieces of the Frame, Giving Good Weight,* and *Table of Contents* McPhee reveals a deep curiosity about and love of nature.

This dual and, I would say, overlapping interest, in nature and in people, complicates McPhee's perspective on the natural world. Recognizing human needs as well as human foibles, he is not always and unequivocally on nature's side; rather, he moves in the penumbra between nature and human society, as much a student of how nature treats us, and we nature, as he is of nature in and of itself. As a result, he addresses (and, as we will see, sympathetically records) various sides of what we have come to think of simply as "environmental issues." His description of the environmental issues facing Alaska in the 1970s suggests the kind of topics he himself grapples with in his writing: "the tension of preservation versus development, of stasis versus economic productivity, of wilderness versus the drill and the bulldozer" (*Coming into the Country*, 79). One might say that McPhee (like David Love, the geologist whom he accompanies in *Rising from the Plains*) "carries within himself the whole spectrum of tensions that have accompanied the rise of the environmental movement" (*Plains*, 180).

As Ch. Perelman and L. Olbrechts-Tyteca have argued, to select a thing for attention is to demonstrate its "importance and pertinency" for the writer (116); presumably, its importance is even greater to a writer who selects it time and again. The frequency with which McPhee has written on nature says much about him and should in itself color the way we read any particular essay touching on environmental issues. Still, the more accurate index of his position is the kind rather than the amount of attention he devotes to the natural world. And McPhee's love of nature is almost palpable in his work. Whether he is gliding peacefully in a bark canoe with its maker, Henri Vaillancourt ("a rite of oneness with certain terrain . . . an act performed not because it is necessary but because there is value in the act itself"; *Bark Canoe*, 25), riding the river in a "wild-water race for eager hacks" (*Pieces*, 71), or hiking in Alaska ("I embrace this wild country"; *Coming into the Country*, 398), McPhee exhibits a kind of youthful exuberance in outdoor activities, a buoyant pleasure in and excitement about nature's offerings. As he says in *Coming into the Country*, "I . . . have liked places that are wild and been quickened all my days just by the sound of the word" (258).

McPhee is also well aware of how much nature has suffered at the hands of greedy or thoughtless people, indifferent to any interests but their own, and he knows that those of us who now enjoy material luxuries must alter our ways. Too often, Americans have listened to the siren call of "a handsome benefit-to-cost ratio" and found themselves stranded with unnecessary, even gratuitous, megaprojects such as the

Lake Dickey Dam, which provides a mere "soupçon" of electricity for the price of nature's beauty (*Good Weight*, 174–75). Too often, they have treated nature like a trash bin, dumping into it the unwanted remains of their bread and circuses: "tires, washing machines, refrigerators, mattresses, and automobiles into the Potomac and Anacostia Rivers" (*Pieces*, 255); "aerosol cans, plastic bottles, boat cushions, sheets of polyethylene, bricks, industrial scum, globs of asphalt, and a tattered yacht flag" into the Hudson (*Encounters*, 109); "two tons of trona . . . into the Green River every day merely from the washing of freight cars" (*Plains*, 195); "thirty-five million gallons of partially treated sewage and forty million gallons of raw sewage into [the Chattahoochee] every day" (*Pieces*, 52).

Criticism of this kind is not unusual in writing about the environment; indeed, we expect nothing less. Nor is McPhee's love of nature especially rare. Certainly, both his dissent and his assent will have strong appeal for like-minded nature-lovers; and if Booth is right, they ought to have at least some appeal for all reasonable people, because they demonstrate that the author has convictions and values what is universally assumed to be worthy of conviction. But explicit criticism of environmental abuse and implicit demonstrations of kinship with nature are unlikely, in and of themselves, to *convert* anyone or to coax the many who are unsure of precisely whom to believe or where to stand on environmental issues. What makes McPhee's criticism more persuasive is that it comes from a man who is not inclined to "stump for public causes" (Howarth, vii). In the context of a volatile public debate in which partisanship and personalities have figured prominently, and in which irrational claims about impending eco-catastrophes have been too often met by scientistic Panglossia, McPhee's ethos seems sane and balanced. His displeasure about our environmental foibles has always been offered *sotto voce*, and it has always been measured. His love of nature never overwhelms his respect for people.

Quoting McPhee's complaints about environmental abuse could easily lead to misrepresentation of his views. Committed to better stewardship of nature he may be, but he is determinedly not "an Environmentalist"—not, that is, one of the fanatical "friars" and "evangelists" (*Basin*, 124) whom the public still thinks of when hearing that word. McPhee is not always (or by temperament, it seems) opposed to the kinds of technology that environmentalists might be expected to condemn as a matter of course, and he is mindful of the complex interconnectedness among ostensibly opposite camps in the environmental wars. He reminds us that corporate projects disliked by environmentalists sometimes give them the opportunity to learn more about the environment (*Good Weight,* 84); that a river remains wild because a timber company owns the land surrounding it (*Good Weight,* 153); that well-intentioned conservationists spend so much time studying a virgin forest that "countless trees have been clearcut elsewhere" in order to print the results of their research ("In Virgin Forest," 23).

The dimensions of McPhee's stance are suggested by his use of the phrase "the control of nature," a phrase with something of a rhetorical history for environmentalists (as he no doubt knew when titling his 1989 collection of essays). From the perspective of America's most famous defender of nature, Rachel Carson, "the control of nature" was a phrase "conceived in arrogance, born of the Neanderthal age of biology and philosophy, when it was supposed that nature exists for the convenience of man" (quoted in Killingsworth and Palmer, 68). From McPhee's perspective, however, the phrase has "bilateral extensions" of meaning (*Control,* 69). Like the "rippling syllables" of the Atchafalaya River, it reminds McPhee not only of human misconduct but also of heroism in the face of natural disasters: "Atchafalaya. The word will now come to mind more or less in echo of any struggle against natural forces—heroic or venal, rash or well advised—when human beings conscript themselves to fight against the earth, to take what is not given, to rout the destroying enemy, to surround the base of Mt. Olympus demanding and expecting the surrender of the gods" (*Control,* 69).

The essays in *The Control of Nature* describe both the heroic and the venal. In "Atchafalaya," we see the venal: a "nation [that] could not afford nature" (6) using its army to wage war against a river: "We harnessed it, straightened it, regularized it, shackled it" (26), says the Army Corps of Engineers, with "a trapezoidal earth dam" (8), a weir, "rock jetties, articulated concrete mattress revetments, and other heavy defenses" (90). In "Cooling the Lava" and "Los Angeles against the Mountains," we see the heroic: people who "would rather defy nature than live without it" (236), but who defy it without waging war, doing in most cases only what they must to protect themselves against the natural dangers they face. Where McPhee's sympathies lie in these particular battles is clear. But if he would prefer to leave nature untouched, he is no fatalist. Unlike those who "oppose everything that comes along" (259)—as the Sierra Club does, according to one of McPhee's subjects—he believes that technology can and should be used. Sometimes it is nature that must be opposed.

The space between "everything" and "sometimes" is where most of us stand on environmental issues, and it is where McPhee makes his appeals. As he says of conservationists and land developers in *Coming into the Country,* only "extremists" are willing to "preserve every bit of the country," and only extremists would "exploit it all": "Everyone else has to think the matter through—choose a point of tolerance, however much the point might tend to one side" (410). Readers familiar with the entire range of McPhee's nonfiction will be aware that the author himself is among those who consistently think matters through rather than prejudging them. His point of tolerance is, as he himself acknowledges, "closer to the preserving side" (410) of environmental debates, but he also demonstrates the ability to distinguish among particular cases. It is this ability that separates him not only from those who would shackle nature but also from the "noisome ecomorphs" (*Control,* 20) who value nature above people. And it is this ability, as much as his open-mindedness, that gives us reason to assent to his rhetoric.

The appeal of McPhee's ethos carries beyond the boundaries of a single essay. Those of us who have charted his work and through it come to know him can see his open-mindedness and discerning tolerance written into the very structures of his nonfiction. I am pointing here to a kind of long-term, implicit ethical appeal, the appeal of particular acts whose meaning is altered when viewed as part of a pattern of behavior. There is, for example, a sense in which McPhee's handling of narrative point of view often has ethical appeal—provided we are aware of his stance in other works and "think of his character" before we read.[1] By sympathizing with various subjects, the author not only confirms that he is open-minded but also coaxes readers into seeing, at least temporarily, as he and his subjects see. He coaxes us, to use a phrase from Booth, into an attitude of "benign acceptance" (*Modern Dogma,* 40).

McPhee's handling of Richard Eckert in "The Atlantic Generating Station" provides an example. As the chief engineer for a proposed nuclear power plant that would float off the eastern coast of the United States—a megaproject that many would consider an environmental nightmare—Eckert makes an easy target. One might expect even McPhee to portray the man less than sympathetically, given the author's love of nature. Yet as he begins describing this project, McPhee seems determined to prevent readers from taking sides before we understand it (and the degree to which impending energy shortages—this is the 1970s, remember—make the project at the very least an option worth examining). Introducing us to Eckert in the opening paragraphs, he persuades the armchair environmentalist in each of us to see that the enemy has a human face. "[L]ean . . . amiable, slightly bald," Eckert is a boyish, mildly eccentric man whose first grand vision of the floating power station came to him almost inadvertently, as he mused early one morning, "wet, naked, and soapy in his shower" (*Good Weight,* 78–79). Details of this sort encourage us to see Eckert as the author himself does—as an unthreatening, even endearing figure. To supplement their effect, McPhee teases us with a comic caricature of an environmental nemesis: Eckert, he says, does "not by appearance in any way suggest the fearsome, two dimensional, fictive American businessman with reinforcing rods in his jaws, emerging from some dark, polluted labyrinth to hand out the wages of fear" (79). The effect of all this is to obviate stock responses. Indeed, after McPhee's descriptions, we are inclined to reject depersonalizing attacks on Eckert. That is when the author tells us this:

> In an anonymous way, [Eckert] would soon be the Antichrist to several hundred thousand people along the barrier beaches of the state [of New Jersey]. Yet he was one of them. And he had not invented the electric toothpick or the electric scalpel or the aluminum beer can or central air-conditioning or the six-thousand watt sauna, or any of the other hardware, large or small, vital or vulgar, that had helped to make a necessity of something that had not existed—not in commercial form—a century before. All those people on the beach had, in a sense, given Eckert his job. (*Good Weight,* 80)

For readers, there would be something almost shameful now in dismissing Eckert's project (and thus McPhee's essay) out of hand. To do so would be to succumb to crude caricatures of complex individuals and simplistic, self-righteous divisions between right and wrong. McPhee is not a mere "fact-writer" here, offering only exposition. He is also persuading us, encouraging us to listen to the approaching account of "The Atlantic Generating Station." If we recognize our complicity in environmental crimes and, rather than pointing fingers, open our minds to the possible benefits of all proposals, we may discover the best available solutions to our environmental problems. If we do not, if instead we reject this unique source of nuclear power before we have even understood what it is and how it might work, our judgment can hardly be considered reliable.

In matters environmental, McPhee consistently suggests that we must avoid extremism of any kind and carefully consider our options— *all* our options—before we act. In this sense, one could call his rhetoric epistemic because it fosters open-mindedness and cooperative inquiry. But his rhetoric is not only epistemic. McPhee is also, implicitly, recommending a position, inasmuch as his sympathetic treatment of Eckert and the floating power plant argues for serious consideration of technological solutions to our problems. To many environmentalists (by no means only those who "oppose everything") this position would be anathema. It does resemble the views of social ecologists, however. As Jimmie Killingsworth and Jacqueline Palmer explain in *Ecospeak: Rhetoric and Environmental Politics in America,* social ecologists may disagree in particulars, but they have in common the belief that technological solutions to environmental problems are possible, provided such solutions are "accompanied or preceded by free and broad access to special knowledge and relevant information as well as by deep psychological and social adjustments" (2). On the evidence of McPhee's writing, "deep" is perhaps too strong a word to describe the social and psychological adjustments he thinks necessary; however, his attempt to ensure that we attend to Eckert's project—and we must remember that he is recommending no more than this—can be seen from one perspective as an attempt to give readers precisely the kind of access referred to by Killingsworth and Palmer. This liberal, middle-ground position can be contrasted, on the one hand, with radical environmentalism (such as deep ecology), which advocates a "mystical communion with nature" (Killingsworth and Palmer, 17), and, on the other, with technocentrism, especially the version supported by traditional scientists. For technocentric traditionalists, good environmentalism is often "a matter of 'efficient environmental management,' of 'cleaning up' after the mess made by necessary modern industrial processes" rather than abandoning those processes (Pepper, 29–30).

In short, McPhee's social-ecological stance situates him precisely between the irrationalists and scientismists described in *Modern Dogma and the Rhetoric of Assent.*

McPhee's "Multiradial" Rhetoric

What I have described thus far is McPhee's social-ecological position on environmental issues and to some extent the ways in which he elicits assent as he states that position. I wish now to examine his most concentrated study of environmental issues, because it reveals most clearly the complex connections among various appeals in his nonfiction. In *Encounters with the Archdruid,* the author gives us few direct, explicit indications of his views; but his handling of his subjects, all of whom indicate clearly where they stand, implies a stance consistent with the position taken in the rest of his nonfiction. McPhee's even-handed treatment of all the major subjects shapes our response to both the author and the issues he addresses in *Encounters with the Archdruid;* in effect, it increases the amount of information we receive on complex environmental topics and at the same time increases our confidence that this information is reliable.

The "archdruid" of the title is Dave Brower, former executive director of the Sierra Club and "its preeminent fang" (*Encounters,* 11); he is, according to McPhee, "the most unrelenting" (87) of environmental evangelists, a man who appears to value trees above people. In what Booth calls the "meaningless logomachy between the adherents of reason" and "the adherents of values or faith or feeling" (*Modern Dogma,* 14), Brower is clearly on the latter side. He seems at times like a parody of Booth's "irrationalist." Says McPhee: "Brower feels things. He is suspicious of education and frankly distrustful of experts. He has no regard for training per se. His intuition seeks the nature of the man inside the knowledge" (87). As someone who values expert opinion and journalistic accuracy, McPhee is clearly disturbed by this attitude. "The force of nostalgia in Brower is such that it can in some instances bend logic" (29). Even worse is the effect of this attitude on the rhetorical climate within a community. When one believes, as Brower does, that "objectivity is the greatest threat to the United States today" (241), one will almost certainly (if inadvertently) begin to treat the audience, and facts, as means to an end. Thus when Brower needs statistics to support his arguments, his standards are less than exacting. "What matters is that they feel right" (86). And when inflated figures are insufficient, he will go even further:

> While Brower was executive director of the Sierra Club, the organization became famous for bold full-page newspaper ads designed to arouse the populace and written in a style that might be called Early Paul Revere. One such ad called attention to the Kennecott Copper Corporation's ambitions in the Glacier Peak Wilderness under the

heading "AN OPEN PIT, BIG ENOUGH TO BE SEEN FROM THE MOON." The fact that this was not true did not slow up Brower or the Sierra Club. In the war strategy of the conservation movement, exaggeration is a standard weapon and is used consciously on broad fronts. (*Encounters,* 37)

As Booth has argued, in what sounds uncannily like a description of Brower, "the prophet and activist who feels strongly that certain values and purposes ought to prevail in the world can have only one rhetorical purpose: to win" (*Modern Dogma,* 77). But winning is a difficult thing to measure. "Conservationists have to win again and again and again" (*Encounters,* 85), says Brower himself. Short-term gains made by questionable practices may not advance one's cause over the long haul, however worthy that cause may be. In Brower's case, exaggeration eventually led to the removal of tax-deductible status for contributions to the Sierra Club (37). And it seems likely (though McPhee does not make the point) that such exaggeration also intensified public suspicion of the environmental movement at a time when public support would have meant a great deal.

Encounters with the Archdruid can teach us much about McPhee's position concerning matters of rhetoric and persuasion because its main character is not just an environmentalist but one of his generation's most single-minded, uncompromising spokespersons for environmentalist causes. Brower's extremism helps us situate McPhee. And clearly, he positions himself far from Brower. Indeed, McPhee is as critical of Brower as he is of any of the major subjects in his nonfiction. This does not indicate an anti-environmentalist stance. We know from passages such as those I quoted earlier that McPhee advocates more cautious, considered use of nature; and, if so inclined, anyone familiar with the terrain could find in his work many additional signs of his love of the natural world. McPhee's treatment of Brower indicates, rather, the author's rhetorical stance: what distresses him more than Brower's romantic reverence for nature is Brower's way of pursuing his cause.

In contrast to Brower's one-sided approach to environmentalism, McPhee gives voice to a plurality of perspectives in the book—not the least of which is the perspective of those who value Brower. The chairman of the President's Council on Environmental Quality "[t]hank[s] God for Dave Brower," because "somebody has to be a little extreme" (*Encounters,* 87). Stewart Udall considers Brower "the most effective single person on the cutting edge of conservation in this country" (5). And McPhee himself suggests that Brower is a complex figure, at times endearing, and his behavior not always "simple to predict" (138). In short, McPhee does not counteract Brower's extremism by treating him as an environmental bogeyman. He tries instead to be even-handed, showing us several sides of Brower and letting us draw our own conclusions.

McPhee also gives us other yardsticks by which to assess the archdruid (as well as environmental issues generally) in the person of the major characters in *Encounters with the Archdruid,* each of whom he treats in similar even-handed fashion. As the U.S. commissioner of reclamation and sometime advocate of dams, Floyd E. Dominy could easily be depicted as a government aide to developers and an archenemy of conservationists; and indeed, with the kinds of telling descriptive details that enrich so much of his work, McPhee seems at times to toy with the idea of painting such a portrait: "His belt buckle is silver and could not be covered over with a playing card. He wears a string tie that is secured with a piece of petrified dinosaur bone. On his head is a white Stetson" (153). But on the whole, after McPhee recounts the commissioner's personal history and shows him in conversation with the archdruid, Dominy emerges as a substantial voice, flawed but neither fool nor ecological bad guy, his views as worthy of consideration as Brower's. The same could be said of another figure in the book, Charles Park, geologist and mineral engineer; he may be optimistic, even naïve, in arguing that "[t]he future can take care of itself" (74), but he is also "more aware of the natural world" than anyone McPhee has met (67). Like Brower, Park and Dominy are not ideological cardboard cutouts but complex individuals whose views warrant "degrees of belief and assent" (*Modern Dogma,* xiii).

By containing David Brower's extremism within a broader, more pluralistic view of environmental issues, *Encounters with the Archdruid* not only clarifies McPhee's position on such issues but also argues for it. His even-handedness is, in effect, a "good reason" for assenting to his position; one does not feel as though he has a hidden agenda, an ecological axe to grind. This appeal is, on one level, ethical in a very traditional sense; it has much to do with the author's "goodwill" toward his various audiences—with his ability to empathize and thus to gain his subjects' as well as his readers' confidence. But something more complicated is happening as well. The fact that McPhee remains open to angles and avenues on which Brower has turned his back, thereby taking into account additional details relevant to environmental problems, effectively improves both his ethos and the substance of his implicit arguments. Not only, we say of McPhee, is this someone who is even-handed; it is someone whose pluralistic perspective gives us more variables with which to assess environmental issues. He is persuasive and/because he is informative; he is informative and/because he is open-minded. Thus it is that McPhee's "multiradial vision" (Howarth, xii) and his pluralistic or dialogical presentation of this vision give us reasons to assent to his position on environmental issues.

Epideictic Appeals in McPhee's Nonfiction

The persuasiveness of McPhee's ethos is strengthened significantly by his use of epideictic appeals. I use the term "epideictic" in much the same way as Perelman, to signify a nonagonistic, laudatory mode of discourse that increases "adherence to the values it lauds" (Perelman and Olbrechts-Tyteca, 50). Epideictic discourse has traditionally been defined as discourse that can blame as well as praise; one can say that a negative example also functions epideictically, presumably to increase aversion to values endorsed by the "blamed" subject. More often, however, the term is reserved for positive models, and it is in this sense that McPhee's rhetoric is frequently epideictic. A rhetor practicing such laudatory discourse is "very close to being an educator" (Perelman and Olbrechts-Tyteca, 52), even though he or she does not advance a thesis or argue explicitly; for as Aristotle says, "To praise a man is akin to recommending a course of action" (1357).

Usually those whom McPhee praises are people of relatively modest accomplishments. A few, such as Bill Bradley and Arthur Ashe, have attained a degree of fame through their achievements, but even these are unassuming figures: though he is "what college students nowadays call a superstar" (*A Sense of Where You Are*, 12), basketball player Bradley nonetheless "dislikes flamboyance, and . . . has apparently never made a move merely to attract attention" (20). (In this regard, he is much like McPhee.) When McPhee's subjects see themselves as larger than life, they usually do so at some cost. They may, for instance, sacrifice their connection with the human community: Brower "is somewhat inconvenienced by the fact that he is a human being, fated, like everyone else, to use the resources of the earth, to help pollute its air, to jam its population" (*Encounters*, 86). Or they may be somehow diminished as a person, becoming, as William Howarth has said of tennis player Clark Graebner, "wholly predictable, doomed to lose because he is not flexible in a changing situation" (xxi). What is important to McPhee is engagement with life and work; and it is this quality, along with a degree of humility, that his more endearing characters share. They are fully attentive to the details of their work, seemingly indefatigable. And their humility leads them to respect not only the complexities of their chosen pursuits but also other people who feel a similar commitment. It should not be surprising that this sounds like a description of McPhee himself; for as Aristotle says, "The ways in which to make [our hearers] trust the goodness of other people are also the ways in which to make them trust our own" (1366a).

Tom Cabot, one of the author's companions on a canoeing trip in Maine, provides us with a good example of how these traits operate in conjunction with positions on the environment that are much like McPhee's own. A man of considerable academic, personal, and professional experience—"qualified to be at least a dozen kinds of snob" (*Good Weight*, 164)—Cabot will nonetheless "walk and talk with anybody" (163); and in "The Keel of Lake Dickey," McPhee quickly and consistently makes us like him. As is often the case, we are first warmed by his physical description: "trim and athletic," toting a rucksack that "must be fifty years old," Cabot is "statistically . . . old and decrepit" but "looks sixty and acts forty" (162). Later, it is Cabot's kindness and sense of humor that win us over. After two paddlers are rescued by McPhee's party of four, one of them, apparently unaware that he was (as we learn from McPhee) clinging to the wrong side of his capsized canoe and that "the river could have kept him," responds to his rescue with "fury, frustration, disappointment—like an athlete who has had his big chance and blown it" (172). Cabot, "more seasoned by far" (142) than even his own experienced companions, might easily take offense at this ungrateful reaction from a somewhat foolhardy novice; but instead he displays a marvelous sensitivity to the needs of others, and camaraderie prevails:

> The other paddler is short and thin, and is shaking deeply from cold. He minimizes it, tries to be nonchalant, but does not seem disappointed to be standing on the bank. His T-shirt is dark grey, and above the left breast are small black letters—"YALE."
>
> Tom Cabot questions him about the shirt, asking if it means that he's a student there.

"Yes. I'm there now."

"And how far along are you?"

"I'm '78."

Over Tom's face comes a small-world smile, and he says, "How about that! I'm seventy-eight, too." (*Good Weight*, 172–73)

This good man, learned, experienced, and sympathetic, also has his opinions on environmental issues; and though McPhee does not play them up, they clearly carry weight in the context of the essay, in which the struggle between preservation and development provides a signifi- cant theme. It is no coincidence that these opinions are close to the au- thor's own: "He knows both sides of the wilderness argument, and he is not *always* with nature in its debate with man" (*Good Weight*, 169; my emphasis). Though his principal concern may be to portray Cabot accu- rately, McPhee also benefits rhetorically from his companion's status as exemplary character.

Many of the most sympathetic subjects in McPhee's nonfiction per- form a similar function. Primarily, they are his expository tour guides as he informs us about the complexities of plate tectonics, or the arcana of foraging, or the Sisyphean frustrations of controlling the Atchafalaya River; but they are also moral guides of a sort, implicitly appealing to us to take an involved yet balanced approach to environmental issues. Among other things, this balance involves the kind of knowledge that can be derived only from a "hands-on" familiarity with nature, as well as the ability to see both sides of the environmental debate. As the geolo- gist David Love says, "Reality is not something you capture on a black- board" (*Plains*, 147). This is why Love—"a frequent public lecturer who turns over every honorarium he receives to organizations like the Teton Science School and High Country News, whose charter is to un- derstand the environment in order to defend it" (180)—stays close to the land ("To compete with Dave, you'd have to do a lot of walking"; 144); and why he is "not always predictable" in his stance on debates be- tween environmentalists and scientists or commercial interests: "It isn't all or nothing," he says. "It doesn't have to be" (*Plains*, 202). This is why Ed Gelvin—"admirably unassuming" (284) and "self-reliant be- yond the usual reach of the term" (*Coming into the Country*, 410), a man who remains in Alaska because "a sense of the place registered higher with [him] than a sense of accumulating wealth" (281)—is puz- zled by an article on Alaskan wolves published by the Friends of the

Earth: "I couldn't believe the misconceptions. Some of the things it said were outright lies. . . . People like the Friends of the Earth and the Sierra Club have the idea that we want to kill all the wolves up here. We like wolves. They're a part of everything else" (296).

Love and Gelvin as well as others whom McPhee clearly likes and encourages us to like, such as Anita Harris (*In Suspect Terrain*), Carol ("Travels in Georgia"), Fred Brown (*The Pine Barrens*), Charles Fryling, and Charles Park (*The Control of Nature*), are not "cocktail environmentalist[s], self-appointed" (*Good Weight*, 108). From firsthand experience, they know nature well, can distinguish among and name its progeny. Fred Brown, for instance, has "a name for almost every rise and dip in the land" (*Pine Barrens*, 21). Fryling is the same: "If you ask him something, he knows. It's green hawthorn. It's deciduous holly. It's water privet. It's water elm" (*Control*, 68). In contrast, Dave Brower can "identify butterflies in flight" (27) but collects rocks "for their beauty alone": "In most cases, he did not know what these rocks were, nor did he appear to care" (*Encounters*, 54–55). McPhee's opinion seems to be that "knowing" means being able to name (perhaps an inevitable position for a writer whose main task is exposition). Moreover, the ability to name is a sign not only of the extent of one's knowledge but of the kind of knowledge one has. Without it, one is like the people with Ph.D.'s of whom Anita Harris complains (*In Suspect Terrain*, 122) or like the anthropologist in "Firewood," who is "the president of Pure Planet, a conservation organization so much above the fruited plain that it did no conservation work of its own but existed solely to encourage other conservation organizations" (*Pieces*, 210)—he can recognize neither a chainsaw nor a pickup truck, and he is in "no hurry to find out" (198) about either. In McPhee's scheme of things, participation and engagement shape knowledge; without them, one's interpretation of problems will be severely skewed.

I want to make it clear that the epideictic functioning of McPhee's nonfiction subjects does not replace or diminish his concern for journalistic accuracy. As Howarth has argued, McPhee "replicates [his subjects] for our judgment as fully as he can" (xxii). If the characters who people McPhee's books move us in the direction of his own attitudes, it is not because the author has dressed each of them up as he wishes and strategically deployed them, like so many toy soldiers, just where his nonfiction requires. Rather, it is because McPhee seems genuinely to like most of them. This attitude enables him to bring out their most endearing qualities—qualities that are likely to reduce faction while at the same time leading to reform in our treatment of the environment. One of the very best reasons we have for assenting to McPhee is that he appears to live by Immanuel Kant's categorical imperative: always treat people as ends in themselves, never as a means only.[2]

Concluding Remarks: Doubts, Degrees of Assent, Consequences, and "Transcendent Values"

This essay has argued that the rhetoric of John McPhee has a suasive function as well as expository and epistemic functions. If we take into account the extent of his writing on nature and examine his explicit statements on environmental issues, his epideictic portraits of subjects who sympathize with his perspective on such issues, and his balanced treatment of diverse views, we can conclude that McPhee recommends a moderate pro-environmental stance, one that resembles that of social ecologists. Drawing on Booth's theory of the "rhetoric of assent," I have also argued that McPhee coaxes us toward taking a similar stance by giving us "good reasons" to assent to what he says.

Obviously, not all the reasons that strike me as warrants for assenting to McPhee will appeal to everyone, especially in the context of such a divisive topic as the environment. My discussion of *Encounters with the Archdruid* identifies at least one audience that is unlikely to be persuaded by McPhee's rhetoric: those who believe that the earth is already in such extreme danger that immediate substantive changes in our conduct are required to preserve it. In this audience we might include David Brower and the "deep ecologists." From their perspective, McPhee's tolerance and even-handedness may seem less like good reasons for assent than attitudes that preserve the status quo in the face of unique and gravely underestimated problems. McPhee has in fact been criticized for being "too cautious" in his treatment of environmental issues (Singular, 50; Hamilton, 54). And from this perspective, his use of epideictic discourse is particularly vulnerable. As Perelman and Ol-brecht-Tyteca have observed, there is "an optimistic, a lenient tendency in epideictic discourse"; it is "practised by those who, in a society, defend the traditional and accepted values . . . not the new and revolutionary values which stir up controversy and polemics" (51). McPhee may, then, preserve the status quo even though he desires change, for "one can protect an interest merely by using terms not incisive enough to criticize it properly" (Burke, 36).

Such doubts about the effect of a rhetoric and an ethos are inevitable. As *Modern Dogma and the Rhetoric of Assent* teaches us, no rhetoric, especially when dealing with complex, value-laden issues such as the environment, can elicit universal or unconditional assent; nor should we expect it to. Rather than asking whether McPhee's reasons prove "true according to abstract methods" (*Modern Dogma*, xii) or can withstand the test of "systematic doubt" (*Modern Dogma,* xvii), we ought to assess them by other criteria. I can, for example, ask myself whether my perceptions of McPhee's ethos are (to paraphrase Booth) "communally validated" by others (146). Elizabeth Giddens, whose reading of McPhee's *Coming into the Country* was considered at the beginning of this essay, provides validation of a kind; for even though her reading disagrees with mine to the extent that she sees in it no suasive dimension, she, too, speaks of McPhee's tolerance, concern for factual accuracy, and willingness to promote "honest inquiry." I can also find a kind of validation in the responses of McPhee's own subjects; as a writer for *Sierra* tells us (Hamilton, 53), even subjects whose portraits were anything but adulatory—such as Theodore Taylor (the physicist in *The Curve of Binding Energy*), David Love, and David Brower—remember McPhee fondly. In addition to finding some degree of communal validation for my assent to McPhee, I can compare his rhetoric to the alternatives. I certainly don't have to rely on his account of Brower to do this; other environmentalist rhetorics are, like McPhee's, there for my analysis.

Finally, we can, as Walter Fisher recommends we do of any rhetoric, ask ourselves two crucial questions about McPhee's rhetoric of assent. First is "the question of consequence": if I adhere to the values implicit in McPhee's nonfiction, what will the effects be—for my concept of myself, for my behavior, for my "relationships with others and society," and for "the process of rhetorical transaction" (Fisher, 379)? Second is "the question of transcendent issue": Are the values implicit in McPhee's nonfiction "those that [in my estimation] constitute the ideal basis of human conduct" (380)? The questions are connected, and our attempt to answer both will be part of the process of comparing McPhee's rhetoric to other rhetorics concerned with environmental issues. If one is firmly convinced that the earth is in grave danger, requiring immediate action, and that the preservation of its health is the ideal basis of human conduct, then one may believe that an agonistic model of rhetorical transaction is appropriate and that whatever persuades people to alter environmentally abusive conduct is right—including the "ecosabotage" practiced by groups like Earth First! I myself prefer McPhee's point of view, especially given that many environmental "facts" are still "warm"—that is, still open to debate (Killingsworth and Palmer, 136). (Were they not, "the environment" would not be an issue.) If everything is connected to everything else, as the deep ecologists like to say, and if we still know too little to assess the condition of the environment precisely, then the best kind of environmentalism seems to me one that involves everybody, working together, sharing information. This is what McPhee implicitly recommends, and it is what his ethos suggests that he implicitly practices. Others might argue militantly for political and personal action; McPhee quietly encourages a cooperative pluralism, in the hope that trust may lead to reform.

Acknowledgments

This essay is a slightly revised version of an article that appeared in *Rhetoric Review* (Fall 1994). I wish again to thank Stuart Brown, Chris Bullock, and Jimmie Killingsworth for their advice on that version of the paper as well as the Social Sciences and Humanities Council of Canada for its generous financial support during my doctoral work.

Notes

1. The phrase is from Aristotle (*Rhetorica*, 1356a), who rules out the rhetorical connection I have made between conduct and act: ethical appeals "should be achieved by what the speaker says, not by what people think of his character before he speaks." For a less restrictive definition of ethos, see Booth, *The Company We Keep*, 8.

2. Asked in a radio interview whether he worries about his subjects' feelings, McPhee responded, "All the time. The first thing I want to do is sketch people as well as I can in their milieu, and the last thing I want to do is to be unfair to them or hurt them" (Gzowski).

Works Cited

Aristotle. *Rhetorica*. Trans. Rhys Roberts. New York: Modern Library, 1954.

Booth, Wayne C. *The Company We Keep: An Ethics of Fiction*. Berkeley: University of California Press, 1988.

———. *Modern Dogma and the Rhetoric of Assent*. Chicago: University of Chicago Press, 1974.

Burke, Kenneth. *A Rhetoric of Motives*. Berkeley: University of California Press, 1962.

Fisher, Walter. "Toward a Logic of Good Reasons." *Quarterly Journal of Speech* 64 (1978): 376–84.

Giddens, Elizabeth. "An Epistemic Case Study: Identification and Attitude Change in John McPhee's *Coming into the Country*." *Rhetoric Review* 2 (1993): 378–99.

Gzowski, Peter. Radio interview with John McPhee. CBC, 17 and 18 December 1990.

Hamilton, Joan. "An Encounter with John McPhee." *Sierra* (May–June 1990): 50–55, 92, 96.

Howarth, William. "Introduction." In *The John McPhee Reader*, vii–xxiii. New York: Farrar, Straus & Giroux, 1965.

Killingsworth, Jimmie, and Jacqueline Palmer. *Ecospeak: Rhetoric and Environmental Politics in America*. Carbondale: Southern Illinois University Press, 1992.

McPhee, John. *Basin and Range*. New York: Farrar, Straus & Giroux, 1981.

———. *Coming into the Country*. New York: Bantam, 1979 (1st ed. New York: Farrar, Straus & Giroux, 1977).

———. *The Control of Nature*. New York: Farrar, Straus & Giroux, 1989.

———. *The Curve of Binding Energy*. New York: Farrar, Straus & Giroux, 1974.

———. *Encounters with the Archdruid*. New York: Farrar, Straus & Giroux, 1971.

———. *Giving Good Weight*. New York: Farrar, Straus & Giroux, 1979.

———. *In Suspect Terrain*. New York: Farrar, Straus & Giroux, 1983.

———. "In Virgin Forest." *New Yorker* (6 July 1987): 21–23.

———. *Pieces of the Frame*. New York: Farrar, Straus & Giroux, 1975.

———. *The Pine Barrens*. New York: Farrar, Straus & Giroux, 1968.

———. *Rising from the Plains*. New York: Farrar, Straus & Giroux, 1986.

———. *A Sense of Where You Are: A Profile of William Warren Bradley*. New York: Farrar, Straus & Giroux, 1965.

———. *The Survival of the Bark Canoe*. New York: Farrar, Straus & Giroux, 1975.

———. *Table of Contents*. New York: Farrar, Straus & Giroux, 1985.

Pepper, David. *The Roots of Modern Environmentalism*. London: Croom Helm, 1984.

Perelman, Ch., and L. Olbrechts-Tyteca. *The New Rhetoric: A Treatise on Argumentation*. Trans. John Wilkinson and Purcell Weaver. Notre Dame, Ind.: University of Notre Dame Press, 1969.

Roundy, Jack. "Crafting Fact: Formal Devices in the Prose of John McPhee." In *Literary Nonfiction: Theory, Criticism, Pedagogy*, ed. Chris Anderson, 70–92. Carbondale: Southern Illinois University Press, 1989.

Schuster, Charles L. "Mikhail Bakhtin as Rhetorical Theorist." *College English* 47 (1985): 594–607.

Scott, Robert L. "On Viewing Rhetoric as Epistemic." *Central States Speech Journal* 18 (1967): 9–16.

Singular, Stephen. "Talk with John McPhee." *New York Times Book Review* (27 November 1977): 1, 50–51.

Vipond, Douglas, and Russell A. Hunt. "The Strange Case of the Queen-Post Truss: John McPhee on Writing and Reading." *College Composition and Communication* 42 (1991): 200–210.

Theodore C. Humphrey

"In a Lifetime of Descending Rivers"

The Art and Argument of John McPhee's "River Essays"

John McPhee has spent "a lifetime descending rivers" ("The Encircled River," 73), the rivers great and small of North America, from youthful summers in north woods camps to communing with the shad anglers of the white hair and AARP set. To account for the rabid opposition of conservationists to dams, he wrote, in "The River" chapter of *Encounters with the Archdruid,* that "rivers are the ultimate metaphors of existence" (159). I think that statement also accounts for McPhee's having written so often and so well of his experiences with rivers for over thirty years. He has written in prose so compelling that his urban readers surely have no trouble imagining their armchairs as canoes or kayaks, or, perhaps, the grumble of urban traffic as distant rapids or the growl of Yukon ice breaking up. He has profiled a sampling of the nation's rivers from east to west, including the Cemocheckobee, the Ochlockonee, and the Chattooga in the southeast. He has taken his readers on the Chattahoochee that flows wild into Atlanta but leaves the city seriously polluted; the Colorado, the Salmon, the Kobuk, and the Yukon in the west; the mighty Mississippi and its heir-apparent, the Atchafalaya, in the Louisiana delta; and the Connecticut and the Delaware in the east, where serious shad anglers await the cry, "They're in the river."

As diverse as his venues are, McPhee's essays on America's rivers are all of a piece and represent an important and compelling aspect of his total artistic achievement because they evoke the uniqueness, beauty, and power of these rivers in rich, entertaining, concrete styles. Furthermore, these essays are not merely travelogues, accounts of an individual's encounters with wilderness with little purpose but to entertain. Instead, they present complex arguments about large and contentious issues: politics and the environment, government and the individual, wilderness and its value to society and its cultures, conservation and ecology as functioning social and political principles, and, ultimately, the critical importance of rivers to the health of American society and its many cultures.

The state of the "natural" world in which McPhee has placed himself is nowhere, not even in Alaska, a "pristine" wilderness. In every instance it is an environment with which human beings have interacted and one that humans have affected. Whether deliberately or accidentally, our species has shaped our natural world, as have other species. Aware of the law of unintended consequences, McPhee often comments on the irony of humanity's attempts to "control" nature not only in his collections of essays *The Control of Nature* (1989) and *Irons in the Fire* (1997) but also in *Annals of the Former World* (1998) and in his *New Yorker* pieces published in 2000 on shad fishing on the Connecticut and Delaware Rivers. While an academic and a prolific and well-respected journalist, he is not an author of "scholarly" monographs. Hence his assumptions about nature, wilderness, and the environment are those of a brilliant individual with a powerful curiosity and a clear and engaging prose style. He is aware of ecological debates; indeed, he staged and reported a now-famous debate between David Brower and Floyd Dominy in which many of the principal environmental issues of our time were illuminated. Oddly, some contemporary environmental scholars such as William Cronon have ignored his work. Susan Kollin in her book *Nature's State: Imagining Alaska as the Last Frontier,* however, at least acknowledges McPhee's effort to "recast depictions of Alaska as a Last Frontier, a place somehow set off and removed from the rest of the United States and the world. Restoring a critique of the political economy of nature writing to discussions of Alaska, McPhee . . . resist[s] writing the region entirely within mainstream landscape convention. . . . [to] challenge and critique the ways nature writers have historically imagined Alaska" (25).

Kollin's critique of "ecocriticism" supports McPhee's "immersion" of himself not as the measure of the particular piece of environment that he is experiencing and on which he is reporting, but as a cultural worker who shapes by his report the public perception of the environment and the debates raging about its worth, preservation, use, and destruction, all stemming from humankind's physical and cultural place within it. Whether deliberately or accidentally, our species (like other species) has shaped our "natural" world and constructed intellectual, emotional, and physical frames around it. We live in the present (mostly) and the short-term past and future. As the wider debates over the definition of concepts such as "wilderness," "conservation," "preservation," "environment," "ecology," and the "exploitation of natural resources" indicate, our efforts to understand our relationship to the physical world have resulted in widely differing social and cultural constructions of "nature" over time. Studying McPhee's principal "river essays" ("A River," "The Encircled River," "Travels in Georgia," "Atchafalaya," and his two recent "shad" essays—"A Selective Advantage" and "They're in the River"—that profile the Delaware and the Connecticut Rivers) reveals his contribution to the debate through his ability to evoke a convincing sense of the uniqueness of a particular river and make clear the basis of his love and passion for each of these rivers.

A major characteristic of the writing in all of these essays and a key to his gaining a large and devoted readership may well be McPhee's ability to bring the reader along on the trip with a strong narrative, accurate and compelling description drawn from keen observation, and a concrete style, all in the service of significant arguments. These essays (which all originally appeared in the *New Yorker*), while entertaining their urban and urbane audiences, always educate us about our stewardship—for good or ill—of America's rivers. They capture the issues that have been and continue to be at the heart of American ecological and political debates at state and federal levels. They make their arguments in part by vividly profiling individual men and women who, while representing various sides of these ongoing debates, remain indelibly their unique selves—whether lock masters or canoe makers, master shad fishermen or biologists, frontier men and women at home on the wild Yukon, ardent conservationists, or dam builders with a drive rooted profoundly in childhood experiences to tame and improve "wild" and "worthless" streams. McPhee's success as a nature writer develops too from how he frames and informs his arguments with his personal experiences of the rivers in question, his authority deriving in large measure from his "going into the territory" himself, immersing himself in the waters and in the lives of the animals and humans who live because the rivers do.

In "A River" (1971), McPhee alternates images of the Colorado River's power, its stunning beauty, and the repose of its surroundings with the give and take of the famous debate between David Brower, the "archdruid" of wilderness and the conservation movement in his capacity as the first executive director of the Sierra Club, and Floyd Dominy, the United States commissioner of reclamation from 1959 to 1969.

Direct head-to-head opponents in the battle over the building of the Glen Canyon Dam and other dams in the arid West, Dominy and Brower emerge from McPhee's prose as passionate, likeable men, each operating out of a principled belief in the correctness and utility of what he does for humankind. (Brower died in November 2000; Dominy, nearing ninety when this essay was written, lives on a farm in Virginia.) McPhee arranged for the two adversaries to debate while on a raft running the Colorado down the Grand Canyon.

McPhee contextualizes the debate by vividly describing the community on the raft and some of the major features they negotiate: the Deubendorff rapids as "a prairie of white water" (181), the Kanab Rapid and its "standing waves six feet high, lots of splash" (225), and the Upset Rapid as "an agglomeration of snapping jaws—the leaping peaks of white water" (229). In contrast to these images of the raw and dangerous power of the river, he writes lyrical passages such as one describing how he and Brower dive into the water of Havasu Canyon and behold a labyrinth with a crystal stream beyond which lay

> a world that humbled the mind's eye. . . . first . . . a cascaded gorge and then . . . the ovate sides of a deep valley, into which the stream rose in tiers of pools and waterfalls. Some . . . were only two feet high, others four feet, six feet. There were hundreds of them. . . . The stream was loaded with calcium, and this was the physical explanation of the great beauty of Havasu Canyon, for it was the travertine—crystalline calcium carbonate—that had both fashioned and secured the all but unending stairway of falls and pools. (235–37)

Here is precisely accurate, sinuous, poetic description, driven with powerful active energy. Such a passage celebrates the "natural" river.

Later in the narrative McPhee contrasts this active beauty of the "managed" river with a grim picture of a Havasu Canyon destroyed beneath hundreds of feet of still water if more of Dominy's dams planned for the Grand Canyon were built. McPhee draws readers into the river—and the debate—and invites them to sort out the conflicting claims as presented by these two vigorous advocates, made very attractive and sympathetic by McPhee's even-handed and respectful profiling of the lives and characters of the two men. Two images sum up, I think, the complexities of the "big dam debate" as presented by McPhee. In the first, Dominy is riding the raft into the teeth of a fearsome rapid while

Brower, who was the first man to climb thirty-three peaks in the Sierra Nevada and had climbed all the Sierra peaks higher than fourteen thousand feet, walks around it. In the second scene, Brower and Dominy are both on the raft as it plunges into Lava Falls, the most dangerous of all the rapids. With these two scenes McPhee invites us to contemplate the intractability of extreme positions and posits the wisdom of the middle course, of respecting each powerful man and respecting his position.

Both narrative and description are emblematic of the entire debate between conservationists and reclamationists. McPhee structures the debate and his readers' responses to it by narrating the run down this living river—ironically made possible by the water released from the Glen Canyon Dam, which Brower had ardently opposed while Dominy had fiercely supported it—through rapids that challenge the strength and knowledge as well as the courage and fortitude of the rafters and past geological treasures that would be destroyed or at least hidden and degraded if further dams were built. Yet "[b]eneath the pink and green limestones are green-gray shales and dark-brown sandstones—Bright Angel Shale, Tapeats Sandstone—that formed under fathoms that held the first general abundance of marine life" (204). In this paragraph as in others offered from an omniscient point of view, the voice of the human mind at work is authoritative—observing, analyzing, and understanding this amazing environment, the river's having "worked its way down into the stillness of original time" (204). Brower suggests that it would be sacrilege to dam the river and stop the "hallowed process" of its cutting the canyon deeper into even earlier time. Dominy rides the boat with bravado and courage, his cigar a lighted beacon glowing through the clashing rapids, even though he "couldn't swim across a goldfish pond" (206); Brower makes his ride in fear seasoned with knowledge and respect. But as the first ascender of many of the highest peaks in the United States, usually alone, he is clearly no coward.

McPhee contrasts the positions taken by Dominy and Brower not only with the contents of their daily debates but also emblematically by presenting both as strong, courageous, admirable men. Setting the two debating aboard the raft running down the Colorado, he reveals in a number of ways (by the ambiguity of the responses of the others on the boat to their debate, for example) the intractability of the issues at hand. McPhee points out that while the uncertainty of the witnesses to the debates might "seem surprising among people who would be attracted, in the first place, to going down this river on a raft, . . . nearly all of them live in communities whose power and water come from the Colorado" (220). Putting the human face on the debate reveals the complexity of "big damn issues." Floyd Dominy, the United States commissioner of reclamation, argues that reclamation is "the father of putting water to work for man—irrigation, hydropower, flood control, recreation." David Brower, the first executive secretary of the Sierra Club, founder of the John Muir Institute for Environmental Studies and Friends of the Earth, and a most ardent conservationist, argues the necessity of preserving wilderness and wildness for less tangible, perhaps, but no less significant reasons.

Coming into the Country (1977), McPhee's most popular book, is about land-use issues in Alaska. Nearly a hundred years of increasingly destructive exploitation have given rise to intense efforts to set aside sections of Alaska in one form or another to preserve significant portions as wilderness. McPhee here explores the fierce debates about further exploitation and preservation and makes the case for preservation of the wilderness by presenting his firsthand experience with several of the major rivers of the state, including the Yukon, the Kobuk, and one of the several Salmon Rivers. In its first paragraph, I count fourteen instances of the first-person personal pronoun. Three-quarters of the paragraph is devoted to a full and joyful catalog of McPhee's immediate sensory participation in the landscape while canoeing down one of the Salmon Rivers—recording how the cold water feels on his head, how his head aches, how the water running down his T-shirt feels pleasurable, how the light reflecting from the water breaks into his eyes, the physical movements of casting his line into the river, his paddle (and his writer's pen) thrusting and guiding his craft. At the end of the trip, he will physically enter the water, swimming and washing in it much as he did years before in the Colorado River in *Encounters with the Archdruid,* suggesting once again a purification ritual by which one may achieve a sacramental relationship with the world.

Before McPhee eases into a discussion of wilderness issues, he sets the hook in his readers and holds us fast with a strong narrative line of his trip down this pristine river. The narrative rips through river water filled with Arctic grayling and salmon and runs between banks covered with tracks of the barren-ground grizzly, moose, and wolf. The river is clearly part of a much larger context, which he celebrates by recording his close and unexpected encounter (while on a long walk near the Salmon) with a large, barren-ground grizzly grazing on blueberries, with his hump vibrating slowly as he engulfs whole plants. In a later unexpected—and close—encounter with a young grizzly playing "lariat salmon" with his latest catch, slinging it around his head, McPhee skillfully positions his audience to respond as he does to the encounter with the barren-ground grizzly, investing both with emblematic significance. We are convinced to do so, I think, because McPhee has earned the right to reflect on the significance of this bear. He writes that coming upon this bear less than a hundred paces ahead of him "stirred me like nothing else the country could contain. . . . What mattered was not so much the bear himself as what the bear implied. . . . He implied a world. . . . This was his country, clearly enough. To be there was to be incorporated . . . into its substance—his country, and if you wanted to visit it you had better knock" (62–72). The narrative of his trip down the Salmon with overnight camping on gravel bars, fishing for dinner, cooking while being very careful not to get the smell of food and fish on one's clothes, and talking and reflecting thus provides a structure that McPhee uses often in his writing. As usual, the narrative structure provides the context for other structures, argumentative and affective—an account of his emotional and intellectual responses to the physical river itself and to the country and its wild inhabitants on either side of the stream, all in the service of his overall argument.

That argument is announced at both beginning and end of the "Encircled River" chapter with a metaphorical action. McPhee dips his rolled bandanna into the waters of the Salmon River and places it around his head—an action representing his physical and intellectual immersion into the water of the Salmon and, by extension, into the debate about designating the Salmon as a wild and scenic river and, by further extension, about preserving not only this watershed but that of other rivers in Alaska as national monuments, preserves, and parks. It is a clever and effective image because, as he points out, the water of the Salmon, captured in the rolled bandanna and placed against the temples, "is a refrigerant and relieving" (5). These natural and subtle images suggest the capacity of wilderness to preserve and heal the nation as a whole and argue for this greater value. McPhee enters the territory of this proposed wilderness area in the company of a state-federal team of experts whose task it is to evaluate the Salmon River and its drainage for preservation (the area became the Kobuk Valley National Park). The title of this chapter, "The Encircled River," is another metaphor related to the encircling bandanna. It means, I suggest, the nature of wilderness, the river as metonym for wilderness, encircled, surrounded by civilization and thus without a safe retreat, under siege and requiring help to understand it and to preserve it.

McPhee develops this argument in a number of ways; perhaps the most interesting involves his blending of images of exploration with images of himself as an explorer who witnesses the telling qualities of the river and its larger contexts. He establishes in the responses of his witness a set of tensions that structure the argument of *Coming into the Country* at every turn along the narrative that provides the sturdy backbone of the book. For instance, in recounting some of the difficulties of traveling down this particular Salmon River, he writes that he "would prefer to walk in water so clear it seemed to be polished rather than to ride like a rocket down a stream in flood. For all of that, another two inches would have helped the day" (74). He is clearly the explorer working his way into the country, into a literal position within the kayak from which he can best experience the myriad elements of the river—the cost in physical pain to the explorer, the qualities of the water at various stages from high flood when it is full of silt and debris to its present low state, too shallow to manage the draft of even a kayak but presenting compensating aesthetic qualities in being "so clear it seemed to be polished . . ." (74). There is a strong suggestion that this kind of wilderness must be earned, and in the earning of it by physical exertion and even pain lies a great deal of its reward. Still, the laconic "another two inches would have helped the day" suggests that humans are, ironically perhaps, too demanding creatures who still fancy themselves "the measure of all things" despite their best efforts to go "into the country" on its own terms. This idea echoes the irony in "A River" that the very run down the Colorado River is itself made possible by regulated releases of stored water from the Glen Canyon Dam.

Another anecdote in McPhee's account emblematically supports his argument for preservation. As he and his companions float and walk down the Salmon, they come upon yet another bear—a young one who has never before seen anything like these three small craft and their passengers; and the outcome is as tension-filled and uncertain as any plotted fiction could hope to create. This scene symbolizes, of course, the fundamental conflict between the desire to maintain the wilderness in an Edenic condition and the desire to exploit the more obvious natural resources of energy and gold at the expense of the more subtle resources of unexploited wilderness. It encapsulates the force and fear of "first contact" between native and intruder and foretells the probable consequences of such encounters if preservation is not achieved. McPhee argues by his choice of detail and metaphor, as well as by the ethical appeals enacted in the rhetorical stance of his persona and his behaviors on the trip, that the wilderness—the river as it races downhill, the bears on the hillside above the Salmon and all they imply—must be preserved.

Book III of *Coming into the Country* celebrates the people and the country alongside the upper Yukon, the state's "eastern interior." It also reveals that the Yukon is quite a different sort of river from the smaller Salmon. During the winter and the summer, it functions as an east-west highway through the middle of the state—solid enough during the long winter and useful as a swiftly moving liquid road in the summer, but treacherous during the "transition" periods.

At Eagle, on Alaska's eastern border, the Yukon is fifteen hundred feet wide from bank to bank. When "breakup" comes in the spring, the river becomes

> like an ore in motion on a giant belt moving toward the Bering Sea. . . . during its times of transition it becomes almost unapproachably inimical. Great floes coming on from upriver roll, heave, compile; sound and surface like whales. Many hundreds of millions of tons of ice, riding a water discharge of two hundred thousand cubic feet per second, go by Eagle at a speed approaching ten miles an hour. . . . The river's edges are lined with ice that is stationary—"shelf ice," "shore ice" . . . is four feet thick but will break apart under a stamping foot. . . . [O]nly a step or two away is the riverborne ice, big masses pounding into one another with a sound like faraway thunder, or, often, like faraway surf. These are muted sounds. For all its weight and speed, the ice moves softly much of the time, fizzing like ginger ale. (200–201)

This passage demonstrates McPhee's mastery of technical language and the rhythms that will best carry evocative and convincing description with the powerful narrative of the river's awakening after a long winter. "The ice comes segmentally from upriver and from the tributary rivers. . . . four hundred miles long. . . . With the ice comes wood. . . . many millions of cords of forest debris. . . . sleepers [logs riding just below the surface]. . . . and preachers [logs with their root structures riding low, bowing and dipping]," providing firewood and building materials to the people at Eagle and the Yupik Eskimos of the western coast (201–2). At all times, the Yukon is a river that requires knowledge, strength, and skill to navigate—and at breakup, not a little luck to navigate in any kind of vessel and stay alive. As the principal river of Alaska and one that must be reckoned with by any plans to exploit natural resources such as oil along the North Slope, its qualities and its traditional contributions to Native American cultures require respect and understanding.

As McPhee describes it, the Yukon is "a big river in a big wilderness" (214), and his profile of it does it justice in part because he lived in a cabin in Eagle for a time, observing the inhabitants and absorbing the river and wilderness culture. The result is a superbly detailed and richly textured account that will not fail to move some of its readers to contemplate the long move north for a "life beyond community, a cabin somewhere up a faraway stream, an existence financed . . . with furs . . . [or] with gold" (216). For other readers the tale is a cautionary one, because life along the Yukon, especially during the bitterly cold winters, is clearly not for everyone. One needs Yukon River water in one's veins to be happy there. McPhee records and summarizes the wonderful talk that takes place at the "river people's equinoctial gathering" (259) as the talk "curved through its long ellipses[,] . . . turned and returned, as always, to the Yukon, to every gravel bar, rock, rip, eddy, and bend—free or under ice" (260).

The Yukon River is central to the culture of the people who make their living along its length; one tends to talk about what is important in one's life and in making a living. At one point McPhee joins Brad Snow in his nineteen-foot Grumman freighter for a 160-mile trip from Eagle to Circle down the Yukon: "six and more fathoms of water, sometimes a mile wide, moving at seven knots. . . . The surface was deceptively calm—it was only when you looked to the side that you saw how fast you were flying" (277–78). Then he describes the sounds the Yukon River makes during this June flow: "the steady sound of sandpaper, of sliding stones, of rain on a metal roof—the sound of the rock in the river, put there by alpine glaciers. Dip a cupful of water and the powdered rock settled quickly to the bottom. At the height of the melting season, something near two hundred tons of solid material will flow past a given point on the riverbank in one minute" (278).

The wild beauty of the country as viewed from the river "resembled Lake Maggiore and might have been the Hardanger Fjord, but it was just a fragment of this river, an emphatic implication of all the two thousand miles, and of the dozens of tributaries that in themselves were major rivers—proof and reminder that with its rampart bluffs and circumvallate mountains it was not only a great river of the far northwestern continent but a river of preëminence among the rivers of the world" (279). A few pages later we find this idyllic passage: "We drifted down the Yukon through a windless afternoon. The fast-flowing water was placid and—with its ring boils—resembled antique glass. Down one long straightaway, framed in white mountains, we saw ten full miles to the wall of the coming bend" (290).

As in each of his river essays, McPhee is very much a part of the scenes in this chapter as an intelligent participant observer. His is a recording, sorting, and evaluating intelligence through whose lens we become conscious of the conflicting cultural constructions of and claims made on its rivers by America's modern and postmodern civilization. Its large and restless population puts rivers to a myriad of uses from the aesthetic to the mundane. Rivers work hard. Rivers provide water supplies for household use, manufacturing, and agriculture and yet serve as well as receptacles for the country's sewage. Rivers transport the production of farms, mines, and manufacturing industries and provide sites for enormous hydroelectric plants. Yet they also serve the people's aesthetic and psychological needs by providing venues for recreation and restoration, for contact with the wild and wilderness. These claims are always complex and often conflict. The implications of cultural and political decisions (both historical and contemporary) about river "control" and "management" reveal the daunting consequences of humankind's efforts to "control" nature, in part because of the enormous complexity of their unintended and unforeseen consequences as well as their successes.

"Travels in Georgia" (1975) presents additional social issues, including urban pollution and wildlife preservation. McPhee travels with Carol Ruckdeschel, Georgia Natural Areas Council biologist, and her council associate, Sam Candler, as they work their way south through Georgia on a number of streams and rivers. They are doing "important conservancy work" by identifying "mini"-areas of natural beauty and ecological significance and getting their owners to register them for preservation. The essay contains brief sketches of the Tallulah River in the north of Georgia (the river of James Dickey's novel *Deliverance* and the movie) and of the Chattahoochee, on which they travel in the company of then-governor Jimmy Carter, who pilots one of two canoes. The essay makes a serious argument in favor of preservation by setting aside small, least damaged riparian areas in Georgia, a state settled by Europeans and Africans over four hundred years earlier and subjected to intense agriculture for most of those years and to industry for at least a hundred.

While this essay is on the whole more notable for its portrait of Carol Ruckdeschel than of the rivers of Georgia, it contains some memorable scenes of rivers, including an unnamed stream being "reamed." An expert dragline operator, Chap Causey, is "channelizing" the stream to "anticipate and eliminate floods, to drain swamps, to increase cropland, to channel water toward freshly created reservoirs serving and attracting new industries and new housing developments" (*John McPhee Reader*, 274). McPhee's account of Causey's work is flat, without overt emotion; but again structure and the juxtaposition of details reveal his strategy of presenting alternate views of complex issues. Just before he details the purpose of "channelization" or "reaming a river," he sketches behind Causey's dragline "a free-flowing natural stream, descending toward the Ogeechee in bends and eddies, riffles and deeps—in appearance somewhere between a trout stream and a bass river" (274). The contrast between its natural appearance (and its natural function as home for trout or bass) and the "new" uses to which the "reamed stream" will be put is clearly representative of the conflict between nature and urban civilization, between the natural world and the world of commerce, a recurring theme in McPhee's "river essays."

A few years later, McPhee finds himself on another river, the "Mighty Mississippi," the "Father of Waters," but this time he is not in a kayak or a canoe. Instead he is a guest aboard the *Mississippi*, "a certain red-trimmed cream-hulled vessel" that carries Maj. Gen. Thomas Sands, the president of the Mississippi River Commission, "down its eponymous river" on his annual inspection. In this way, McPhee "immerses" himself in the history of the Mississippi River, human struggles to live along it, and the consequences of that struggle. He personifies the river and the history of its "desires" over the last three thousand years to get to the Gulf of Mexico as fast as it can. In doing so, it "built" most of Louisiana with enormous loads of mud and silt, chiefly from the vast drainages of the uplifting and degrading Rocky Mountains, changing its main channel roughly every thousand years to sweep its upstream gifts in building arcs across its delta or spreading its deposits here and there through openings along the sides of the main channel.

But as European settlement progressed, settlers began to build up a levee system, causing the sediments to be shot farther and farther downstream into the abyssal plain of the Gulf of Mexico. As a consequence, "the whole deltic plain, a superhimalaya upside down, is . . . subsiding" ("Atchafalaya," 57) "out of sight" (63) and is not being replenished, leaving the channel of the river incongruously higher than the country through which it travels. McPhee writes that erosion of the coastal marshes has cost Louisiana a million acres in a hundred years, a very fast (in contrast to geological time) alteration of the environment. Thus "the river goes through New Orleans like an elevated highway" (61), with the city now unnervingly below the level of the river. Furthermore, ever since the Atchafalaya captured the Red River in the 1950s, this former tributary has been seducing the Mississippi's present channel into shifting itself to the southwest. The Mississippi's inclination has been to say "Yes!" and shift westward; if (or when) the Atchafalaya's courtship is successful, the Mississippi will become a tributary of the Atchafalaya, and its waters will flow by a steeper gradient and shorter route to the Gulf. However, as McPhee laconically puts it, "in the interval since the last shift Europeans had settled beside the river, a nation had developed, and the nation could not afford nature. . . . Nature, in this place, had become an enemy of the state" ("Atchafalaya," 6–7).

McPhee's historical survey in "Atchafalaya" of the efforts since the eighteenth century to control the Mississippi's flows and floods suggests that humankind's hubris is alive and well. Although the river itself had built "natural" two- or three-foot levees along the riverbanks, humans have built on this model of nature by adding ever-increasing heights to the levees until they currently reach over thirty feet in many places. The battle to control the Mississippi River has been joined since before the Civil War principally by the United States Army Corps of Engineers because virtually the entire economy of the United States depends on maintaining the Mississippi down its 300-mile-long "traditional" route through Baton Rouge and New Orleans. Even though shorter by over a hundred miles, the western route of the Atchafalaya will not win the battle without a fight; too much has been invested over the last 200 years by the European settlers—including the settlement of New Orleans—to allow the upstart river to capture the Mississippi. Therefore, the U.S. Army Corps of Engineers has been seeking to control the Mississippi River and force it to be true to its present course by constructing a series of dams, shipping locks, and other control structures to protect shipping and property. This mission is arguably a losing battle against the forces of the Mississippi and the increasingly insistent claims of its rival and, some think, heir-apparent, the Atchafalaya—and one that has had and continues to have unforeseen consequences.

McPhee identifies and characterizes the warriors along the front line and their weapons of choice. He draws upon the elements of narration, argument and structural framing, description, scene, detail, dialogue, and, as usual, the voice of an "intimate" and well-informed observer of the struggle. McPhee seeks to make clear just how powerful an adversary the forces of water flow and gravity are to business as usual along the length of the Mississippi River and its tributaries but acknowledges the awesome ambition—some would call it arrogance, others heroism— of the Army Corps of Engineers to save the heart of U.S. manufacturing and commerce, which it calls the American Ruhr. The Army Corps of Engineers has always seen its mission in terms of defending the country's vital interests by building structures wherever needed, "doing battle" at whatever cost.

McPhee contextualizes his story with a historical survey of the river and European settlement along its banks and the ultimately futile efforts to control its rampages by constructing ever higher and more elaborate levees. Even adding more and more "control structures" (huge devices to manage the outflow of enormous floodwaters) is, as McPhee says, attacking "Antaeus without quite knowing who he was" (43). Perspective counts for much. Thus it is difficult to imagine the volume of water concentrated at the Old River Control structure just a few miles north of Baton Rouge. The drainage of the Mississippi is so huge that the volume of water would have at times, as McPhee memorably puts it, caused Noah to send for ship's carpenters. But even they would be dwarfed by the immensity of the river—its size, its sounds, its velocities.

McPhee as always introduces a number of important "on the ground" or "in the water" characters who are on the front lines of efforts by the state to make these two mighty rivers do what national and local economic and political interests dictate. He characterizes them skillfully through dialogue and description of their appearance and working habits and contexts, capturing the essence of the man or woman by the telling detail—a gesture of hand or speech, a physical prop. McPhee puts human faces on the forces in play. Norris F. Rabalais and LeRoy Dugas are both seasoned workers, "two Cajuns" at ground zero in the "battle of the Mississippi." Rabalais works for the U.S. Army

Corps of Engineers as the lockmaster at Old River Control, the navigation lock that "drops" ships out of the Mississippi and into the Atchafalaya, and worked as a construction inspector during the building of the navigation lock at Old River, part of the effort to keep the river a servant rather than a threatening hydraulic enemy of the state. LeRoy Dugas has worked at Old River Control since 1963 and managed the ten-pier bridge or "sill, or weir" ("Atchafalaya," 11) put on line in 1963 to control the outflow from the Mississippi to the Atchafalaya. McPhee alternates brief, striking portraits of Rabalais and Dugas with crisp descriptions of the engineering devices, with their construction—and their failure—woven into the overall analysis. (He also establishes his own quality as an "honorary" Cajun when Rabalais calls McPhee a "coonass" —slang for Cajun—because his bandanna for the day is red.)

In 1973 the control structure failed under the relentless battering of the Mississippi, which hammered the structure with barely imaginable forces. Ten years after the Corps of Engineers had built the "control" structures at Old River and "put them on line"—in McPhee's words— "a slab of water six stories high, spread to the ends of perspective," assaulted the Old River Control structure. This structure weighed two hundred thousand tons yet vibrated under this attack like a flimsy shack when a fully loaded freight train thunders by. "Nowhere were velocities [of the flow] greater than . . . where the waters made their hydraulic jump, plunging . . . into the regime of the Atchafalaya" (28). McPhee's verbs and nouns, his metaphors for the water, and his similes for the everyday power of the river combine to make his point. Other authorities such as Oliver Houck (a law professor at Tulane), Sherwood Gagliano (an independent costal geologist and regional planner), Raphael Kazman (emeritus professor of hydrological engineering), and Thomas Sands of the Corps of Engineers provide information and commentary for all sides of the debate over controlling the river.

McPhee's *New Yorker* essays about shad fishing in the Delaware and in the Connecticut (published in 2000) provide excellent recent examples of his techniques and their effects. In "A Selective Advantage," he gives the reader a feast of information about the characteristic behaviors of shad (*Alosa sapidissima*) through the expert testimony of Boyd Kynard (research behaviorist at the S. O. Conte Anadromous Fish Research Center in Turners Falls, Massachusetts) as well as a detailed sketch of Kynard himself. A fishing trip that McPhee and Kynard take one day in South Hadley, Massachusetts, gives the essay its narrative line, onto which McPhee grafts a body of scientific and ecological detail about shad and oral narratives about encounters with the fish and with those who fish for them. Submitting a shad's scale to the laboratory for scientific analysis reveals a great deal about the age, gender, and "secret" life of the fish as it moves from its birthplace as high in the chosen watershed as its parents' genetic superiority has made possible, down to the ocean and, years later, back up the river of its genesis.

In pursuit of the shad, McPhee is chest deep in the river, casting his darts shoulder to shoulder with other anglers who just happen to be experts on the behavior of this species, and neck deep in facts and stories about the fish. Validating their reports and discoveries with his own enthusiasm for this beautiful animal, McPhee again baptizes his audience by immersing himself and them into the river and repeating the sacred words of the experts' scientific wisdom.

McPhee's analysis of the life habits of shad and of his kayaking on the Salmon River stand as metaphors for his methods of research and writing. They provide both the substance of his reports and the validation for their content and quality, yielding the all-important ethical appeal that Aristotle avers is central to the success of any argument. Through his creation of a particular narrative persona as well as the substance of his report, cast in luminous prose, McPhee has created a body of work that will long endure. His task as a writer is to convince his reader of the truth of his work. A large measure of McPhee's genius and success as a writer is how he meets this challenge by identifying in often unexpected yet completely apt ways with his subject without appearing to be narrowly partisan, doctrinaire, or strident. His first response seems to be to create a narrative persona that wins assent and respect, establishing, in Aristotelian terms, his ethical appeal so that he is trusted and respected as a truthful reporter.

Perhaps the best autobiographical report about McPhee's "writerly persona" occurs metaphorically in his description of how shad move upriver, apparently in response to first light—"an optimal time, when muscles are rested" ("Selective Advantage," 72). He remarks that their actions remind him "of what I do all day (nothing). I sharpen imaginary pencils and look out real windows. The light of a computer screen seems far too bright to me. I kill hours, hoping for distraction, and complain bitterly when distraction occurs. Three, four, five P.M. Nothing whatever accomplished. The day coiling like a spring. Nothing is worse than a lost day. Panic rises, takes over, and I write until I go home at seven, thinking like a shad" (74). The unexpected comparison not only delights but suggests a fond yet insightful immersion in his subject. It is not every writer who would identify not only with the shad's behavioral response to light but also with its feelings. His implied metaphor is that he is driven to write just as the shad is driven to get upstream to spawn and, motivated by "light," moves in fits and furious starts.

This quality of McPhee's writing habits, while certainly not unique to him, is worth noting because in his hands it is a powerful technique. Why is it so powerful? I think it is a central quality of his writing, whether his subject is basketball players gone to politics, the effects of plate tectonics, bears feeding in the Alaskan tundra, or the rivers of his world. McPhee is of the species *Homo scribblerus,* his behavior like that of *Alosa sapidissima,* the shad. At the heart of his art is his abiding curiosity about the world, a kind of instinctual drive to fulfill his destiny by going "into the country"; and his total command of the resources of language—his poet's ability to create the apt image with a pleasing economy of words—enables him to describe his rivers' appearances and behaviors, their contexts and contents, their history as well as their effects on humanity and wildlife. Also, because each work advances his larger "writerly" purposes to make complex and subtle arguments, the intensity of attention to a river as river varies from book to book, essay to essay. Analysis of the specific techniques of his art in four of his major "river essays" reveals how they change with his purpose and arguments yet meet the challenges inherent in different subjects to yield works that not only are eminently readable but also are enduring creative nonfiction.

Two of McPhee's signal gifts to his readers create the solid foundations of his essays. The first is his exhaustive research, characterized by scholars of creative nonfiction as "total immersion." Numerous trips to relevant sites, hundreds of spiral-bound note card packs, and months if not years spent in the field garner a huge body of facts—observations, experiences, character notes, conversations, descriptions, colors, and technical data. McPhee's second gift is his capacity for doggedly thinking and rethinking his voluminous materials, organizing and reorganizing them into a form that suggests an organic and inevitable enactment of his central idea. Once his argument presents itself, demands admission, and throws out red herrings and false scents, McPhee is ready to write.

But without the wealth of facts, the researched and experienced detail, there would be no apt images or "hot" words to reveal such arcane matters as rates of flow, the forces that give rivers their mystery and their life. McPhee traces their origins and suggests their nature thereby; he wants his readers to know about the life that exists not only in the water itself but along its edges; as with his geological essays, his human experts help him make serious sense out of the raw data that his perceptions and research bring in. He wants to show how human beings use and regard rivers and how their lives affect the rivers.

McPhee always amplifies his extraordinary personal experiences, acquired in a lifetime of descending rivers, with the testimony of experts profiled in such detail that the figures of Carol Ruckdeschel, Bob Fedeler, Floyd Dominy, David Brower, Norris F. Rabalais, LeRoy Dugas, and Boyd Kynard become part of his—and our—experience of the rivers. As a consequence his prose engages the reader on multiple fronts in multiple ways. McPhee's mind as revealed in his writing is a wondrous piece of intellectual Velcro that sticks to his subject and consequently to his reader. Each of his works is based on solid research and an inexhaustible capacity for creating beautiful and persuasive structures for essays that are in part the narrative of human struggles with nature, in part a description of awesome natural forces, and in part a homily on human pride. By narrating in detail his personal experiences of the rivers, McPhee helps his readers understand the tensions between preservationists and exploiters, between dam builders and free-river advocates, between channelization and a natural riparian environment for free-flowing streams and rivers. He puts human faces on these issues by profiling the men and women on both sides of the argument, including those whose positions one thinks are not McPhee's, a strategy that acknowledges the enormous complexity and competing claims of environmental debates.

The phrase "immersion journalism" accurately describes much of McPhee's research strategy: intense research over time, visiting and revisiting his informants in their "native habitats." It also takes on a kind of literal application in McPhee's "river essays" since he actually immerses himself in the waters of nearly every one of his subject rivers and spends much time on the waters in crafts ranging from kayaks and canoes to river towboats. He always goes "into the country" and thus into his subject deeply, returning time and time again to gather the facts. But the most critical and significant dimension of McPhee's immersion is intellectual, as he interviews, observes, and converses with a company of experts and authorities, gathering testimony, facts, and anecdotes.

Near the beginning of the Dominy-Brower section of *Encounters with the Archdruid,* entitled "The River," appears a striking metaphor that describes the platform on which the debate takes place and thus suggests how it is to be understood. The raft they are on is made of two neophrene bananas connected to a rubber barge, giving it "both lateral and longitudinal flexibility. . . . The raft is informal and extremely plastic. Its lack of rigidity makes it safe" (204). This metaphor surely suggests McPhee's own position, one of flexibility and openness yet designed to ensure survivability and endurance; but his technique is to expound with metaphor and arrangement, not with overt argument. By having both Brower and Dominy spend part of each day arguing their respective positions, he allows the readers to draw their own conclusions—or so it may seem.

One may see his technique at work in the passage in which he juxtaposes against this description of the river raft—the means by which thousands of people can with reasonable safety float the river—a dense paragraph describing the rock through which the Colorado now slices. "Isolation wilderness . . . rims . . . a mile above us and, in places, twelve miles apart. All the flat shelves of color beneath them return the eye by steps to the earliest beginnings of the world—from the high white limestones and maroon Hermit Shales of Permian time to the red sandstones that formed when the first reptiles lived and the vermilion cliffs that stood contemporary with the earliest trees" (204). The paragraph continues in a masterful description (by color and quality of the rock) of the entire geological history of the canyon. McPhee sets the geological history and the natural beauty of such a rare piece of the country against the utility of impounded water put to various social uses. He presents the stakes imagistically and structurally in this debate between preservation and reclamation and does not simplify them.

In his "lifetime of descending rivers" and writing about them, McPhee has demonstrated how he investigates, masters, and reports on his subject, always putting himself literally and immediately into the scene, becoming deeply informed if not, indeed, an adept. The very title of *Coming into the Country* reveals how he practices "immersion journalism": he enters the country (and the water), immerses himself in it, taking "psychological" possession of it by the fact of his physical experience of it. While this method is certainly not unique to McPhee (Thoreau famously does the same thing in the passage in *Walden* where he describes what he has taken for himself in his walk across a neighboring farm), he thereby authenticates the effect of the descriptions and narrations that comprise his "true report." He celebrates his subject in powerful and convincing and seemingly artless prose. Elsewhere I have described McPhee's "travel writing" as essentially spiritual, as gracing the landscape with his "authenticating eye" ("John McPhee's Spiritual Journeys"). It is, I think, difficult to overstate the rhetorical effect of this method. The persuasive power of the personal experience is hard to beat because it constitutes a first-rate and compelling ethical appeal. When McPhee's language and images are wrought entirely from his firsthand experience with the river, we are persuaded by the inescapable authenticity of his report that his conclusions are just and true.

McPhee's authorial persona is an attractive, wryly ironic man, sufficiently self-deprecating to avoid egotism yet wise enough to be a good companion on any excursion. He is at home in the outdoors, a keenly observant and well-informed member of the party, but one who seeks to learn what the others know rather than to lecture them on the subject. McPhee is a strong observer of the region upon whom—to judge from the depth of his reports—little is lost, a perceptive and credible reporter of the facts not only about the environment but also about human participation in it. McPhee reveals this persona in a series of scenes— one, for example, that shows him getting awkwardly into a kayak, breaking a toe in the process (74) but continuing the trip, and another in which he wryly confesses himself to be "an advanced, thousand-deaths coward with oakleaf clusters" (92) who imagines all the catastrophic possibilities for any situation. Over the period of the trip McPhee develops this character more fully. He is no whiner. He gets on with it. He shoulders his load. He figures out how to pack his kayak to carry all his stuff. He paddles with skill and competence. He takes humorous solace in a certain remedy (distilled in Kentucky) for "snakebite" above the Arctic Circle. Still, he confesses to a "mild nervousness" after hearing a campfire story about the unfortunate writer who pitched his tent unthinkingly on a bear trail; all that was found of him the next morning was a pencil.

The details of McPhee's reportage and of his emotional and intellectual responses to the encounter make the scene fully realized and convincing. The depth of his report convinces us of the honesty and the truth of what he writes. Given a "choice between hiking and peeling potatoes," he says he "would peel the potatoes" (52–53) because his is an active imagination full of "what-if." We readers are close enough to the bear—and to McPhee's shoes—to believe every word. McPhee has made a deft rhetorical stroke. He is no braggart, no blow-hard. We trust him now as one whose vision of the country and the river and its surroundings we may safely adopt because he has so solidly situated the ethical appeal in the detailed narrative of the encounter and its effect on him and his companions. This is no small achievement: in nearly incalculable ways it advances his argument that to preserve the wilderness is indeed to preserve our humanity.

Other elements of McPhee's craft (including, quite significantly, illustration) contribute to his argument. For instance, he presents a wealth of details about the Salmon River, a "riff" on its qualities as a natural stream, including the significance of the tracks of animals along the river and their part of the total picture. He details the history of human efforts to "control" the Mississippi and the Atchafalaya. McPhee records contrasting views of the rivers at hand: one preserved as a national wild river, another a wild stream drowned as a lake. He reports conflicting opinions about the best uses and nature of the Colorado. The structures, the wealth of vivid detail, the clarity of each narrative, the dialogue, the scenes of his actions in each river, and the contextualizing particulars of proposals to keep a river wild or to tame it combine to make a single but complex argument: wilderness must be set aside and preserved from exploration. But human pride—the hubris that is both humankind's glory and its curse—and greed create a powerful cultural tension that McPhee explores in his work. The question at hand is: "What should be the fate of all this and all these waters?" And he leaves his readers with no doubt about the correct answer.

McPhee's contribution to the larger environmental debate is essentially his testimony about some of the ways in which humanity creates, alters, destroys, or "controls" our physical environment. He teaches us to understand something of that process but even more, to revel in our natural world, celebrating our romantic capacity for awe and joy as well as benefiting and sometimes suffering from our capacity to make and wield tools. McPhee's writing reveals that any attempt to "control nature"—no matter how useful—is temporary, as is our stay as a species. (*Annals of the Former World* provides a useful antidote to hubris.) Two images from his "river essays" perhaps may serve to sum up McPhee's contributions to the literature of humanity's relationship to the physical world: McPhee's encounter with the barren-ground grizzly bear and its implied vision of "a whole land, with an animal in it" ("The Encircled River," 71); and Floyd Dominy and David Brower riding together down the "wild" Colorado River on water stored behind Glen Canyon Dam and released in controlled stages to allow such a trip and much else besides.

To buttress his complicated and balanced arguments, McPhee has always added appeals to authority, bringing the testimony of experts to bear on the issues. Over the course of his career his perspective has always been multiple, complex: at once appreciative and analytical, sensory and scientific. This, I think, is the essential quality of McPhee's mind, of his approach to any subject of his gaze. We see that quality, for instance, in his magnum opus, *Annals of the Former World,* in which he travels across the United States in the company of different geologists to learn the details and significance of each area's geology and its contributions to the economic well-being of its residents.

McPhee typically embeds subtle but powerful metaphors within personal anecdotes to extend the range and force of his arguments. He establishes himself as a proxy for his readers, engaging in his wilderness adventures not as an expert but as one of us traveling in the company of experts. As "one of us," he receives instructions throughout the trip. Like us, he often hears what he is told, but he is not always able to execute the lessons perfectly. In "The Encircled River," to cite but one example, he narrates the beginning of his trip down the Salmon. It includes instructions on getting into his kayak, some awkward efforts, pain, humility, but, finally, movement down the stream and into a rich encounter with Alaskan wilderness. Despite the instructions, he flops backward into the kayak, almost rolling it over; but, he writes, because of low water levels "the day would hold, if nothing else, practice in getting in and getting out of a kayak. . . . The problem of getting in was . . . complicated by generally doing so in the middle of rapids. In the first such situation, I lost all coordination, lurched backward on the boat, nearly sat in the river, and snapped a toe, ripping the ligaments off the second joint" ("The Encircled River," 73–74).

This kind of personal anecdote serves metaphorically as a parable instructing those who seek to understand the complex values of wilderness both to influence its wise preservation and to disseminate that knowledge. McPhee as a physical explorer, our proxy, encounters the wilderness directly as a traveler who pursues understanding and enlightenment through the pleasures and the pains of experience. He has to make crucial decisions in the middle of rapids. McPhee is all of us in this unfamiliar environment. He is humbled as he acquires new knowledge. He exhibits courage and stamina in the face of painful experiences. He continues the journey despite injury and displays a capacity to learn from his experience and to submit to its necessity, but not to be deterred from his goal. The snapped toe suggests the inherent precariousness of humankind's relationship with wilderness as well as the painful and humbling truth of our limitations. "Pride goeth before a fall" is an ancient proverb, here enacted within the context of a large and engaging argument about the complexities facing human beings who must, McPhee argues, humble themselves to understand the wilderness and make wise decisions about its fate "in the middle of rapids."

Many other anecdotes including the archetypal encounter with the barren-ground grizzly, majestic in his dominance of the scene (58), the encounter with the four-year-old bear toward the end of the trip playing "sling the salmon" (94), and the earlier encounter with the "Eskimo girls" (42) ages nine and eleven who innocently press against McPhee eye to eye likewise compel the reader vicariously to enter his experience and then ponder its significance within his larger arguments. The instructive metaphor embedded within a strongly narrated anecdote is a signal quality of McPhee's style.

McPhee does not in truth write for the naïve reader. Through his experiences and his expert witnesses on several sides of difficult issues, however, readers can improve their felt understandings of the complexities and the intractability of the issues. Building the Glen Canyon Dam and attempting to control the paths and behaviors and consequences of the Mississippi River are neither all good or all bad, but they appear to be necessary and pragmatic. Without being merely didactic, McPhee illustrates that a balance, a tension, exists between humankind's nature and the pristine wilderness. His issues may at first be too hard for most of us to think about. But by going down the rivers with him, we learn as he learns from his experiences and his experts; at the same time, we respond through his writing to the power and beauty of each river. It is an old tension, an old issue: When Adam and Eve were evicted from the Garden of Eden, they were faced with having to make a living in the dreary world according to the Law of the Harvest and without understanding the Law of Entropy. McPhee argues, I think, that we need to understand both.

Works Cited

Cronon, William. "Introduction: In Search of Nature." In *Uncommon Ground: Rethinking the Human Place in Nature,* 23–68. New York: W. W. Norton, 1995, 1996.

————. "The Trouble with Wilderness; or, Getting Back to the Wrong Nature." In *Uncommon Ground Rethinking the Human Place in Nature,* 69–90. New York: W. W. Norton, 1995, 1996.

Gutkind, Lee. *The Art of Creative Nonfiction: Writing and Selling the Literature of Reality.* New York: John Wiley & Sons, 1997.

Humphrey, Theodore C. "John McPhee's Spiritual Journeys: The Authenticating Eye." In *Issues in Travel Writing: Displacement, Empire, and Spectacle,* ed. Kristi Siegel, 165–78. New York: Peter Lang, forthcoming 2002.

Kollin, Susan. *Nature's State: Imagining Alaska as the Last Frontier.* Chapel Hill: University of North Carolina Press, 2001.

McPhee, John. *Annals of the Former World.* New York: Farrar, Straus & Giroux, 1998.

————. "Atchafalaya." In *The Control of Nature,* 1–92. New York: Farrar, Straus & Giroux, 1989.

————. "The Encircled River." In *Coming into the Country,* 5–95. New York: Farrar, Straus & Giroux, 1977.

————. "Encounters with the Archdruid." In *The John McPhee Reader,* ed. William Howarth, 189–231. New York: Farrar, Straus & Giroux, 1976.

————. *Irons in the Fire.* New York: Farrar, Straus & Giroux, 1997.

————. "A River." In *Encounters with the Archdruid,* 153–245. New York: Farrar, Straus & Giroux, 1971.

————. "A Selective Advantage: Shad Fishing in the Connecticut River with B. Kynard." *New Yorker* (11 September 2000): 70–82.

————. "They're in the River." *New Yorker* (10 April 2000): 72–80.

————. "Travels in Georgia." (Originally published in *Pieces of the Frame,* 1975.) In *The John McPhee Reader,* ed. William Howarth, 267–308. New York: Farrar, Straus & Giroux, 1976.

Pearson, Michael. "John McPhee." In *Twayne's United States Authors* on CD-ROM. New York: G. K. Hall & Co., 1997.

Rick Van Noy

A Plate Tectonics of Language

Geology as a Vernacular Science

> In the vernacular of geology, your nose was on the outcrop. Through experience with structure, you reached for the implied tectonics. Gradually, as you gathered a piece here, a piece there, the pieces framed a story. *Annals* (380)

In his essay "Some Principles of Ecocriticism," William Howarth (editor of *The John McPhee Reader* and Princeton colleague) explains that ecology is a "vernacular science," used to "read, interpret, and narrate land history" (74). Based on that definition, geology, too, should be a "vernacular science," as geologists tell the story of a land developing over hundreds of millions of years. Yet, to read *Annals of the Former World*—a volume of 600-plus pages that attempts to understand how, over geologic time, physical America came to be as it is today—is to encounter a language that is anything but vernacular. McPhee gives us the geologist's lingo, which is far from familiar or "native" to most of us ("vernacular" from Latin *verna*, native). Beneath its plutons, grabens, horsts, gabbros, catsteps, and slickensides, however, are terms and phrases with a familiar sound to their sense—discordant batholiths, mosaic conglomerates, welded tuffs, bulldozed hash. On the one hand, there is a scientific discourse, unfamiliar to the untrained ear. On the other hand, there is another language, more familiar and descriptive, complementing but also competing with it. In the words of literary critic Mikhail Bakhtin, these discourses—scientific and rhetorical—are in "dialogue" with one another.

Too much of the scientific language would be more clatter, like mineral engineer Charles Park's pick banging against the rock in the first third of *Encounters with the Archdruid*. But roll back the lingo—and the layers of rock—and McPhee is writing the story of a science made familiar, a geology that retains its own complicated nomenclature but that is also made understandable to lay audiences. His goal in *Annals,* as he describes it in his preface, was to present science in a "form and manner that was meant to arrest the attention of other people while achieving acceptability in the geologic community" (9). The geological terms certainly "arrest" our attention, disorienting us in a way that necessitates a language more comprehensible, even metaphorical. Yet he must not make it too literary, so as not to lose "acceptability" among scientists. Just as McPhee describes geologic plates colliding, uplifting, and intermingling, he brings together two seemingly incompatible modes of expression, "rhetoric" and "science," to show that rhetorical and literary devices are necessary components for a linguistic understanding of complex geological concepts.

As Howarth presents it, ecology is a science closely related to a history of verbal expression. The natural, descriptive sciences remained bound to words of local, vernacular origin until Linnaeus compiled his *Systema Naturae* (1734), a treatise that used Latin to create a categorical taxonomy or naming system. "The dead language was static and hierarchical, imposing on nature the fixed ranks of kingdom, phylum, class, order, family, genus, species" (Howarth, 72); but then along came Charles Darwin, who wanted to describe a more active, changing biology. "As a vernacular science," Howarth writes, ecology was widely adapted by many disciplines to describe the relationships between nature and culture. Rapid "settlement and spoilage" of American land after 1900 spurred the rise of ecological concepts to describe regional biomes, but not all scientists greeted the trend warmly. Scientist Marston Bates objected to ecology replacing natural history because ecologists were too "literary, using rhetoric and symbols instead of precise data" (74). Ecology found its voice by studying the properties of species, their distribution across space, and their adaptive course in time. So, as a science and system of knowing, ecology had to develop a vocabulary supple enough to describe the changing, dynamic variations of life, "a broader discourse of ecological story" (74).

Geology, too, has had to lift itself out of a flat taxonomy to something more dynamic, active, and changing. It also studies the properties of species (in this case, rock) and their distribution across space and time. And to do so, it has had to develop a language of process, one at times even literary. Yes, geology has its complex nomenclature (like the Linnaean one); but the words themselves, when they roll off the tongue, express a kind of onomatopoeia for McPhee, containing within them enough "resonance to stir the adolescent groin" (32). Words like "pulsating glaciers," "radiolarian ooze," and "orogeny" (the "swelling" of mountains) contain an unknown but exotic (and erotic) charge. Like kids exchanging "dirty" words or slang on a playground, we may not know their meanings but giggle with delight when they are said. They help form the bonds of a particular group; before their meanings are really clear to us, however, there must be a sense to go with the sound. Geology, McPhee says, has a certain amount of "literary timbre" (133). The unfamiliar expressions (like the referent-rocks they describe) contain an echo of something we can understand, but they must also be placed in the context of another language. As McPhee sees it, geology is a discipline that must continuously rely on rhetorical devices and figurative language to make itself known. The vernacular is, of course, distinguished from the elevated language of literature, but McPhee relies on literary tropes to bring complex geological processes into the realm of the everyday. While he is fascinated with the idiom and specialized dialect of geology, he is also interested in translating that language into some kind of shared ken.

McPhee's best-known metaphor is the one to describe "deep time": hold your arms spread wide to represent all the time on earth, and wipe out human history with a nail file. Stephen Jay Gould, Harvard professor of geology and zoology and author of *Time's Arrow, Time's Cycle: Myth and Metaphor in the Discovery of Geological Time,* says that the notion of "deep time" threatens the idea of "human domination," replacing it with "an almost incomprehensible immensity, with human habitation restricted to a millimicrosecond at the very end" (2). Thomas Bailey has also argued that the effect of McPhee's exploration of deep time has been to displace the human ego from its privileged center to the "longer patterns of nature" (212).

But while the concept of deep time is "almost incomprehensible" and may unsettle us, more often the tropes McPhee uses in the *Annals* help us focus on complex geological concepts, bringing them closer to home. He explores the overlapping of two different epistemologies: the more abstract measuring of space by scientists and the cognitive mapping of poets and writers. A scientific or topographical map reduces what is immense to a scale that the mind can understand, but the details are still not brought into any definition. Cognitive maps focus on the minute, the particular, the local, and they give rise to words: "Let me tell you where I've been." More frequently than abstract "deep time," McPhee keeps the "blind man feeling the elephant" parable in view (63, 380), the subjective geologist/humans grappling to understand their "place" and the language they use to describe it and make it their own. As much as he may disorient and defamiliarize us with the notion of deep time, making the "terrain" underneath us "suspect" (228), more often in *Annals* he helps to orient us by depicting those who specialize in becoming more familiar with the physical earth. Though volcanoes on the sea floor have an "arresting" feature—their tops cut off—they are "spread out around the Pacific bottom like Hershey's Kisses on a tray" (127). The geological phrases and concepts may unsettle us, may remove us from our ordinary habits of perceiving our surroundings, but the other language provides a counterpoint, since its function is to communicate rather than "arrest our attention." To explain the volcanoes on the sea floor, called guyots, Harry Hess presented an "essay in geopoetry," describing the earth as a "dynamic body" whose surface is "swept clean" every three to four hundred million years (quoted in *Annals*, 128).

Contemporary historians of science and Gould himself advance the theory that science is not really objective: it is socially embedded; its theories are not simple deductions from observed facts of nature but a complex mixture of social and cultural ideology (if unconsciously expressed) and empirical data ("Specious Critics," 34). So late nineteenth century explanations of nature, coinciding with the rise of capitalism and industrialism, opted for metaphors of machinelike parts working together in an "economy" (one of Thoreau's chapters in *Walden*). While disciplines such as geology, ecology, and cartography give us empirical tools for understanding nature, our interaction with it consists of much more than observing or analyzing in a disinterested scientific manner. If we are to comprehend nonhuman nature, we must bring our human language and our culture. For McPhee, the subjectivity of science frees it to be written and explained, even if with potentially destabilizing metaphors. "With their four-dimensional minds, and in their interdisciplinary ultraverbal way, geologists can wiggle out of almost anything," he writes. For example, the explanation for why the San Andreas fault is moving to the right but the surface of the earth is moving to the left has quite a bit of "legerdemain." "Harry Houdini had legerdemain when he got out of his ropes, chains, and handcuffs at the bottom of the Detroit River" (612). Though a science, geology accommodates magic and also descriptive wonder at the natural world.

In late nineteenth century geology, when the nation turned from the Civil War to the vast spaces that lie to the west, one notices the prevalence of the aesthetic of the sublime. Two former directors of the U.S. Geological Survey, Clarence King and John Wesley Powell, repeatedly referred to the places (the Sierra Nevadas and the Colorado River, respectively) they surveyed in the 1870s by evoking the romantic (and unscientific) emotion when one, in essence, viewed the face of God. Powell later concluded that the Grand Canyon was "the most sublime spectacle on earth" (*Canyons of the Colorado*, 390). Geologist Clarence Dutton (who worked under Powell on the survey) wrote in his *Tertiary History of the Grand Canyon District* (1882) that the Grand Canyon "is the sublimest thing on earth" (143). Such descriptions can be read in terms of manifest destiny, patriotism, and pride in the national landscape, although they also suggest that geology had not quite been lifted yet from theological metaphor. Though becoming better known through science, geological processes—the interior of the earth's crust—were still explained by the geologist's interior. These geologists did not "discover" that the sublime existed "out there" in nature but expected to see it that way, blending the surveyor's sense of how nature could be objectively measured with the denizen's sense of how it could be intuitively and subjectively felt.

One also notices in these earlier geological descriptions the presence of architectural metaphors. King finds grottos, minarets, obelisks, and amphitheaters; Powell finds doors, columns, walls, tables, and temples. Paul Shepard in *Man in the Landscape* theorizes that "rocks of certain angular shapes may always mean 'man-made structure' to European-Americans because of an indelible association of form with human works." He likens it to biological "imprinting," where the place becomes an image in the mind as much as a force in nature (274). The terms were also used to reinforce the notion of the sublime: the physical environment is built that way, not by accident.

The geology that McPhee describes is one that emerges not from the 1870s but from the 1970s, "wild, wierdsma" geology in a "leather-jacket" (*Annals,* 32) and shades, a Peter Fonda in *Easy Rider.* During this period, the view of how mountains came up and canyons went down, how seabeds rifted and continents crept, was itself "shifting, upthrusting, subducting." Plate tectonics, "the giddy new geology," said that continents floated on some twenty crustal plates, sixty miles thick, kept in motion by a phenomenon no one was quite sure about (Skow,

90). By the late 1960s and early 1970s the theory had caught on among geologists. Most agreed, for instance, that India rammed (and is still ramming) into Tibet at high speed, heaving up former ocean floor to create the Himalayas. Hence "[t]he summit of Mt. Everest is marine limestone" (*Annals*, 124). Plate tectonics reveals that there is "no consecutive story of deposition, just mountains of bulldozed hash" (125). And geology seemed to reflect the chaos of the culture at large. Like the geology one hundred years ago, it kept its ties to the vagaries of language and the subjectivity of the sense of place, because all knowledge is "situated" within a particular culture and context (Harraway, 188). The assemblage of rocks was viewed as a meaningless pile of debris, afterproduct of a natural "revolution," rather than a "sublime" creation.

Before the plate tectonics revolution took to the streets, "how the mountains came up was not absolutely defined, but the story seemed clear, even if the authorship was somewhat moot, and it was the story of rhythmically successive orogenies, chapter headings in the biography of the earth" (*Annals*, 220). In writing that story, geologists have even referred to mountains as "punctuation marks" because they took so little time in the overall formation of the "story" (220). Clarence King draws on literary devices to present the history of the Sierra as unfolding in a five-part drama:

> First, the slow gathering of marine sediment within the early ocean, during which incalculable ages were consumed. Second, in the early Jurassic period, this level sea-floor came suddenly to be lifted into the air and crumpled in folds, through whose yawing fissures and ruptured axes outpoured wide zones of granite. Third, the volcanic age of fire and steam. Fourth, the glacial period . . . with huge dragons of ice crawling down its slopes, and wearing their armor into the rocks. Fifth, the present condition, which the following chapters will describe (25).

King's language ("yawing fissures and ruptured axes") seems intended to meet his audience with the same force he describes. Even the slow-working glaciers come like fiery-hot "dragons of ice," "wearing their armor into the rocks." This kind of "catastrophic" theory allows for descriptive, metaphorical language rather than static taxonomy. Because of its emphasis on violent, sudden change, it can be viewed as a forerunner to plate tectonics theory. It implies that nature offers stories not readily available to the untrained eye and that the geologists delve back into the past to interpret them. Their information is more than evidentiary and something they sense and conceive. Through inference and imagination, geologists relate these temporal narratives to the reader. Whatever their scientific accuracy, because of their emphasis on violent rifts and eruptions, these stories make for more compelling literature.

In telling nature's story, words retain an attachment to cultural memory, which explains the prevalence of theological metaphors in the 1870s and prevalence of more anthropocentric metaphors in our own, more secular age. The crusts in the Great Basin "suggest stretch marks" (*Annals,* 46). In Appalachia, McPhee writes, there are "stubs" of rock, "pulses" of orogenies, and "bald" mountains (186). In addition to implying a place for each organism, this personification illustrates that nature is knowable and that every aspect of it can be recognized the way one would recognize and refer to the people who live in one's neighborhood. Geological features form part of an orderly "body," and geologists can "study" parts of this living organism as they would pages in a book. "Rocks are the record of events that took place at the time they were formed," Anita Harris says. "They are books. They have a different vocabulary, a different alphabet, but you learn how to read them" (156–57). Just as anatomy differs from person to person, and no one book says the same thing to different people, each moment of the geological record will be different, depending on which body is being examined and who is doing the reading.

The nature-as-book metaphor has always been used by geology. Sir Charles Lyell used it in his *Principles of Geology* but not optimistically: "The book of Nature is the book of fate" (336). In the original *Exploration of the Colorado River and Its Canyons,* John Wesley Powell says that that the gulches, canyons, and alcoves of the Grand Canyon are part of the "library of the gods": "he who would read the language of the universe may dig out the letters here and there, and with them spell the words, and read, in a slow and imperfect way, but still so as to understand a little, the story of creation" (194). Like Harris, Powell uses the book metaphor to suggest that the levels of rock are like leaves of a book, implying an accessible natural order that we may "dig out," though Harris does not use the theological terms. Instead, she describes a language, a "vocabulary," an "alphabet"—an order not built by God but always constructed and arranged by humans. According to geographer Yi-Fu Tuan, this kind of meaning-making helps distinguish a more locally defined area from abstract ideas. "What begins as undifferentiated space becomes place as we get to know it better and endow it with value," a process that must begin and end with language (6). In profiling geologists such as Harris in the terms they used to describe and give value to their surroundings, McPhee helps pry geology loose from anonymity; he helps give a language and story to the land.

McPhee himself has observed that geology is a "descriptive, interpretive science," not only classifying what the eye sees but also evoking change that it cannot see (*Annals*, 379, 31). Geologists can detect traces of the earth's forces in that topography, scars of geological time, revealing not only "deep time" but also a "deep map" (to use William Least Heat-Moon's term) rather than a superficial one. They delve through the exterior to reveal the interior and make nature, often muted in our technological age, talk. According to William Howarth, "[McPhee is] helping us to see processes that are invisible. He's giving language to the land" (quoted in Hamilton, 96).

Nature becomes a character in this process. Diamonds, McPhee says, "shoot like bullets" through the earth's crust (155). Nonetheless, they are reluctant to play this role. "They want to be graphite, and with a relatively modest boost of heat graphite is what they would become, if atmospheric oxygen did not incinerate them first. They are in this sense, unstable—these finger-flashing symbols of the eternity of vows, yearning to become fresh pencil lead" (156). Noting that the last Ice Age stopped around Ebbets Field, vanished home of the Brooklyn Dodgers, he writes: "When a long-ball hitter hit a long ball, it would land on Bedford Avenue and bounce down the morainal front to roll toward Coney on the outwash plain. No one in Los Angeles would ever hit a homer like that" (161). Diamond and baseball metaphors help locate geology in human history, in a specific time and place.

As a character, nature is an agent and force of change, acting rather than acted upon. "Geologists tend to be strongly influenced by the rocks among which they grew up" (297). They inherit the vernacular of their places. Californians start with "highly deformed rock," while David Love, Wyomingite, has a little of everything. Along with the orogeny of that highly geological state come the yarns about Love's father, John, who rode with Butch Cassidy and Sundance, and mother, Wellesley-educated Ethel Waxham, who arrived in Rawlins on the stagecoach, subdued a sheep ranch, and wrote an epic diary. David Love speaks in the vernacular of Wyoming: some items are "store-bought," and coffee brewed right would "float a horseshoe." Blankets are "sougans," and a tarpaulin is a "henskin." "In the flavor of his speech the word 'ornery' endures" (322). Indeed, the dramatic landscape of the region's history is closely intertwined with Love's family and cultural history, and he was drawn to be a geologist the way "someone from Gloucester, Massachusetts, would be drawn to be a fisherman" (350). James Hutton, who wrote that he could read "in the face of the rocks the annals of a former world," became the father of modern geology by roaming around regions of his native Scotland and his backyard farm, peeling off layers of moss to reveal layers of rock below (*Annals,* 74). Anita Harris has a New Yorker's skepticism and thinks plate-tectonic theory, though correct in many respects, has considerable bunk in it. If Love is the cowboy, Harris is the urban Sherlock, detecting her way through territory close to home, the Delaware Water Gap.

Stephen Jay Gould has criticized McPhee for celebrating field geology over that performed in the laboratory, a conflict, he writes, "with long tendrils, for it also evokes such basic contrasts as romantic and mechanical approaches, or holistic and analytic procedures" (*Time's Arrow,* 69). Hutton, Gould shows, developed his major contribution to the field—the notion of cyclicity in deep time (that is, though parts of the earth are ruined by erosion, there is a restorative force that repairs it to permit life and agriculture)—*a priori,* based on cause and effect analysis and influenced by Isaac Newton's Second Law. It was conceived in Hutton's mind as a machinelike model before the theory could be confirmed in the field.

But such a view of *a priori* knowledge is certainly not absent from McPhee's book. When geologists are in the field, they bring a set of cultural practices with them and can transform (through metaphor) what is verifiable into another kind of knowledge. Whatever theory (such as cyclical theory) or analogy they may be working with allows them to re-perceive what they see in a new way. In the words of Mikhail Bakhtin, any linguistic utterance is made up of a "background" of opinions, points of view, and value judgments, so that an idea presented before us lapses into "open orientation," complicating the path of description toward to the "object" (281). Within such a space, Bakhtin writes, alternative versions of reality, "like mirrors that face each other," "force us to guess at and grasp for a world" that is multileveled and varied (414–15). An "open conversation" begins between these (former) worlds and points of view, so that what emerges are shifting, even paradoxical profiles of the place presented before us. "At any location on earth," McPhee writes, "as the rock record goes down into time and out into earlier geographies, it touches upon tens of hundreds of stories, wherein the face of the earth often changed, changed utterly, and changed again, like the face of a crackling fire" (37)

McPhee does focus primarily on fieldwork but in a way consistent with his overall emphasis on profiling the language of the "field" of geology. He places geologists in their home settings to convey both the vernacular of where they live and the vernacular of their professional lives. Standing in her hometown of Brooklyn, New York, Harris can see "the annals of a former world" beneath the sweep of city. Instead of the Parachute Jump and Cyclone at Coney Island, Harris runs her eye across the scene but sees New Jersey diabase, Fordham gneiss, Inwood marble, and Manhattan schist. In the sand, she sees the elements of a geological history side by side with the Pepsi-Cola cans, sand-coated pickles, and paper plates (160). "Brooklyn is a pitted outwash plain," she says, adding: "Brooklyn means broken land" (157). Harris draws connections between place names and their geological features. Driving through New York, she calls out geological details the way Fred Brown calls out directions in the Pine Barrens, narrating the stories of place and the insider's landscape as they drive (*The Pine Barrens,* 19). While some places are not even identified on maps, "Fred had a name for almost every rise and dip in the land" (21). What to others is an ordinary or even blank landscape to Brown and Harris is a landscape encoded with a special language, a vernacular of place. Both Brown and Harris are environmentally literate, schooled in the respective languages of their places. In *Mapping the Invisible Landscape,* Kent Ryden writes that "this sort of [environmental] literacy," "as with any language," "is best gained through incessant practice and exposure; also with any language, those who cannot read it will see the text as a meaningless jumble" (72). According to Ryden, this kind of vernacular language "as opposed to formal biological taxonomies . . . provide[s] an especially good indication of environmental literacy" and a good "indication of regional consciousness and a sense of living in a distinctive place" (78).

In her youth, Harris did not know the geological details; she was not geologically or environmentally literate. But coming back to her native environment now, she can appreciate it in a new way. Before, "she didn't know from geology," McPhee says, changing the common phrase from she "didn't know from Adam" (165). In other words, she had not discovered her own creation myth. Geology changes her "cognitive map" and gives her a feel for the landscape beneath what the eye normally sees. In thinking about paintings and the Hudson River School, Anita Harris suggests

> a sense of total composition—not merely one surface composition visible to the eye but a whole series of preceding compositions which in the later one fragmentarily endure and are incorporated into its substance—with materials of vastly differing age drawn together in a single scene, a composite canvas not only from the Hudson River School but including everything else that had been part of the zones of time represented by the boats, gravels, steeples, cows, trains, talus, cutbanks, and kames, below a mountain broken upon by a river half its age. (192)

Holding her lens to the sand at the Indiana Dunes, Harris can almost *see* the "world in a grain of sand": "I see little fragments of igneous rock. I see amphibiote and red jasper. . . . I see red iron-oxide-coated quartz grains. You can see right through the quartz. I see little pieces of carbon. I see green chert. I see a bug crawling through the sand" (274). She sees not the Blakean universe, however, but something at once more particular and local: the composites of a geological history illegible to most of but written in the available "ledger."

McPhee writes that geologists are often able to see something they call the picture. "The oolites and dolomite—tuff and granite, the Pequop siltstones and shales—are pieces of the Picture" (62). The creatures and chemistry that go with them are parts of the composition. The problem with the picture is that 99 percent of it is missing, washed away, melted down, or broken up. "The geologist discovers lingering remains, and connects them with dotted lines" (62). At this point, geology becomes more imaginative than descriptive. "Geologists," he writes, "inhabit scenes that no one ever saw, scenes of global sweep, gone and gone again, including seas, mountains, rivers, forests, and archipelagoes of aching beauty rising in volcanic violence to settle down quietly and then forever disappear—*almost* disappear" (64). In the subjective imagination, McPhee goes on to say, the geologist rebuilds the archipelago (64).

Despite satellite technology and microprobes, David Love insists on walking the topography, getting a feel for the land. Love has, McPhee claims, a "geologic map of Wyoming in his head" (295). Love has first-hand geology, "all in one mind," rather than "pieced together from papers and reports," maps and atlases (379). "To compete with Dave," a fellow geologist says, "you'd have to do a lot of walking" (379). McPhee is profiling a process, where the landscape of one's region is mapped not onto paper but into thought and memory. Ultimately, he helps us see the "picture" and gives us a better "sense of where you are."

In doing so, McPhee describes how geologists draw inferences from available facts: "To go back this way, retrospectively, from scene to shifting scene, is to go down the rock column, groping toward the beginning of the world. There is a firm ground some of the way. Eventually, there comes a point where inference will shade into conjecture. In recesses even more remote, conjecture may usurp the original franchise of God" (217). Geologists "see, infer, extrapolate, conjure, discover, and describe" long-veiled and innumerable worlds until they get the "Picture" (641). But the picture for McPhee and the geologists he profiles is more like a moving one than the static taxonomies of Linnaeus. In *Rising from the Plains,* the third book of the *Annals,* McPhee shifts the master metaphor from "picture" to "narrative." David Love assembles "a story in his mind," a "sequential narrative" of the history of the Yellowstone Valley, and McPhee writes that Love can "see it in motion now, in several ways responsively moving in the present" (374). Eldridge Moores, central character of book four, *Assembling California,* also sees something more like a moving picture: "like most geologists, [Moores also] carries in his head a portfolio of ancient scenes, worlds overprinting previous worlds. He sees tundra in Ohio, dense forestation on New Mexican mesas, the Persian Gulf in the Painted Desert" (541). The geologists McPhee presents remind us that geologic structures are not static forms in the landscape: they are "seen" as they are encountered and re-created by the geologist even as they are were created in nature. Finally, they are reinterpreted and re-presented by McPhee himself, so that we too might get the "picture."

To read these geological volumes "assembled" by McPhee is to come away with the feeling all writers strive to attain: for a brief moment, the earth moves. McPhee explodes the passive, static, map-view of a geological landscape, creating a volatile, organic sense of place beneath the map's smooth skin: "If you look on a world map at Antarctica, South America, Africa, and Australia, you virtually see them exploding away from one another. You can reassemble Gondwana [a former continent] in your mind and then watch it come apart" (560). Maps deal with surfaces, showing the "uppermost formations in present time, while indicating little of what lies farther down and less of what is gone from above" (185). Unlike a verbal description, which may always be suspected of subjectivity, a map offers a seemingly indisputable representation of the world. But at any given coordinate on a map, the "world will have changed too often to be recorded in a single picture," writes McPhee. It will have been at one time below fresh water, at another, brine; it "will have been mountainous country, a quiet plain, equatorial desert, an arctic coast, a coal swamp, and a river delta, all in one Zip Code" (185). Below this surface is an alphabet, "phrases and clauses" not yet assembled into a narrative. Words give the land a different form and shape from maps, making a "deep" space in the mind, evoking a changing sense of place in ways that maps or static taxonomies never can. A picture would provide a fixed, authoritative representation, but geology depends on a fluid, variable language to make its subject known, since the rocks themselves are moving. As such, "there remains in geology plenty of room for the creative imagination" (185)—as there remains in geology plenty of room for the vernacular landscape.

In order to make his subject known, McPhee must continually *vernacularize* it by employing metaphor or simile. "There's a little bit of the humanities that creeps into geology," he writes, "and that's why I'm in it" (24). In "Crossing the Craton," the last of the *Annals*, McPhee writes about how the midcontinental rift system stopped rifting and was, in the vernacular, "snuffed out." "In the language of geology," he writes, "grabens were squeezed upward and became horsts." In the language of everyday, "it was as if the Red Sea were to stop widening while its floor came up to stand higher than the shores" (659). Rocks like Devil's Tower are called volcanic chimneys; they're also known as volcanic necks. A xenolith "is a rock from around the margins of the neck that fell into the magma when it was soft. Like a bit of chocolate in a cookie, it is a foreign body with its own age and its own history, distinct from the stuff it went into" (649). In *Basin and Range*, McPhee again draws on food for his comparison: xenoliths are "blobs of the country that fell into the magma and became encased there like raisins in bread" (20). New Jersey's Hammer Creek Conglomerate is "polka-dotted headcheese rock, sometimes known as puddingstone" (41). The Appalachian Mountains are folded "like a tubal air mattress, like a rippled potato chip" (42). Whether evoking raisins or chocolate chips, potato chips or headcheese, McPhee helps us bring the rocks closer to home, bringing the outcrop into the kitchen.

Beneath my hometown are layers of experience and story that an out-sider would not understand the full meaning and nuance of. Geology, to McPhee, is a metaphor for that kind of experience, extracting and writ-ing the accretion of stories that compose this insider's landscape. Many of us ignore the historical depth associated with familiar places; but like a protruding outcrop, it is right there under our nose. The vernacular names insiders apply to their regions consolidate a strong sense of iden-tity and belonging, and McPhee helps bring the outsider in. The lan-guage of these experiences will be lost to those not conversant with them, and some of us may never become comfortable with the language of geology. Geology is, admittedly, more abstract than ecology. With lit-tle training, most of us can see and intuit the interactions of species at work in our back yard—but that is exactly the point. Geology may de-pend more on knowing the language. Once you begin to read it, "[i]t pays to put your nose on the outcrop," says Anita Harris (20). Roadcuts become like "posters" for a dramatic play, "advertising the dramatic events, suggesting their narratives, fabrics, and structures" (286).

On one level McPhee is fascinated with the specialized "vernacular of geology" itself and has stuck his own nose out on the outcrop to trans-late it (380). It is an insider's game, and he has to "go native" to gain ac-cess to it, traveling with geologists through roadcuts "like barnyard poultry pecking up rock" (62). The Green River Basin in Wyoming is not to be confused with the Green River Basin that was in Wyoming. One is on the surface and the other is under it. Terracettes (small ter-races) of Council Bluffs are also called catsteps (626). Because the lithic sandstone in Ledges State Park is so weathered, it is "punk rock" (626). Referring to roadcuts, geologists note that highway departments will "hair everything over" by scattering grass seed (23). Geologists "debate in a language exotic in itself, and shuffle like a blackjack deck the strati-graphic units of the world" (233). There is a language that is exotic, na-tive to only a few; but there is also one that is more vaguely familiar and, by consistently employing metaphor, can become more native to layper-sons. Reporting on a conversation between two geologists riding in a car in Vermont, "amidst Black Angus meadows and roll-mop hay, over plank bridges" (233), McPhee replays their esoteric vocabulary, con-trasting it with the bucolic scene. "It doesn't matter that you don't un-derstand them. Even they aren't sure if they are making sense. Their purpose is trying to" (234). Geologists have acknowledged McPhee's own efforts in "trying to" by recognizing him as one of their own. The

American Institute of Professional Geologists (AIPG) awarded him its 1997 Outstanding Achievement Award, "as an individual who exemplifies excellence in the writing of geological nonfiction" ("AIPG," 34).

In reaching for explanations, the "implied tectonics," geologists literally probe the depths of the world. McPhee writes about the rock component most widely employed in the quest for dating rock. Zircon has become, according to geologist Randy Van Schmus, "the workhorse of the Precambrian." And "zircon" is derived from the old French *jargon,* which had the same ultimate source as "gargle." Jargon is indeed a "workhouse" in geology, and the words themselves something to gargle in the throat (646–47). But beneath that jargon, itself a form of vernacular, is another kind of language. Though isolated layers and elements of geology have specialized terms, the processes that bring them together rely on stories and depend on more familiar models. As McPhee replays the processes for us, the respective languages of geology and the everyday almost begin to fold and fault in on themselves like geologic plates. Finally, the explanations harden like cooling lava to form a "mantle."

In a 1993 article for *Discovery* magazine, McPhee describes a trip to the Liberty Science Center in his home state of New Jersey. The center is designed to fascinate urban children and inspire some to become scientists. "The idea behind the museum's various discovery rooms is that if something especially arrests your interest you can take it further" ("Don't Scare Them Off," 95). In *Annals of the Former World,* McPhee both arrests our attention and helps us to take it further. He asks an elemental question in the *Discovery* article: how can we make science stick? He is asking the same question in the *Annals* too.

McPhee is a layman, an outsider, learning to speak as a "native" so that gradually "verbal deposits [will] thicken" (33). Ironically, he draws on geology to explain what happens when language becomes vernacular, when it reaches its angle of repose. Though "zircon" may sound extraterrestrial, McPhee peppers the *Annals* with enough imagery, story, analogy, and vernacular so that gradually, a "piece here, a piece there," the pieces frame a story—and stories are the central means through which cultures organize their surroundings. McPhee describes eventually learning about all the elements that really compose granite (what could be more "solid"?). Relax, he says: "The *home* terms still apply" (34; emphasis added). "They say granodiorite when they are in church and granite the rest of the week" (34). Foundational terms of geology are indeed "home" terms: the bottom, Precambrian floor is a "basement," though it is stacked with "plates," "mantles," and "crusts." The annals of a former world now become a more familiar, internalized one. Long-dead strata are brought in more closely, so that we too might be in-habit with this language and consequently better inhabitants of our present worlds.

Works Cited

"AIPG Honors AGI Executive Director, Marcus Milling, Other Professional Geologists." *Geotimes* (December 1997): 34.

Bailey, Thomas C. "John McPhee: The Making of a Meta-Naturalist." In *Earthly Words: Essays on Contemporary American Nature and Environmental Writers,* ed. John Cooley, 195–216. Ann Arbor: University of Michigan Press, 1994.

Bakhtin, Mikhail. *The Dialogic Imagination: Four Essays.* Trans. Caryl Emerson and Michael Holquist. Austin: University of Texas Press, 1981.

Dutton, Clarence E. *Tertiary History of the Grand Canyon District* (1882). Santa Barbara: Peregrine, 1977.

Gould, Stephen Jay. "On the Origin of Specious Critics." *Discover* (January 1985): 34.

———. *Time's Arrow, Time's Cycle: Myth and Metaphor in the Discovery of Geological Time.* Cambridge: Harvard University Press, 1987.

Hamilton, Joan. "An Encounter with John McPhee." *Sierra* (May–June 1990): 50-\55, 92, 96.

Harraway, Donna. *Simians, Cyborgs, and Women: The Reinvention of Nature.* New York: Routledge, 1991.

Howarth, William. "Some Principles of Ecocriticism." In *The Ecocriticism Reader,* ed. Cheryl Glotfelty and Harold Fromm, 69–91. Athens: University of Georgia Press, 1996.

King, Clarence. *Mountaineering in the Sierra Nevada* (1872). Ed. Francis Farquhar. Lincoln: University of Nebraska Press, 1997.

Lyell, Sir Charles. *Principles of Geology, Being an Attempt to Explain the Former Changes of the Earth's Surface by Reference to Causes Now in Operation.* London: Murray, 1830–33.

McPhee, John. *Annals of the Former World.* New York: Farrar, Straus & Giroux, 1998.

———. "Don't Scare Them Off." *Discover* 14(11) (November 1993): 95–98.

———. *Encounters with the Archdruid.* Farrar, Straus & Giroux, 1971.

———. *The Pine Barrens.* New York: Farrar, Straus & Giroux, 1968.

Powell, John Wesley. *The Exploration of the Colorado River and Its Canyons.* New York: Penguin, 1987 (*Canyons of the Colorado,* 1895).

———. *The Exploration of the Colorado River of the West and Its Tributaries.* Washington, D.C.: GPO, 1875.

Ryden, Kent. *Mapping the Invisible Landscape.* Iowa City: University of Iowa Press, 1993.

Shepard, Paul. *Man in the Landscape: A Historic View of the Esthetics of Nature.* New York: Ballantine, 1967.

Skow, John. "Review of *Annals of the Former World*." *Time* (6 July 1998): 90.

Tuan, Yi-Fu. *Space and Place: The Perspective of Experience.* Minneapolis: University of Minnesota Press, 1977.

Barbara Stevens

John McPhee's *Annals of the Former World*

Geology, Culture, and a Fountain of Metaphor

What we are talking about is using the material of natural history, geography and anthropology to open up the dilemmas of the late twentieth century.

Barry Lopez (cited in Trimble, 6)

There's always something in the rocks that will give you the answer you are looking for.

John McPhee (*Annals,* 627)

The best way to learn about any neighbourhood is the way small boys do it—explore.

John Wiebenson (cited in Wood, 193)

The "literary nonfiction" of John McPhee provokes dilemma. Heavy with the connotations of both art and hard fact, his corpus of over three decades, encompassing topics from oranges to nuclear physics, from baseball to crofting in the Scottish islands, straddles the boundaries of distinct genres and confounds notions of classification and category. How, laments William Howarth (vii), can one order such diversity? Indeed, how can one adequately define a nonfictional reportage that is packed with the "narrative tricks" of the creative artist? Many, it seems, have tried; while the issue has ostensibly been settled—for "literary non-fiction" has been neatly described as the "third way to tell a story" (Pearson, 13)—it is Howarth who perhaps most honestly expresses the predicament of the critical analyst: "no one," he points out, "has a proper name for [McPhee's] brand of factual writing" (vii).

While the variety and mode of McPhee's corpus provoke dilemma, his authorial identity also arouses perplexity. Indeed, as the writer of many works focusing on the natural world (including *The Survival of the Bark Canoe, The Pine Barrens,* and *Encounters with the Archdruid*), McPhee has been perceived as the "most effective literary advocate for environmentalism" (Pearson, 22). Yet he frequently confounds the conventions of the environmental genre by upholding a landscape neither entirely natural nor entirely cultural, ultimately asserting no clear winner in the environmental debate. Brian Turner identifies this as a "dual and overlapping interest in [both] nature and people [that] complicates McPhee's perspective on the natural world" (168); and McPhee himself, it seems, resists facile categorization. Michael Pearson, for example, describes him as a man who, while "bristl[ing] at being defined simply as a nature writer," is "a nature writer malgré lui" (100). Notwithstanding such authorial perplexities, it is McPhee's geologic opus *Annals of the Former World,* a work spanning a dozen years and of course examining nature resolutely at ground level, that most forcefully confronts—indeed, opens up and illuminates—"the wider dilemmas of the late twentieth century." After all, "landscape," it has been said, "is an analogue of the human condition or at least of our communications" (Hobbs, 44). The shifting and mobile geologic landscape that McPhee explores and elucidates is strikingly analogous to the shifting contours and complex terrain of contemporary cultural theory. McPhee himself calls geology a "fountain of metaphor" (*Annals,* 31) and describes the rocks he encounters as "windows into the world" (36); his scrutiny of the revolutionary theory of plate tectonics that emerged in the 1960s situates the geologic landscape, as spatial metaphor, at the heart of the study of concurrent and insurgent theoretical discourse, particularly the moving and "compound" landscapes (Gregory, 122) of critical human geography.

The essence of the theory of plate tectonics, outlined in McPhee's tetralogy, is the notion of evolving and dissolving lands, for "the story is that everything is moving. . . . The earth is a dynamic body with its surface constantly changing" (*Annals,* 119, 128). Indeed, while each volume of *Annals* explores aspects of the "new" geology, it is *Basin and Range* (Book I) that summarizes plate tectonic theory. Plate tectonics, as McPhee reveals, does not recount a single narrative but rather touches upon tens of hundreds of lithic (Greek *lithos* = stone) stories. This is a story in which everything is moving "in varying directions and at different speeds" (120); the disparate worlds of lithic history and space collide and intermingle in a welter of disassembled earth. It is a story far removed, in fact, from the steady rhythm of the rock and landscape formation of an "old" geology that embraced the notion of neat stratigraphy—the "layer cake" school of established geologic thought. Plate tectonics is a story, therefore, that in only one decade overturned all geologic vision, a "change as profound as Darwinian evolution, or Newtonian or Einsteinian physics" (119). Certainly by the end of the 1960s the ordered and steady rhythm of established geological theory, serenely described as the "symphony of the earth," was sidelined. The "symphony," as McPhee (pursuing the musical allusion) asserts, "had come to the last groove and was up in the attic. Mountain building had become a story of random collisions, unpredictable whims and the motions of the plates, which when continents collided or trenches otherwise jammed could give up going one way and move in another" (126).

Certainly, from the beginning of Book I notions of stability and reliable orientation are questioned. Indeed, although McPhee and his geologic guide begin *Basin and Range* in a specific location—"73 degrees 57 minutes and 53 seconds west longitude and 40 degrees 51 minutes and 14 seconds north latitude" (*Annals,* 19)—their coordinates patently and inevitably can remain only a temporary description, "as if for a boat on the sea" (19); the reader's location, both literally from the first scene on the George Washington Bridge at 9 A.M. and figuratively in the world of geologic knowledge, is consistently changing and challenged. McPhee inexorably slides on the colliding plates of tectonics and moves in his exploration of diverse landscapes; the doyen of fact-writing refutes, in his very first sentence, any notions of a stable world: "The poles of the earth have wandered. The equator has apparently moved . . ." (19).

In the early 1970s Marxist geographer Henri Lefebvre asserted that the " 'real' can never become completely fixed . . . it is constantly in a state of mobilisation" (cited in Gregory, 366), and the movement inherent in McPhee's geologic world is reflected in the sphere of critical human geography. Indeed, Lefebvre formed the vanguard of a new cultural geography that sought to question established modes of critical thought by placing shifting space at the center of a social theory preoccupied with rigid and linear historicism. Lefebvre's was a geography recognizing the validity of difference and hybridity, the key theoretical claim of which was that spatial relations must not only be seen but must necessarily be seen as multiple, mobile, and contested.[1] Lefebvre himself urged a "turbulent spatiality" (Gregory, 356), and the work of many cultural geographers exemplifies this thrust toward a restless reformulation of the interpretative terrain. Edward Soja, for example, employing his own term "postmodern geography," describes the restructured contemporary theoretical world as one of "[u]nprecedented heterogeneity, [of] fragments flying every which way. . . . a larger landscape . . . a dynamic contradiction filled dialectic of space and time, human agency and structural constraint, a historical geography that is played out at many different scales" (*Postmodern Geographies*, 157).

Soja's evocation of such dynamism and fragmentation is a striking echo of McPhee's lithic vitality and discord. Indeed, McPhee's evocation of and passion for the new, diverse, and dynamic geologic "tune" of tectonics is an apt metaphor for what Soja perceives as the "recomposition" of a carceral conventional critical theory of mere historicism. Unless we recognize the importance of space and its diversity, Soja suggests, we become entrapped in an understanding limited by its one-dimensionality. Soja describes a new critical geography not only "attuned to . . . [the] call for increased attention to spatiality" (*Postmodern Geographies*, 6) but also attuned to the creative recombination of time, history, and space. It is a geography of what Soja terms "spatial reawakening" (6); and McPhee's vital and potent geology—"the whole thing is alive . . . it is live country" (*Annals*, 45–46)—metaphorically refutes the torpor of an atrophied critical tradition in which space "was treated as the dead, the fixed, the undialectical, [and] the immobile . . ." (Michel Foucault cited in Soja, 4). Soja articulates this dialectic space—somewhat aptly, in view of McPhee's identity as a "third-way" storyteller—in the notion of "thirdspace," a realm with affinities to the juxtaposed, conflicting, and mixed spheres of McPhee's landscape. This realm seeks not merely to combine but to transcend and reform, akin to McPhee's perplexing literary nonfiction, the opposing spheres of what Soja terms "first space"—a space of "concrete materiality . . . [in which] things [are] empirically mapped" (*Thirdspace*, 10)—and "second space"— a space of mental or cognitive forms—to create a realm in which "everything comes together . . ." (56).

Derek Gregory similarly focuses on reformed geographic theory as a mobile and developing entity, a series of overlapping, contending, and colliding discourses that transcend both the "utopian gestures" of cognitive thought and the coherent totality of empiricism. He cites James Clifford to elucidate the instability of the new critical agenda—and Clifford's alpine metaphor is particularly apt here: "We ground things now on a moving earth. There is no longer any place of overview (mountain-top) from which to map human ways of life, no Archimedian point from which to represent the world. Mountains are in constant motion" (cited in Gregory, 9).

Of course, the lack of overview and the refutation of generalization suggested by Clifford imply the need for "new ways of seeing" our land-scapes[2]—both physical and theoretical. Indeed, the obverse of the gen-eral remains the particular; and the notion of landscape proximity, the interpretation of detail, informs the work of both Gregory and McPhee and is crucial to a deeper understanding of any complex terrain.

Gregory's revelation of a reformed human geography certainly rec-ognizes a multiplicity of detailed and chaotic histories and space, as op-posed to a geographic tradition that invoked the world as coherent and distanced totality. By the end of the nineteenth century, what Gregory terms the "enframing" of the world—the rendering of the world as a detached object to be viewed—had become characteristic of the geo-graphic mode. Without a "separation of the self from [the] 'picture' [it seems], it bec[a]me impossible to grasp 'the whole'" (Timothy Mitchell cited in Gregory, 37). It is impossible to "dissipate the glare which arises from a multiplicity of objects at once presenting themselves to view" (Goldsmith cited in Gregory, 22). In contrast to this singular overview, however, Gregory seeks not to dissipate but to embrace the "glare" of diversity. In aptly geologic terms, therefore, he calls for a close-up view, a "multi-levelled dialogue [that pays] scrupulous attention to the junc-tures and fissures [the spaces] between many different histories . . . [one] that reopens contact with the hermeneutics of everyday life and repositions theory much closer to the ground" (416, 80).

Gregory's rebellious theoretical preoccupation with proximity is sig-nificant, for the necessity of such contact with the "landscape" is reiter-ated constantly and literally by McPhee's faction of geologic "revolu-tionaries"—the geologists who guide him through the intricacies of the geologic landscape. They do not write about geology from a distance, do not "sit in high councils figuring out how the earth works" (*Annals,* 379). They are field oriented—they know geology, as McPhee con-stantly points out, from having found it out themselves. Thus, from Kenneth Deffeyes's *Basin and Range* counsel to "stick [your] eyeballs on this one" (99) to David Love's *Rising from the Plains* admonition that "reality is not something you can capture on a blackboard" (381) and his practice of "hands on" geology (on horseback or on foot, gathering fragments of the world with his own eyes and his hammer), notions of geologic and theoretical proximity become remarkably analogous. Indeed, while Deffeyes displays unflinching familiarity with the geologic terrain ("he put it in his mouth and chewed it"; 38), the seeing and touching of the landscape, "leaning against it with a hand lens" (512), "picking and prying [at it] a roadcut at a time" (476), by all of McPhee's geologist guides becomes symbolic of the conceptual excavations of Soja, Gregory, et al.

The theoretical notion of the "multi-levelled" with its connotations of new and previously unexplored dimensions is constantly expressed in McPhee's narrative. Certainly, McPhee, akin to Gregory, eschews the validity of the merely two-dimensional: "The history of the earth may be written in rock, but [its] history is not coherent on a geologic map, which shows a region's uppermost formations in present time, while indicating little of what lies farther down and less of what is gone from above . . . the appearance of the world [has] changed too often to be recorded in a single picture" (*Annals,* 185).

McPhee's geologists are mentors patently conversant with other dimensions, both spatial and temporal. They are interpreters able to decode the cryptic rock record, the " 'books' [that] have a different vocabulary, a different alphabet" (*Annals,* 157), who can "think in two languages, function on two different scales . . . [tutors] free[d] from . . . conventional reactions" (129). Kenneth Deffeyes, for example, illuminates new dimensions, sees beyond the reassuring coherence and constraints of landscape conventions. A scene perceived by McPhee in purely picturesque terms—a scene that forms a metaphor for the ordered conventional cultural landscapes described by Gregory—is typically re-viewed by Deffeyes: "The Humboldt River, blue and full, was flowing toward us, with panes of white ice at its edges, sage and green meadow beside it and dry russet uplands rising behind. I said I thought that was lovely. He said yes, it was lovely indeed, it was one of the loveliest angular unconformities I was ever likely to see" (68). Indeed, Deffeyes is constantly and literally deconstructing the landscape, breaking the surface with his geologist's pick and carefully hoarding and assimilating the fragments he finds. He refers many, many times to the Big Picture, cautioning McPhee against a singular landscape vision, advising him to look beyond the limits of generality: "The oolites and dolomite—tuff and granite . . . are pieces of the picture. The stories that go with them—the creatures and the chemistry, the motions of the

crust . . . may well, as stories, stand on their own, but they are all fragments of the Picture" (62).

While spatial imprecision and diversity are repeatedly realized in
McPhee's tetralogy, the notion of temporal disorientation remains an
equally important element in the geologic metaphor I employ, for time
is a central theme in his work. Gregory's theoretical "multi-levelled dialogue" is thus realized temporally in McPhee's various and tumultuous
histories, encompassing both the minutiae of geology and the details of
humanity. Indeed, for McPhee the elements of human and geologic
time remain not separate and distinct but conjoined and compounded—
the human instants he constantly juxtaposes with the vast geologic past,
as Susan Maher points out, "sharing in [the geologic record] of compression and fragmentation" (41). It is a record in which every scene, including the human scene, is temporary and "only fragments remain,
[only] summations and moments" (Maher, 41). Kenneth Deffeyes's fer-
vent pursuit of "noble metal," for example, renders the human histories
as equally enticing as the lithic. For the evidence of nineteenth-century
mining, "the hand-forged ore buckets [and] square nails" (*Annals*, 108)
that he upturns in his scavenging of mill-tailings and dumps, is significantly perceived by Deffeyes not as unimportant or peripheral to the geology but as valid and exciting—as "good [a] litter" (108) as the "handsome mess" of geologic rubble. In fact Deffeyes's "catholic
enthusiasms," akin to those of McPhee himself and all of his geologist
mentors, always extend beyond the singular and form a striking analogy
for a new theoretical agenda that embraces "different ways of seeing
time and space together, 'vertical' and 'horizontal' dimensions of being
in the world freed from the imposition of inherent categorical privilege"
(Soja, *Postmodern Geographies*, 12).

McPhee's *Assembling California* geologist, Eldridge Moores, clearly
remains crucial to negotiating the multidimensional. After all, he constantly embraces a wider picture in which a broadened vision enables a
broadened understanding. The "better to understand California," for
example, McPhee "follows [Moores] to analogous geological field areas
[worldwide]" (*Annals*, 436). Indeed, Moores's "wider" picture not only
includes greater lithic exploration but also explicitly includes humanity.
For he has "read widely in Greek history as well as geologic history"
(436). And the "big chunks of serpentine—smooth as talc, mottled
black and green" (36) that lie on each of his two porches—remain symbolic of the conjunction of diverse spheres; his own threshold is an anal-

ogy for the creative juxtapositions, both spatial and temporal, of the new critical theory.

Certainly, it is in *Assembling California* that the concept of corrupted time—of jumbled and messy histories—is rendered most explicit, for McPhee memorably likens the disordered Californian landscape to the "draped, hung, arched [and] folded [imagery] of Dali's watches" (*Annals*, 513). His allusion is clearly to Salvador Dali's disturbing entropic image *The Persistence of Memory*, a surreal work that oversteps the borders of a delineated landscape tradition by challenging perceptions of space, art, landscape memory, and time itself. Dali's central figure is ghostlike, a suggestion of ephemeral humanity upon the "timeless" landscape covered with a distorted clockface and encircled by further misshapen timepieces, each displaying a different time. Indeed, Dali's notion of temporal disorder—of the necessarily multifaceted nature of history—is, for McPhee, a key narrative device: he repeatedly places human and geologic histories together in a casual and seamless synthesis. His evocation of the by-products of humanity, for example, mirrors the outpourings of the geologic process itself: "long after the truck had gone, the cloud hung stinking in the air. The [volcanic] ash had been launched in several eruptive episodes" (*Annals*, 454). Similarly, early in *Basin and Range*, a moment from the natural world of two hundred and fifty million years ago is contiguous with the cultural present: "There are fossil burrows in the slate—long stringers where Triassic animals travelled through the quiet mud. . . . There is a huge rubber sandal by the road, a crate of broken eggs, three golf balls. Two are very cheap, but one is an Acushnet Titleist. A soda can comes clinking down the Interstate, moving ten miles an hour" (22–23). These examples represent a mere fraction of the multitude of syntheses found in McPhee's opus.

Significantly, these compound histories occur by the highway: for McPhee, it is by the road that the fragments of the "Big Picture" seem most apparent. The interstate repeatedly connects the components of his annals. His restless soda can clinking down the road becomes a graphic and memorable icon, a vivid detail we cannot ignore—its noisy and eternal journey beating the mantra of progress and movement so central to late twentieth century cultural and critical thought. In the contemporary study of deep landscape and space, the concept of stasis is patently not an option. Edward Soja, for example, posits "voyages of exploration . . . [along many] different routes" (*Postmodern Geographies*,

248, 243) in order to achieve a practical understanding of the restructured theoretical terrain. And his work, akin to McPhee's odyssey, is a search to reveal "other spaces" and hidden geographical texts—an exploration of the unseen. Journeying also remains a central trope of Derek Gregory's contemporary geographical imagination. For the metaphor of traveling, as he points out, inevitably calls into question static discourses that may claim to erase particularities and transcend notions of multiplicitous time and space. Gregory perceives the discourses of critical human geography as necessarily mobile—a "cross-border traffic" (12) of ideas, a series of "travelling" discourses moving from site to site that facilitate a landscape vision embracing new and ever changing perspectives. Gregory terms this "geography in [its] expanded sense" (11), and the notion of transgression and exploration—the infringement of the limits of established temporal-spatial thought—is fundamental to his argument.

Like McPhee, who strives to feel the difference between the old geology and the new, to sense how the science has settled down a decade after its great upheaval in the 1960s, Gregory welcomes existing boundaries, perceiving structured and logical landscape order (expressed in his favorite analogy as defined cartographic spaces) as less a repressive than a constructive element in the exploration of a wider and more complete "landscape." For the fixed and inert places of conventional landscape "totality," marked noted and named, effectively make "possible the particulars of other journeys" (Gregory, 25) by positively defining the active, living, and unrealized "blank spots" of time and space. While Henri Lefebvre rejects the concept of such definite and boldly marked limiting boundaries, perceiving social spaces as distinguishable yet not separable—spaces that frequently "interpenetrate one another and/or superimpose themselves upon one another" (86)—the notion of traveling also forms an essential element of his theories. The concept of networks and pathways, for example, is for Lefebvre key to the disclosure of new horizons concealed by conventional categories. Indeed, his mesh of pathways, which "ha[ve] more in common with a spider's web than a drawing or plan" (118), crosses the linear logic of structured landscapes to gain access to alternative spaces of representation, to "counterspaces" that challenge the dominant spatialities and "re[veal] . . . the space [that is inevitably] appearing in the ruins" (Gregory, 394) of convention's collapsing referentials. Thus Lefebvre's trajectory, like Gregory's, and ultimately like McPhee's journey to new geologic knowledge, is a form of traversal, a dis-covery of the blank spots and a dis-closure of the space between the lines of the definitive landscape "map."

Deep landscape knowledge, in John McPhee's terms, "requires prodigious travel" (*Annals,* 474), and the road remains a significant and central factor in his explication of the "mobile" landscape. After all, McPhee's intellectual momentum, in terms of geologic understanding, is sustained by the physical act of movement. He describes the "road [as] a portal . . . a proscenium arch" (23) to a complex and elaborate landscape drama—a "window" leading the imagination into the earth. And while his journey encompasses every kind of trail from dirt road to mountain ledge, it is alongside the restless highway that McPhee gains a clear, intimate, and revelatory view of his subject. "Roadcuts," said geologist Karen Kleinspehn, "are essential to do geology . . . a godsend" (23); and McPhee's voyage of exploration aptly begins with essentials— in what Lefebvre might have termed a landscape "counterspace"—in the high, dark roadcut of the Palisades Sill, pressed up against the rock-wall by the windbooms of juggernauts and assaulted by the needle-sharp shriek of the truckers' air horns. Here McPhee stands face to face with movement and speed, with discord and chaos, and the notion of critical transgression—of Lefebvre's interpenetration, or of what Soja termed "lateral mapping" (*Postmodern Geographies,* 2)—is physically realized in Kleinspehn's hard-hitting sideward landscape exploration: "she hits [the rockwall] again and again—until a chunk of some poundage falls free . . . geologists have fungoed so much rock off the walls they may have set them back a foot . . ." (20–21).

Indeed, the concepts of transgression and travel—and hence, I suggest, progress—remain inextricable in each of the sections of McPhee's epic geologic adventure. Geologist Anita Harris of *In Suspect Terrain* (Book II), for example, begins her trip west on I-80 not merely with her vehicle, but with her "rockhammer, her sledgehammer, her hydrochloric acid and [McPhee]" (*Annals,* 182). While she describes the three key things in the science of geology as "travel, travel and travel" (234), it is the road that primarily facilitates her understanding: "If it weren't for this roadcut, I'd never be able to measure the rocks" (210); and it is also the road that enables her transgression—enables her to practice what Derek Gregory termed geography in its expanded sense and to confront the close-up view. Hence, walking the narrow spaces between the interstate's "concrete guard wall[s] and the rock" (195), Harris and McPhee quite literally overstep the landscape boundaries to explore the previously unrealized landscape "blank spots"—the chaotic subsurface structure. They experience, in fact, the "flickers and glimpses" of a thousand million years of space and time: "As we moved along beside the screaming trucks we were averaging about ten thousand years per step. The progression was not uniform, of course. There might be two million years in one fossil streambed, and then the next lamination in the rock would record a single season—on one flaky surface a single drop of rain" (198).

The notion of flickering glimpses of diverse realities—the medley of jumbled images invoked and embraced by McPhee—is suggestive of a form of frenzied film show before which the bewildered viewer must succumb passively to the chaos of disordered takes. Certainly, the plethora of perspectives created by this contemporary transformation of the "landscape" vision induces foreboding. After all, a transdisciplinary voyage into the tumult of "deep space" and what I will term "deep history" (for history and space cannot be separated, each space having, of course, its own history) negates the concept of the earth as a coordinated and easily understood whole—as a "condens[ed] region [of] oneness, [and its] principle of 'terrestrial unity'" (Gregory, 40). Derek Gregory expresses such disorientation in map-making terms. For if the worldview from a single perspective maps a landscape of completeness, then the multiple perspectives of contemporary theory generate what Gregory can describe only as "cartographic anxiety" (70). After all, how can we map inconsistency, irregularity, and eternally provisional boundaries?

Many, as Gregory points out, have articulated this loss of unity and certainty. Michel Foucault asserted, for example, that insecurity is inevitable; our "repugnance to . . . difference and the epistemological mutation of history" (12, 11) is an understandable reaction in the face of rupture, dispersion, and dissolution of reassuring and established coherence. Of course, as Foucault continues, we are "afraid to conceive of the Other" (12). For as uninterrupted continuities prepare us, lead us, and provide us with a "privileged shelter for the sovereignty of our consciousness" (12), so the discontinuities of contemporary social theory leave us exposed, confused, and lost; the disruption of any neatly charted land renders us knee-deep in the quagmire of uncertainty—the "shifting sands . . . [in which our] every goal [seems to] ha[ve] disappeared" (Gregory, 122, 149). Indeed, while the path to unity always leads us back to a "stilling of the waters [and a] domestification of the dread" (Gregory, 143), so the path to multiplicity that Gregory endorses inevitably leads us to uncertainty and even danger.

The dilemmas inherent in critical social theory are made manifest in McPhee's symbolic landscape. While he embraces notions of uncertainty and convolution, for example—"I don't want to look at a topic from just one perspective . . . I want to look at the *complexities*, to come up with a piece of writing in greater dimensions" (quoted in Hamilton, 54; emphasis added)—he also recognizes the desire for stability and the dread of chaos. Of course, McPhee points out, people will want to perceive the landscape as immutable and the writhing lithic turmoil as finished. For what Leonardo Seeber referred to as the "principle of least astonishment" (*Annals*, 604) is a basic human psychological need, and "there is no greater betrayal than when the earth defaults on the understanding that it stay still underfoot" (605).

The notion of contention, however, pervades McPhee's work and echoes Derek Gregory's own engagement with the concept of threat. In an eschewal of passivity, Gregory advocates a form of "guerilla warfare" on the immutable, a participation in the "wag[ing] [of the] war on totality" (143). Indeed, the fervor of the plate tectonics revolution—which geologist Eldridge Moores describes as analogous to warfare: "The causal excitement of it was something like landing on Guadalcanal in the middle of the action of a 'noble war' " (*Annals*, 134)—clearly recalls the notion of conflict invoked by Gregory. His concept of an active engagement with new territory, with new and splintered mapping, is echoed repeatedly in McPhee's exploration of the geologic landscape. For McPhee's geologist guides constantly seek to (re)express the evolution and dissolution of the existing landscape. Kenneth Deffeyes in *Basin and Range,* for example, continually subverts cartographic authority—the conception of the world as an enframed and fixed totality—by confidently "sketch[ing] in . . . alternative lines" (141) on the Exxon regional map. Indeed, his physical contact with the map itself ("he places his hands on the map . . . and hold[s] between them a large piece of California [and] the coast [lies] against his belly"; 141) constitutes a form of territorial assault and instantly revokes the security of an inviolable cartographic landscape authority.

While McPhee, moreover, is constantly and literally standing on shifting earth, the material beneath his feet—irrefutably "crumbly, loose, weathered [and] unstable . . . a pyramid side of decomposing shards"

(*Annals,* 109)—is analogous to his own premeditated, contested, and unstable narrative. The rigorous planning and composing for which he is renowned[3]—the "structural order . . . [that] is the main ingredient of his work" (Howarth, xv)—finds a form appropriate to tectonic dynamism. Thus as we journey with McPhee the lithic fragments of which he speaks and on which he stands are mirrored in a mobile text that juxtaposes an ordained jumble of narrative elements and that compels our engagement—our participation in the conflict. McPhee is directing, and we are in the picture: from anecdote to fact, from scientific data to literary device, from the wider history of geologic theory to the personal diary extracts of a single Wyoming homesteader, we are fighting for annexation and control of the narrative. Edward Soja cites John Berger to express the essence of his "postmodern" geographies, and Berger's evaluation of the modern narrative may be constructively applied to McPhee's own challenging geologic chronicle: "We hear a lot about the crisis of the modern novel. What this involves, fundamentally, is a change in the mode of narration. It is scarcely any longer possible to tell a straight story sequentially unfolding in time and this is because we are too aware of what is continually traversing the storyline laterally. . . . Such awareness is the result of our constantly having to take into account the simultaneity and extension of events and possibilities" (*Postmodern Geographies,* 22).

McPhee delights, it seems, in imparting all the particulars of a landscape that is inherently difficult to understand, traversing the storyline laterally, and taking into account extended possibilities. For geology per se is not simple. It is a jumble not only of rocks, histories, and stories, but of words—a new and complex language with which to contend. For example, a cactolith, according to the American Geological Institute's *Glossary of Geology and Related Sciences,* is a "[q]uasi-horizontal chonolith composed of anastomosing ductoliths, whose distal ends curl like a harpolith, thin like a sphenolith, or bulge discordantly like an akmolith or ethmolith[!]" (*Annals,* 33). And the "new" geology reveals complexities beyond the singular. What had previously been described, for example, as "[t]he granite of the world, turned out to be a large family of rock that included granodiorite, monzonite, syerite, adamellite, trondhjemite, alaskite and a modest amount of true granite" (34). Thus the new geologic vocabulary, as McPhee (and the reader) struggles to understand, is a language of multiple meanings in which even the "normal" is a duality—" 'normal' meant at right angles. 'Normal' also meant a fault with a depressed hanging wall" (32)—and the concept of normality itself frequently seems elusive and impalpable.

The complexity of McPhee's shifting tectonic terrain, a terrain of many dimensions, is a compelling metaphor for the dialectical and conflictive space of contemporary critical human geography. Indeed, the geologic fusion of history and space, of landscapes and stories, that so elegantly mirrors a cultural geography of simultaneous relations and meanings is finally rendered explicit in McPhee's *Assembling California* earthquake—the climax of his lithic journey and the most tangible evidence of tectonic theory. McPhee is at the end of the road. He has come, with a man named Araullo, "down the trail" (*Annals*, 620) and jumped over water to a wide, flat boulder overlooking the Pacific Ocean. But the landscape is still moving. The driveways of San Francisco are breaking "like crushed shells"; the redwoods are swaying; cracks, fissures, and fence-posts are "jumping." And in contortions analogous to Edward Soja's "twisted" temporal and spatial orders, even the "double yellow lines are making left lateral jumps" (611). Landscape constraints (exemplified by this most potent symbol of cultural restriction), like the material and intellectual contexts of modern critical theory, "have begun to shift dramatically" (Soja, *Postmodern Geographies*, 10).

Indeed, using McPhee's geology as a powerful metaphor, notions of coherent, separate, and linear history/ies and spaces are transformed; and a new "landscape" rhythm is introduced. A new discordant tune is unavoidably played, and the fundamentals of limited and constrained social and geographic theories are dispersed and diffused: "Coastal bluffs [and] mountain cliffs . . . fall. . . . The piano moves. Jars filled with beans shatter. Wine pours from breaking bottles. A grandfather clock falling—its hands stopping at 5:04—lands on a metronome, which begins to tick" (*Annals*, 613). As landslides move away from the earthquake's epicenter, McPhee's physical terrain literally and forcefully echoes a kaleidoscopic intellectual terrain that, as Soja points out, is no longer easily mappable; for it no longer appears with its "familiar time-worn contours" (*Postmodern Geographies*, 60). There's always something in the rocks, said McPhee, that will give you the answer you are looking for. The answer is, thus, that the landscape—geologic and cultural—is still moving, the Big Picture is not static. McPhee, the "archetypal wayfarer" (Pearson, 62) and the gatherer of complexities, must be content that the dilemma continues.

Acknowledgments

I would like to thank the Arts and Humanities Research Board of the British Academy for its financial assistance when this work was first undertaken as part of a doctoral dissertation.

Notes

1. This reconfigured critical human geography, of course, forms only part of a wider and restructured postwar cultural, political, and theoretical context encompassing many elements: from the breaking down of the certainties in the system of art classification to New Marxism, the political affiliate of the artistic and cultural avant-garde; from feminism to postmodernism, two of the most important political-cultural currents of the last three decades. Indeed, Edward Soja describes the 1960s as a period when "virtually every social science discipline seemed to spawn a reawakened radical fringe" (*Postmodern Geographies*, 45).

2. This phrase, famously, belongs to art critic John Berger, whose questioning of modes of narration—visually and otherwise—is a recognition of the complexity and reconfiguration of the contemporary cultural terrain.

3. See William Howarth's introduction to *The John McPhee Reader* for an in-depth description of McPhee's process of composition.

Works Cited

Foucault, M. *The Archaeology of Knowledge*. London: Tavistock, 1972.

Gregory, D. *Geographical Imaginations*. Cambridge, Mass.: Blackwell, 1994.

Hamilton, J. "An Encounter with John McPhee." *Sierra* (May/June 1990): 50–96.

Hobbs, R. *Robert Smithson: Sculpture*. Ithaca: Cornell University Press, 1981.

Howarth, W. (ed.). *The John McPhee Reader*. New York: Farrar, Straus & Giroux, 2000.

Lefebvre, H. *The Production of Space*. Oxford: Blackwell, 1998.

Maher, S. N. "Deep Time, Human Time and the Western Quest: John McPhee's *Rising from the Plains*." *South Dakota Review* 30(1) (Spring 1992): 36–45.

McPhee, John. *Annals of the Former World*. New York: Farrar, Straus & Giroux, 1998.

Pearson, M. *John McPhee*. Boston: Twayne, 1997.

Soja, E. *Postmodern Geographies*. London: Routledge, 1989.

————. *Thirdspace: Journeys to Los Angeles and other Real-and-Imagined Places.*
    Oxford: Blackwell, 1996.
Trimble, S. (ed.). *Words from the Land.* Reno: University of Nevada Press, 1995.
Turner, B. "Giving Good Reasons: Environmental Appeals in the Nonfiction of
    John McPhee." *Rhetoric Review* 13(1) (Fall 1994): 164–82.
Wood, D. *The Power of Maps.* London: Routledge, 1992.

III

The Writerly Challenges of McPhee

The four essays in part three examine, in different ways, aspects of that particular signature that represents McPhee's style and form. Librarians and bibliographers have long recognized what these essayists identify: McPhee is all over the place and resists classification and categorization. He defies boundaries between fiction and journalism, for example, which explains in large part his influence and attraction. These essays explore just a few of those boundary sections. Meta Carstarphen's essay locates McPhee in a history of English-language journalism and, in her study of two early titles, probes his literary journalism in the service of social criticism. Kathy Smith reads McPhee's first book, *A Sense of Where You Are,* as a means of contrasting journalistic and novelistic traditions and standards; she shows McPhee carving out his own territory in overlapping some of these contrary standards. Dan Philippon, like Alan Weltzien, looks closely at *The Control of Nature,* but from a pedagogical perspective. His essay describes some of the challenges of teaching McPhee in a college classroom and defining comparative bioregionalism in the process. Finally, Susan N. Maher's essay comprehensively studies McPhee's deep interest in codes and the implications of decoding. She reviews several more recent McPhee titles in order to assess his status as a "cultural encoder" and "decoder." Together, this quartet provides more insights into McPhee's unique terrain and identity as a master of literary nonfiction.

Meta G. Carstarphen

Traveling in Social Spaces

John McPhee's Dichotomies in Levels of the Game *and "In Search of Marvin Gardens"*

Historically, the rhetoric of travel writing has exploited the dichotomy of difference versus the cultural norm in order to point readers to some new understanding about themselves and their places within the world. Infused with ideas about power and privilege, travel writing during its heyday in seventeenth- and eighteenth-century literatures featured powerful narratives that helped to shape worldviews about global relationships, even into the current millennium. In more modern times, especially during the last two decades of the twentieth century, travel writing metamorphosed into a celebrated genre of opportunity that reconstructed the idea of travel from a necessary activity for commerce to a leisure-driven one for well-heeled individuals. So the paradigm for adventure had shifted from challenge to consumption, as travel narratives celebrated a new kind of privilege. More often than not, travel writing reflected the mores of economically advantaged classes. And these values not only put the power to define the world around us through travel writing in the hands of a few published authors but also established a romantic formula for those travels. Even as the impetus for travel has changed dramatically over four centuries, from state-sponsored to personal exploration, the resulting travel narratives resonated with classic themes: foreign climes, exotic adventures, strange environs, and even stranger inhabitants.

John McPhee, a journalist with a long career at the prestigious *New Yorker* magazine, wrote prolifically after a time when some reporters initiated a different style of reportage, dubbed the New Journalism. Tom Wolfe and Truman Capote, reporter/writers of the 1960s, were two of the best-known names behind this phenomenon. What was "new" about this writing was the scintillating merger of fact with fiction and of detail with compelling narrative. Leaving behind the journalistic penchant for "objective" facts, New Journalists contended that the story-beneath-the-story was worth as much attention as the surface. This artful interpretation of the world of reality as opposed to the world of fantasy led to a growing body of work recognizable as literary nonfiction, of which journalistic writing became a subset. McPhee's abundant work embraces many of the characteristics of the New Journalism tradition, primarily a willingness to insert a "first-person" viewpoint, to include scrupulous detail in the narrative, and to juxtapose multiple, often marginalized, voices within the text.

Almost prescient of this shift is the "social" writing of John McPhee as exemplified in two of his classic works, *Levels of the Game* and "In Search of Marvin Gardens." He subverts the rhetoric of travel writing and privilege, however, by turning its classic worlds inside out. The interplay of early journalism and travel writing invites theoretical comparisons to McPhee's writing by showing how both traditions inform his attention to detail and style. But is he an essayist, a creative writer, or a reporter? Certainly, all three descriptions are apt.

McPhee can be both topical and obscure, and his work can invoke both the personal and the measured objectivity of the best reporting technique. Two essays that exemplify this conundrum force readers to navigate into infrequently visited terrain, America's social spaces. McPhee wrote *Levels of the Game* and "In Search of Marvin Gardens" during a time when the United States was grappling with the confounding elements of race and class in its most profound way since the Civil War. Riots and civil unrest, social experiments and the "Great Society," dominated the news stories of the late sixties and early seventies.

Such was the turbulent world in which McPhee reported and wrote *Levels of the Game* and "In Search of Marvin Gardens." More than any of his other works, these two essays carried the unmistakable subtext of a nation's curiosity and angst about race and class. As a journalist/writer in the forefront of this profession now suddenly being assailed for its own flaws and biases, McPhee was in a unique position to record worlds in transition. Like the historic journalists before him venturing out from safe habitats, he had the enormous privilege of being able to use the authority of his work to establish a historical record of particular moments in time. Rather than choosing to reassert long-standing racial and social hierarchies, McPhee discovered a different way of telling familiar stories.

As a writer who has defied facile classification, McPhee brings to bear in *Levels of the Game* and "In Search of Marvin Gardens" structures that borrow from both journalistic and literary techniques. Perhaps he would be reluctant to call himself a journalist, despite a stint as a staff writer for *Time* magazine and his long association with the *New Yorker.* Certainly, critical assessment of him as a "type" varies, though most classify him as more than a journalist. Ronald Weber, while conceding that McPhee works like a journalist, characterizes him as a writer who writes above the formula, though he is not quite willing to designate him a "literary journalist" (116). William Howarth, by contrast, insists that McPhee is "not one of the so-called New Journalists, those celebrities who parade their neuroses or stump for public causes" (vii). And Sharon Bass says that McPhee defies easy classification because of the breadth of his work but nonetheless believes that he should be placed "beyond the realm of the traditional essayist and squarely at the center of the emerging literary journalistic tradition" (344).

A full appreciation of McPhee's writing must include a consideration of the journalistic streams from which his works emerge. In truth, his scrupulous reportage and reliance upon observation, his penchant for travel, and his essayist style recall some of the earliest, still-enduring journalistic traditions. Placing McPhee within the historic tradition of what it means to be a journalist/writer evokes a sensibility that is eminently literary, although it rarely communicates that attribute today. When the word for this new kind of timely writing was coined in the late seventeenth century, it defined a distinctly writerly persona. According to *The Oxford English Dictionary,* the word "journalist" came into use in 1693 as almost a synonym for "Epistle-Writer," although by the time Joseph Addison first used the word in 1712 it referred to a female correspondent who provided news from her "journal" (607).

This nascent form of what came to be known as journalism had one of its best showcases in the writings of eighteenth-century British essayists Joseph Addison and Richard Steele. Many years after the first English-language newspaper, the *Oxford Gazette,* appeared in England in 1665, Addison and Steele debuted their first publishing collaboration, the *Tatler* (Wilson and Wilson, 23). As much a celebration of literary style as a recounting of the current news, this twice-weekly publication peppered its items with a decidedly subjective—and apparently popular—writing style. This proved to be so appealing that their other collaborative paper, the *Spectator,* created a persona of the same name for the publication. A gossipy character, "The Spectator" became the narrative alter-ego for

Steele, anticipating by nearly two centuries the intrusion of journalists as characters within their own works. For example, in "In Search of Marvin Gardens," McPhee "creates" a first-person board game player who moves through an imaginary game of Monopoly while other passages describe more objectively the "real" Atlantic City neighborhoods.

As has been the historic pattern, each new incarnation of a communication medium builds upon the successes of its predecessors. Journalists writing for the early newspapers borrowed many of the tools of authors and journal writers who preceded them. Ironically, at the same time, the *form* of journalism moved closer toward a "diarist" style that highlighted facts and events at the expense of context and story. From its earliest incarnations, journalism has always been about the business of news. In his brilliant study of the progression of news throughout history, Mitchell Stephens connects the historic flow of literacy and the human need to know with the evolution of news as product. In time, that product became defined by what he calls the "journalistic method," a praxis for reporting the news involving primarily the use of enterprise, observation, and investigation (Stephens, 229).

Regarding American journalism's "worship" of objectivity, David T. Z. Mindich scrutinizes what ultimately became a hegemonic formula for newswriting. As he observes, "If American journalism were a religion, as it has been called from time to time, its supreme deity would be 'objectivity'" (1). Tracking journalism's development through much of the nineteenth century, Mindich notes that objectivity became entrenched as part of the journalistic code in the 1890s, paralleling the recognition of journalism as a professional enterprise (114).

Twice during the twentieth century the phrase "new journalism" was coined to characterize a shift in newswriting and reporting that reigned as the dominant form of the day. When "new" journalism emerged a second time, McPhee became one of its more prominent practitioners. The earlier incarnation of "new" journalism emerged in the century's first decade and was quickly renamed "yellow journalism." A by-product of circulation battles between two newspaper titans, William Randolph Hearst and Joseph Pulitzer, this "new" kind of journalism gloried in the sensational and elevated scandal and intrigue (Wilson and Wilson, 134). The language characteristic of this type of reportage was often florid and dramatic, carrying with it a decided point of view that frequently lambasted or extolled its subject in no uncertain terms.

In the 1960s Tom Wolfe resurrected the name "new journalism" and became one of its most dedicated advocates. However, this incarnation defined itself as a form capable of successfully combining "objective detail with personal opinion" (Perkins et al., 1155). In order to avoid the excesses of the earlier period, these New Journalists were far less eager to exploit the bizarre with lurid prose and loud headlines. Instead, practitioners of this New Journalism like McPhee gave themselves permission to interject their views by making one subject more dominant than another or by adding heretofore hidden background or context in order to create empathy for a subject.

Compelling characters and a connection to the issues of the day are evident in both *Levels of the Game* and "In Search of Marvin Gardens." Ostensibly written about a semifinal match between African-American tennis player Arthur Ashe and his Anglo opponent Clark Graebner, *Levels of the Game* appears to miss the mark as far as chronicling significant sports events. As critic William Howarth notes, this game was not decisive in either man's career (129). "In Search of Marvin Gardens" takes its title from ruminations about the Monopoly board game as well as from shifts in urban development in New Jersey. The social contexts of race and class of the late sixties and seventies made McPhee's musings on these topics eminently topical. Employing the techniques of the New Journalism—a tradition with which he should be aligned—McPhee has used subjectivity and character portrayal to make such abstract and difficult concepts in the social arena appear imminently personal and accessible.

With a journalistic heritage that arose from the sensibilities of literary writers, contemporary forms of journalism have expanded the continuum between "diaristic" and "journalistic" with news-writing protocols that make a distinction between "hard" news and "soft" news, respectively. Hard news, more like diary writing, presents facts with little elaboration. By contrast, soft news describes the longer-format, less-urgent topics that newspapers carry. Dominated by "lifestyle" stories describing anything from recipes to celebrity profiles, soft news articles seem trivial compared to hard news stories. Hard news is the privileged discourse of daily newspaper writing, ruling the all-important front page with bold headlines. It is the acknowledged format for the serious (and by implication the most important) content of the paper. But McPhee pushes the soft news continuum by inculcating perspectives on the serious issues of race and class in both *Levels of the Game* and "In Search of Marvin Gardens." The social concerns of the New Journalists of the 1960s and 1970s challenged the historic division within journalism between "serious" hard news and "trivial" soft news. McPhee, writing in this tradition, also challenges the detached reliance upon facts and the formulaic writing of mainstream journalism. Moreover, the end results of his work, pointing as they do to meaning and truth beyond the surface narratives, attempt to reassert balance in how readers interpret their worlds.

Anyone familiar with McPhee's body of work knows that he is a mobile writer. He travels to distinct geographic places to write, and his writings are marked by the strong sense of place evoked by his adventures. The whole enterprise of "travel writing" is problematized by its roots in exploration and colonization, however, because the massive works generated during the eighteenth and nineteenth centuries created such iconic beliefs about "difference" that many remain in place today.

While the culmination and synthesis of the objective method in journalism may have occurred in the nineteenth century, the philosophical underpinnings for its dominance began with seeds planted in the eighteenth century and even earlier. The "age of reason" privileged European intellectualism against other streams of knowledge. The "other" in this worldview invariably had the face of color, as British and European powers sought to consolidate their power through slavery and conquest of such places as Africa, India, and the Americas. Journalists and travel writers sent home their reports of foreign and inferior lands to eager audiences, sustaining a "rhetoric of privilege" emanating from these texts. This privilege derived from the seemingly objective way the facts about such travels appeared, bolstered by the authority of both firsthand observation and printed text. Similarly, objective news writing would later dominate journalism, based upon the reporter's ability to observe facts and get a written report about them into print faster than anyone else.

Contemporary scholar Mary Louise Pratt's study of travel writing illuminates this genre as a rhetoric of conquest. Looking at texts some 300 years before the eighteenth century, she identifies a shift in what she calls the "maritime" paradigm of travel writing. During this premodern newspaper era, books carried exploration news in a dominant construct that focused, Pratt notes, on "technical observations of coastal border, geographic land forms and horizon" (24). By the mid-1800s such travel writing shifted to "interior exploration," which enabled new knowledge to be built upon neophyte systems of "discovery, sampling and labeling of all kinds" (24). Furthermore, travel accounts that were now being carried in newspapers and books were pivotal, in a real promotional sense, to this era's dominant metaphor of "reason." Notes Pratt: "Journalism and narrative travel accounts . . . were essential mediators between the scientific network and a larger European public. They were central agents in legitimating scientific authority and its global project" alongside Europe's other ways of "knowing the world and being in it" (29).

Not surprisingly, this way of understanding the known world gave Europe ascendancy over other territories—a reality that was borne out by domination, both physical and economic. Pratt sees little that has changed in the major travel writing motifs as practiced during the 1960s and 1970s. In her view, travel writing in the latter part of the twentieth century fueled the insatiable needs of a growing travel industry that exoticized foreign "paradises" as a commodity for these business interests (221). Ideologically, the narratives about such idyllic or exotic places, when considered against a subtext of Western superiority, did little more than offer "degraded, countercommodified" versions of postcolonial reality (210).

For the New Journalists of the late twentieth century, the opportunity to re-create writing that could record reality yet offer multiple possible "levels of meaning" was the professional challenge of the era. Their nonformula "formula" opened up all kinds of exploration of the real world. Like travelers from previous eras, New Journalists also set out from the safe and distant vantage points of objective fact-gathering to venture into the interior nuances of storytelling and truth. And few have done it better than McPhee.

McPhee's work, then, demonstrates a keen ability to marry the ethos of a working journalist (a writer searching for the truth in facts) and the pathos of a storyteller (a writer searching for the truth in imagined realities). It seems he releases his well-researched works into the imaginative minds of his readers. Like a seasoned traveler advising neophytes about the adventures before them, however, McPhee "guides" his readers carefully, using detail and metaphor to help them navigate through these texts and landscapes.

For instance, in "Travels of the Rock," McPhee ostensibly focuses on the repair of the actual Plymouth Rock while ruminating on the history, geology, and possible origins of the "oldest symbol of the New World" (188). His presumption—an axiom in journalistic writing—is that the audience brings no knowledge to the subject. Therefore, he densely surrounds the underlying simple premise about the monument's restoration with lots of fact and detail.

By contrast, McPhee's aim in *Levels* and "Marvin Gardens" may have been inverted, particularly because the subjects of race, poverty, and achievement are ones about which ostensibly everyone is knowledgeable or least holds strong opinions. Strategically, he writes about subjects that everyone "knows" about, but he invalidates that knowledge by bringing so much that is new and fresh to the discussion. Thus, as readers guided by McPhee's particular sense of how we should traverse his narrative and what we should see, we are all uninitiated travelers into these new worlds of possibilities. We have lost our own rhetoric of privilege, race, class, and social dynamics because McPhee injects copious details into these two essays in order to reform, rather than inform, the readers' sensibilities.

Just as explorers did so many centuries ago, McPhee's writing in *Levels of the Game* and "In Search of Marvin Gardens" offers himself as traveler, explorer, and journalist of new worlds. In 1968 few documents fully framed the worlds of race, class, and society so acutely as *The Kerner Report*. Its effect upon society and journalism was profound and could provide an important context for McPhee's own engagement of socially tinged issues.

Fueled by urban rebellions that exploded in many American cities during the "long hot summer" of 1967, President Lyndon Johnson appointed the National Advisory Commission on Civil Disorders or Kerner Commission in July 1967. He charged this committee with answering three salient but basic questions about the violence: "What happened? Why did it happen? What can be done to prevent it from happening again?" (*Kerner,* ix). Seven months later, on 1 March 1968, the commission issued its findings. In a reprinting of the original report twenty years later, in 1988, journalist Tom Wicker wrote that the validity of the sweeping recommendations was enhanced because of the moderate composition of the commission membership. These recommendations included ideas from "specifics on jobs, housing, schools, police procedures, newspaper practices," to large abstractions like "community attitudes" (xvii). Wicker suggests that the committee's findings were likely to resonate with much of America, given the "safe" composition of its membership.

Certainly, journalists in every part of the media were intricately involved with the story of *The Kerner Report* (named after commission chairman Otto Kerner, then the governor of Illinois). Journalists had covered the riots that spawned the report. Journalists spread the word of *The Kerner Report*'s findings. And, much to the dismay and embarrassment of the profession, journalism was found to be a contributing factor in the unrest and came under harsh criticism from the report's authors. Chapter 15, "The News Media and the Disorders," soundly criticized the media for being out of touch with their audiences—failing to report on the underlying causes of the tensions and, when they did, offering inaccurate and sensational portrayals (363). Moreover, the industry's professional performance was severely compromised by what the committee discovered was an appalling lack of staff diversity along racial and social lines. The legacy of the Kerner Commission report haunted journalism three decades later, as newspapers continued to grapple with the challenges of trying to create racial parity among their reporters and in their coverage (Carstarphen, 2). Whatever McPhee's own thoughts were about race relations in the United States at that time, both *Levels of the Game* and "In Search of Marvin Gardens" show an intellectual curiosity about these issues that was neither predictable nor condescending.

Levels of the Game centers on a semifinal tennis match between Arthur Ashe and Clark Graebner, who in 1968 were competing against each other to win the men's singles match played at Forest Hills (Howarth, 129). At the essay's end, McPhee is grounded firmly at the sidelines of this game, recording with technical precision some of the actual play: "Serve, return, volley—Ashe hits a forehand into the tape" (McPhee, *Levels*, 156). But at the beginning McPhee is interested in building his narrative around a more compelling subject than a sports match. In time, Ashe was destined to become the best-known African-American tennis player in the history of the game before the achievements of today's Williams sisters. But in 1968, when the match took place, Americans in general knew very little about this man, who was quiet, self-possessed, and in the eyes of some aloof and unknowable.

In *Levels of the Game*, McPhee immediately plunges readers into his subject with an extended quotation from Ronald Charity: "People say that Arthur lacks the killer instinct. . . . And that is a lot of baloney. Arthur is quietly aggressive—more aggressive than people give him credit for being. You don't get to be that good without a will to win" (*Levels*, 129). Several sentences later readers learn that Charity was a self-taught aficionado of tennis who gave Ashe his first lessons in the game.

Thus, Ashe's character is partially revealed through the eyes of his earliest tennis mentor. Throughout the essay, in successive passages and intercuts, the unknowable Ashe becomes more transparent as layers peel away. Significantly, the opening quotation of the essay tells us salient information about Ashe the tennis player as opposed to Ashe the "Negro" tennis player.

Only several sentences later do we get a subtle introduction to the racial undertones of what it means to be an African-American tennis player in 1968. McPhee does not have to give statistics about privilege and discrimination; nor does he "sensationalize" Ashe by objectifying his race. In the traditional practices of standard journalism at that time—which demanded that the most important facts go first—Ashe's ethnicity would have been a prominent part of the inverted pyramid. Thus, McPhee resists an easy formula by failing to flag Ashe's race in the first paragraph of his essay. This deliberate choice speaks volumes about McPhee's diminution of his own privilege as a "white" writer about a "black" subject. In a very deliberate way, he has "leveled" the playing field between journalist and subject—and ultimately the readers—by inviting us to be partners in his discovery of Arthur Ashe's personhood.

Nevertheless, the race and class differences between Ashe and his opponent are not irrelevant to McPhee's storytelling. Ashe's opponent, Clark Graebner, is just as casually introduced. After an extended introduction to Ashe and information about his formative years, we meet his opponent at play during this intense match in which they are both engaged. As Graebner, a formidable competitor, faces off with Ashe, McPhee evokes a Goliath towering over his David: "He [Ashe] is uncomfortable looking uphill at Graebner, who hits another serve of almost unplayable force but just close enough to be reached" (*Levels*, 135). Next we learn of Graebner's accomplished wife, herself a world-class tennis player, and later of his dentist father, with whom he engaged in father-and-son tournaments during his youth.

By contrast, Ashe was born to a father who worked multiple jobs to support his family and Arthur's expensive sport yet who could barely read or write. Ashe got his start in the game by playing with Ronald Charity in Richmond, Virginia, on "four hard-surface courts [that] were built at Brook Field, a Negro playground about two miles from the heart of the city" (*Levels*, 130). Graebner, an only child, grew up in Ohio, with easy access to the game that would dominate his later life:

> The Cleveland Skating Club had four cement indoor tennis courts
> and ten *en-tout-cas* outdoor courts, so Clark spent a high proportion
> of his formative years there, making the trip every afternoon on "the
> rapid," and going home, after office hours, with his father. (The ten-
> nis facilities are now called the Calvary Tennis Club and are a separate,
> integrated organization, because "a citizen do-gooder," as Mrs.
> Graebner describes him, noted some years ago that the courts were on
> public land rented from the city, and therefore membership should be
> open to all. The solution was to create the Calvary Club.) Skating
> Club members could join Calvary or not, as they chose, and the
> Graebners immediately signed up. (146)

The contrast in the two players' access to tennis, an uncommon sport
in the 1950s, communicates poignantly and vividly the caste differences
between Ashe and Graebner. United by their youthful love for the
sport, they nevertheless were products of their particular time and space.
When Ashe's ability outgrew the limitations of the public tennis courts,
his father placed him in the hands of a wealthy black doctor who personally supervised Ashe's continued excellence with the protection of
his private tennis court. The Graebners, in contrast, quietly skirted
around the public use of their facilities by forming a "private" club
within a club. As a writer, McPhee neither condemns these segregated
times nor extols them. Yet the common superiority of these two cham-
pions is rendered in such individual terms through these experiences
that the tennis match itself becomes more than a game—it becomes an
iconic match of excellence against an archaic order of things. As the title
implies, and as McPhee himself writes some 1,000 words into this essay,
"Ashe wants to level things." By the end of the essay, readers are left to
meditate on how many levels there truly are to this game and to the
game of life in 1969.

As an observer, journalist, and shaper of word images for a vast audience, McPhee wrote from a position of privilege. On the whole, this is
true of all United States journalists, who always write under the protec-
tive veil of the First Amendment, which, in part, excludes government
control or sanction of the press. In contradistinction to early British
journalists, who were indeed routinely subjected to the pleasure or displeasure of their monarch or other officials, this privileged space carries
enormous power. It can also, potentially, lead to a great abuse of power.

In a different approach, and with a much shorter exposition, "In

Search of Marvin Gardens" displays McPhee's affinity for highlighting ironic consciousness by intercutting two types of narrations and blending them into one. Unlike *Levels,* which is built upon the contrasts or differences between its two protagonists, "Marvin Gardens" actually patches together "similar" words and phrases to construct a poignant piece about urban decay and privilege.

With its overt motif borrowed from a board game about economic dominance, however, "Marvin Gardens" has other subjects to explore. Once again, McPhee sets up a dialogue of two different perspectives. Here he writes in first person, opening in cryptic style with the beginning of a game of Monopoly: "Go. I roll the dice—a six and a two. Through the air I move my token, the flatiron, to Vermont Avenue, where dog packs range" ("Search," 310). As McPhee-the-narrator moves around the playing board, McPhee-the-writer intercuts these interludes with scenes from the real-life places named. While his unnamed opponent buys "St. Charles Place" in a seemingly benign game, the real "St. Charles Place" is brought into vivid reality through his descriptive prowess: "The sidewalks of St. Charles Place have been cracked to shards by through-growing weeds. There are no buildings. Mansions, hotels once stood here. A few street lamps now drop cones of light on broken glass and vacant space behind a chain-link fence that some great machine has in places bent to the ground. Five plane trees—in full summer leaf, flecking the light—are all that live on St. Charles Place" (310).

Marvin Gardens, as game fans know, is the name of a location on the popular board game Monopoly, created in the early 1930s by Charles B. Darrow ("Search," 311). Monopoly immortalized the familiar sites of Atlantic City, then a middle-class resort enclave. But the Atlantic City of the late sixties and early seventies was quite different. Touched by the urban unrest and grinding poverty that had affected so many cities across the nation, Atlantic City was a textbook example of poverty and neglect. Race is also the subtext in this essay; and once again, McPhee is concerned with subtleties rather than overt blandishments.

After opening sentences that announce the roll of dice and landing on "Vermont Avenue," McPhee takes us to an actual street in the next paragraph that seems to have absolutely no connection to the innocuous board game. This street is vividly presented, with images of "ruins, rubble fire damage, open garbage" ("Search," 310). In the board game segments, streets with names familiar to Monopoly players—Illinois, St.

Charles Place, Indiana—are sold off for increasingly higher values in this duel between the McPhee persona and his opponent, described as a "tall, shadowy figure" (310). Yet with each transaction, the intervening segments continue to describe dismal environs and hardened residents. McPhee introduces the first of the many people he describes in this neighborhood with vivid detail: "She wears dungarees and a bright-red shirt, has ample breasts and a Hadendoan Afro, a black halo, two feet in diameter" (311).

McPhee resists the default cliches such as "urban blight," "predominately black," "ghetto," or "inner-city" to communicate this neighborhood. Instead he creates richly nuanced portrayals of urban neglect. Later in the essay, when McPhee does use a term such as "bombed-out ghetto," the words have meaning built upon his careful construction of a scene instead of our own stereotyped imaginings. In time, he will expose the true irony of Monopoly, juxtaposing the commercially successful game and pop culture icon against the enduring socioeconomic strains among races, classes, and ethnic groups.

As the essay progresses, it reveals a saga about the decline of what was once a resort area, juxtaposed with a history of how the Camden & Atlantic Land Company monopoly was constructed. This late nineteenth century consortium of real estate and railroad investors built profits upon the control of train travel into Atlantic City and its surrounding neighborhoods. McPhee succinctly describes this group as "founders, fathers, forerunners, archetypical masters of the quick kill" ("Search," 312).

One of the classic "sites" of the Monopoly game is the jail, which McPhee renders in brilliant, understated commentary. In the board game, an unfortunate roll of the dice can send a promising player to jail and out of the action during pivotal times. The McPhee persona ruefully reflects on his own experience during the second game of this series as an example: ". . . I go immediately to jail, and again to jail while my opponent seizes property. He is dumb-foundingly lucky. He wins in twelve minutes" ("Search," 313).

More chilling are McPhee's descriptions of the "real" jail in Atlantic City. In the board game, players may evoke the penalty "Go Directly to Jail, Do Not Pass Go" if they select the wrong playing card. In the real jail, occupants are imprisoned for such crimes as hitting a jitney driver, stealing a car, or carrying a pistol in a purse. The facilities are dingy, and the food is questionable. As an example of jail life, McPhee chronicles a white teenager who makes bail and leaves after one night and a sixteen-year-old black male who cannot make bail and who languishes for days in a lonely cell. The inhabitants who stay incarcerated for any length of time seem to have two qualities in common—they are poor and marginalized. Near the end of the essay, McPhee reveals in his understated way that one of the city's early financial barons, Alexander Biddle, punched a streetcar conductor with his fist and "did not go to jail" ("Search," 319). The irony is complete.

Ultimately, these two narratives, the historical and the present, converge in McPhee's real and imagined search for "Marvin Gardens." In his actual reportage, he easily finds the real-life counterparts of all the Monopoly game sites except Marvin Gardens; and his repeated questions to himself and to the people he meets accentuate his quest. Simultaneously, during his imagined board game series (as he is locked into a property acquisition struggle with his opponent), the McPhee persona discovers that unless he "buys" the Marvin Gardens "property," he will lose the game and the series. As in *Levels of the Game,* McPhee inserts a phrase that seems to be the thematic topic of this piece, repeating at strategic structures the observation that he and his opponent "[b]lock upon block, gradually, are canceling each other out . . ." ("Search," 310). As financial wealth in the "play" world accumulates, while financial ruin spreads in the real one, McPhee seems to ask readers to weigh the cost of rampant economic greed against the loss of social opportunity and neighborhood integrity. In the end, he does find the elusive "Marvin Gardens" of the title—the only board game landmark that was not readily identifiable. Discovered as a middle-class enclave adjacent to Atlantic City, Marvin Gardens has survived with something of its past splendor by hiding itself—literally—from the teeming city life outside its guarded environs.

Can such "protection" last forever? Insulated against the changes around it, the real Marvin Gardens remained a neighborhood unto itself, protected by financial stability, police oversight, and a tightly designed residential enclave not subject to the vagaries of changing business or social trends. Because of its "success" in retaining vestiges of its former glory, is a Marvin Gardens–style insularity the answer to the problems that beset us? It does not seem that McPhee is lauding this as a formula, yet the nuanced essay is certainly designed to give readers pause about how communities form, survive, and ultimately deteriorate.

The strong socioeconomic underpinnings of community and urban privilege vs. urban blight are very much woven throughout, an example of how McPhee subverts what we may believe about privilege and advantage. In the face of an economic system that lauds competition and success, "In Search of Marvin Gardens" calls into eloquent question the rightness of unbridled monopolies and the roles that class, race, and luck can play in winning.

From the tennis courts of an exclusive sport to the real neighborhoods that inspired the board game Monopoly, McPhee brilliantly redefines the world around us through skillful comparison, scrupulous reporting of detail, and an inverted rhetoric of privilege. In the tradition of classic travel writing, he does indeed expose readers to new worlds— our own. Unflinchingly honest, yet beguiling in his storytelling technique, McPhee resists writing that simply reiterates past frameworks; instead he creates new ones that serve as guides into our own neighborhoods and social relationships.

When travel writing flourished in an era of great colonial expansion for Europeans, the substance and subtext of what was written took on the aura of those quests. Themes of conquest and economic opportunity necessarily infused descriptions of new lands and new peoples. And, as comparisons were made and strengthened, travel writing reached a level of prose that eventually distinguished it from the category of "letter-writing" as a literary category all its own. Echoing the craft of these seventeenth- and eighteenth-century explorers, McPhee creates the leisurely sensibility of a ship explorer whose only witnesses to the marvels seen are pen and paper. Like elegantly crafted "letters home," his essays invisibly adopt the form of these early travel journalists and take us into places we have never been and perhaps never will visit. McPhee's writing is ultramodern, however, in its subtext and use of detail to communicate a point of view, while maintaining an objective space for readers to find their own personal meaning within his works. By combining the best of "old" and "new" journalistic traditions, McPhee's work is a harbinger of what writing within the social spaces of an increasingly diverse society could become.

As an organic writer, McPhee constructs his final stories through a laborious process, essentially parsing tons of facts and rearranging them in a narrative construction cemented by his own keen intuition and observation. Howarth observes that the work that resulted from McPhee's

system of writing created a literary journalism as distinct as Arthur
Ashe's tennis performances:

> McPhee wants to create a form that is logical but so unobtru-
> sive that judgments of its content will seem to arise only in the
> reader's mind. And he also wants to stay loose himself, free to en-
> counter surprises within the pattern he has formed. . . .
>
> Arthur Ashe plays in McPhee's preferred style, unpredictably
> full of contours and strata. Writing is the same sort of game: he has
> spent a long time learning to move against a habitual thought or
> phrase, which is always the easiest, oldest rut to follow.
>
> The resulting prose style, rare in modern journalism, is fresh,
> strong, unaffected, and yet entirely idiosyncratic. (Howarth,
> xvi–xvii)

Works Cited

Addison, Joseph, and Richard Steele. *Selections from the Tatler and the Spectator.*
Introduction and notes by Robert J. Allen. New York: Holt, Rinehart &
Winston, 1962.

Bass, Sharon. "John McPhee." In *A Sourcebook Of American Literary Journalism: Representative Writers in an Emerging Genre,* ed. Thomas B. Connery, 343–52. Westport, Conn.: Greenwood Press, 1992.

Carstarphen, Meta G. "Journalism in the 'Contact Zones': An Ethnographic
Study of Reporting and Race." Unpublished manuscript presented to the
Poynter Institute for Media Studies, St. Petersburg, Fla., 4 June 1998.

Howarth, William L. "Introduction." In *The John McPhee Reader,* ed. William
L. Howarth, iii–xvii. New York: Random House, 1976.

*The Kerner Report: The 1968 Report of the National Advisory Commission on
Civil Disorders.* Preface by Fred R. Harris and new introduction by Tom
Wicker. New York: Pantheon Books, 1988.

McPhee, John A. "In Search of Marvin Gardens." In *The John McPhee Reader,*
ed. William L. Howarth, 309–20. New York: Random House, 1976.

——— "Levels of the Game." In *The John McPhee Reader,* ed. William L.
Howarth, 129–56. New York: Random House, 1976. (Also available in
book form.)

———. "A Narrative Table of Contents." In *Annals of the Former World.* New
York: Farrar, Straus & Giroux, 1998.

———. "Travels of the Rock." In *Irons in the Fire.* New York: Farrar, Straus &
Giroux, 1997.

Mindich, David. *Just the Facts: How "Objectivity" Came to Define American
Journalism.* New York: New York University, 1988.

The Oxford English Dictionary: Vol. 5, H–K. London: Oxford University Press, 1970.

Perkins, George, Barbara Perkins, and Phillip Leininger. *Benet's Reader's Encyclopedia of American Literature*. New York: HarperCollins Publishers, 1991.

Pratt, Mary Louise. *Imperial Eyes: Travel Writing and Transculturation*. New York: Routledge, 1992.

Spurr, David. *The Rhetoric of Empire: Colonial Discourse in Journalism, Travel Writing, and Imperial Administration*. Durham: Duke University Press, 1993.

Stephens, Mitchell. *A History of News: From Drum to Satellite*. New York: Viking Penguin, 1988.

Weber, Ronald. *The Literature of Fact*. Athens: Ohio University Press, 1980.

Wilson, James, and Stan Le Roy Wilson. *Mass Media/Mass Culture*. 4th ed. New York: McGraw-Hill, 1998.

Kathy Smith

John McPhee Balances the Act

> "You know," he explained to Lapham, "that we have to look at all these facts as material, and we get the habit of classifying them. Sometimes a leading question will draw out a whole line of facts that a man himself would never think of."
>
> William Dean Howells, *The Rise of Silas Lapham*

The idea that authors are *subjects* of and to their own narratives was explored with rigor in postmodern hermeneutics, according to Marxist, Feminist, Psychoanalytic, Reader-Response, New Historic, and other critical literary theories. Applied to literary journalism, the concept demonstrates how celebrated writers such as John McPhee work the complex interstices between facts and the observation and treatment of facts. When literature and journalism meet, truth telling, while not necessarily based on a less "objective" set of criteria, is less transparent. The recounting of history depends on a point of view, an authoring subject; it therefore cannot be represented "as it is." Literary journalists remind us that the world "as it is" (the world as slippery phenomena) cannot emerge neat and whole, because it is not neat and whole, from the chronicler's pen. McPhee's authorial *contract* with the reader, his agile blending of literary and journalistic techniques, makes him seem to "disappear" into history, makes the writing process seem naturally to emanate from history. But the writing mind has always mediated between what is real and what is interpreted, regardless of genre. McPhee's disappearance takes place not because the history he tells is more "true" but because of his artful manipulation of material.

While my use of the two concepts "writing subject" and "contract" will take on context in the course of this chapter, a brief explanation may help guide the following discussion. The choice of the phrase "writing subject" is a deliberate one meant to heighten the awareness that a writer or author at once subjects, is a subject of, and is subject to the material composed in the act of writing itself. The conventions of journalistic writing impose boundaries meant to contain and maintain objectivity and to limit rhetorical and narrative choices. When one calls oneself a journalist, therefore, one takes up a judicial position in regard to differentiating between fact and fiction. As a writer in the more general sense, however, and as a manipulator of the material he fashions into story, McPhee constantly crosses and tests those boundaries. He poses as a paradoxical figure, both crafty and innocent, who reveals himself in the position he takes up within the contract. As he does so, the two categories of fact and fiction blur (a claim I hope to substantiate later on).

When we regard the author as a "subject" of writing itself, the effect on the contract (understood in journalism as a tacit agreement with the reader and the ostensible story subject to make a true accounting) is to substitute anxiety for assurance. If we expect truth and verifiability from this true story, then we must impose artificial restraints on the story line. This is where journalism's codes come in, protecting the true from the story. McPhee may well be regarded by most nonfiction writers as a master tactician when it comes to maintaining both the integrity of the journalism profession and the art of writing. When the two collide, the reader-writer contract can be reassessed to discover what has been understated. If the narrative is labeled "nonfiction," then the obvious assumption is that the event takes a privileged place in its relationship to writing. The new contract written by literary journalists, among whom McPhee must count, disturbs this assumption by calling into question the priority of the event over writing. One might indeed say that in the new contract writing always precedes the event.

In his introduction to *The John McPhee Reader,* William Howarth calls attention to McPhee's "transparency" in social settings and its importance to his role as reporter:

> A good reporter, he moves through crowds easily, absorbing names, details, snatches of talk. He inspires confidence, since people rarely find someone who listens that carefully to them. Around Princeton, old neighbors and schoolmates remember him fondly, if not well. He cultivates a certain transparency in social relations, a habit derived from practicing his craft. To see and hear clearly, he keeps his eyes open and mouth shut.[1]

Howarth continues—for the bulk of the introduction is concerned with McPhee's process of composition and his theory of writing—by noting

McPhee's almost fanatical preoccupation with controlling the story's structure. Howarth's description points to an interesting conflict, one that seems endemic to the craft of literary journalism: the reporter adopts an attitude of cozy selflessness, a kind of partisan nonpartisanship, taking on the solid and respectable aspect of a nonjudgmental witness in order to be privy to the "essential" subject. Later, the reporter metamorphoses into a willful usurper or supersleuth, imposing order, center, logic, and meaning.

The story, one is led to imagine, both writes itself—possesses a natural internal order—and, at the same time, needs to be shaped. McPhee's titles are revealing: *A ROOMFUL of Hovings, LEVELS of the Game, ENCOUNTERS with the Archdruid, PIECES of the Frame.* The metaphors are spatial and structural. They produce an arrangement that seems to partake of the subject's own particular structure. They illustrate McPhee's desire to control and make sense of the real in a conventionally novelistic way, where plot, character, setting, and mood develop in a framework based not on a traditionally historical model of temporal progression, like a chronicle or a list, but on a narrative one, where the author takes liberties with the order and structure of events so that the story advances strategically along thematic lines. On the written level, the synthesis of the world and the written word results in something like what Howarth calls a "true replica" (xiii) in his introduction. Of course the phrase has much more resonance than Howarth can begin to discuss there.

A provocative indirection may discover for us a useful analogue to this notion of the true replica. In *Image, Music, Text,* French literary critic Roland Barthes writes: "The function of narrative is not to 'represent,' it is to constitute a spectacle. . . . Narrative does not show, does not imitate. . . . 'What takes place' in a narrative is from the referential (reality) point of view literally *nothing;* 'What happens' is language alone, the adventure of language, the unceasing celebration of its coming."[2] Seen from Barthes's point of view, the news story as narrative cannot be fully apprehended merely as an *effect* of an event that, having taken place in time, is transposed into a new time of linguistic adventure. The replica certainly bears resemblance to a truth that the author monitors, anatomizes, and then reproduces, making careful rhetorical choices. These choices, however, are not based on a model of reality established through recitation or observation of fact, or not merely so.

The assumption one makes with narrative in general is that the more appropriate the literary figure chosen to represent a real phenomenon, the truer the replica. To avoid the trap of this circular logic, Barthes proposes the "spectacle" of language itself, which serves as its own referent, its own remark on itself. It may seem almost perverse to read McPhee, of all people, through Barthes. But Barthes's articulation of the writing adventure is clearly relevant to any discussion of labels—both McPhee's own and those used by others to describe his work. Barthes's theory of language in its limited use here provides a means of seeing something that McPhee cannot readily reveal about how he prepares us for reading.

Labels and titles obviously cause us to think in a certain summary way about a subject. They act as symbols of the total information contained in a text or a body of texts, and they perform a function of identification. McPhee insists on the appropriateness of one clear label—"nonfiction"—when he says: "Things that are cheap and tawdry in fiction work beautifully in nonfiction because they are true. That's why you should be careful not to abridge it, because it's the fundamental *power* you're dealing with. You *arrange it and present it.* There's lots of artistry. But you don't make it up" (emphasis added).[3]

Without gainsaying the "power" of McPhee's truth, we can still insist on the gap between it and its image in the text. By referring again to Howarth's introduction to the *Reader,* we find an example of a more conventional critique of representation. Howarth engages the problem of attempting to define the character of a work by laws and labels as follows:

> He packs an impressive bag of narrative tricks, yet everyone calls his work "non-fiction." This label is frustrating, for it says not what a book is but what it is *not.* Since "fiction" is presumably made up, imaginative, clever, and resourceful, a book of "non-fiction" must *not* be any of those things, perhaps not even a work of art. If the point seems a mere quibble over terms, try reversing the tables: are Faulkner's books on Mississippi "non-history" just because they are novels?[4]

The question of naming is crucial here. When McPhee talks rather ominously about the "power" of "nonfiction," and when Howarth discusses the misappropriation of the generic label, my sense is that they are treating narrative as a flexible category, the power of "tawdriness" of which can depend on what it is called. While both McPhee and Howarth might question the value of judging works according to strict conformity with generic codes, both would agree that in order to maintain the integrity of the subject one must follow certain established journalistic practices.

Since McPhee's style has typically been praised for its dramatic scenic quality and its almost visceral presence, we might pose a more visual metaphor for the true replica. In Hollywood parlance, a photographic image is "true" inasmuch as it represents the view in the frame. But the replication accrues meaning in a totalized "image system" that defines the value of a particular frame or angle. The single photo has a certain correspondence to reality but gains coherence only in the total system of the film. The photolike realism of McPhee's writing scenes, by analogy, tends to divert any uncertainty about the authenticity of the subject. The match between image and representation tends to be regarded as natural and true to the extent that the film offers a coherent sum of images.

If we return to McPhee's story "A Sense of Where You Are,"[5] we discover that much of the pleasure of reading it, and much of its coherency, come through the play on the central metaphor of place. A sense of belonging where you are is crucial; without knowledge of place Bradley's game is unplayable. The *place* of place, however, is difficult to determine because it continually reactivates the chance for movement. Movement is possible in this game (of basketball and of writing) because one is aware of position. The concept of place is unthinkable without its supplement, movement.

For McPhee, and for the hero of his story, a sense of where you are determines the quality of play and openness, the degree of choice among nearly unlimited options. This developed sixth sense also operates by closing down options that break the rules or threaten to violate the logic or reason of the game. The sense of place makes sense only when there is a consensus, an agreement to play by the rules. It is ultimately hierarchical. To know one's place is to be aware of the possible positions in the system of placement. Knowing where you are requires the appropriate valuation of proportion, dignity, and self-confidence in the context of the game. It is in this context that we must begin to read this story.

The title "A Sense of Where You Are" inspires a certain reliability and establishes propriety. It seems a logical starting place for a story on basketball, a game of placement. In this reading of Bill Bradley as a master of the game, all the "facts" point back to McPhee's title. Bradley's character is a remarkable one inasmuch as he has control of all possible actions within his given sphere. McPhee sets him apart from the other players because he has observed that Bradley's superior ability lies in his willingness to spend countless hours "rehearsing the choreography of the game" ("A Sense of Where You Are," 14).

An obvious connection between game and genre should be made here on the basis of the order internal to both. The concepts "game" and "genre" are imagined as sets of rules outside of which one can no longer play or work without fear of infraction, confusion, or the introduction of a new order of play. Play, which is vital to games, can never be freed in this sense. The writing model and the game plan must be executed within certain limited spheres and agreed-upon boundaries. Professionalism demands this, as does reason. When *free* play becomes a dimension of the game, there is little possibility that play can continue. In fact, play will be stopped and a forfeit imposed in order to regain game integrity and to protect against the further violence of rule-breaking. Literary journalism has shown that when genre opens to incorporate play, writing forms become subject to new scrutiny and a new set of rules that will attempt to contain the effects of the border crossing. Because a certain conception of historical truth is at stake when this crossing happens in journalism, the rules for writing "objectively" are systematically enforced.

The border crossing points to the very feature of genre that gives it the constant capacity for crossing over to be something it is not. Genre, like place, is both itself and not-itself at the same time, a paradoxical logic articulated most rigorously in "poststructuralist" thinking. This philosophy attempts to explain how genre, a structural concept that determines order, law, and placement, manifests doubt about the very possibility of certainty, fixity, and meaning. Law, or genre, then, introduces its own supplement. We might apply this reasoning to literary journalism by regarding the "novelistic" as a supplement to the "nonfiction." In a sense, the novel is added to the journalistic account. This addition points to a lack in the original text. It occupies the space where the "missing words" should or might have been. The novel is also a substitute for the factual report, what originally appeared in the text, since it directly challenges the fullness of that text's account. The supplement of fictional techniques in journalistic writing both makes up for and reveals a lack. The supplement, then, can be regarded as a feature of genre that is always possible.

We might draw another parallel between Bradley's basketball game and McPhee's writing, both games of pivots, pics, set-ups, and rebounds—games of will and containment. The components of Bradley's play adapt peculiarly well to McPhee's. McPhee ascribes various key qualities to Bradley: vision, discipline, concentration, freeing oneself up for the big play, understanding the "geometry of action" ("A Sense of Where You Are," 16), honing the "hunting" instinct, knowing the terrain, and manipulating the balance of power. All of these components might be made to fit a McPhee composite. In fact, they might be made to fit many a "master narrative" of heroism. The play in both games is made to appear heroic, and the definition of heroism continually turns on mastering logic of place and the paradox of play.

Having a sense of where you are, learning what to do and then doing it as well as or better than your original models, is the hallmark of Bradley's character. Bradley's sense of place is nowhere more convincingly dramatized than in McPhee's replaying of a certain practice session on foreign turf:

> Last summer, the floor of the Princeton gym was being resurfaced, so Bradley had to put in several practice sessions at the Lawrenceville School. His first afternoon at Lawrenceville, he began by shooting fourteen-foot jump shots from the right side. He got off to a bad start, and he kept missing them. Six in a row hit the back rim of the basket and bounced out. He stopped, looking discomfited, and seemed to be making an adjustment in his mind. Then he went up for another jump shot from the same spot and hit it cleanly. Four more shots went in without a miss, and then he paused and said, "You want to know something? That basket is about an inch and a half low." Some weeks later, I went back to Lawrenceville with a steel tape, borrowed a stepladder, and measured the height of the basket. It was nine feet and seven-eighths inches above the floor, or one and one-eighth inches too low. (7)

This remarkable sixth sense bestows a high degree of infallibility on Bradley that the other players do not have. Bradley is so sure of himself and his game that he is able to construe the difference of an inch and a half from a distance of fourteen feet. McPhee is also performing here. He has set up what rhetorician Michael Jordan calls a "situation structure" to combine the effects of subjective assessment and verifiable information.[6] He is also able to assess from his journalistic distance, a distance he foreshortens by his perfect knowledge of the writing game and his capacity to find and manipulate the "fundamental pattern."

Neither objective data nor opinions alone suffice to satisfy McPhee's desire for complete coverage of a situation or subject, so he provides both. But by linking point of view so intimately with observed data, and thereby rendering a type of "proof," he avoids inviting the kind of scrutiny that accompanies the literary journalist's writing adventure when point of view and perspective become "too" subjective. This strategy works continuously throughout McPhee's piece. It is repeated as a kind of balancing act, an inconspicuous weighing and meting out of perspective and fact so that the thing itself seems to supply narrative structure and value.

Another example might serve to elaborate my point that McPhee's style takes on resemblance to truth in direct proportion to his ability to exemplify the logic of his theme: a sense of movement in place. Throughout the story, McPhee's prose illustrates an ability to allow Bradley to *speak for himself,* matching the rhythm of the writing with the motion and fluidity of Bradley's style. The need to explain the elegance of Bradley's strategy becomes less urgent if the writing itself reflects the movement of his "dance," a repeated metaphor for his game. Clearly nature is being improved upon by artifice. Like Bradley, McPhee always sets up for the next move. McPhee's ability to structure the narrative hinges on his faith in the importance and power of his performance to create meaning. Just as Bradley moves "for motion's sake, making plans and abandoning them" just to keep the basketball narrative going, giving it structure and place, so, too, McPhee moves around his subject, angling first this way and then that to provide the most spectacular view in an associative and highly structured system of value (16–17). He creates a portrait of Bradley that takes shape during skilled and close observation. That picture is also shaped according to the coherency of words and images with the overall writing plan, the "fundamental pattern" of which is to provide depth and balance.

In the following passage, McPhee sets out to substantiate his own ideas about Bradley's "most remarkable natural gift . . . his vision":

> During a game, Bradley's eyes are always a glaze of panoptic attention, for a basketball player needs to look at everything, focussing on nothing, until the last moment of commitment. . . . Bradley's eyes close normally enough, but his astounding passes to teammates have given

> him, too, a reputation for being able to see out of the back of his head. To discover whether there was anything to all the claims for basketball players' peripheral vision, I asked Bradley to go with me to the office of Dr. Henry Adams, a Princeton ophthalmologist, who had agreed to measure Bradley's total field. (19)

The doctor finds that Bradley has an abnormally large peripheral field of vision. McPhee also discovers, after further investigation, that Bradley probably affected his own field of vision by practicing looking at objects out of the corners of his eyes as a kid. The findings corroborate McPhee's initial hunch and fit in well with the specific motif that Bradley's talent is as much acquired as natural.

What is more interesting about this example stylistically is the way fact follows opinion. McPhee's observations of Bradley's eyes, which during a game "are always a glaze of panoptic attention," lead him to suggest the visit to the doctor's office. It appears that these astute *observations* have led to the "discovery" of the *new fact* of Bradley's super-normal field of sight, without which the comment that Bradley "can read the defense as if he were reading Braille" would be merely a pretty metaphor (20). The focus is on verification; only after the trip to the doctor, and only after having all the collected material and notes at his disposal, does McPhee construct this specific image system. This point is worth noting because it emphasizes the importance of the balance I have been talking about, between the real in literary play and the novel-istic techniques in structuring the real. At the same time it makes the play—here the positioning of certain events in a certain sequence—seem less a product of a personal narrative imposition than a fitting cast to an identifiable subject or an external referent.

McPhee constantly goes back to the scene in order to verify the truth, as if without the verification we might not appreciate the value of Bradley's performance or the reliability of McPhee's word. What must be noted here is the perhaps obvious implication that nothing unsettles or mystifies if it can be structured and if that structure partakes of reality itself, not as the manufacturing of a metaphor for the real, but as a vision of the real—the empirically verifiable—as fundamentally structured. Logic, order, and meaning are the by-products of this structure. A hier-archy of value can be assigned around an implied center. This structure is the ground for the ideology of objectivity in journalism, and McPhee toes the line by preserving the center. He demystifies the story by certifying the facts. But despite McPhee's insistence on the power of truth, the way in which representation occurs always depends on artifice. The author disguises himself as recorder in order to temper the mediation between fact and story and to promote the "real illusion" that structure itself provides a natural and absolute system of identification rather than a true replica that is produced in the midst of narrative adventure.

I would like to make a brief comparison with the work of another literary journalist, at least as adept at journalistic sleight of hand as McPhee, to show how craftily, if quietly, McPhee's prose operates on a story. Like Tom Wolfe, McPhee acknowledges the artifice of fictional technique, but more covertly. He conceives of the fictional part as a kind of glossy finish on the printed image. When we see Bradley throwing a ball "like a pinch of salt" ("A Sense of Where You Are," 4) into the basket without looking behind him, we are faintly cognizant of authorial license, precisely because these images stand out from the "factual voice" that has previously been established. These particular images are not arbitrary; they, too, seem almost factual, fitting the fact of Bradley's leg strength and his supernormal range of vision, respectively. The secret of both Bradley's and McPhee's total game plans, however, remains mysteriously undisclosed.

In most of McPhee's work, the language sounds confident and playful but not sarcastic or hyperbolic. It is measured and polite, not extreme, and it is comprehensive but includes few stage bows, the summary and attention-getting authorial gestures that mark Wolfe's prose. Wolfe and McPhee use voice in opposite and symmetrical ways to produce the same rhetorical effects. If we compare two passages, the first from Wolfe's *Radical Chic* and the second from another McPhee work entitled *Encounters with the Archdruid,* we find a similar play on voice and point of view resulting from a very different writing style. In the following excerpt, Wolfe clearly speaks *for* an impersonal subject—a subject, nonetheless, with an idiom all its own. Because Wolfe needs to create a context and a story for the subject, a subject that has no access to his overarching plan and cannot fully or effectively grasp itself within that context, he must control the selection and arrangement of information. In this particular instance, Wolfe's narrative design must fit the theme of social unease that results when radical meets chic or "black rage" and "white guilt" celebrate their hip collision. The effect, however, is of an intimate, very personal voice speaking for itself, without a script:

Cheray tells her: "I've never met a Panther—this is a first for me!" . . . never dreaming that within forty-eight hours her words will be on the desk of the President of the United States. . . .

This is a first for me. But she is not alone in her thrill as the Black Panthers come trucking on in, into Lenny's house, Robert Bay, Don Cox the Panthers' Field Marshal from Oakland, Henry Miller the Harlem Panther defense captain, the Panther women—Christ, if the Panthers don't know how to get it all together, as they say, the tight pants, the tight black turtlenecks, the leather coats, Cuban shades, Afros. But real Afros, not the ones that have been shaped and trimmed like a topiary hedge and sprayed until they have a sheen like acrylic, wall-to-wall—but like funky, natural, scraggly . . . wild . . .

These are no civil rights Negroes *wearing gray suits three sizes too big*—[7]

Wolfe's positioning of himself above and around the subject allows him to make the comparison between an Afro and a topiary hedge. Clearly, Wolfe needs to stand in for the subject in his own interests and in the interests of the story. His assumption is that by doing this, by adopting the language of the subject yet maintaining distance, he can provide fuller and more complete coverage of the event.

In the McPhee excerpt that follows, the subject also only *seems* to speak for itself. McPhee is obviously allegorizing the conflict in order to dramatize the first encounter between the conservationist and former Sierra Club director David Brower (the archdruid) and the dam builder Floyd Dominy, United States commissioner of reclamation. At the same time, McPhee also appears to be having a little fun at Brower's expense. Still, he does not want to appear to preempt the story with the flashiness of his own associations, so he starts off the section by attributing his analogy to a particular view and by representing that view in the third person. The point of view is calculated to create a sense of the author's having researched the conflict carefully enough so that the metaphor develops as a natural analogue to the conflict:

In the view of conservationists, there is something special about dams, something—as conservationist problems go—that is disproportionately and metaphysically sinister. The outermost circle of the Devil's world seems to be a moat filled mainly with DDT. Next to it is a moat of burning gasoline. Within that is a ring of pinheads each covered with a million people—and so on past phalanxed bulldozers and bicuspid chain saws into the absolute epicenter of Hell on earth, where stands a dam.[8]

McPhee is careful to mention right away that his comments represent the view of the conservationists since such a disclaimer automatically registers at a level of objectivity and balance that appears to be missing from the previously quoted Wolfe piece. Bulldozers and bicuspid chain-saws are not necessarily more "objective" elements in a story that dramatizes the conflict of development versus conservation than are tight pants, leather jackets, and Cuban shades in a story on the new black power. But the voices that render those ingredients appear to have a different relationship to the narrative. While Wolfe appears to be intimately involved, McPhee seems distanced and apart. In fact, one might say that Wolfe is habitually speaking *through* his subjects, using them as media, whereas McPhee is the medium through which his subjects speak.

Clearly, however, any neutral pose is illusory, and intimacy with or distance from the subject is impossible to measure. Both McPhee and Wolfe manipulate the voice of the subject to legitimize their own authorial acts and to give credibility to the story line, just as the story line must, since the genre demands it, seem to take form from the subject's voice. The literary journalists' assumption that the voice of the subject is a natural force (as opposed to writing, which supposedly has no emotional impact of its own) helps us to understand how writers depend on the reciprocity of world and word and how voice is used in narrative as a representation of ideal form or natural law.

In most journalistic writing, the personal mark of story arrangements obtrudes as little as possible on the record. What Hayden White calls history's "narrativization" appears to follow the natural order of the subject:

> Since its invention by Herodotus, traditional historiography has featured predominantly the belief that history itself consists of a congeries of lived stories, individual and collective, and that the principal task of historians is to uncover these stories and to retell them in a narrative, the truth of which would reside in the correspondence of the story told to the story lived by real people in the past. Thus conceived, the literary aspect of the historical narrative was supposed to inhere solely in certain stylistic embellishments that rendered the account vivid and interesting to the reader rather than in the kind of poetic inventiveness presumed to be characteristic of . . . fictional narratives.[9]

When the voice of the subject speaks *through* McPhee, when he makes himself "transparent," the law of journalism's genre (i.e., of objectivity) acts as a naturalizing agent. The subject's voice is taken from its own presumed raw nature and recontextualized so that the objective account can penetrate and balance the emotional authenticity of the originating source. This complementarity is both meaningful and illusory: It is not *natural* itself but is rather a matter of convention, by which representation is established as a legitimate means of assuring some immediate apprehension of the world. The referencing, therefore, of literary journalism in terms of an organic correspondence, a natural fit between world and story, protects authorial license in acts of representation. It also wards off the inclination to examine the notion of the "natural" and writing's function of denaturalization.

McPhee is a kind of latter-day Herodotus in that he seems to embellish without fictionalizing. He practices a style at once scrupulously accurate and boldly participatory and metaphorical, a style that has influenced successful "second generation" literary journalists like Mark Kramer and Tracy Kidder and, one easily imagines, countless eager journalism students learning the literary craft.[10] McPhee is not taught in courses on fiction and the American novel as are other nonfiction writers like Joan Didion, Norman Mailer, and Hunter Thompson; but in terms of my reading of the fictional act, where imagination, world, and text overlap, he leans into the "fictional space" of the novel, although less conspicuously, as much as any of the writers mentioned earlier.

Returning to the story at hand, we see, in fact, that McPhee sets Bradley up, as surely as Bradley sets up for a jump shot. He begins with a "curious event" that occurs before a play-off game during Bradley's senior year at Princeton:

> The game was played in Philadelphia and was the last of a triple-header. The people were worn out, because most of them were emotionally committed to either Villanova or Temple—two local teams that had just been involved in enervating battles with Providence and Connecticut, respectively. . . . A group of Princeton boys shooting basketballs miscellaneously in preparation for still another game hardly promised to be a high point of the evening, but Bradley, whose routine in the warmup time is a gradual crescendo of activity, is more interesting to watch before a game than most players are in play. (4)

The rest of the paragraph describes in dramatic sequence Bradley's performance of "expandingly difficult jump shots" that go "cleanly through the basket with so few exceptions that the crowd began to murmur." Finally, after a series of "whirling reverse moves," more "jumpers," and sweeping "hook shots in the air" he begins to move "in a semicircle around the court. First with his right hand, then with his left, he tried seven of these long, graceful shorts—the most difficult ones in the orthodoxy of basketball—and ambidextrously made them all. The game had not even begun, but the presumably unimpressible Philadelphians were applauding like an audience at an opera" (4). The crescendo of the play is at least matched by the crescendo of the written play as it moves dramatically to re-create the movement of the crowd's involvement from bored passivity to appreciative engagement. The comparison between the game and the opera further dramatizes the action on the court, and it works so well to evoke the requisite response of suspense and release that we forget it is McPhee's *own* assumption that the Philadelphians are "unimpressible."

McPhee offers a considered dramatization of material; and his artistry informs the facts, just as his careful attention to detail earns for him (as it does for Wolfe) the poetic license to identify the subject through his metaphorical treatment of it. It allows him to be able to claim, for example, that "basketball is a hunting game . . . a player on offense either is standing around recovering his breath or is on the move, foxlike, looking for openings, sizing up chances . . ." (16). In McPhee's and Wolfe's careful attention to the reconstruction of the voices of their subjects we never hear the nostalgic or self-conscious voice of the author who cannot quite reclaim the subject, as we do, for example, in Sara Davidson's, Norman Mailer's, or Joan Didion's work. Instead, they both rely on the subject's "natural" voice to make the limitations of writing and the work of the author seem to disappear.

An important question for the practice of journalism, then, is how a writer who takes up a position that claims to be balanced and neutral can make value judgments at the same time. One way of examining this question is to regard the recorded event not only as a narrative re-creation but as a version of history that was deemed apt and legitimate enough to record in the first place. Howarth's introduction to "Encounters with the Archdruid" in *The John McPhee Reader* is, in this context, an interesting prelude, in that he tells us McPhee had already planned the book before finding his protagonist. The plan, he writes, "was a bit formulaic; it resembled Boswell's jostling of Dr. Johnson into conversations of quotable prose." However, he defends the use of this formula, an excellent example in at least one respect that McPhee is absolutely impartial "on the issues he dramatizes."[11] It is worthwhile quoting the rest of Howarth's short commentary on the piece because, even as he underscores McPhee's set-up of the balanced equation, he demonstrates how an uncritical notion of balance can be made to serve impartiality:

> For every point Brower scores on the beauties of wildness, his opponents respond with sensible defenses of progress. . . . Brower is no mere Druid, a worshipper of trees, nor are his adversaries simply out to exploit the land. . . . The story exemplifies how facts lend themselves to McPhee's imaginative handling; the lake, river, dam, and raft become his emblems of rigidity or flexibility, expressing a scale of values without forcing him to "take a position" on these controversial issues.[12]

We may be able to agree with Howarth about the surface effects of the story: it provides balanced views, the characters are not one-dimensional (good or bad subjects), and the landscape seems to work as symbol of the conflict being recounted. There is something odd, however, in the claim that McPhee can maintain a creditable *distance* between expressing value and taking a position. In fact, all the way through the story he is telling us how to respond by giving either Dominy or Brower the last word, by making one seem heroic in one instance, a coward or fool the next. While McPhee may not be assigning an absolute value either to irrigation or to the preservation of the natural form of the river, he is clearly taking the position that in relative terms, *nature*—in this case the Colorado River—must ultimately be allowed to speak for itself. McPhee wants to convey the idea that balance resides in nature and so, too, in the narrative. Of course, the story has been selected according to a specific criterion of conflict that seems to call for arbitration, which, as always, is the task of the author. Moreover, since nature in this case has no clear voice of its own—one might say it is forcefully mute—McPhee must provide it with one.

The way in which the news is selected for presentation is the subject of several studies on media practice. The importance of the "story" feature—how much drama the event can promise to news presentation—is clearly high on the list of necessary characteristics. As Hayden White writes, it is the drama of the story "line" that reinvests reality with truth: "The authority of the historical narrative is the authority of reality itself; the historical account endows this reality with form and thereby makes it desirable by the imposition upon its processes of the formal coherency that only stories possess." The position of neutrality becomes more difficult to imagine when we understand that selection of story material hinges on specific cultural practices that may not be flexible enough to accommodate events that do not fit the routine. "Events," White continues, "are real not because they occurred but because, first, they were remembered and second, they are capable of finding a place in a chronologically ordered sequence. . . . Unless at least two versions of the same set of events can be imagined, there is no reason for the historian to take upon himself the authority of giving the true account."[13] Part of the problem in claiming neutrality, then, is that the fiction/nonfiction categories do not remain separate despite the insistent implication of objectivity in the nonfictional label. McPhee claims a fundamental "power" for the historical real, but not until the real is packaged and reported and changed with effects does the event become part of our narrative history, part of our structure of meaning.

If we agree, therefore, with White and with Barthes that history somehow postdates its own packaging, then we can begin to measure the effects of the linguistic spectacle on journalism. The label "literary journalism" has the capacity to force a new way of reading news as an adventure of language. It does not make changes in the text. The text itself is plural—we may believe it if it is labeled "nonfiction" or we may suspend belief if it is labeled "novel"; one story contains the difference within itself to allow completely varied readings, at the instigation of a word. But the label has helped refocus attention on the role of narrative in determining news value and allowed a more complete and sophisticated understanding of the way in which a story takes on meaning.

Although the role that various narrative strategies play in "uncovering" history is not underplayed at the surface level of the text in McPhee's work, the assumption of categorical differences between nonfictional and fictional discourses remains intact. McPhee regards fiction as an interfering or distorting mechanism that endangers the process of the recovery work; and he dismisses the notion that nonfiction and fiction have common aspects (their substitution of language for events) as a secondary philosophical concern, unrelated to the business of reproducing objective accounts of reality. For McPhee, the distinction between fact-gathering in the field and invention on the page is predicated, as in Wolfe's work, on the accepted notion of objectivity; it is the quest for knowledge itself that is at stake when two genres collide. I refer again to White: "Myths and the ideologies based on them presuppose the adequacy of stories to the representation of the reality whose meaning they purport to reveal. When belief in this adequacy begins to wane, the entire cultural edifice of a society enters into crisis, because not only is a specific system of beliefs undermined but the very condition of possibility of socially significant belief is eroded."[14]

For journalists, the possibility that an objective narrative devised precisely for the purpose of preserving reality in a recognized and shared body of knowledge is working at the service of a "myth" or an "ideology" is already to approach the state of crisis. In order to preserve the metaphors that lend credibility to the discovery of real knowledge, and the "condition of possibility" for emerging truth, authors need a verifiable, empirical world in which to insert themselves. In McPhee's case, there is a kind of fearlessness in the prose that is achieved by the easy conjunction of fact and metaphor. He does not confront the interesting contradiction that truth can be mediated by arrangement and presentation and that the power of truth is a function of its representation in the text—in other words, that truth and representation reflect one another but do not necessarily converge.

This is an especially vital point in regard to McPhee since his work has the character of an equation. As I suggested earlier, he balances the need for subjective assessment of his subject (his metaphorical treatment of it) with the objective field of collected data. In the process, language—the structure of the equation—becomes the instrument by which reportorial objectivity—the cornerstone of generic law for journalism—is both reasserted and dismantled. The paradoxical position for McPhee is that he both desires the power of narrative to convey the real and resists its continual and infinite power to distort it. White writes: "Narrative becomes a problem only when we wish to give to real events the form of story. It is because real events do not offer themselves as stories that their narrativization is so difficult."[15] Without structure, without a "moral" order of meaning, events look like mere compilations of information, lists that have no connection with human intercourse. In McPhee's meticulously crafted writing, which appears so painstakingly true to life and which posits a natural correspondence between subject and style, the contradiction nevertheless remains: the subject is clearly *fashioned* and at the same time supposedly undisturbed in its essential nature. There is a clear irony in the configuration. The structure and codes of McPhee's writing resist denaturalization precisely because of his unwillingness to acknowledge the narrative invasion of an "objective" subject.

History unfolds as an interpretive and performative gesture of recovery. It is personal and provisional and in that sense objective. In the balance McPhee attempts to preserve, there is no security of objectivity but rather a reconfirmation of the determining, subjective feature of the law of narrative that presents truth by imposing order. Because McPhee is both spectator of the real and manipulator or player in its representation, he is in a position to produce and stage the heroism of his subject that is both Bradley's game and his own game of literary journalism. The assumed value of the fundamental pattern of the court play is the same one that seems to characterize McPhee's writing activity. Perhaps it is this very neat formula itself that remains still to be reevaluated, for it may be only those who, like McPhee, clearly operate according to the fundamental pattern of journalism who can most easily, if unwittingly, twist its logic and stretch its rules.

The operative assumption in literary journalism is that if we desire the certainty of order we must recognize that we gain it at the price of its mediation through systems of meaning designed to control the reading process. For McPhee, that understanding is both the given from which he begins to write and the burden he refuses fully to disclose. What then becomes of objectivity when it is only the *sense* of where you are (the sixth and nonverifiable sense) that is translatable into language, already a metaphor for the place of the absent thing? What if this place is also a "nonplace," the point that is always in motion? McPhee's fictionalizing act, whether he acknowledges it or not, is grounded in the same logic as all narrative—one that seeks, through illusion, a perfect apprehension of the world. In stubbornly resisting the fiction label, McPhee comes no closer to the world of fact. On the contrary, his work only reaffirms the need for literary journalists to maintain a certain play between the verifiable and the fictional, which invests the facts with a common value. He participates in the fictionalizing act because he takes up this illusory position of balance when he attempts to narrow the gap between narrative versions of history and the definitive real and because he so completely forces his metaphors to conform to a "naturalistic" reading of the subject, as if they belonged outside of writing.

John McPhee *reinforces* the importance of a feature of his method that, at the same time, he seeks to *reform:* a sense of privilege without involvement. This position creates moral as well as aesthetic tension. How does one remain uninvolved in a position of privilege? How does one remain distant and close simultaneously? What effects does the dilemma of privileged noninvolvement have on the story and the story sources, on the writing of journalism and the genre itself?

McPhee obviously uses the nonfiction label in an attempt to tip the scales and to underplay the fictional elements of the book. The equivalence between the aesthetic use of a label and its appropriateness to truth is partly achieved—and we are reminded of this quite graphically in Howarth's introductory comments to "Encounters with the Archdruid"—by an imposition on the material that has been composed with the label in mind. In imagining the breakdown of genre and the dysfunctional and misleading fact/fiction dichotomy, the possibility of the third story emerges—one that is not necessarily a synthesis of the two (the novel and the report) but is instead an expression of the ambiguous in and out movement as the necessary movement of writing itself. With McPhee, the movement remains unconscious of the text, and the label sticks as a sign of the story's grounding in one representational mode. The balance he effects, however, the fictional poise of it, remains to negotiate and color and finally to narrate the facts.

This is not to say that facts are not facts. It is important that McPhee retain the label "nonfiction" so that the subject of his narrative can produce the power that he speaks of, the power of legitimacy conferred by the label that promises a true story. By now, though, it should be clear that the object of this chapter is to examine the true story as a contradiction in terms that the rethinking of journalism as literary has helped to begin. For McPhee, the struggle to make and assign order to the world out there and the replication of that ordered world in the text meet in the writing process. The novelistic design of the text affords him the satisfaction of finding the one "best place" for the facts, by placing them inexorably at the mercy of invention.

Notes

1. William Howarth, introduction to *The John McPhee Reader,* ed. William Howarth (New York: Vintage Books, 1977), viii.

2. Roland Barthes, "Introduction to the Structural Analysis of Narratives,"

in *Image, Music, Text,* trans. Stephen Heath (New York: Hill & Wang, 1977), 124.

3. McPhee quoted in *The Literary Journalists,* ed. Norman Sims (New York: Ballantine Books, 1984), 3.

4. Howarth, *McPhee Reader,* vii.

5. John McPhee, "A Sense of Where You Are," in *The John McPhee Reader,* 3–21 (hereafter cited in the text).

6. Michael P. Jordan, *Rhetoric of Everyday English Texts* (London: Allen & Unwin, 1984), 89.

7. Tom Wolfe, *Radical Chic and Mau-Mauing the Flak Catchers* (New York: Bantam, 1970), 8.

8. John McPhee, *Encounters with the Archdruid* (New York: Farrar, Straus & Giroux, 1971), 158.

9. Hayden White, introduction to *The Content of the Form: Narrative Discourse and Historical Representation* (Baltimore: Johns Hopkins University Press, 1987), ix–x.

10. See Sims, *The Literary Journalists,* a collection of interviews with and stories by literary journalists. "Second generation" literary journalists discuss the influence of writers like McPhee on their work.

11. Howarth, *McPhee Reader,* 189.

12. Ibid., 189–90.

13. White, *The Content of the Form,* 20.

14. Ibid., x.

15. Ibid., 5.

Daniel J. Philippon

"Academic Air"

Teaching *The Control of Nature*

In a 1993 interview, Michael Pearson asked John McPhee to respond to a quotation from "John McPhee Balances the Act," Kathy Smith's interpretation of his work in the 1990 essay collection *Literary Journalism in the Twentieth Century*. Smith said, as Pearson quoted: "McPhee's fictionalizing act, whether he acknowledges it or not, is grounded in the same logic as all narrative, one that seeks, through illusion, a perfect apprehension of the world" (Smith, 225). McPhee's response to Smith's claim was, for the most part, dismissive. "That's just academic air. Of course, there's definite truth in it, the idea that all writing is fiction. I agree with the idea if you express it in a certain way. You can't exactly reproduce human life; everything is a little bit of illusion. So what? Ho, hum. Basically, the whole thing is academic air. Everyone knows that at the start. The important gradation in the whole thing is that you get as close as you can to what you saw and heard" (Pearson, "Profile," 82).

I have the same mixed feelings about McPhee's response as I have about much of his work. On the one hand, his comment is refreshing in its matter-of-factness: acknowledging that all representations are to some degree constructions, but then saying, in effect, get over it, move on; to dwell on this fundamental characteristic of writing at the expense of what is being represented is, in a sense, to miss the whole point of writing. On the other hand, McPhee seems, at least in this brief exchange, a bit too quick to dismiss interest in what Smith calls his "fictionalizing act." By claiming that writers, particularly "literary journalists" like himself, simply try to "get as close as [they] can to what [they] saw and heard," McPhee fails to acknowledge the fact that, if all writing is fiction, then any number of ways might exist for writers to represent their ideas and experiences successfully—success being an idea that, in this example, McPhee chooses to represent through a metaphor of distance: "closeness." Furthermore, his comment that he agrees with Smith's idea "if you express it in a certain way" suggests that successful writing depends not only on the writer but also on the rest of what rhetoricians call the "four coordinates of discourse": writer, reader, text, and context.[1]

It is with this "academic air" in mind—the idea that successful writing could take many forms and that its success depends not only on the writer and the text but also on the reader and the context—that I wish to discuss my own experiences teaching *The Control of Nature* (McPhee's twentieth book, published in 1989). I do so in three stages: first, by describing the particularities of the book and the course; second, by outlining some of the strengths and weaknesses of the book and how I have tried to make it "come alive" in the classroom; and, finally, by suggesting that both the subject and the method of McPhee's writing apply equally well to teaching. In particular, I want to argue that undergraduate students are, like the subjects of McPhee's books, "real people in real places" and that the central question he raises in *The Control of Nature*—whether and how to exert control—applies equally well not only to McPhee's own writing but also to the teaching of environmental issues or the teaching of any controversial issue, for that matter.

The Book and the Course

Like most of McPhee's work, *The Control of Nature* consists of pieces of writing originally published in the *New Yorker*: "Atchafalaya," "Cooling the Lava," and "Los Angeles against the Mountains." Although the book won the John Burroughs Medal for Distinguished Natural History in 1990, it is as much a book of travel writing, science writing, and war correspondence as it is a book of natural history. In its first part, "Atchafalaya," McPhee examines the history and consequences of a U.S. Army Corps of Engineers project called Old River Control, whose purpose is to keep the Mississippi River from changing its course and bypassing the billion-dollar industries that lie between New Orleans and Baton Rouge. In "Cooling the Lava," the second part, McPhee travels to Iceland to survey its residents' attempts at controlling the flow of another portion of nature in motion—lava—and compares their efforts to those taking place on another island: Hawaii. And in "Los Angeles against the Mountains," McPhee turns his attention from exploding mountains to disintegrating ones, detailing the struggles of Angelenos to control the debris flows that regularly cascade down from the San Gabriel Mountains, often taking cars, houses, and people with them.

For the past two years, I have used *The Control of Nature* as one of the principal texts in an undergraduate elective course I teach called "In Search of Nature."[2] The course is a three-credit, semester-long, introductory survey of ideas of nature in Western culture in which my students and I explore some of the many perspectives through which human beings have envisioned and affected the nonhuman world, including ethics, aesthetics, science and technology, economics, politics, and religion. We read *The Control of Nature* in the section of the course on science and technology, in which we ask the question: how have scientific and technological developments affected both ideas about nature and the physical realities of nature? Given the constraints of time, I have my students read only the first and last sections of the book: "Atchafalaya," in the context of a case study on the U.S. Army Corps of Engineers, and "Los Angeles against the Mountains," in a case study on natural disasters.

Just as there are many ways for writers to represent their own experiences and ideas faithfully, there are many ways in which *The Control of Nature* may be taught, other than my own. A quick survey of online syllabi reveals that the book is being used in a wide range of courses in the sciences, social sciences, and humanities (including geology; hydrology and water resources; wetland ecology and management; forest resources; environmental science; earth science; geography; landscape architecture; science, technology, and society; environmental studies; conservation and natural resources; environmental politics; environmental history; American studies; nature writing; environmental literature; and composition). Although my course fulfills a requirement for a degree in Natural Resources and Environmental Studies offered by the University of Minnesota, it might best be termed a course in the "environmental humanities" or the ways in which environmental literature, history, and ethics interact.

My course, therefore, offers a particular perspective through which to evaluate the success of *The Control of Nature*. Like all of my courses, "In Search of Nature" concerns a controversial subject, so questions of advocacy and balance are always at the front of my mind when assigning and teaching texts—a fact I address at the end of this essay. In addition, because my course is about neither literary criticism nor composition, I do not assign *The Control of Nature* as part of McPhee's oeuvre, or introduce the book by reference to his reputation, or ask the students to catalog the fine points of McPhee's style. Instead, I ask them to read it as they think most general readers would: as a descriptive account of its stated subject—the control of nature—and to judge it on its ability to convey the richness of life as they know it. In part because I do not ask them to approach the book as a literary artifact, I think my students tend to be less self-conscious about their reading—and less reverent about the text—than students in a typical English class might be.

So what do they think?

Strengths and Weaknesses

Some students love the book, finding its descriptions of the characters and techniques involved in the battle between humans and nature to be nothing short of riveting. Others, more typically, find it "somewhat interesting," but certainly not a book they would pick up on their own. More than a few, however, find it to be "dry" and "wordy," and it is these reactions that interest me most. One student's comment is characteristic of the responses generated by this last group of students:

> Several portions of this text were boring as a result of how it is written and what information it contained. For example, the section titled "Atchafalaya" was not understandable because I was unable to picture the key subject. . . . Also, this was written more as a story, a broken up story that was difficult to follow. In "Los Angeles against the Mountains," McPhee kept switching from person to person. It was difficult to keep track of who everyone was and what his or her part in the San Gabriel Mountains was.

Using this student's response as a guide, and keeping in mind Kathy Smith's claim about McPhee's "fictionalizing act," I would like to organize my comments about the strengths and weaknesses of *The Control of Nature* according to the categories traditionally used for close readings of fiction—setting, plot, and characters.[3]

Setting

My student's comment that she was "unable to picture the key subject" of "Atchafalaya"—the Old River Control structure—speaks to the first set of strengths and weaknesses in *The Control of Nature*, concerning its setting.

Unlike many of McPhee's other books, *The Control of Nature* is set in three different locations, most of which are unfamiliar to undergraduates who do not live in or have not visited these places. By limiting my students' reading to the American portions of the book, I am able to reduce this problem somewhat (since even fewer undergraduates have been to Iceland), but the problem still remains: for many students, the lower Mississippi and the canyons of the San Gabriels are *terra incognita*. This geographic unfamiliarity also extends to culture and language—"Atchafalaya," for instance, is hardly a household word in the United States—and to technology—the catchment basins around Los Angeles are no more easily pictured than the Old River Control structure along the Mississippi.

Although a reader's unfamiliarity with the setting of a book can hardly be considered a weakness of the book itself, the challenge such unfamiliarity poses in the classroom does point to alternate ways of presenting geographic information. Why, for instance, are there no maps, photographs, or illustrations in the book, save a few sketches of houses in "Cooling the Lava" (122–24) and a single line drawing in "Los Angeles against the Mountains" (226)? Surely even the most highbrow reader of the *New Yorker* would appreciate a cartographer's treatment of the Atchafalaya, or a photographer's perspective on the San Gabriels, or an artist's rendition of Cajun country.[4] That such visual rhetoric is not present in *The Control of Nature* is surely one of the many reasons why readers and critics have termed McPhee's writing "*literary* journalism": journalism that is as interested in manipulating language as it is in conveying information.[5] How many illustrations, I wonder, could *The Control of Nature* safely include before it would no longer be considered "literary"? And to what degree would the type and function of those illustrations help to signify its genre to the reader?

Of course, no clearer testament to McPhee's considerable "literary" talents could exist than the fact that so many readers *have* been able to envision the places and feats of engineering he describes, based solely on his words and their own prior experiences. Yet I wonder, as Christopher Lehmann-Haupt did in his *New York Times* review of *The Control of Nature,* what image readers would take away from some of McPhee's more technical passages, such as this sentence from "Atchafalaya": the towers of the Old River Control Auxiliary Structure "are separated by six arciform gates, convex to the Mississippi, and hinged in trunnion blocks secured with steel to carom the force of the river into the core of the structure" (Lehmann-Haupt, C21; McPhee, *Control,* 52). In this case, a picture (or map or other illustration) certainly could have aided the descriptive process.[6]

In my course, I take several steps to augment McPhee's descriptions of his settings. In a lecture on the environmental history of science and technology, I present maps that illustrate the changes in the courses of the Mississippi and Atchafalaya Rivers over time. In our case study on natural disasters, I show a video clip depicting a mudslide similar to the debris flows that McPhee describes in "Los Angeles against the Mountains." And throughout our reading of *The Control of Nature* I ask my students to visit some of the many excellent websites devoted to the geographic, cultural, and technological particularities described in both sections of the book.[7]

More effective than any of these indoor exercises, however, is a field trip my students and I take to the Upper St. Anthony Falls Lock and Dam, a U.S. Army Corps of Engineers structure on the upper Mississippi River, located only a few miles from our St. Paul classroom. Completed the same year as Old River Control (1963), the Upper St. Anthony Falls Lock and Dam is situated at mile 854 on the Mississippi River in Minneapolis (the Old River Control structures are located between river miles 312 and 315, about fifty miles northwest of Baton Rouge). While not nearly as extensive as the structures at Old River, the Minneapolis lock and dam nevertheless function quite literally as concrete reference points to help students appreciate the size and character of the attempts to control the flow of the Mississippi throughout its length. We begin our trip in the visitors' center, learning more about the history of the Corps of Engineers and the falls; but the highlight of our visit is our tour with Lockmaster Steven Lenhart, who takes us outside, atop towering concrete walls, to demonstrate the opening and closing of the lock's giant steel doors, whenever river traffic allows. No written explanation, even one by John McPhee, could possibly convey the sound of those huge doors creaking shut or the sight of hundreds of gallons of water rushing from that lock—not to mention the feelings of fear that accompany a quick dash across the narrow mesh walkways that separate visitors from the turbulent waters beneath.[8]

The opportunity for such field trips that *The Control of Nature* presents is one of the clear strengths of the book as a classroom text. But one need not live along the Mississippi to find suitable examples of urban infrastructure to compare to Old River Control or to the catchment basins of Los Angeles. As Emily Hiestand wrote recently about the touristic potential of urban infrastructure, "A whole genre of monuments to human ingenuity and nature's forces exists in our very midst, as big as life, laced with miracles and wonders, and yet so little remarked as to be almost invisible. Do we overlook these places on purpose, because they make up a shadow city on which the fashionable city rests?" (132). Her visits to wastewater treatment facilities and fish-processing plants illustrate that these structures, too, should be part of the "field" that is the stated subject of such trips. "Visits to infrastructure facilities," writes Hiestand, echoing McPhee, "give the traveler techie info, good shoptalk, insight into the big sustainability puzzles, more fun than you might imagine, and also deep respect for the souls who build and tend these places" (132). Such visits are, in effect, like walking through real-life versions of David Macaulay's *The Way Things Work*.

Just as *The Control of Nature* is a good companion text for field trips into the urban infrastructure, it also offers an excellent starting point for what might be termed "comparative bioregionalism" or the comparison of the environmental and human histories present in one's own bioregion to those present in another. The book provides a particularly good model for this process, as students are able, through their reading, to compare and contrast the efforts of residents in two or more different regions to live amidst the challenges of a changing nonhuman environment. Although the needs and desires of urban residents are the driving force behind the stories McPhee relates, one need not live in a city to find examples of the interactive character of urban, suburban, and rural landscapes. Exurban aqueducts, power stations, and commercial distribution centers all provide examples of the kind of interrupted pastoral found in "Atchafalaya."

To enhance this comparative bioregional study, I provide students with a handout containing such questions as these:

- Do you think the environment in which the Twin Cities developed is well suited for human inhabitation? Why or why not? Could residents better conform to their environment? If so, how?
- Identify three ways in which people attempt to control nature in and around the Twin Cities. Where, when, why, and how do these attempts take place? Are these activities necessary for people to live here?
- Is there any place human beings could live that would not entail

the control of nature? What would this ideal human environment look like? Does it exist?

Armed with the answers to questions such as these, students can then begin to add their own chapters to *The Control of Nature,* investigating the ways in which the same kinds of characters and concerns present in McPhee's book also exist in their own communities. The process of acquiring such local knowledge often reveals to students that they were in fact as unfamiliar with their own environment as they were with the environments that McPhee describes, and it reminds them that he, too, was once unfamiliar with the places he describes until he began to study them in detail. Local knowledge, in other words, can transform students' opinions not only about the control of nature but also about *The Control of Nature*. As my students soon discover, had McPhee chosen to write about the Twin Cities, they might very well have said the same thing about his treatment of their environment as Jack Miles, book editor of the *Los Angeles Times,* says about his treatment of L.A. "Los Angeles against the Mountains," Miles writes, is "the finest of the three essays in this volume" and even "one of the finest that McPhee has ever written" (4)—a perfect example of the kind of influence the setting of a book can have on one's opinion of it.

Plot

In addition to an inability to picture the infrastructure of "Atchafalaya," this student also complained that the essay "was written more as a story, a broken up story that was difficult to follow." Considering all the praise that has been lavished on the "architectonics" of McPhee's writing, this is a noteworthy comment. William Howarth, for instance, in his excellent introduction to *The John McPhee Reader,* dwells at length on how McPhee works, detailing the process by which he brings structure to the information he has gleaned from interviews, site visits, and library research. "Writers have infinite options for order," Howarth observes, "and McPhee delights in playing any that do not violate his story's 'logic.' A book on tennis can imitate the game's back-and-forth, contrapuntal action; but it can also resemble a mountain climb, with an ascent, climax, and descent arranged in pyramidal form. The choice is McPhee's: either find an idea for order *in* the material or impose one *upon* it, selecting what Coleridge called the 'organic' and 'mechanic'

principles of structure" (xvi). Following Howarth, other critics have
continued to explore the elements of McPhee's structure.[9]

When I first encountered my student's comment about the narrative
of "Atchafalaya," I was concerned that the student might have been a
victim of our time, expecting McPhee's stories to unfold in outline
form, like so many PowerPoint presentations.[10] But my student is hardly
alone in finding *The Control of Nature* to be "broken up" and "difficult
to follow." The environmental historian Stephen Pyne, for example,
writing in the *New York Times Book Review*, noted:

> The enormity of the stories [in *The Control of Nature*] strains at tradi-
> tional formulas, even those that have served Mr. McPhee—an extraor-
> dinary literary engineer—so well in the past. . . . Instead the narrative
> emulates the rhythms of the natural flows it describes, each time en-
> countering another monument to human assertion or absurdity.
> There is no single persona to represent either side. Almost everyone is
> implicated, and nearly everything is diffused. There are at times too
> many images, too many episodes, too many persons, a constant ravel
> of comments interrupted by an occasional flood of storytelling. (22)

To help first-time readers see the underlying structure of a text, I usually do try to provide an outline of its main points, which, for a book,
often takes the form of an annotated table of contents. As O. Alan
Weltzien has observed (this volume), the structure of *The Control of
Nature* is the same "A-B-C over D" pattern that McPhee first used in
Encounters with the Archdruid, as well as a variation on the home-away-
home pattern traced by Michael Pearson in *John McPhee*. *The Control of
Nature*, however, lacks the unifying presence of a David Brower to hold
its three sections together. Tracing the structure of the individual essays
is more difficult, since their architectonics are not always readily apparent, much like the layers of rock McPhee describes in *Annals of the Former World*. As William Howarth has noted, McPhee's essays "are carefully organized, but not in normal time sequences" (viii). In a
conversation with Norman Sims, McPhee explained how the structure
of "Travels in Georgia" (from *Pieces of the Frame*) resembles a lowercase
e, for instance, whereas the structure of *A Roomful of Hovings* could be
compared to an uppercase Υ ("Literary Journalist," 13–14). "Readers
are not supposed to be aware of structure," McPhee has argued, "but its
logic may bring them into the story" (Pearson, *John McPhee*, 29).

For students who find his stories "broken up" and "difficult to follow," however, an outline is often a necessity; and while the intended structure of his essays may be known only to McPhee, I attempt to provide students with a possible framework for each of the essays we examine from *The Control of Nature*. "Atchafalaya," for example, seems to me to contain at least three distinct sections, the first consisting of an introduction to the Mississippi River (3–9), Old River Control (9–15), and the U.S. Army Corps of Engineers (15–26). This is followed by McPhee's discussion of the various attempts to control flooding in the Mississippi River Basin during the Flood of 1973 (26–30), before the Flood Control Act of 1928 (30–42), and after the Flood Control Act of 1928 (43–55). Finally, the essay concludes with a discussion of the human interests in the Mississippi River Basin, including those of the residents of New Orleans (55–64), the Bayou (64–78), Morgan City (78–86), and the U.S. Army Corps of Engineers (86–92). "Los Angeles against the Mountains," however, seems to me to function contrapuntally, with stories of the debris flows and the destruction they cause alternating with discussions of the construction of the debris basins, the causes of the debris flows, the environmental and human history of the San Gabriels, the ignorance of the debris flow problem by realtors and home buyers, and the issue of where to put the debris captured by the basins. Whether McPhee would agree with these readings or not is, to some degree, beside the point, since I challenge my students to create their own outlines showing how they think the essays are organized, as both a means to encourage their close reading of the texts and a demonstration of the way meaning emerges collaboratively from the interaction of reader, writer, text, and context.

Characters

My own sense of the contrapuntal structure of "Los Angeles against the Mountains" is echoed by my student's comment that "McPhee kept switching from person to person" in that essay and that "[i]t was difficult to keep track of who everyone was and what his or her part in the San Gabriel Mountains was." The issue that concerns her, in other words, is the large number of characters that he employs to tell his stories in *The Control of Nature*.

In "Los Angeles against the Mountains," for instance, we meet, in order of appearance, Bob and Jackie Genofile and their two teenage children, Kimberlee and Scott, all residents of Shields Canyon (183–84);

the late Roland Case Ross, emeritus professor of biology at California State University (187); Cliff Hamlow, basketball coach at Azusa Pacific College (188); John McCafferty, a bulldozer driver (190); Gary Lukehart, John Caufield, and John Marcellino, all residents of Glencoe Heights (189–91); Donald Nichols, an engineer with the Sedimentation Section of the Hydraulic Division of the Los Angeles County Department of Public Works—or "Flood," as it is known (193); Reyner Banham, late professor of the history of architecture at University College, London (195); Chris Terracciano, driver of a Flood truck (198); Wade Wells, a hydrologist with the U.S. Forest Service (204); Edwin Harp, a debris-flow specialist from the U.S. Geological Survey (206); Charles Colver of the U.S. Forest Service (209); Dan Davis and Hadi Norouzi, engineers with Flood (217); Amos and Elva Lewis, Cal and Mary Drake, and Gabe Hinterberg, all of Hidden Springs (216–17); Mike Rubel, owner of a 22,000-square-foot castle in Glendora (222); Leon Silver, Barclay Kamb, Andre Ingersoll, and Vito Vanoni, all scientists at the California State Polytechnic University (225–31); Mel and Barbara Horton, who live in John Burroughs's former home in Pasadena Glen, and their daughter Alison, who lives in Alaska (237); Dennis and Susan McNamara, residents of Glendale (243); Aimee Miller and her husband, who was Frank Sinatra's piano accompanist (244); G. Henry Stetson, the hatmaker (245); Peter Fay, a professor of history at Caltech (246); Marilyn Skates and James Dubuque, who lived near the Big Tujunga (247); Richard Crook, a consulting geologist (248); Arthur Cook, acting city manager of Glendora, and Sally Rand, also of Glendora (250); a handful of unnamed realtors (252–54); Carl Gunn, another resident of Glendora (255); Chakib Sambar, vice-principal of Crescenta Valley High School (256); Miner Harkness, a resident of Sierra Madre (257), and his wife, Sara, an intensive-care nurse, and their two sons and daughters (263); Joanne Crowder, the Harknesses' neighbor (263); and John Tettemer, acting chief deputy engineer with Flood, and Arthur Bruington, his colleague (269), among others.

To be fair, a few of these folks are referred to only in passing; but equally few, such as the Genofiles and Miner Harkness, could be said to loom considerably larger than the rest. Some, like Thoreau's loon, appear at one point in the essay and then disappear, only to reemerge later in the same essay. But most are simply part of the vast human landscape that pervades all of the essays in *The Control of Nature*.

That so many people should be referred to in a single essay might not surprise long-time readers of McPhee, since in interview after interview he has described his work as concerning "real people in real places" or what he has termed "sketches of people in backgrounds in which they work" (Shabecoff, 22).[11] As Michael Pearson nicely summarizes, "McPhee's goal . . . is to allow the issues to come to life through the individual drama" (*John McPhee,* 100). Yet many of my students, like the one quoted above, have difficulty keeping such a large number of characters straight; and as a result they tend to see McPhee's essays, as he himself wrote of the debris flows, "like bread dough mixed with raisins" (*Control,* 185). For this reason I distribute a character list like the one given above for each essay, including the name, occupation, location, and page number for each of the major characters. This may not solve the problem of keeping track of McPhee's characters, but it at least provides a starting point.

What emerges from the discussions my students and I have about all these characters is that they can essentially be boiled down to two types—the hero and the expert—that William Howarth first identified in his introduction to *The John McPhee Reader* (xx–xxiii). McPhee's heroes are not heroes in the comic-book sense, of course, but in the mythological sense—the sense in which we are all heroes, engaged in the quests that are our daily lives. Like Emerson's "representative men" (and women), McPhee's heroes are interesting not just in themselves, but also for the roles they play in the larger narrative he is tracing.[12]

Whereas Howarth sees the expert as constituting "the broad base for this pyramid of heroes" (xxii), I see something slightly different, at least in *The Control of Nature.* To me, McPhee's heroes and experts represent two sides of the ongoing tension in contemporary environmentalism between technical experts and the general public—a tension well documented by Rachel Carson in *Silent Spring.* What makes McPhee more than just a popularizer of scientific and technological expertise is his ability to demonstrate that these are really two sides of the same coin. Bob Genofile and Mike Rubel, for instance, display their own brand of engineering expertise in "Los Angeles against the Mountains." In the same way, expert geologists find themselves as much in need of aesthetic fulfillment as do members of the general public: "Why would a geologist live in the San Gabriels?" McPhee asks Leon Silver, who replies: "Great views" (229–30). *The Control of Nature* provides a good example of the ways in which science and technology both mediate human interactions with the nonhuman world as well as a good example of the ways in which human nature mediates the application of science and technology to nature.

Subject and Method

Of all the characters in *The Control of Nature,* the most important is the one we notice least: the narrator, or McPhee himself. Although he selects the setting, structures the plot, and describes—if not interacts with—all the other characters in the book, he reveals remarkably little information about his own life and views. This is of course no accident. "I think authors can get between the reader and the work," McPhee once told Michael Pearson. "A piece of writing is something in which the figure of the author is just one component" ("Profile," 86).

Whether McPhee's strategy is a strength or a weakness is a subject of some debate. William Howarth, for one, believes that "the greatest of his virtues, *contra* the New Journalism, is that readers need not know him to appreciate his writing" (xi). But David Quammen—like McPhee, a winner of the John Burroughs Medal (in 1997 for *The Song of the Dodo*)—feels quite strongly otherwise. In one of his "Natural Acts" columns, Quammen describes *The Control of Nature* as a "small, cautious" book whose author "had seen much but . . . had refused to conclude anything" and has "no evident thoughts or opinions of his own" (30). Instead, he is "a dutiful journalist with a narrow view of his job and a determination to remain innocent of metaphysics" (31).

This debate interests me in part because it interests my students. One year, for instance, when we read *The Control of Nature* alongside Bill McKibben's *The End of Nature*—an intensely activist book—students who loved McKibben's strongly held views hated McPhee's lack of them and vice versa. More importantly, the debate interests me because it also raises the question of how I as a teacher should position myself in the classroom. McPhee's role as a "literary journalist" is not that far removed from my role as a teacher: we both convey expert knowledge to an audience of generalists, we both try to keep our audience interested and entertained, and we both tell stories. But what kind of storyteller should I be? Should I, like McKibben, advocate for a particular conclusion or course of action, based on the information I present; or should I, like McPhee, remain neutral, a "dutiful journalist"? McPhee's own preference, at least in terms of his writing, is clear from several interviews he has given, including one with Bob Sipchen following the pub-

lication of *The Control of Nature*. "I want the judgments to be performed by the reader," McPhee said. "There are some people who think
that one ought to be more forceful in one's judgments and have an ax to
grind. I don't want to grind axes in my writing. But I want to have
plenty of axes out there for others to do their own grinding on" (15).

My own preference for teaching resembles McPhee's preference for
writing: I want the judgments to be performed by the student. But I
would agree with several critics of McPhee's writing who observe that
his apparent objectivity is in fact a rhetorical stance. No one is ever
wholly neutral—not McPhee and certainly not me. In the same way that
McPhee expresses his preferences through his "fictionalizing act"—his
selection of setting, plot, and character—I express mine through my selection of subject matter, teaching methods, and personal behavior. We
both choose from among many effective ways to present our information, and we both function as only one of the four coordinates of discourse. We both, in short, breathe the same "academic air."[13]

McPhee's rhetoric of objectivity shares several features with my own.
As Elizabeth Giddens has argued, McPhee's writing "affirms the need
for mutual trust and openness in any ethical rhetorical exchange" (378)
and manifests "the broad objectives of promoting honest inquiry, debate, and attitude change" (380). Similar concerns motivate my teaching: primarily the Socratic belief that the unexamined life is not worth
living, from which follows a set of secondary values such as honesty,
human dignity, and rationality (values that almost all educational institutions embrace) as well as such social goods as the value of civic engagement. And, just as Brian Turner has suggested that McPhee seeks
to remain objective within a particular value system, addressing and
sympathetically recording "various sides of what we have come to think
of simply as 'environmental issues' " (168), I choose to make my own
environmental values explicit by including the following note on the syl-
labus for "In Search of Nature":

> Just as medical education is biased toward health, and legal education
> is biased toward justice, this course is biased toward sustainability. It
> begins with the assumption that environmental health and environ-
> mental justice are desired goals. Such an assumption does not, how-
> ever, imply that you must be an "environmentalist" to succeed in this
> course. In fact, we will spend much of the course discussing the dis-
> agreements that exist regarding environmental issues. While I will try

to present the course material as objectively as possible, you should always think critically about the information you receive. Ultimately, my goal is to demonstrate not only that it is possible to distinguish between better and worse environmental choices, but also that good citizenship involves cultivating the knowledge and skills to make such choices wisely.

The Control of Nature succeeds in my classroom, I think, not only because its setting, plot, and characters provide me with a wide range of teaching opportunities but also because its subject and method effectively model the subject and method of good teaching. As several critics have observed, McPhee's rhetoric of objectivity stems from his interest not only in nature but also in human nature. In Brian Turner's words, McPhee "moves in the penumbra between nature and human society, as much a student of how nature treats us, and we nature, as he is of nature in and of itself" (168). My own teaching shares this subject with McPhee's writing, but I have the added advantage of my audience being present for debate and discussion. Like McPhee's stated subject, my students are "real people in real places"—heroes of everyday life who inhabit places unique in both time and space—and their presence in the classroom makes all the difference. Like McPhee's readers, they are co-creators of meaning, each interpreting the text in a different context—each reading, in effect, his or her own version of the text.

If the central question of *The Control of Nature* is whether and how humans should exert control over the nonhuman environment, this same question can be applied with equal force to McPhee's own writing and to the teaching of controversial issues: what are we to do with a multiplicity of voices? McPhee's method, I would argue, applies equally well in both cases. A rhetoric of objectivity—fostering a sympathetic hearing of all voices, from within a particular system of values—not only allows McPhee's readers to come to their own conclusions but also allows my students to come to theirs. If there is a politics here, it is a democratic politics of prefiguration, which entails modeling, in one's own behavior, the behavior one wishes to see adopted by others—the classic example being the peace activists whose protests embody a philosophy of nonviolence. A teacher who seeks to achieve a society in which all voices receive a fair hearing, in other words, must first provide a fair hearing for all the voices in the classroom. While I am hesitant to overstate the significance of this rhetorical stance—well modeled by *The*

Control of Nature—it does seem to me to represent a crucial insight into what may be the major dilemma of environmental politics: how to strike a balance between totalitarianism and anarchy. If that is what constitutes McPhee's "dutiful journalism," I will take it any day.

Notes

1. According to this view, McPhee might rightly object to my placing too much weight on a few words he uttered in the context of one interview, which can hardly be considered definitive. In another interview, he further acknowledged the function of the reader and the context: "a writer, in my view, is the less creative partner than the reader, and 97% (or whatever you want to say) of the *creativity* that's going on in a piece of writing is being done by the reader. A writer is tossing out the things with which the reader makes pictures in the mind. The pictures, of course, depend on the frame of reference of the reader" (Vipond and Hunt, 204).

2. The other texts in the course include Emerson's *Nature* and Thoreau's "Walking," Jon Krakauer's *Into the Wild,* John C. Ryan and Alan Thein Durning's *Stuff: The Secret Lives of Everyday Things,* Rachel Carson's *Silent Spring,* and a course packet of more than twenty related essays. In previous versions of the course I have also taught William Cronon's edited collection *Uncommon Ground: Rethinking the Human Place in Nature,* Bill McKibben's *The End of Nature,* Jean Hegland's *Into the Forest,* and Michael Pollan's *Second Nature: A Gardener's Education.* Two books that offer a different perspective on the same subject as *The Control of Nature* are Theodore Steinberg's *Slide Mountain; or, The Folly of Owning Nature* and *Acts of God: The Unnatural History of Natural Disaster in America.*

3. Thomas Bailey offers his own compact assessment of the strengths and weaknesses of McPhee's environmental writing in "John McPhee: The Making of a Meta-Naturalist":

> The strengths of McPhee's vision are not hard to find: a style that allows him to portray the beauties and realities of the natural world as few writers ever have; a sense of order that allows for striking and powerful comparisons; an ability to juxtapose difficult questions in a way that insures that the reader will become his partner in the making of meaning; and a relentless mind that questions and probes and never settles for the easy answer. His weaknesses are equally obvious: his appetite for technological or professional detail often exceeds that of even a devoted reader; and his fascination with the human personality leads him at times to load the dice against the David Browers of the world and come down on the side of a free enterprise humanism that, despite its charm, poses grave risks to a healthy biota on a healthy planet. (212)

4. I am not alone in this complaint. See Stephen MacDonald's review of the book in the *Wall Street Journal.*

5. For years McPhee has taught a course at Princeton called "The Literature of Fact"—which, he stresses, was titled by the university, although his acceptance of the title indicates that he must have achieved at least some level of comfort with it (Sipchen, 1). For more on McPhee as a "literary journalist," see chapter 2 of Michael Pearson's *John McPhee.*

6. A frequent complaint of reviewers is the abundance—some would say overabundance—of detail in McPhee's writing. "McPhee is a lover of small details," says Michael Pearson. "He is the kind of man who draws intricate directions on the back of cocktail napkins" ("Profile," 78). If only he had included a few of those drawings in the book!

7. An interesting theoretical question concerns the degree to which a textbook can be considered "good" if it cannot stand alone. Were I teaching a literature class, I would justify using all these ancillary materials as a way to illustrate the writer's craft; but if I need all these materials just to get students to understand the book, is it worth using the book at all? This question, like my previous one about the role of illustrations in literary journalism, is really a version of that much-debated question "what is literature?"—which itself reflects the romantic view of literature as aesthetic and contemplative, not active and persuasive (a view that rhetorical critics obviously reject).

8. All of these sights, sounds, and emotions are components of what David E. Nye (*American Technological Sublime*) calls the technological sublime.

9. See, for example, Barbara Lounsberry's "John McPhee's Levels of the Earth"; Jack Roundy's "Crafting Fact"; and W. Ross Winterowd's "John McPhee and the Craft of Writing."

10. See Ian Parker's essay "Absolute PowerPoint." I was also concerned that my student may have been so conditioned to expect an "extreme" encounter with nature to be rendered with a similar narrative extremity (such as we find in Jon Krakauer's *Into the Wild*) that McPhee's matter-of-fact narration might have seemed "difficult to follow." I do not, however, believe this was the case.

11. See also Hamilton, "Encounter with John McPhee," 52; Pearson, "Profile," 83; Sims, "Art of Literary Journalism," 17; and Vipond and Hunt, "Strange Case," 207.

12. For more on McPhee's heroes as Emersonian "representative men," see Barbara Lounsberry's "John McPhee's Levels of the Earth"; and chapter 4 of Michael Pearson's *John McPhee.*

13. For other perspectives on advocacy in the classroom, see the collection *Advocacy in the Classroom: Problems and Possibilities,* ed. Patricia Meyer Spacks.

Works Cited

Bailey, Thomas C. "John McPhee: The Making of a Meta-Naturalist." In *Earthly Words: Essays on Contemporary American Nature and Environmental Writers,* ed. John Cooley, 195–213. Ann Arbor: University of Michigan Press, 1994.

Carson, Rachel. *Silent Spring.* New York: Houghton Mifflin, 1994.

Cronon, William (ed.). *Uncommon Ground: Rethinking the Human Place in Nature.* New York: Norton, 1996.

Emerson, Ralph Waldo, and Henry David Thoreau. *Nature/Walking.* Boston: Beacon Press, 1991.

Giddens, Elizabeth. "An Epistemic Case Study: Identification and Attitude Change in John McPhee's *Coming into the Country.*" *Rhetoric Review* 11(2) (Spring 1993): 378–99.

Hamilton, Joan. "An Encounter with John McPhee." *Sierra* 75(3) (May/June 1990): 50–55, 92, 96.

Headlam, Bruce. "The War with Nature." *Toronto Star,* 14 October 1989, M28.

Hegland, Jean. *Into the Forest.* New York: Bantam, 1998.

Hiestand, Emily. "Real Places." *Atlantic Monthly* 288(1) (July/August 2001): 130–36.

Howarth, William L. "Introduction." In *The John McPhee Reader,* ed. William L. Howarth, vii–xxiii. New York: Farrar, Straus & Giroux, 1976.

Krakauer, Jon. *Into the Wild.* New York: Anchor, 1997.

Lehmann-Haupt, Christopher. "Oh, to Still the Floods and Quench the Fires." *New York Times,* 3 August 1989, C21.

Lounsberry, Barbara. "John McPhee's Levels of the Earth." In *The Art of Fact: Contemporary Artists of Nonfiction,* 65–106. New York: Greenwood, 1990.

Macaulay, David. *The Way Things Work.* Boston: Houghton Mifflin, 1988.

MacDonald, Stephen. "Going against the Flow." *Wall Street Journal,* 3 August 1989, A9.

McKibben, Bill. *The End of Nature.* New York: Anchor, 1990.

McPhee, John. *Annals of the Former World.* New York: Farrar, Straus & Giroux, 1998.

———. *The Control of Nature.* New York: Farrar, Straus & Giroux, 1989.

———. *Encounters with the Archdruid.* New York: Farrar, Straus & Giroux, 1971.

———. *Pieces of the Frame.* New York: Farrar, Straus & Giroux, 1975.

———. *A Roomful of Hovings.* New York: Farrar, Straus & Giroux, 1968.

Miles, Jack. "McPhee on Debris." *Los Angeles Times Book Review* (30 July 1989): 4.

Nye, David E. *American Technological Sublime.* Cambridge, Mass.: MIT Press, 1994.

Parker, Ian. "Absolute PowerPoint: Can a Software Package Edit Our Thoughts?" *New Yorker* (28 May 2001): 76–87.

Pearson, Michael. *John McPhee.* New York: Twayne, 1997.

———. "Profile: John McPhee." *Creative Nonfiction* 1 (1993): 76–87. (Reprinted as "Twenty Questions: A Conversation with John McPhee." *Creative Nonfiction* 6 [1996]: 103–15.)

Pollan, Michael. *Second Nature: A Gardener's Education.* New York: Delta, 1993.

Pyne, Stephen J. "A War against the World." *New York Times Book Review* (6 August 1989): 1, 22.

Quammen, David. "Muscling Nature." *Outside* 14(12) (December 1989): 29–32, 34, 36.

———. *The Song of the Dodo: Island Biogeography in an Age of Extinctions.* New York: Scribner, 1996.

Roundy, Jack. "Crafting Fact: Formal Devices in the Prose of John McPhee." In *Literary Nonfiction: Theory, Criticism, Pedagogy,* ed. Chris Anderson, 70–92. Carbondale: Southern Illinois University Press, 1989.

Ryan, John C., and Alan Thein Durning. *Stuff: The Secret Lives of Everyday Things.* Seattle: Northwest Environment Watch, 1997.

Shabecoff, Philip. "Defying Nature May Be the Only Choice." *New York Times Book Review* (6 August 1989): 22.

Sims, Norman. "The Art of Literary Journalism." In *Literary Journalism: A New Collection of the Best American Nonfiction,* ed. Norman Sims and Mark Kramer, 3–19. New York: Ballantine, 1995.

———. "The Literary Journalist." In *The Literary Journalists,* ed. Norman Sims, 3–25. New York: Ballantine, 1984.

Sipchen, Bob. "Mountains from Molehills: Speck by Speck, Writer John McPhee Compiles Scary Tale of L.A.'s Slippery Geology." *Los Angeles Times,* 6 August 1989, pt. 6, pp. 1, 14–15.

Smith, Kathy. "John McPhee Balances the Act." In *Literary Journalism in the Twentieth Century,* ed. Norman Sims, 206–27. Oxford: Oxford University Press, 1990.

Spacks, Patricia Meyer (ed.). *Advocacy in the Classroom: Problems and Possibilities.* New York: St. Martin's Press, 1996.

Steinberg, Theodore. *Acts of God: The Unnatural History of Natural Disaster in America.* New York: Oxford University Press, 2000.

———. *Slide Mountain; or, The Folly of Owning Nature.* Berkeley: University of California Press, 1995.

Turner, Brian. "Giving Good Reasons: Environmental Appeals in the Nonfiction of John McPhee." *Rhetoric Review* 13(1) (Fall 1994): 164–82.

Vipond, Douglas, and Russell A. Hunt. "The Strange Case of the Queen-Post Truss: John McPhee on Writing and Reading." *College Composition and Communication* 42(2) (May 1991): 200–210.

Weltzien, O. Alan. "John McPhee and the Question of Environmental Advocacy" (this volume).

Winterowd, W. Ross. "John McPhee and the Craft of Writing." In *The Rhetoric of the "Other" Literature,* 79–83. Carbondale: Southern Illinois University Press, 1990.

Susan Naramore Maher

"Pentimento in the Hide"

Cracking Code with John McPhee

> The business end of most running irons is a short simple line. It becomes a red-hot stylus for metamorphic sketching. The business end of some running irons is as broad and flat as a playing card. You use that to blot out what you can't change. Be warned, though: there is pentimento in the hide—a history readable from within.
>
> John McPhee, *Irons in the Fire*

The work of John McPhee, like so much I value in life, entered into my view serendipitously. In 1979, as a new teaching assistant at the University of Wisconsin at Madison, I shared a large office with five other students. We each had a square of space marked by bookcases, small area rugs, and whatever else we could devise to claim some autonomy, some patch of privacy in an otherwise open and public room. One of my office mates, C. Topf Wells, kept a well-stocked and eclectic bookcase that I would visit when I needed a break from my particular corner. Topf never minded my diagonal beelines to his corner, where I would finger his titles and browse through book jackets. One day, I pulled a volume called *Oranges* from a shelf. It was by a writer named John McPhee. "Great book," Topf declared. "Go ahead and take a look." I imagined the book must be a novel, perhaps something quite contemporary with that stripped-down title, something self-reflexive and self-consciously ironic. I imagined I might hate it, but I took *Oranges* with me anyway—and from that first encounter I was hooked on John McPhee. His exacting, precise way with language, his narrative experiments, his vivid, carefully limned portraits, and his keen interest in so many facets of work and life have hooked many a reader and earned him high praise.

Among the writerly virtues that attracted me to McPhee's evolving oeuvre is his ability to decode for his readers an unfamiliar way of life or thinking and to textualize it lucidly, intelligently, and accessibly. He decodes worlds for us. Semiotician Wendy Leeds-Hurwitz informs us that

> codes are culture-bound and context-specific. The rules for their use are not self-evident, not readily available to everyone presented with a particular sign. Not all people are party to the same codes: There must be a group available to support the particular agreements of any code, this group being what is generally called members of a culture. Only a legitimate member of the group using the code has the knowledge to appropriately interpret the meanings of any sign. (59)

McPhee's genius is entering into a cultural group—orange growers, academic geologists, brand inspectors, for instance—gaining knowledge of their work and thus the competency "to appropriately interpret" a group's code for his readers, who are not always "party" to the meanings. Making professional codes accessible and legible is crucial to much of McPhee's work.

While any dictionary provides a concise definition of decipherment and decoding—"to convert (as a coded message) into intelligible form; to recognize and interpret . . . to discover the underlying meaning of"—a thesaurus overflows in McPhee-like cataloging with analogues. Crack, crack the cipher, find the meaning, read hieroglyphics, read, spell out, puzzle out, make out, work out, piece together, find the sense of, find the key to, solve, resolve, enucleate, unravel, unriddle, disentangle, read between the lines: McPhee's narratives "puzzle out" such translation work, reading for us the pentimento in the hide, the history "readable from within." Author and text mediate worlds for us, bringing us into domains at times arcane, restrictively professional, and little known.

Metaphorically, decoding carries multiple meanings, becoming itself an operative metaphor for reading McPhee. Ciphers and codes have a long history in warfare. During war decoders work urgently to translate the enemy's signs, protecting the community of soldiers and citizens. In a number of McPhee's essays, an analogous sense of urgency propels the narrative. Lives and livelihoods are at stake. For instance, a war metaphor is central in "Los Angeles against the Mountains." Humans, at war against the natural world, attempt to decode its secrets in an effort to control nature. The elegant if arcane science of this "war" also begs translation. Deciphering the work of geologists who read the rock, McPhee presents a cautionary tale. Those who ignore the San Gabriels' pentimento in the rock do so at their own risk. Los Angeles, shadowed by "disassembling mountains" (236), awaits many disasters. In this work and others, McPhee asks us to consider the consequences, even dangers, of human choice—in this case of people who "would rather defy nature than live without it" (236). Part of McPhee's epistemology, as Brian Turner argues, is "writing [that] is . . . value laden, and has a suasive function. . . . He implicitly and explicitly recommends stances" (166–67). By challenging his readers with the ability to know the multivalences of a given situation, McPhee opens them to the ethical dimensions of human behavior. As in true war, cracking code becomes a necessary moral as well as survival function.

Additionally, decoding may suggest a mentorship or student-teacher relationship. To understand unfamiliar codes, one needs guidance. McPhee's acts of decoding are eminently social, involving the help of knowledgeable experts. David Espey has noted that McPhee is no lone traveler trying to understand an experience as solo translator (167). In McPhee's nonfiction, then, the choice of guides and scouts—what Espey calls the "traveling companion" (167)—distinguishes his narrative form. McPhee as writer attempts to decode for the reader-student the information his guides provide. In this sense, his persona assumes the mask of writer-teacher, introducing his readers to the intricate, accumulated wisdom of a professional culture. Yet McPhee often shares with his readers the role of student. His is no "magisterial gaze" (Boime, 1–2), declaiming authoritatively upon the scene, translating without hesitation or doubt. The humility of this narrative stance—McPhee humbling himself to the subject matter—is part and parcel of his purposeful, social rhetoric. To decode is to learn, to counter unfortunate or unwitting ignorance.

Finally, decoding can be play with all its pleasures. In "Irons in the Fire," McPhee tells us that "[not] all brands are letters or numbers. You will see a range cow branded with a ladder, a leaf, a mitten, a mountain, a Boeing, a bow tie, or a fissioning bomb. In Minden, Nevada, the Hellwinkels' brand is COD. In Austin, Nevada, the Saraluguis' brand is COW" (10–11). Such alliterative cataloging and such playful punning express the pure joy of manipulating and translating the code of branding into readable text. McPhee's linguistic virtuosity remains one of his signature skills; the pleasure he takes in presenting the lexicon of other disciplines, professions, and communities delights his readership. This essay, too, plays with the rich metaphors of encoding and decoding to explore the nuanced interchange of reportage and play, suasiveness and art, that marks McPhee's mature period.

Coming into McPhee's essays, then, is no static act. His variability is legendary, as is his itinerancy. McPhee's narratives challenge his readers, engaging them in a creative exchange. They must meet him halfway. Over the years his essays have taken on added complexity, starting with the landmark *Coming into the Country* (1977), running through the innovative volumes of *Annals of the Former World* (1981–1998), and continuing in recent volumes like *The Control of Nature* (1989) and *Irons in the Fire* (1997) or the increasingly personal occasional pieces in the *New Yorker*. In this mature period, his perspective has shifted from a balanced pastoralism to a less comforting stance that posits human vulnerability, mischance, and evil against a backdrop of a changing, at times violent natural system—"a system inherently at odds," Thomas C. Bailey insists, "with any social or economic system men and women have ever devised" (195). This more somber note was first sounded in *Encounters with the Archdruid* (1971) and deepened in *Rising from the Plains* (1986). Standing amidst the ruins of his parents' ranch, geologist David Love, McPhee's central figure in *Rising from the Plains,* admits ambivalence: " 'At places like this, we thought we were doing a great service to the nation. In hindsight, we do not know if we were performing a service or a disservice. Sometimes I think I might regret it. Yes. It's close to home' " (214). Here a once thriving community now decays, and the individual voice sounds into the shadows of the dead past. Love, Job-like in the wilderness, questions his inheritance and a century's boosterism.

McPhee, noted for his balanced rhetoric that "arouses one's sense of community" and "elicits assent to the values for which he stands" (Turner, 165), in this later period allows for more dissonance, contradiction, and uncertainty in his writing. As McPhee himself has stated, "The final sixth of *Rising from the Plains* is an environmental montage of tensions between geological discovery and environmental preservation. David Love . . . contains within himself the essence of the struggle . . ." (*Annals,* 11). In this work and others, the struggle is never completely resolved. In an interview with Jared Haynes, McPhee insists, "It seems to me that life is not simple, it's complex. There are always many factors. In some instances, you have to pull a lever and vote, but there's always something to be said on the various sides. . . . My goal is life in the round, not instructions on what lever to pull" (Haynes, this volume). The struggle, the choices, the possibilities: in the human realm, ambiguity often clouds our desire for clear, forthright answers.

Yet this very ambiguity has heightened McPhee's desire to decode what he cannot read, to provide metaphorical bridges for himself and his readers into new territory. Life's very complexity encourages closer inspection, an eye for detail, the skill to translate. Understanding and translating cultural code is a complicated exchange, as Leeds-Hurwitz makes clear, involving encoding—"to convey information through that code"—and decoding, "to interpret information from the code" (61). McPhee's texts involve both processes. As Jack Roundy puts it, "His aim in writing fact pieces is nearly always to lead the reader to unfamiliar territory . . . whose mysteries he will then reveal" (81). Such revelation, however, is rarely absolute. In *Annals* Sharon Bass sees McPhee dropping a "plainness of speaking" noticeable in earlier writings and embracing "the very mystery and magic of the dense material of geologic vocabulary" (346). By the time McPhee is following brand inspector Chris Collis around a sizable portion of Nevada in "Irons in the Fire," he admits, "Stare as I will at the cattle, I have to ask him what the brands are. I'm not just suggesting that the brands are unfamiliar. I'm saying that I can't even see them" (6). Lacking "the accomplished eye" of Collis (7), McPhee assumes the role of student. His education parallels that of the reader, both becoming more appreciative than adept, more knowledgeable about than practiced in the brand inspector's art. Roundy's understanding of McPhee's "lexicon" is informative: introducing his readership to "a presumably alien vernacular," McPhee "invokes the familiar world to help the reader see an unfamiliar one" (84–85). Creating "analogical bridges," he brings the uninitiated reader into "the 'exotic terrane' of his subject" (Roundy, 88). But McPhee does not mind admitting when his own sight is flawed, when "I can't even see."

Making professional codes accessible and legible can be a long process. McPhee has been particularly honest about his difficulties in writing the completed *Annals,* starting with *Basin and Range:* "I was in over my head and I kept saying, 'What am I doing? Why am I doing this? How did I get into this?' more intensely than I had done with anything else" (Haynes, this volume). Trying to decode the outcrops with geologist Anita Harris, McPhee confesses: "But I was so at sea. I could feel my neck turning red as Anita would talk in front of the outcrops at the Delaware River Gap. I didn't understand one word. I was scribbling everything down and I understood nothing." Two years later, though, McPhee's notes made sense. "When I look at them now," he says, "they look like a map of my hometown. But when I scribbled those notes down and typed them up, I had no idea what they meant" (Haynes, this volume). The frustration of not knowing, not seeing, not understanding—a process his readers often share with him—compelled a dogged McPhee to keep trying. Once he cracked the code, writing the *Annals* moved apace. His readers move through a similar process in many of his essays, stumped at first by a lack of orientation; yet as McPhee's texts provide definition and translation, his readers, too, proceed with confidence into new terrain.

In the later writings, McPhee's struggles with the unfamiliar reveal a humanizing narrative voice and provide both comic relief and a truthful assessment of any journey's incompletion. Sometimes the writer is more plain John Watson than brilliant Sherlock Holmes, more foot soldier than general, more student than teacher. Because of this inversion, these later writings, with their technical and intellectual complexity, particularly fascinate me. Ranging over McPhee's recent repertoire, from "Los Angeles against the Mountains" (*The Control of Nature,* 1989); to the tour de force conclusion of *Assembling California* (1993) as the Loma Prieta earthquake rips through the Bay area; and through the essays "Irons in the Fire" and "The Gravel Page" (*Irons in the Fire,* 1997), we witness McPhee's fascination with decoding as he attempts to read the complexities of landscapes and human nature. In the process, we do not receive absolute conclusions, steady reassurances, or easy answers. McPhee's "relentless mind that questions and probes" carries us along "in a way that insures that the reader will become his partner in the making of meaning" (Bailey, 212). It is "participation and engagement" that matter, not total assent (Turner, 179). In traversing unfamiliar territory, we enter a literary world of nuance, ambiguity, and contingency—a world we must decode if we are to imagine it and learn from it.

In each of these four works, McPhee grapples with a new professional lexicon and grammar. Learning to read an unfamiliar world—the complex array of rock and assemblage that is California; the cryptic cattle brands in Nevada; the intriguing gravel page that betrays murderers—constitutes a central incitement in McPhee's evolving canon. None is a simple act of reading.

Reading the earth is key to understanding the odds for surviving catastrophes in California. Los Angeles has nowhere to go in what McPhee calls "the confrontation of the urban and the wild" ("Los Angeles," 184). Squeezed between the Pacific Ocean and the San Gabriels, Los

Angelinos have aggressively pursued development on unstable ground. The San Gabriels loom nearly ten thousand feet above the city: "Shedding, spalling, self-destructing, they are disintegrating at a rate that is also among the fastest in the world," McPhee announces (184). Humans map L.A. streets, impose an order upon this landscape, only to have their efforts erased in monumental debris flows year after year. To contend with and control nature, Los Angeles has built a series of dams and debris basins replete with channels and concrete crib structures to catch the falling mountains. The reservoir systems that feed into the city also catch and trap the San Gabriels, though the original planners had no idea their lakes would serve this purpose. In one dam structure alone, the San Gabriel Dam, annual cleaning of the reservoir once removed "twenty million tons of mountain" (194). When the mountains do move—"The places change. Volumes differ. There are vintage years" (203)—neighborhoods look like war zones.

Citizens depend upon city planners, engineers, contractors, geologists, and others to read the San Gabriels' lexicon correctly. Yet the urge to develop and profit from development runs up against the gained experience and knowledge of the experts who study the mountains. Even they can be lulled into complacency; even a home engineered to survive the mountains' assault can end up a potential tomb, as Bob and Jackie Genofile discover. Bob, a general contractor, has understood the mountains enough to construct a home "made of concrete block with steel reinforcement, sixteen inches on center" (185). Built to withstand a falling mountain, Bob's home earned the nickname "the fort." Such hubris offers a challenge that the mountains answer.

Comfortable in their Shields Canyon home, the Genofiles wake up one night to disaster. By morning light, they see the following scene: "There was a white sedan under the house eaves crushed to half its height, with two large boulders resting on top of it. Near the pool, a Volkswagen bug lay squashed. Another car was literally wrapped around a tree, like a C-clamp, its front and rear bumpers pointing in the same direction. A crushed pickup had boulders all over it, each a good deal heavier than anything a pickup could carry" (199). The mountains have tossed artifacts of our fast-moving culture around like matchbox toys. The rumblings of deep time—the transformation of the California coast under the pressure of merging plates—have exposed the vulnerability of the human present. Freeways penetrate the San Gabriels, giving people a sense of control; on some days smog veils the peaks, allowing busy

humans to ignore their presence. The imperatives of moving, competing, consuming, living humans diminish the mountains' significance.
Yet the San Gabriels overwhelm the city.

To gain advantage, geologists, structural engineers, and other scientists gauge the "oversteepening" angles that near "the angle of maxi-
mum slope" (207), measure the rainfall, and record seismic events. Ordinary citizens, whose desires lead them up into the mountains for air,
view, and perspective, depend upon these trained men and women to
decode the mountains correctly. Rock slides, debris flows, fires, and
earthquakes are part and parcel of the mountains' rise above the Pacific.
But Los Angelinos, modern lotus eaters, refuse to read the geologic
truths around them. McPhee asserts that "the geologic time scale does-
n't mean a whole lot in a place like Los Angeles. In Los Angeles, even
the Los Angeles time scale does not arouse general interest" (203). The
science that decodes southern California's tectonic complexity goes unheeded most days.

Leon Silver, a geologist at Caltech, explains the risks of living in the
mountains to McPhee. On the mountain front, where so many people
live, "the whole front face of the San Gabes is processed" (229). McPhee
asks, "Why does anybody live there?" Silver responds, "They're not well
informed. Most folks don't know the story of the fire-flood sequence.
When it happens in the next canyon, they say, 'Thank God it didn't happen here'" (229). The code revealing nature's relentless, at times devas-
tating, creative processes is all there to be read. The signs of earthquake
sketched on the surfaces and traced as sonic echoes; the semiotics of fire
and flood; the visible symbols of strewn boulders and debris miles from
their origins lie awaiting interpretation. "The forces of development are
hard to oppose," says Vito Vanoni, professor emeritus at Caltech. "Most
people who buy property in those areas never see the map and wouldn't
know what they were looking at if they saw one" (232). But even those
who have studied the mountains' encryption, geologists like Vanoni,
move into the mountains. Above the smog line, in country that brings
the urban into sudden interface with wilderness, homeowners seek
refuge from the city below. The view is stunning. To canyon dwellers,
such pleasing country, in the short term, negates the dangers of living
on processed rock. After debris flows, neighbors rebuild; and few move
out permanently. Even the initiated stay, perhaps in a bid to make at
least something stable in a land disposed to unraveling.

Los Angeles, in McPhee's story, is a place where everything "is disposable" (195). Living in such temporal uncertainty, residents reflect the gamut of emotional responses: indifference, anxiety, apprehensiveness, *joie de vivre*. Despite days that give the name "Pacific" credence, Los Angeles "has not been everlastingly serene" (183). Debris does not flow from the mountains continuously; its cycles are punctuated. Between the fire-flood cycles, earthquakes, and erosion and "the way people think" lies "a great temporal disparity" (202–3). But the geological record bespeaks the dangers: if significant fires are followed by heavy rainfall, then "the flint hits the steel, . . . the sparks fly into the flash-pan . . . the debris mobilizes" (215). How, then, is one to read the rocks correctly? McPhee provides no sure answer. The probability of disaster is well understood by scientists, engineers, public servants, and many citizens, but what should be done with that knowledge? Crib and dam structures provide qualified assurance; building stronger homes pro-vides another. Disassembling whole communities to protect the people who live in them would provoke civil troubles. Arresting develop-ment—and the money that makes fortunes—is equally problematic. When even a man as knowledgeable as Vito Vanoni defends his right to live in the San Gabes, it is harder to move people than it is to move mountains.

Willful misreading of the geological lexicon continues as a theme in McPhee's longer work *Assembling California*. Those who study the pieces of California—whose life's work is assembling its stories—under-stand the calculated risks of living on such new, evolving terrain. But the population as a whole prefers ignoring the risks or believing the scien-tists and engineers have created safer conditions. California's geologic story is complex, and many of the pieces remain buried under the ground until a seismic event dramatically provides new evidence. The Loma Prieta earthquake in October 1989, in the lexicon of geologists, was just such an "illegible" event (289). While the earth's surface records "an enigma of weird random cracks," the earth's depths hide the truer signatures of past traumatic events (288). Because California is a complex assemblage of suspect terrains that have over eons merged into the North American plate, its hard-to-read depths require sophisti-cated yet fallible instruments for the scientists' decoding. The geologists themselves must become superb readers of the earth's record: "With their four-dimensional minds, and in their interdisciplinary ultraverbal way, geologists can wiggle out of almost anything" (289). McPhee ad-mires geologists, who observe "messy" nature, synthesize their acquired knowledge, and make the "random rock . . . frame a cohesive story" (24). "Never shy about metaphors," geologists are master wordsmiths, whose scientific art parallels McPhee's narrative art. Their own work inspires the architecture of *Annals*. His coda piece, *Assembling California*, in particular represents one of the most complex "contrapuntal arrangements" (David Chapman's wonderful metaphor; 75) McPhee has ever written. Through narrative assemblage as complex as the Coastal Range mélange, *Assembling California* plots human history at those points where geology becomes destiny. In a story that clarifies both the rational and irrational impulses underlying human migration, McPhee reconstructs vestiges, traces, exotica, palimpsests, and memories—all lost or forgotten, all unfamiliar ground—that speak to the ephemera of all we know.

Reading complex geology, understanding its lexicon, is no easy thing. Guided by geologist Eldridge Moores, McPhee translates for the reader a geologic record as cryptic as any code—a difficult, messy record that is necessarily incomplete. McPhee has talked about the need to "deal with [a subject] on its own terms" (Singular, 50). California, he writes, is "a boneyard of exotic" (*Assembling California,* 231). Quite literally, California exists because of multiple suturings of exotic terrains: tectonic energy—moving, breaking, and building land masses—directs the process. With each new collision, rocks metamorphose, stratigraphy bends and bows, volcanoes erupt, earthquakes distend the surface. The geologic record in much of California "cannot be read in sequence" (192)—in other words, whatever linear process produced the landscape now reads like a modernist or postmodernist text. In *Assembling California,* as in all the *Annals,* McPhee seeks to decode the geological lexicon into a more familiar tongue and lead the reader to understand the unfamiliar language of geologists describing what they see. In country as enigmatic and potentially violent as California, it is essential that humans learn the history readable from within the rock and encoded by geologists.

Yet the Loma Prieta fault took even these master interpreters by surprise. Its momentous energy reminded them of the blank spaces on the page, unfamiliar territory yet to be mapped. The consequences of misreading the rock are considerable in a land as unstable as California. Millions of people cleave to the hills and mountains, live in the valleys and lowlands of the San Francisco area. Here, where the San Andreas fault deviates, where the strain of grinding plates builds, people have constructed homes, institutions, businesses—a whole culture. They all must ask, "What are the odds the big one will strike in my lifetime?" Of course, they all hope it will not. Indeed, as McPhee believes, "the big one" is "a chimeric temblor . . . as if some disaster of unique magnitude were waiting to happen." In fact, "[a] big one will always be in the offing" (253). In California, the human world is poised for collision with the natural world: "As the strain rises through the years, the scales of geologic time and human time draw ever closer, until they coincide" (285). Geologists bank on the known. The San Andreas fault system has been studied now for a number of generations through field studies, seismic recorders, ultrasonic searches, and other instrumentation. Thanks to these efforts, much of this "idiosyncratic" fault line is now legible (261). When an illegible temblor occurs, however, when a new page in the story suddenly snaps open, geologists are forced to acknowledge the unknown, to revise their own tendency toward "the principle of least astonishment" (278). Even those trained to decipher the rock can stumble.

Human knowledge of complex natural systems is always incomplete. The assembling of California is itself an unfinished business. Its narrative—replete with truncations, vestigial evidence, and buried truths—precludes a definitive reading. And the catastrophic earthquakes that loom large in the human story are merely short footnotes in California's geologic history. In 1906 an earthquake measuring 8.3 on the Richter scale devastated San Francisco and made the San Andreas fault line infamous. The San Andreas is not just a simple line etched up California, zipper style. Other faults accompany it, a system of splintery features, many "illegible" and cryptic, leaving no surface traces of their existence (289). The Loma Prieta earthquake has reminded geologists of just how incomplete their lexicon is. Unknown to geologists before this event, the Loma Prieta, a slammer of an earthquake, announced itself before a national audience. Who can forget the televised images of Candlestick Park swaying, the Marina District burning, and the pancaked Nimitz Freeway becoming a burial ground? Five minutes after five in the afternoon, "the scales of geologic time and human time draw ever closer, until they coincide" (285). The rest, as they say, is history.

McPhee's replaying of the Loma Prieta earthquake, second by second, makes for dramatic reading. Starting at the deepest epicenter ever recorded along the San Andreas (59,800 feet) and following the pressure waves, shear waves, and surface waves that rock the "serene" land,

McPhee's re-creation is a resounding, tour de force conclusion, one of the best segments he has ever written. Fourteen seconds into the quake,

> [t]he shock reaches Stanford University, and sixty buildings receive a hundred and sixty million dollars' worth of damage. The university does not have earthquake insurance.
>
> The waves move on to San Mateo, where a woman in a sixteenth-floor apartment has poured a cup of coffee and sat down to watch the third game of the World Series. When the shock arrives, the apartment is suddenly like an airplane in a wind shear. The jolt whips her head to one side. A lamp crashes. Books fall. Doors open. Dishes fall. Separately, the coffee and the cup fly across the room.
>
> People are dead in Santa Cruz, Watsonville has rubble on the ground, and San Francisco has yet to feel anything. (292–93)

For twelve pages, McPhee re-creates in pulsing detail the waves of destruction that burst forth from the temblor's epicenter. Human time meets geologic time. Despite scientific efforts to decode the assemblage of California, despite all precautions people might take to prepare for such an event, the arrival of the unknown exhilarates, terrifies, and clarifies life for all in its path.

Geologists claim a space in McPhee's pantheon of everyday heroes. Though their efforts to unravel the earth's meanings go unheeded at worst or remain incomplete at best, they provide crucial interpretations for those who choose to live in California's unstable places. In the introduction to the *Second John McPhee Reader*, David Remnick suggests that the *Annals* inspire a "complicated pleasure" (xiv). "These books are not always easy," he admits, "filled as they are with Whitmanic catalogues of minerals and pyrotechnic attempts to explain nothing less than the textures and the movements of the earth" (xiv). In *Assembling California,* the mineral is gold; and the pyrotechnic style reflects the dramatic measure of the land. When geologic time and human time meet and part, California merges into our collective memory, leaving behind an imprint that both stirs and discomforts.

In *Irons in the Fire,* McPhee continues to highlight the unnoticed work that often exposes uneasy truths. This time, that which requires decoding is not necessarily the land, but the humans who enact their small dramas upon it. Chris Collis, in "Irons in the Fire," tries to foil cattle rustlers in eastern Nevada. For forensic geologists like Ron Rawalt, in "The Gravel Page," evidence of sand, soil, and crushed rock has helped solve a number of killing events, from Japan's balloon bombs launched to terrorize western states during World War II to simple, brutal murder. They seek answers in the gravel page. Brand inspectors and forensic geologists read land and human nature, seeking an inventory of meaning to arrive at truth. In both essays, McPhee is an uncertain decoder searching for a way into an unfamiliar professional language to translate it for the reader.

An effective brand inspector must know the "Nevada Livestock Brand Book," "which describes and sketches thirty-seven hundred and forty-three brands" ("Irons in the Fire," 4), and must know the country, "every wash, draw, arroyo, dip, and depression in a country where a hundred miles is as far as the eye can see" (28). Rustlers, with their running irons, gooseneck trailers, and cunning born of greed, take advantage of this vastness to outwit authorities. Both parties know the lay of the land, its signature grammar. Collis is expert in decoding brands, though McPhee, a greenhorn, finds the whole enterprise "unfamiliar" and unreadable: ". . . by and large I see only a few disjunct lines, not whole letters and whole numbers and geometric forms. I could not tell a Lazy S from a Rolling M if my life depended on it, or a Running F from a Lazy Walking A" (6). While Collis reads brands with little effort, McPhee suffers from the frustration of illiteracy. The rustler attempts to foil inspectors. The running iron, "a red-hot stylus," recodes a brand, blotting out the original design. Yet the cow's hide never lies, and therein sits a tale: "a history readable from within" (9). McPhee delights in the varied cipher of the brand, and his prose joyfully plays with its subject. But for Collis and others, the brand protects livelihoods; its system of signs is part of a larger effort to ensure that the big business of cattle proceeds honestly. Rancher Norman Sharp tells McPhee: " 'Some people steal because they're hungry. Others for a lark. And for a third group it's a way of life. If it wasn't for Chris, they could come into the desert here, load up, and be in Kansas in a few days' " (50).

To beat the odds against rustlers, Collis must prove a master reader of many signs, from dust on the horizon to "the story of roping and loading written into the sage" (46). Writing, reading, narrating: McPhee makes these the operative metaphors as he decodes Collis's work and the decoding of brands. Even a brand sequence like the Cross L next to the H over L followed by the H Hanging L reminds McPhee of "a scribe bent over his table in Beijing building a composite character" (45). Collis, like a scribe, works with signs, but his is not the studied work of a scholar. He takes his semiotic knowledge out into the basin and range country of Nevada.

To succeed against rustling, inspectors "read and record tracks and signs as thoroughly as possible," creating a "chain of evidence" that tells a commanding, irrefutable story (46). Forensic geologists work the same way. For McPhee, pebbles from the Platte River, each representing a distinct origin, serve as an opening metaphor for the unique work of forensic geology. At heart is a science born of codes, the signatures left by soil and rock and sand. "Mineral grains and microfossils," he informs us, "can narrate a story" ("The Gravel Page," 87). With the assistance of a cadre of geologists, McPhee narrates three stories "concentrated in military puzzles and egregious crimes" (89). Each is a story of violence that requires decoding "the gravel page." McPhee lightly peppers his essay with strategic quotations from Sir Arthur Conan Doyle's fiction and borrows his metaphoric title from *The Hound of the Baskervilles*. The game is very much afoot as McPhee interviews forensic geologists who helped protect the U.S. mainland from Japanese aerial bombs during World War II and who helped solve two murders later in the twentieth century.

Minerals, crystal chemistry, isotopic composition, and microfossils can be as distinctive as fingerprints. In geologist Karen Kleinspehn's lingo, they can be "diagnostic" ("The Gravel Page," 82). McPhee wonders about his own fate were he to commit the "unthinkable" and "run off to Florida." What would happen were his van to be found? He responds: "Jim Swinehart or someone like him could have determined the provenance of each pebble in the group—and the distance of transport, and the presence and absence and percentages of rock types—and told anyone who needed to know that I had perpetrated whatever it was on a gravel bar in the main stem of the Platte River west of the line of glacial advance and east of the hundredth meridian" (87). Special Agent Ronald Rawalt, McPhee's representative scientist and guide, is trained to decode the gravel page. With books, maps, instruments, and common sense, forensic geologists assist in solving any number of crimes. A little soil in a wheel well or on a body can undo a criminal.

Forensic geologists are expert cross-checkers. Color, texture, and mineralogy help with the initial decoding. Collecting "alibi samples" (89) helps establish or eliminate possible locations of crime. The process is painstaking yet ultimately revealing. The Federal Bureau of Investigation has unraveled numerous crimes with the aid of forensic geologists.

Had Walter Osborne, alias of felon Joseph Corbett, Jr., realized the revelatory power of soils, he might have more thoroughly disposed of his
yellow Mercury outside Atlantic City, New Jersey. Gasoline and matches
were not good enough. The murderer of Adolph Coors III thought he
had covered his tracks well, though FBI agents were able to uncover his
purchases, his movements, and his itinerant work life. With fingerprints
filed when the murderer applied for a Colorado driver's license, the FBI
discovered that Osborne was a former San Quentin resident named
Corbett.

The FBI investigators used "dozens of ways" to assemble the murder
story ("The Gravel Page," 96). But without the soil samples found on
Corbett's burned hulk of a vehicle, they could not have proved defini-
tively that Corbett was near Ad Coors's ranch in the mountains. Working backward in time, the gravel page revealed first the signature "sands,
silts, paper fibres, cinders, glass wools, and black slags" of the Atlantic
City dump (100). The next deposition disclosed sharp, fresh sand grains,
all distinctive in origin: Pikes Peak granite, "a geology that stands alone,
and can write its name in dust" (96); Front Range granites; hogsback's
Dakota Group quartzose sands; and Morrison Formation clays (101).
This layer connected Corbett's junked Mercury to Colorado. The following deposit damned him: soils from "the country around Coors'
ranch," placing Corbett "within a couple of miles of the crime scene"
(101). Unwittingly, Corbett "had been writing his itinerary on the bottom of his car" (100). The cipher cracked, trained eyes decoded the narrative, and a violent crime played out against breathtaking scenery was
solved.

Barbara Lounsberry has commented: "For McPhee, rendering accurately the complexity of any natural and human setting . . . is the con-
summate artistic challenge" (66). His is a "gradient way of seeing," providing "panoptic perspective" (66). In "The Gravel Page," McPhee's
sleuths prove just how challenging it is to develop a gradient view, for
essayist, forensic expert, and reader alike, especially when their delimit-
ing must conjoin geologic fact and variant human behavior. McPhee
tracks the forensic teams that solve violent acts. He brings us intimately
into their professional worlds and translates the operative codes that inform their work. In late 1944 Ken Lohman and others working for the
Military Geology Unit of the U.S. Geological Survey were given the
task of decoding signature minerals in sand samples taken from *fusen
bakudan*—balloon bombs. From Alaska to California and east to

Saskatchewan and Michigan, balloons descended or dropped bombs. What cracked the code of this mystery, pivotal to home-front defense, were microscopic algae called diatoms. Given "a palmful of sand," Lohman, Julia Gardner, Clarence Ross, and Kathryn Lohman conducted a "subtle," incisive analysis of the evidence ("The Gravel Page," 111–12). Diatoms signaled beach sand. With that knowledge, Lohman's team examined small mollusks, the mineral assembly, the foraminifera; they pored over the papers of geologist Hisashi Kuno, eliminating "chunks of country" (111). The work required patience and stamina, assiduousness and collective brain power. With a tiny sample, in a crowded fifth-floor lab in the Interior Department thousands of kilometers from Japan, American geologists read minute evidence, refined their search layer by layer, and pinpointed three possible balloon launching sites. One of them, the beach at Ichinomiya near Tokyo, was near the Ninth Army Technical Research Laboratory. Evidence only microns large directed the Army Air Corps in its bombing of Ichinomiya and halted *fusen bakudan* production. Between 1944 and 1945 Lohman and company created a process of geologic detective work that serves as a model of scientific forensics to this day.

Five decades later, using parallel methodology, FBI geologist Ron Rawalt was called upon to solve the murder of Drug Enforcement Administration agent Enrique Camarena Salazar. Watching news coverage, Rawalt immediately noticed a discrepancy between the soil on the dead man and the ground he lay on. He smelled a cover-up. It took two trips to Mexico, first disguised as DEA agents and second returning as the FBI agents they were, for Rawalt and colleague Michael Malone to expose the truth. Camarena's body, in advanced decay, "had begun to undergo the process known as mummification. The skin resembled leather" ("The Gravel Page," 127). Yet this dead man spoke: a teaspoonful of soil remaining on his clothes and skin gave forensic geologists a mineral assemblage to decode. Examining the sample, Rawalt read important traces: "The globularity of the grains spoke of slow deposition in a sedimentary basin, of water deposits interlayered with ash flows from intermittent volcanic events. The soil from Camarena spoke of mountains" (128–29). Because 98 percent of the sample was unremarkable, Rawalt turned his keen eye toward 1 percent of the mineral content. A distinctive "big indicator" in the soil was cristobalite crystals, "vesicles full of cristobalite" (129).

Following such incremental work, McPhee's text works in tandem, bringing the reader into the professional's lab, translating for the reader a puzzling detective's lingo. We are taken step by step into physical and psychological depths: how does one read the evidence? How does one decipher human corruption? What patterns justice? Ron Rawalt's cunning decipherment finds its match in McPhee's prose and his readers' creative induction. In a needle-in-a-haystack exercise, Rawalt next combed maps and scientific papers. His colleague, Chris Fiedler, sums the problem up: " 'Initially you have the whole country of Mexico in which to find where a teaspoon of soil came from' " (130). The big break came when Rawalt took his results to an unidentified scientist at the Smithsonian. She had expertise in volcanology and had done field-work near Guadalajara. She knew intimately "the unusual hue of the rose glass": it was "specific to a Jalisco state park called Bosques de la Primavera" (130). Importantly, this mineral was found only in this park and the mountain slopes contained in it.

With knowledge in hand, Rawalt and Malone systematically, painstakingly undermined the Mexican authorities' cover-up. In tense, dramatic prose, McPhee replays the difficulty of avenging Camarena in a corrupt system. The Mexican Federal Judicial Police, criminal *pistoleros,* and drug lords worked together and were often interchangeable. Rawalt remembers: " 'You were told that in essence you cannot trust anybody but the D.E.A. Your life is at danger. Do not go to dinner. Do not go for a job without going in groups. An easy way to tell the good guys from the bad guys down there was by the armament they were carrying' " (137). In search of the burial site, already armed with the soil sample's story, Rawalt and Malone had to decode the unfamiliar, potentially fatal signs of the Mexican criminal's coded behavior. AK-47 rifles signify drug traffickers. If an MFJP officer carried an AK-47, look out—" 'he's a traffickers' *pistolero*' " (138). With their every movement watched and recorded, Rawalt and Malone beat the odds and finished their detective work.

Backhoes, cadaver dogs, and geologic know-how combined in the final deciphering of murder. Working in terrain heavy with "the smells of lead, cordite, powder, and decay," Rawalt tested multiple samples to find an exact match (146). Finally, under his field microscope, he saw the signature two cristobalites and the rose-colored quartz, shaped like sugar crystals. The soil under the microscope matched that on Camarena's body. A combination of exacting lab and fieldwork brought the body home. The reader, joined in this process of cracking code, shares in the exhilaration of hard work completed. Such pleasures—a crime solved, a code cracked, an artful text finished—provide decided compensation in our otherwise morally compromised world, where wars continue and human corruption remains a constant.

In a personal interview with Michael Pearson, John McPhee explains the creative exchange that defines his nonfiction: " 'The reader is the most creative thing in a piece of work. The writer puts down the words and the reader creates a scene. Writing is literally in the eye of the beholder. . . . Creative reading is the issue' " (Pearson, 18). "Braiding many things together," McPhee's readers, in his words, "[create] the author" (18). Part of the joy of creative reading, of collaborating with McPhee, is the process of decoding. Since first reading *Oranges* over two decades ago, I have joined him in puzzling out such disparate topics as geology, nuclear physics, building canoes, branding cattle, collecting art, playing basketball or tennis, and, most recently, fishing for shad in northeastern rivers. In each work, he eases his reader into a world that engenders its own cultural code. Guided by professionals and experts from all walks of life, McPhee's readers expand their circumscribed worlds, test their patience for abundant knowledge and new nomenclature, and open to the "gradient way of seeing" that provides such satisfaction after accepting his writerly challenge.

Over the years, I have learned to read "pentimento in the hide" and so much more. Such histories "readable from within" make cracking code with John McPhee a signature effect of his prose. Richard Parkinson suggests: "Decipherment and reading can be metaphors for understanding another culture" (12). McPhee, master of so many codes, multiple cultures, has in over three decades published significant "cultural texts" (Parkinson, 12). Scanning and unraveling diverse aspects of human production and natural history, McPhee's oeuvre marks the vitality and elevates the aesthetic significance of literary nonfiction as a contemporary genre.

Works Cited

Bailey, Thomas C. "John McPhee: The Making of a Meta-Naturalist." In *Earthly Words: Essays on Contemporary American Nature and Environmental Writers*, ed. John Cooley, 195–213. Ann Arbor: University of Michigan Press, 1994.

Bass, Sharon. "John McPhee." In *A Sourcebook of American Literary Journalism*, ed. Thomas B. Connery, 343–52. New York: Greenwood, 1992.

Boime, Albert. *The Magisterial Gaze: Manifest Destiny and American Landscape Painting c. 1830–1865.* Washington, D.C.: Smithsonian Institute, 1991.

Chapman, David. "Forming and Meaning: Writing the Counterpoint Essay." *Journal of Advanced Composition.* 11(1) (1991): 73–81.

Espey, David. "The Wilds of New Jersey: John McPhee as Travel Writer." In *Temperamental Journeys: Essays on the Modern Literature of Travel,* ed. Michael Kowalewski, 164–75. Athens: University of Georgia Press, 1992.

Leeds-Hurwitz, Wendy. *Semiotics and Communication: Signs, Codes, Cultures.* Hillsdale, Mich.: Lawrence Erlbaum, 1993.

Lounsberry, Barbara. *The Art of Fact: Contemporary Artists of Nonfiction.* New York: Greenwood, 1990.

McPhee, John. *Annals of the Former World.* New York: Farrar, Straus & Giroux, 1998.

———. *Assembling California.* New York: Farrar, Straus & Giroux, 1993.

———. *Coming into the Country.* New York: Farrar, Straus & Giroux, 1977.

———. *The Control of Nature.* New York: Farrar, Straus & Giroux, 1989.

———. *Encounters with the Archdruid.* New York: Farrar, Straus & Giroux, 1971.

———. "The Gravel Page." In *Irons in the Fire,* 81–147. New York: Farrar, Straus & Giroux, 1997.

———. "Irons in the Fire." In *Irons in the Fire,* 3–56. New York: Farrar, Straus & Giroux, 1997.

———. "Los Angeles against the Mountains." In *The Control of Nature,* 183–272. New York: Farrar, Straus & Giroux, 1989.

———. *Rising from the Plains.* New York: Farrar, Straus & Giroux, 1986.

Parkinson, Richard. *Cracking Code: The Rosetta Stone and Decipherment.* Berkeley: University of California Press, 1999.

Pearson, Michael. *John McPhee.* Twayne's United States Author Series 674. Ed. Frank Day. New York: Twayne, 1997.

Remnick, David. "Introduction." In *The Second John McPhee Reader,* ed. Patricia Strachan, vii–xvii. New York: Farrar, Straus & Giroux, 1996.

Roundy, Jack. "Crafting Fact: Formal Devices in the Prose of John McPhee." In *Literary Nonfiction: Theory, Criticism, Pedagogy,* 70–92. Carbondale: Southern Illinois University Press, 1989.

Singular, Stephen. "Talk with John McPhee." *New York Times Book Review* (27 November 1997): 50–51.

Turner, Brian. "Giving Good Reasons: Environmental Appeals in the Nonfiction of John McPhee." *Rhetoric Review* 13(1) (1994): 164–82.

Notes on Contributors

Meta G. Carstarphen is an associate professor of journalism at the University of Oklahoma in Norman. Her book reviews and commentaries appear frequently in the *Dallas Morning News* and *Our Texas* magazine. She is the co-editor of *Sexual Rhetoric: Media Perspectives on Sexuality, Gender, and Identity* (1999).

Jared Haynes received degrees from Dartmouth College and Humboldt State University. He was hired in 1989 by the University of California, Davis, to teach composition to upper-division students. He specializes in scientific writing and technical grammar as well as legal writing. Haynes's varied research interests include Renaissance science, James Joyce, and the cognitive development of college students. He has also published interviews with Stephen Jay Gould and Roger Angell.

William Howarth is professor of English at Princeton University. He focuses his research on the literature and history of North America. His thirteen books include *Nature in American Life, The John McPhee Reader, The Book of Concord, Traveling the Trans-Canada, Mountaineering in the Sierra Nevada,* and *Walking with Thoreau.* Former editor-in-chief of *The Writings of Henry D. Thoreau,* he serves on the editorial board of *Environmental History* and is chairman of the board for the Center for American Places. He has taught at Princeton since 1966, offering courses in English, American Studies, Environmental Studies, and humanities computing.

Theodore C. Humphrey is emeritus professor of English at California State Polytechnic University, Pomona, California. He gardens, hikes the local mountains, and writes and publishes on twentieth-century American novelists and nonfiction writers.

Barbara Lounsberry is the nonfiction editor of the *North American Review,* the oldest literary magazine in the United States. Her books include *The Art of Fact: Contemporary Artists of Nonfiction* (1990); *The Writer in You* (1992); *Writing Creative Nonfiction: The Literature of Reality* (co-edited with Gary Talese, 1996); and *The Tales We Tell: Perspectives on the Short Story* (co-edited with Susan Lohafer, 1998). She is currently completing a book on Virginia Woolf's diaries.

Susan Naramore Maher is professor of English at the University of Nebraska at Omaha, where she contributes to the Women's Studies and Environmental Studies programs. She has published widely on the literature of the American West, including John McPhee's *Rising from the Plains*. In 2001 she served as president of the Western Literature Association. Currently, she is at work on a book-length project (*Deep Maps: The Literary Cartography of the Great Plains*) that will trace the burgeoning field of literary nonfiction in this region.

Michael Pearson, director of the Creative Writing Program at Old Dominion University, has published four nonfiction books. *Imagined Places: Journeys into Literary America* was named a Notable Book of the Year by the *New York Times Book Review* in 1992. It was reissued in paperback in 2000 by Syracuse University Press. In 1999 he published *Dreaming of Columbus: A Boyhood in the Bronx*. He has written extensively on John McPhee.

Daniel J. Philippon is an assistant professor of rhetoric at the University of Minnesota, Twin Cities, where he teaches courses in environmental rhetoric, history, and ethics. He is the editor of two books of nature writing from the Johns Hopkins University Press: *The Height of Our Mountains: Nature Writing from Virginia's Blue Ridge and Shenandoah Valley* (co-edited with Michael Branch, 1998) and *The Friendship of Nature: A New England Chronicle of Birds and Flowers* by Mabel Osgood Wright (1999). He is currently completing a study of the role nature writers have played in the formation and development of environmental organizations in America.

Norman Sims is chair of the Journalism Department at the University of Massachusetts at Amherst, where he teaches reporting, freedom of the press, the history of journalism, and literary journalism. He edited *The Literary Journalists* (1984) and *Literary Journalism in the Twentieth Century* (1990) and co-edited *Literary Journalism* (1995). He has known John McPhee since 1982.

Kathy Smith received an M.A. in fiction writing from the University of New Hampshire and a Ph.D. from the University of Massachusetts, Amherst. A former journalist, newspaper editor, and teacher, she has published poetry, essays, and nonfiction. Smith served for twelve years as program director for the New Hampshire Humanities Council, where she developed public humanities programs and wrote grants.

Barbara Stevens, although living and working in Dorset, England, is completing her Ph.D. at the University of Derby. Her dissertation, placing contemporary cartographic and geographic concepts alongside recent photographic and literary landscape representations, explores the notion of a remapped and remappable Californian landscape and space.

Brian Turner is an associate professor in the Centre for Academic Writing at the University of Winnipeg, Manitoba (Canada), where he teaches courses on composition, rhetorical criticism, and rhetorical theory. His articles have appeared in *Journal of Teaching Writing, Rhetoric Review, Textual Studies in Canada, Teaching English in the Two-Year College,* and *WPA: Writing Program Administration.* Currently, he is working on a book about ethos in the nonfiction of McPhee, Edward Abbey, Wendell Berry, and Barry Lopez.

Rick Van Noy grew up on the same brunswick shale as John McPhee. He has worked as a technical writer and now teaches technical writing, composition, environmental literature, and American literature at Radford University. His essay "Surveying the Sublime" will appear in *The Greening of Literary Studies.* He is also working on a book called *Surveying the Interior: Literary Cartographers and the Sense of Place.* With his wife, Catherine, he is raising two children, Sam and Elliot, in the New River Valley.

O. Alan Weltzien is professor of English at the University of Montana–Western, in Dillon. He teaches a grab-bag of courses including, occasionally, creative nonfiction and contemporary nature writing. In summers he likes to climb mountains in and out of Montana. He has published articles in *Montana: The Magazine of Western History, WLA: Western American Literature,* and *ISLE: Interdisciplinary Studies in Literature and Environment,* among other journals. He is editor of *The Literary Art and Activism of Rick Bass* (2001) and has completed a memoir, *At Home on Camano: Summers in a Puget Sound Life,* currently in circulation among publishers.

Index